Lecture Notes in Computer Science　　12582

More information about this subseries at http://www.springer.com/series/7409

Diganta Goswami · Truong Anh Hoang (Eds.)

Distributed Computing and Internet Technology

17th International Conference, ICDCIT 2021
Bhubaneswar, India, January 7–10, 2021
Proceedings

Editors
Diganta Goswami
Indian Institute of Technology Guwahati
Guwahati, India

Truong Anh Hoang
University of Engineering and Technology
Hanoi, Vietnam

ISSN 0302-9743   ISSN 1611-3349   (electronic)
Lecture Notes in Computer Science
ISBN 978-3-030-65620-1   ISBN 978-3-030-65621-8   (eBook)
https://doi.org/10.1007/978-3-030-65621-8

LNCS Sublibrary: SL3 – Information Systems and Applications, incl. Internet/Web, and HCI

This Springer imprint is published by the registered company Springer Nature Switzerland AG
The registered company address is: Gewerbestrasse 11, 6330 Cham, Switzerland

Preface

This volume contains the papers selected for presentation at the 17th International Conference on Distributed Computing and Internet Technology (ICDCIT 2021) held during January 7–10, 2021, in Bhubaneswar, India.

From its humble beginnings, the ICDCIT conference series has grown to a conference of international repute and has become a global platform for Computer Science researchers to exchange research results and ideas on the foundations and applications of Distributed Computing and Internet Technology. An additional goal of ICDCIT is to provide an opportunity for students and young researchers to get exposed to topical research directions of Distributed Computing and Internet Technology.

This year we received 99 full paper submissions. Each submission considered for publication was reviewed by about three Program Committee (PC) members with the help from reviewers outside the PC. Based on the reviews, the PC decided to accept 17 papers – 13 regular papers and 4 short papers – for presentation at the conference, with an acceptance rate of 17%.

We would like to express our gratitude to all the researchers who submitted their work to the conference. Our special thanks goes to all colleagues who served on the PC, as well as the external reviewers, who generously offered their expertise and time, which helped us select the papers and prepare the conference program.

We were fortunate to have three invited speakers – Ajay D. Kshemkalyani from the University of Illinois at Chicago, USA, Martin Gogolla from the University of Bremen, Germany, and Nguyen Le Minh from Japan Advanced Institute of Science and Technology, Japan. Their talks provided us with the unique opportunity to hear the leaders of their field. The papers related to the talks were also included in this volume.

A number of colleagues have worked very hard to make this conference a success. We wish to express our thanks to the Local Organizing Committee, organizers of the satellite events, and many student volunteers. The School of Computer Engineering, Kalinga Institute of Industrial Technology (KIIT), Bhubaneswar, the host of the conference, provided various support and facilities for organizing the conference and its associated events. Finally, we enjoyed institutional and financial support from KIIT Bhubaneswar. Particularly, we express our sincere thanks to Achyuta Samanta, the Founder of KIIT Bhubaneswar, for his continuous support to ICDCIT since its inception. We express our appreciation to all the Steering Committee members, and in particular Prof. Hrushikesha Mohanty and Prof. Raja Natarajan, whose counsel we frequently relied on. We are also thankful to D.N. Dwivedy for his active participation in ICDCIT. Our thanks are due to the faculty members of the School of Computer Engineering, KIIT Bhubaneswar, for their timely support.

The conference program and proceedings were prepared with the help of EasyChair. We thank Springer for continuing to publish the conference proceedings.

We hope you will find the papers in this collection stimulating and rewarding.

January 2021   Diganta Goswami
                                                     Truong Anh Hoang

Organization

General Chair

Laxmi Parida   IBM, USA

Program Committee Chairs

Diganta Goswami   IIT Guwahati, India
Hoang Anh Truong   VNU-UET, Vietnam

Conference Management Chair

Manjusha Pandey   KIIT, India

Organizing Chair

Jagannath Singh   KIIT, India

Finance Chair

Chittaranjan Pradhan   KIIT, India

Publicity Chair

Hrudaya Kumar Tripathy   KIIT, India

Registration Chairs

Bindu Agarwalla   KIIT, India
Abhaya Kumar Sahoo   KIIT, India

Session Management Chairs

Sital Dash   KIIT, India
Saurabh Bilgaiyan   KIIT, India

Publications Chair

Junali Jasmine Jena   KIIT, India

Student Symposium Chairs

Manoj Kumar Mishra	KIIT, India
Amiya Ranjan Panda	KIIT, India

Industry Symposium Chairs

Phani Premaraju	KIIT, India
Siddharth Swarup Rautaray	KIIT, India

Project Innovation Contest Chairs

Ajay Kumar Jena	KIIT, India
Krishna Chakravarty	KIIT, India

Steering Committee

Maurice Herlihy	Brown University, USA
Gérard Huet	Inria, France
Bud Mishra	Courant Institute, NYU, USA
Hrushikesha Mohanty	KIIT, India
Raja Natarajan	TIFR, India
David Peleg	WIS, Israel
R. K. Shyamasundar	IIT Bombay, India

Program Committee

Arup Bhattacharjee	NIT Silchar, India
Santosh Biswas	IIT Bhilai, India
Duc-Hanh Dang	VNU-UET, Vietnam
Ashok Kumar Das	IIIT Hyderabad, India
Meenakshi D'Souza	IIIT Bangalore, India
Anh Nguyen Duc	University College of Southeast Norway, Norway
Christian Erfurth	University of Applied Sciences Jena, Germany
Antony Franklin	IIT Hyderabad, India
Sasthi Charan Ghosh	ISI Kolkata, India
Diganta Goswami	IIT Guwahati, India
Arobinda Gupta	IIT Kharagpur, India
Truong Anh Hoang	VNU-UET, Vietnam
Chittaranjan Hota	BITS Pilani, India
Dang Van Hung	VNU-UET, Vietnam
Hemangee Kapoor	IIT Guwahati, India
Dac-Nhuong Le	Haiphong University, Vietnam
Ulrike Lechner	Bundeswehr University Munich, Germany
Partha Sarathi Mandal	IIT Guwahati, India
Ganapathy Mani	Purdue University, USA

Hrushikesha Mohanty	KIIT, India
Arijit Mukherjee	TCS Research and Innovation, India
Krishnendu Mukhopadhyaya	ISI Kolkata, India
Dmitry Namiot	Lomonosov Moscow State University, Russia
Raja Natarajan	Tata Institute of Fundamental Research, Mumbai, India
Atul Negi	SCIS, University of Hyderabad, India
Himadri Sekhar Paul	TCS Research and Innovation, India
Sathya Peri	IIT Hyderabad, India
P. S. V. S. Sai Prasad	University of Hyderabad, India
Tho Quan	Ho Chi Minh City University of Technology, Vietnam
Ramaswamy Ramanujam	Institute of Mathematical Sciences Chennai, India
Shrisha Rao	IIIT Bangalore, India
K. Sreenivas Rao	IIT Kharagpur, India
Debasis Samanta	IIT Kharagpur, India
Chayan Sarkar	TCS Research and Innovation, India
Nityananda Sarma	Tezpur University, India
Somnath Tripathy	IIT Patna, India
T. Venkatesh	IIT Guwahati, India

Additional Reviewers

Hrishav Bakul Barua
Gaurav Bhardwaj
Hieu Vo Dinh
Barun Gorain
Aayush Grover
Aditya Gulati
Abhay Jain
Karishma Karishma
Rakesh Matam
Kaushik Mondal
Minh Thuan Nguyen
Nam Nguyen
Pradip Pramanick

Nemi Chandra Rathore
Durga Bhavani S.
Muktikanta Sa
Dibakar Saha
Ashok Sairam
Ranbir Sanasam
Sinchan Sengupta
Roohani Sharma
S. P. Suresh
Ha Nguyen Tien
Trung Tran
Gopalakrishnan Venkatesh

Contents

Invited Talks

The Bloom Clock for Causality Testing.......................... 3
　Anshuman Misra and Ajay D. Kshemkalyani

Model Development in the Tool USE: Explorative, Consolidating
and Analytic Steps for UML and OCL Models..................... 24
　Martin Gogolla

ReLink: Open Information Extraction by Linking Phrases
and Its Applications... 44
　Xuan-Chien Tran and Le-Minh Nguyen

Cloud Computing and Networks

Energy-Efficient Scheduling of Deadline-Sensitive and Budget-Constrained
Workflows in the Cloud....................................... 65
　Anurina Tarafdar, Kamalesh Karmakar, Sunirmal Khatua,
　and Rajib K. Das

An Efficient Renewable Energy-Based Scheduling Algorithm
for Cloud Computing... 81
　Sanjib Kumar Nayak, Sanjaya Kumar Panda, Satyabrata Das,
　and Sohan Kumar Pande

A Revenue-Based Service Management Algorithm for Vehicular
Cloud Computing.. 98
　Sohan Kumar Pande, Sanjaya Kumar Panda, and Satyabrata Das

Interference Reduction in Directional Wireless Networks 114
　Manjanna Basappa and Sudeepta Mishra

Distributed Algorithms, Concurrency and Parallelism

Automated Deadlock Detection for Large Java Libraries 129
　R. Rajesh Kumar, Vivek Shanbhag, and K. V. Dinesha

DNet: An Efficient Privacy-Preserving Distributed Learning Framework
for Healthcare Systems 145
　Parth Parag Kulkarni, Harsh Kasyap, and Somanath Tripathy

Memory Optimized Dynamic Matrix Chain Multiplication Using Shared
Memory in GPU.   160
  Girish Biswas and Nandini Mukherjee

Graph Algorithms and Security

Parameterized Complexity of Defensive and Offensive
Alliances in Graphs.   175
  Ajinkya Gaikwad, Soumen Maity, and Shuvam Kant Tripathi

A Reconstructive Model for Identifying the Global Spread in a Pandemic . . .   188
  Debasish Pattanayak, Dibakar Saha, Debarati Mitra,
  and Partha Sarathi Mandal

Cost Effective Method for Ransomware Detection:
An Ensemble Approach.   203
  Parthajit Borah, Dhruba K. Bhattacharyya, and J. K. Kalita

Social Networks and Machine Learning

Exploring Alzheimer's Disease Network Using Social Network Analysis. . . .   223
  Swati Katiyar, T. Sobha Rani, and S. Durga Bhavani

Stroke Prediction Using Machine Learning in a Distributed Environment. . . .   238
  Maihul Rajora, Mansi Rathod, and Nenavath Srinivas Naik

Automated Diagnosis of Breast Cancer with RoI Detection Using YOLO
and Heuristics.   253
  Ananya Bal, Meenakshi Das, Shashank Mouli Satapathy,
  Madhusmita Jena, and Subha Kanta Das

Short Papers

An Efficient Approach for Event Prediction Using Collaborative Distance
Score of Communities.   271
  B. S. A. S. Rajita, Bipin Sai Narwa, and Subhrakanta Panda

A Distributed System for Optimal Scale Feature Extraction and Semantic
Classification of Large-Scale Airborne LiDAR Point Clouds   280
  Satendra Singh and Jaya Sreevalsan-Nair

Load Balancing Approach for a MapReduce Job Running
on a Heterogeneous Hadoop Cluster   289
  Kamalakant Laxman Bawankule, Rupesh Kumar Dewang,
  and Anil Kumar Singh

Study the Significance of ML-ELM Using Combined PageRank
and Content-Based Feature Selection.   299
    Rajendra Kumar Roul and Jajati Keshari Sahoo

Author Index   309

Invited Talks

The Bloom Clock for Causality Testing

Anshuman Misra and Ajay D. Kshemkalyani$^{(\boxtimes)}$ ⓘ

University of Illinois at Chicago, Chicago, IL 60607, USA
{amisra7,ajay}@uic.edu

Abstract. Testing for causality between events in distributed executions is a fundamental problem. Vector clocks solve this problem but do not scale well. The probabilistic Bloom clock can determine causality between events with lower space, time, and message-space overhead than vector clock; however, predictions suffer from false positives. We give the protocol for the Bloom clock based on Counting Bloom filters and study its properties including the probabilities of a positive outcome and a false positive. We show the results of extensive experiments to determine how these above probabilities vary as a function of the Bloom timestamps of the two events being tested, and to determine the accuracy, precision, and false positive rate of a slice of the execution containing events in the temporal proximity of each other. Based on these experiments, we make recommendations for the setting of the Bloom clock parameters. We postulate the *causality spread hypothesis* from the application's perspective to indicate whether Bloom clocks will be suitable for correct predictions with high confidence. The Bloom clock design can serve as a viable space-, time-, and message-space-efficient alternative to vector clocks if false positives can be tolerated by an application.

Keywords: Causality · Vector clock · Bloom clock · Bloom filter · Partial order · Distributed system · False positive · Performance

1 Introduction

1.1 Background and Motivation

Determining causality between pairs of events in a distributed execution is useful to many applications [9,17]. This problem can be solved using vector clocks [5,11]. However, vector clocks do not scale well. Several works attempted to reduce the size of vector clocks [6,12,18,20], but they had to make some compromises in accuracy or alter the system model, and in the worst-case, were as lengthy as vector clocks. A survey of such works is included in [8].

The Bloom filter, proposed in 1970, is a space-efficient probabilistic data structure that supports set membership queries [1]. The Bloom filter is widely used in computer science. Surveys of the variants of Bloom filters and their applications in networks and distributed systems are given in [2,19]. Bloom filters provide space savings, but suffer from false positives although there are no false negatives. The confidence in the prediction by a Bloom filter depends on the

© Springer Nature Switzerland AG 2021
D. Goswami and T. A. Hoang (Eds.): ICDCIT 2021, LNCS 12582, pp. 3–23, 2021.
https://doi.org/10.1007/978-3-030-65621-8_1

size of the filter (m), the number of hash functions used in the filter (k), and the number of elements added to the set (q). The use of the Bloom filter as a Bloom clock to determine causality between events was suggested [16], where, like Bloom filters, the Bloom clock will inherit false positives. The Bloom clock and its protocol based on Counting Bloom filters, which can be significantly more space-, time-, and message-space-efficient than vector clocks, was given in [7]. The expressions for the probabilities of a positive outcome and of a false positive as a function of the corresponding vector clocks, as well as their estimates as a function of the Bloom clocks were then formulated [7]. Properties of the Bloom clock were also studied in [7], which then derived expressions to estimate the accuracy, precision, and the false positive rate for a slice of the execution using the events' Bloom timestamps.

1.2   Contributions

In this paper, we first give the Bloom clock protocol and discuss its properties. We examine the expressions for the probability of a positive and of a false positive in detecting causality, and discuss their trends as the distance between the pair of events varies. We then show the results of our experiments to:

1. analyze in terms of Bloom timestamps how the probability of a positive and the probability of a false positive vary as the distance between a pair of events varies;
2. analyze the accuracy, precision, and the false positive rate for a slice of the execution that is representative of events that are close to each other. The parameters varied are: number of processes n, size of Bloom clock m, number of hash functions k, probability of a timestamped event being an internal event pr_i, and temporal proximity between the two events being tested for causality.

Based on our experiments, we

1. analyze the nature of false positive predictions,
2. make recommendations for settings of m and k,
3. state conditions and analyze dependencies on the parameters (e.g., n, pr_i) under which Bloom clocks make correct predictions with high confidence (high accuracy, precision, and low false positive rate), and
4. generalize the above results and state a general principle (the *causality spread hypothesis*) based on the degree of causality in the application execution, which indicates whether Bloom clocks can make correct predictions with high confidence.

Thus our results and recommendations can be used by an application developer to decide whether and how the application can benefit from the use of Bloom clocks.

Roadmap: Section 2 gives the system model. Section 3 details the Bloom clock protocol. Section 4 studies properties of the Bloom clock, discusses ways to estimate the probabilities of a positive outcome and of a false positive, and predicts the trends of these probability functions as the temporal proximity between the events increases. Section 5 gives our experiments for the complete graph and analyzes the results. Section 6 gives our experiments for the star graph (client-server configuration) and analyzes the results. Section 7 summarizes the observations of the experiments and discusses the conditions under which Bloom clocks are advantageous to use. It also postulates the *causality spread hypothesis* and validates it. Section 8 concludes.

2   System Model

A distributed system is modeled as an undirected graph $(\mathcal{N}, \mathcal{L})$, where $\mathcal{N}$ is the set of processes and $\mathcal{L}$ is the set of links connecting them. Let $n = |\mathcal{N}|$. Between any two processes, there may be at most one logical channel over which the two processes communicate asynchronously. A logical channel from P_i to P_j is formed by paths over links in $\mathcal{L}$. We do not assume FIFO logical channels.

The execution of process P_i produces a sequence of events $E_i = \langle e_i^0, e_i^1, e_i^2, \cdots \rangle$, where e_i^j is the jth event at process P_i. An event at a process can be an *internal* event, a *message send* event, or a *message receive* event. Let $E = \bigcup_{i \in \mathcal{N}} \{e \mid e \in E_i\}$ denote the set of events in a distributed execution. The causal precedence relation between events, defined by Lamport's "happened before" relation [10], and denoted as $\rightarrow$, induces an irreflexive partial order $(E, \rightarrow)$.

Mattern [11] and Fidge [5] designed the vector clock which assigns a vector V to each event such that: $e \rightarrow f \iff V_e < V_f$. The vector clock is a fundamental tool to characterize causality in distributed executions [9,17]. Each process needs to maintain a vector V of size n to represent the local vector clock. Charron-Bost has shown that to capture the partial order $(E, \rightarrow)$, the size of the vector clock is the dimension of the partial order [3], which is bounded by the size of the system, n. Unfortunately, this does not scale well to large systems.

3   The Bloom Clock Protocol

The Bloom clock is based on the Counting Bloom filter. Each process P_i maintains a Bloom clock $B(i)$ which is a vector $B(i)[1, \ldots, m]$ of integers, where $m < n$. The Bloom clock is operated as shown in Algorithm 1. To try to uniquely update $B(i)$ on a tick for event e_i^x, k random hash functions are used to hash (i, x), each of which maps to one of the m indices in $B(i)$. Each of the k indices mapped to is incremented in $B(i)$; this probabilistically tries to make the resulting $B(i)$ unique. As $m < n$, this gives a space, time, and message-space savings over the vector clock. We would like to point out that the scalar clock [10] can be thought of as a Bloom clock with $m = 1$ and $k = 1$.

The Bloom timestamp of an event e is denoted B_e. Let $\mathcal{V}$ and $\mathcal{B}$ denote the sets of vector timestamps and Bloom timestamps of events. The standard vector comparison operators $<$, $\leq$, and $=$ [5,11] apply to pairs in $\mathcal{V}$ and in $\mathcal{B}$. Thus, for example, $B_z \geq B_y$ is $\forall i \in [1, m], B_z[i] \geq B_y[i]$. The Bloom clock mapping from E to $\mathcal{B}$ is many-one. $(\mathcal{B}, \leq)$ is a partial order that is not isomorphic to $(E, \rightarrow)$.

Algorithm 1: Operation of Bloom clock $B(i)$ at process P_i.

---

1 Initialize $B(i) = \bar{0}$.

2 (At an internal event e_i^x):
   apply k hash functions to (i, x) and increment the corresponding k positions mapped to in $B(i)$ (local tick).

3 (At a send event e_i^x):
   apply k hash functions to (i, x) and increment the corresponding k positions mapped to in $B(i)$ (local tick). Then P_i sends the message piggybacked with $B(i)$.

4 (At a receive event e_i^x for message piggybacked with B'):
   P_i executes
   $\forall j \in [1, m], B(i)[j] = max(B(i)[j], B'[j])$ (merge);
   apply k hash functions to (i, x) and increment the corresponding k positions mapped to in $B(i)$ (local tick).
   Then deliver the message.

Proposition 1. *Test for $y \rightarrow z$ using Bloom clocks: if $B_z \geq B_y$ then declare $y \rightarrow z$ else declare $y \nrightarrow z$.*

4   Properties of the Bloom Clock

We have the following cases based on the actual relationship between events y and z, and the relationship inferred from B_y and B_z.

1. $y \rightarrow z$ and $B_z \geq B_y$: From Proposition 1, this results in a true positive.
2. $y \rightarrow z$ and $B_z \ngeq B_y$: This false negative is not possible because from the rules of operation of the Bloom clock, B_z must be $\geq B_y$ when $y \rightarrow z$.
3. $y \nrightarrow z$ and $B_z \ngeq B_y$: From Proposition 1, this results in a true negative.
4. $y \nrightarrow z$ and $B_z \geq B_y$: From Proposition 1, this results in a false positive.

Let pr_{fp}, pr_{tp}, and pr_{tn} denote the probabilities of a false positive, a true positive, and a true negative, respectively. Also, let pr_p denote the probability of a positive. To evaluate these probabilities, we need $pr(y \rightarrow z)$ and $pr(B_z \geq B_y)$. As we do not have access to vector clocks, we cannot evaluate $y \rightarrow z$ as $V_y \leq V_z$. So we estimate $pr(y \rightarrow z)$ as the probability that $B_z \geq B_y$, which is the probability of a positive, pr_p. So the estimate of pr_{fp} is $(1 - pr_p) \cdot pr_p$, from Case (4) above. However, the second term pr_p can be precisely evaluated, given B_y and B_z, as $pr_{\delta(p)}$, where

$$pr_{\delta(p)} = \begin{cases} 1 & \text{if } B_z \geq B_y \\ 0 & \text{otherwise} \end{cases} \tag{1}$$

So $pr_{fp} = (1 - pr_p) \cdot pr_{\delta(p)}$. Also, $pr_{tp} = pr_p \cdot pr_{\delta(p)}$ from Case (1) above. Further, as a negative outcome $(B_z \not\succeq B_y)$ is always true from Cases (2,3) above and a negative outcome can be determined precisely, $pr_{tn} = 1 - pr_{\delta(p)}$. Thus,

$$
\begin{aligned}
pr_{fp} &= (1 - pr_p) \cdot pr_{\delta(p)}, \\
pr_{tp} &= pr_p \cdot pr_{\delta(p)}, \\
pr_{tn} &= 1 - pr_{\delta(p)}
\end{aligned}
\tag{2}
$$

If $pr_{\delta(p)}$ were not precisely evaluated but used as a probability, we would have:

$$
\begin{aligned}
pr_{fp} &= (1 - pr_p) \cdot pr_p, \\
pr_{tp} &= pr_p^2, \\
pr_{tn} &= 1 - pr_p
\end{aligned}
\tag{3}
$$

We now show how to estimate pr_p using Bloom timestamps B_y and B_z.

Definition 1. *For a vector* X, $X^{sum} \equiv \sum_{i=1}^{|X|} X[i]$.

For a positive outcome to occur, for each increment to $B_y[i]$, there is an increment to $B_z[i]$. The number of increments to $B_y[i]$, which we denote as c the *count threshold*, is $B_y[i]$. The probability pr_p of $B_z \geq B_y$ is now formulated. Let $b(l, q, 1/m)$ denote the probability mass function of a binomial distribution having success probability $1/m$, where l increments have occurred to a position in B_z after applying uniformly random hash mappings q times.

$$
b(l, q, 1/m) = \binom{q}{l} \left(\frac{1}{m}\right)^l \left(1 - \frac{1}{m}\right)^{q-l}
\tag{4}
$$

Observe that the total number of trials $q = B_z^{sum}$. Then,

$$
b(l, B_z^{sum}, 1/m) = \binom{B_z^{sum}}{l} \left(\frac{1}{m}\right)^l \left(1 - \frac{1}{m}\right)^{B_z^{sum} - l}
\tag{5}
$$

The probability that less than the count threshold $B_y[i]$ increments have occurred to $B_z[i]$ is given by:

$$
\sum_{l=0}^{B_y[i]-1} b(l, B_z^{sum}, 1/m)
\tag{6}
$$

The probability that each i of the m positions of B_z is incremented at least $B_y[i]$ times, which gives pr_p, can be given by:

$$
pr_p(k, m, B_y, B_z) = \prod_{i=1}^{m} \left(1 - \sum_{l=0}^{B_y[i]-1} b(l, B_z^{sum}, 1/m)\right)
\tag{7}
$$

Equation 7 is time-consuming to evaluate for events y and z as the execution progresses. This is because B_z^{sum} and $B_y[i]$ increase. A binomial distribution

$b(l, q, 1/m)$ can be approximated by a Poisson distribution with mean q/m, for large q and small $1/m$. Also, the cumulative mass function of a Poisson distribution is a regularized incomplete gamma function. This provides an efficient way of evaluating Eq. 7.

For arbitrary event y at P_i, to predict whether $y \to z$ where events z occur at P_j, there are at first true negatives, then false positives, and then true positives as z occurs progressively later. As $B_z^{sum} - B_y^{sum}$ increases, we can predict the following trends from the definitions of pr_p and pr_{fp}.

1. pr_p, the probability of a positive, is low if z is close to y and this probability increases as z goes further in the future of y. This is because, in Eq. 7, as B_z^{sum} increases with respect to B_y^{sum} or rather its m components, the summation (cumulative probability distribution function) decreases and hence pr_p increases.

   This behavior is intuitive because intuition says that as z becomes more distant from y, the more is the likelihood that some causal relationship will get established from y to z either directly or transitively, by the underlying message communication pattern.

2. pr_{fp}, the probability of a false positive, which is the product $(1 - pr_p) \cdot pr_p$ using Eq. 3, is lower than the two terms. It will increase, reach a maximum of 0.25, and then decrease.

   If Eq. 2 were used, then $pr_{fp} = (1 - pr_p) \cdot pr_{\delta(p)}$ would be higher for a positive outcome. Once $B_z \geq B_y$ becomes true, it steps up from 0 and then as z goes into the future of y, it decreases. Given a positive outcome, if $B_z \geq B_y$ and z is close to y (B_z^{sum} is just a little greater than B_y^{sum}), there are two opposing influences on pr_{fp}: (i) it is unlikely that "a causal relationship has been established either directly or transitively from y to z by the underlying message communication pattern", and thus $1 - pr_p$ and pr_{fp} should tend to be high; (ii) it is also unlikely that "for each $h \in [1, m]$, $B_z[h] \geq B_y[h]$ due to Bloom clock local ticks only (and not due to causality merge for $y \to z$)", and thus pr_{fp} should tend to be low. As z goes more distant from y, the likelihood of influence (i) that a causal relation has been established increases, resulting in a lower $1 - pr_p$ and hence lower pr_{fp}. This $overrides$ any conflicting impact of the likelihood of influence (ii), that $\forall h, B_z[h] \geq B_y[h]$ due to local ticks only and not due to causality merge for $y \to z$, increasing and thus increasing pr_{fp}.

   Based on the above reasoning, it is not apparent whether Eq. 2 or 3 is better for modeling pr_{fp} behavior. However, Eq. 2 uses the full range of $[0,1]$ (as opposed to $[0,0.25]$), and uses an approximation only for $pr(y \to z)$ and not for $pr(B_z \geq B_y)$.

We remind ourselves that these probabilities depend on B_y, B_z, k, and m, and observe that they are oblivious of the communication pattern in the distributed execution.

We are also interested in calculating the accuracy, precision, and false positive rate of Bloom clocks. Accuracy (Acc), precision ($Prec$), recall (Rec), and false positive rate (fpr) are metrics defined over all data points, i.e, pairs of events, in the execution. Let TP, FP, TN, and FN be the number of true positives, number of false positives, number of true negatives, and the number of false negatives, respectively. Observe that FN is 0 as there are no false negatives. We have:

$$Accuracy = \frac{TP + TN}{TP + TN + FP + FN}, Precision = \frac{TP}{TP + FP},$$
$$Recall = \frac{TP}{TP + FN}, fpr = \frac{FP}{FP + TN} \tag{8}$$

Recall is always 1 with Bloom clocks. Given events y and z and their Bloom timestamps B_y and B_z, there is not enough data to compute these metrics. So we consider the slice of the execution from y to z and define the metrics over the set of events in this slice.

We observe that many applications in distributed computing require testing for causality between pairs of events that are temporally close to each other. In checkpointing, causality needs to be tracked only between two consistent checkpoints. In fair mutual exclusion in which requests need to be satisfied in order of their logical timestamps, contention occurs and request timestamps need to be compared only for temporally close requests. For detecting data races in multi-threaded environments, a causality check based on vector clocks can be used; however, in practice one needs to check for data races only between events that occur in each other's temporal locality [14,15]. In general, many applications are structured as phases and track causality only within a bounded number of adjacent phases [4,13]. Thus, in our experiments to measure accuracy, precision, and false positive rate, as well as the probability of positives and the probability of false positives, we consider an execution slice that is relatively thin.

There is a trade-off using Bloom clocks. m can be chosen less than n, for space, time, and message-space savings. But for acceptable precision, accuracy, and fpr, and a suitable pr_{fp} distribution, an appropriate combination of values for the clock parameters m and k can be determined.

5   Experiments for the Complete Graph

In the complete graph, we assume a logical channel between each pair of processes. This experiment consists of a decentralized system of processes asynchronously passing messages to each other over shared memory. The processes are scheduled in a fair manner and are identical to each other. Even though FIFO channels are not maintained, a majority of messages arrive in order. The parameters of this experiment are *number of processes (n)*, *size of Bloom clock (m)*, *internal event probability (pr_i)*, and *number of hash functions (k)*. Each event can be uniquely identified with a *Global Sequence Number (GSN)*. An event is modelled as an object with the following attributes: (i) vector timestamp, (ii) Bloom timestamp, (iii) GSN, (iv) executing process ID, (v) sending process ID, (vi) receiving process ID, (vii) physical timestamp.

The main program establishes shared memory, creates n processes and supplies them with parameters pr_i, k, and m. It then waits for all processes to complete execution and analyzes the distributed execution log. Shared memory consists of an integer tracking GSN, a message queue containing messages (send events) yet to be received, and an execution log containing all events executed at any point of the distributed execution. All processes maintain a local queue containing messages asynchronously pulled from the shared message queue. Message receive events are executed by processing messages one at a time from the local queue with probability $(1 - pr_i)/2$. Send events are executed with probability $(1 - pr_i)/2$. For each send event the sending process randomly selects a receiving process from the other $n - 1$ processes. Processes execute internal events with probability pr_i. All executed events are pushed into the global execution log. Send events are also pushed into the global message queue.

Each process maintains its own vector clock and Bloom clock which are ticked in accordance to the vector clock and Bloom clock protocols, whenever an event is executed. The event object stores the local process's revised clocks as its vector and Bloom timestamps. In addition to this, upon executing an event, each process increments the global GSN variable by 1 and stores it in the event object. Whenever a process increments the global GSN counter, it has to acquire a lock. This is done to prevent race conditions on the GSN counter as it is stored in shared memory. Other operations that are required to be atomic and around which locks are used include accessing the global message queue in shared memory containing messages that are waiting to be retrieved. Each process continues to iterate and execute events until the GSN reaches n^2. Once all processes terminate, the main program analyzes the execution to compute precision, accuracy, and fpr of the Bloom clock protocol from the execution log. The execution log contains approximately n^2 events at the end of the execution.

The main program computes causal relationships of pairs of events in the execution slice beginning with the event with GSN = $10n$ (to eliminate any startup effects) and until the last event (with GSN = n^2) in steps of 100. This means that the sample that we use to check for causality predictions consists of a series of events where two closest events have a difference of 100 in GSN. Further, the number of pairs of events for which we tested for causality was approximately $n^4/10^4$. The main program compares causality predictions of the Bloom timestamps of events with predictions of vector timestamps and classifies the Bloom clock predictions as true positives, false positives and true negatives. The precision, accuracy, and fpr are computed over this execution slice. We intentionally chose an execution slice with n events per process because in practice, causality tests are applied to pairs of events in the temporal proximity of each other. Had we chosen a larger execution slice, we expect the metrics would have improved.

Finally, in this section and the next on experiments with the star configuration, each reading reported is the average of at least 3 runs of each setting of the parameters indicated. Also, in Sects. 5.2 to 5.4, where indicated, each reported reading is also averaged over multiple settings of m and/or k for simplicity of presentation of results; the impact of varying each individual parameter is clear when the results of all experiments are considered.

5.1   Number of Processes

We ran the decentralized experiment for $n = 100$ to $n = 700$ in increments of 100 to ascertain scalability of Bloom clocks. Parameters were fixed to maintain uniformity of results with $pr_i = 0$, $k = 2$, and $m = 0.1 * n$. The results are compiled in Table 1. A visual representation of the trend can be seen in Fig. 1. We see that as n increases Bloom clock performance improves considerably. Accuracy increases from 85.2% for $n = 100$ to 95.7% for $n = 700$ and the *fpr* drops from 20.3% for $n = 100$ to 7.4% for $n = 700$. Since Bloom clocks are not prone to false negatives, a critical method of measuring performance is to calculate the ratio of positive predictions that are correct to overall positive predictions. Precision measures exactly that. We observe that precision increases from 64.4% for $n = 100$ to 90.7% for $n = 700$. Overall from Table 1, we conclude that Bloom clocks are highly scalable.

Table 1. Variation of metrics with n

n	Precision	Accuracy	*fpr*
100	0.644	0.852	0.203
200	0.781	0.905	0.145
300	0.833	0.926	0.118
400	0.856	0.935	0.107
500	0.883	0.947	0.089
600	0.897	0.953	0.081
700	0.907	0.957	0.074

5.2   Internal Event Probability

We ran the decentralized experiment for fixed $n = 200$ and averaged metrics over $m = 0.1 * n, 0.2 * n, 0.3 * n$ and $k = 2, 3, 4$ for individual values of pr_i in order to observe the variation of metrics with pr_i. The results are shown in Table 2. We observed that by introducing more relevant (and therefore timestamped) internal events in the decentralized execution, the performance of Bloom clocks deteriorates significantly. So with an increase in send events and thus message-passing, i.e., a relative decrease in the number of relevant timestamped internal events, more causal relationships get established among events across processes, which get captured through the merging of Bloom clocks at receive events. This results in a higher fraction of the number of pairs of events being related by causality and a smaller fraction of the number of pairs of events being concurrent. Bloom clocks performed best at $pr_i = 0$. We generalize this observation as the *causality spread hypothesis* later in Sect. 7.2.

The practical implication of setting $pr_i = 0$ is that most of the relevant events at which clocks tick are send and receive events, and only a few internal events (of interest to the application) cause the clocks to tick. In contrast, with a high

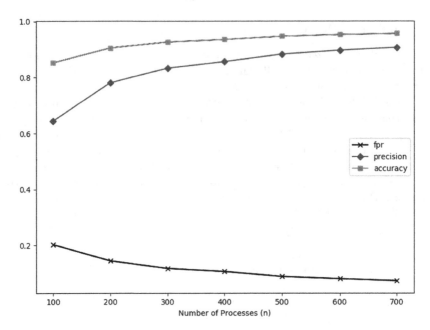

Fig. 1. A plot of metrics vs. number of processes for decentralized execution

Table 2. Variation of metrics with pr_i

pr_i	Precision	Accuracy	fpr
0	0.807	0.918	0.125
0.90	0.609	0.847	0.201
0.95	0.311	0.760	0.269
1	0.101	0.773	0.232

value of pr_i (such as 0.9 at which 90% of events at which clocks tick are internal events), accuracy and precision drop significantly, and fpr increases significantly. Thus, Bloom clocks are practical only when the percentage of relevant events (where clock ticks) that are internal events is small.

5.3   Number of Hash Functions

We ran the decentralized experiment for fixed $n = 200$ and fixed $pr_i = 0$ and averaged metrics over $m = 0.1 * n, 0.2 * n, 0.3 * n$ for individual values of k to check the variation of Bloom clock performance with respect to k. The results are shown in Table 3. We observe that the effect of changing the number of hash functions does not have a quantifiable effect on Bloom clock performance.

Table 3. Variation of metrics with k

k	Precision	Accuracy	fpr
2	0.804	0.917	0.126
3	0.809	0.919	0.124
4	0.808	0.919	0.124

5.4 Size of Bloom Clock

We ran the decentralized experiment for fixed $n = 200$ and fixed $pr_i = 0$ and averaged metrics over $k = 2, 3, 4$ for individual values of m to check the variation of Bloom clock performance with respect to m. The results are shown in Table 4. As expected, Bloom clock performance improves, but by up to 4.3% points, as m increases from $0.1 * n$ to $0.3 * n$. The improvement seems intuitive because with a larger number of indices the probability of hash function outputs mapping to the same indices reduces, due to which there is a lower probability of false positives.

Table 4. Variation of metrics with m

m	Precision	Accuracy	fpr
$0.1 * n$	0.784	0.906	0.143
$0.2 * n$	0.811	0.920	0.122
$0.3 * n$	0.827	0.929	0.109

In addition, we ran the experiment with scalar clock ($m = 1$ and $k = 1$) instead of Bloom clock, in order to investigate improvement in metrics for Bloom clock over scalar clock. We compared Bloom clock of size $m = 0.1 * n$ and $k = 2$ to scalar clock at various values of n for $pr_i = 0$. The results are presented in Table 5. We observe significant performance improvements over scalar clock by utilizing Bloom clock at all values of n – precision was 0.06 to 0.11, accuracy was 0.07 to 0.09, and fpr was 0.10 to 0.12 better.

Table 5. Bloom clock vs. scalar clock

n	Bloom Clock			Scalar Clock		
	Precision	Accuracy	fpr	Precision	Accuracy	fpr
50	0.492	0.788	0.266	0.434	0.713	0.368
100	0.644	0.852	0.203	0.542	0.769	0.318
200	0.781	0.905	0.145	0.672	0.835	0.248

5.5   Plots for pr_p and pr_{fp}

We ran the decentralized experiment for fixed parameters $n = 100$, $pr_i = 0$, $k = 2$ and $m = 0.1 * n$ to obtain plots for pr_p, and pr_{fp} computed using Eqs. 2 and 3. These plots demonstrate the behavior of Bloom clocks throughout an execution as the temporal proximity between events y and z varies, using just the Bloom timestamps of the two events being compared for causality. For these plots we fix event y with $GSN = 10 * n$, which is 1000, to allow for any startup transient effects, and compare its Bloom timestamp with all events z with $GSN = 10*n+1$ to $GSN = 4500$ ($\sim n^2/2$). This slice of the execution is adequate to capture all the trends. The x-axis of Figs. 2, 3 and 4 is the GSN of z and the y-axis is the probability being plotted.

Figure 2 shows a plot of pr_p as a function of GSN. We observe that as GSN increases, the probability of a positive prediction increases and flattens to around 1 between $GSN = 3500$ and $GSN = 4000$. This is because as the distance between two events increases, there is a higher probability of a causal relationship being established either directly or transitively. The split view of pr_p vs. GSN allows us to observe that most false positives occur in the middle of the distribution while all true negatives occur within the first half of the execution. This is due to the fact that initially the probability of a true negative is very high because the probability of a causal relationship being established is lower.

Figure 3 shows plots for $pr_{fp} = (1 - pr_p) \cdot pr_{\delta(p)}$ (Eq. 2) vs. GSN. We observe that Bloom clocks correctly predict the probability of false positive being 0 for all true negatives in the execution. Most of the false positives are distributed in the middle of the execution slice; the pr_{fp} jumps from 0 to large values once false positives start occurring and then gradually decreases as GSN increases. The (few) false positives that occur towards the end of the execution slice are not captured correctly with low values of pr_{fp}. The probability of false positive for a majority of true positives is below 0.25; however, for the initial few true positives, the pr_{fp} is inaccurately evaluated as being high. This probability pr_{fp} (for the true positives) rapidly decreases to 0 as GSN increases.

Figure 4 shows plots for $pr_{fp} = (1 - pr_p) * pr_p$ (Eq. 3) vs. GSN. As expected, pr_{fp} has values below 0.05 for most true negatives and true positives and reaches a maximum value of 0.25 in the middle of the execution where most of the false positives reside. Thus, the pr_{fp} is inaccurately evaluated as being low for the false positives in the middle of the execution slice.

Thus, Figs. 2, 3 and 4 confirm the theoretical predictions made in Sect. 4. Equation 2 uses a range of $[0,1]$ for pr_{fp}, gives a high pr_{fp} to the initial few true positives, and does not seem to capture the two conflicting influences on pr_{fp} described in Sect. 4 when the GSN of z is just a little greater than the GSN of y. Equation 3 uses a range of only $[0,0.25]$ and inaccurately gives a low pr_{fp} for the false positives in the middle of the execution slice.

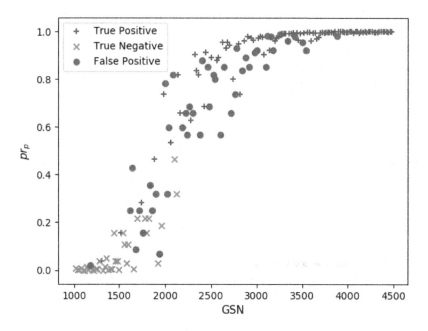

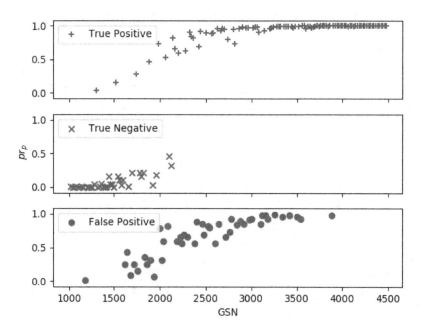

Fig. 2. pr_p vs. GSN, showing combined view and split view

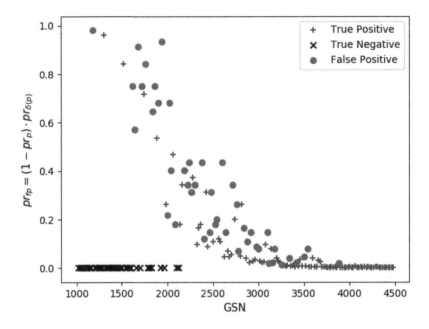

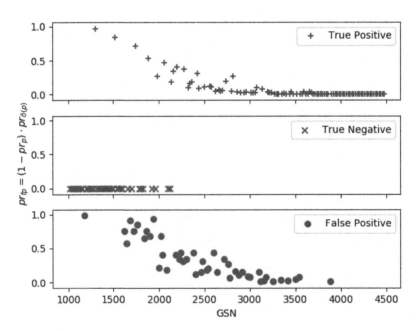

Fig. 3. $pr_{fp} = (1 - pr_p) \cdot pr_{\delta(p)}$ using Eq. 2 vs. GSN, showing combined view and split view

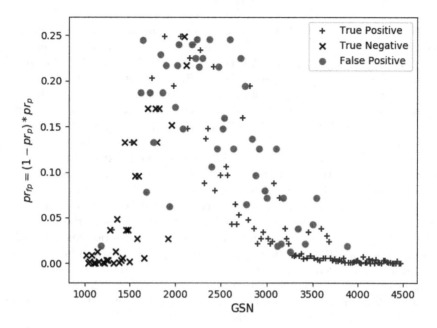

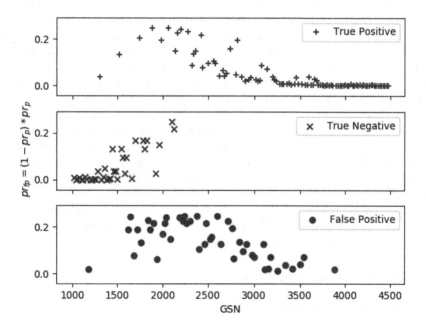

Fig. 4. $pr_{fp} = (1 - pr_p) \cdot pr_p$ using Eq. 3 vs. GSN, showing combined view and split view

6   Experiments for the Star Graph

We set up an experiment with a client-server architecture to investigate how faithfully the Bloom clock determines causality. Client processes connect to a multi-threaded server accepting TCP connections. Each server thread connects to a single client. The internal event probability, pr_i was set to 0. All message sends were synchronous and blocking and receives were blocking. Each client consisted of a process and had its own vector clock and Bloom clock. The server had a single vector clock and a single Bloom clock shared across all threads.

The server threads used a single lock to make sure that there were no race conditions on the vector clock and the Bloom clock while executing events. We did not use locks at the client end because GSN was not maintained. Further, not using locking mechanisms allowed interleaving of client processes.

Each client sent n messages to the server and received n corresponding messages from the server. This resulted in overall $O(n^2)$ events in the execution. Post execution, each 100th event was taken from the execution log containing all the events from the execution to create a sample of events to be compared for causality. Each event y was compared to each other event z to determine if Bloom clock correctly classified whether $y \rightarrow z$ or $y \nrightarrow z$. The correctness of the Bloom clock prediction was ascertained by comparing it with the prediction from vector clock. The results for the client-server experiment for $k = 2$ are shown in Table 6.

As can be seen from the results, Bloom clock performs quite well with high values of precision and low *fpr*. The first four rows are for $m = 0.1 * n$ and the last four rows are for $m = 0.05 * n$. We observed that for a small Bloom clock of size $m = 3$ for $n = 50$, the accuracy is high at 100% (There was one false positive, but rounding off to three decimal places results in the stated accuracy value). The difference in precision, accuracy, and *fpr* for smaller Bloom clocks as compared to larger Bloom clocks is not significant, therefore it is safe to say that for this configuration, smaller Bloom clocks perform well. The reason for strong performance of Bloom clock is that there are a lot of merge events with a centralized process, and the inherent message pattern at the server resulted in automatic and widespread distribution/broadcasting of information contained in individual Bloom clocks among all client processes. The server is always up to date with a client's Bloom clock after it executes a receive event corresponding to a message send event from the client. We generalize the reasoning behind the good performance of the Bloom clock for the client-server configuration by postulating the *causality spread hypothesis* in Sect. 7.2.

7   Observations and Discussion

7.1   Summary of Results

The results of the experiments are summarized as follows.

1. In predicting the causality between events y and z using their Bloom times-tamps, we observe the following.

Table 6. Results for client-server experiment with $k = 2$

n	m	Precision	Accuracy	fpr
50	5	0.985	0.992	0.015
100	10	0.990	0.995	0.010
125	13	0.991	0.996	0.009
150	15	0.995	0.997	0.005
50	3	100	100	0
100	5	0.996	0.998	0.004
125	7	0.997	0.998	0.003
150	8	0.997	0.998	0.003

(a) The probability of a positive pr_p increases relatively quickly from 0 to 1 as z occurs after but in the temporal vicinity of y.

(b) The probability of a false positive pr_{fp} is 0 or close to 0 except when z occurs later than but in the temporal vicinity of event y. As z occurs later at a process, the probability spikes up from 0 to a high value but soon comes down to 0 as the occurrence of z get temporally separated from the occurrence of y. Some true positives have a non-zero value of pr_{fp}.

2. As the number of processes n increases, the Bloom clock performance improves significantly – the accuracy and precision increase, and the fpr decreases.

3. When the number of internal events at which the clock ticks is low relative to the number of send events, precision, accuracy, and fpr all improve significantly. Thus, with relatively more send events, performance of Bloom clock improves. With more send events, causality between more pairs of events is established. On the other hand, if the number of internal events being timestamped is high with respect to the number of send events, Bloom clocks do not perform well.

4. The number of hash functions k used in the Bloom clock protocol does not impact much the precision, accuracy, and the fpr. Hence, it is advantageous to use a small number (such as 2 or 3) of hash functions.

5. The precision, accuracy, and the fpr improved by a few percentage points as the size of the Bloom Clock m was increased from $0.1 * n$ to $0.3 * n$. The impact is noticeable but not much. Hence, this suggests that small-sized Bloom Clocks can be used to gain significant space, time, and message-space savings over vector clocks. As a baseline for comparison, we also measured the precision, accuracy, and fpr for Lamport's scalar clocks. The scalar clocks performed noticeably worse.

6. For the client-server configuration, Bloom clocks performed exceedingly well.

Bloom clocks are seen to provide a viable space-, time-, and message-space-efficient alternative to vector clocks when some false positives can be tolerated. Bloom clock metrics improve as the number of processes increases. Bloom clock sizes can be 10% or even lower of the number of processes, and can handle churn transparently when processes join and leave the system. The probability of a false positive is high only when the two events occur temporally very close to each other. However, Bloom clocks do not perform well when the fraction of timestamped events that are internal events is not very low. In the next section, we generalize this behavior using the *causality spread hypothesis*.

7.2   Causality Spread

After conducting experiments to track causality using the Bloom clock for multiple architectures and varying parameters, we develop a hypothesis to help system engineers and software developers figure out whether the Bloom clock is a good fit for a given application. This hypothesis is stated only from the application's perspective. We hypothesize that with an increase in spread of causality in an execution, i.e., with a larger proportion of events related by causal relationships, Bloom clock performance (i.e., confidence in its predictions) increases. We define and compute the *causality spread*, α, as the ratio of the number of ordered pairs of events that are causally related, that is, *total positives*, to the sum of all ordered pairs of events compared for each execution. The set of events that we include in the computation of causality spread are the *relevant events* for the application.

Definition 2 (Causality spread α)

$$\text{Causality spread } \alpha = \frac{Total\ Positives}{\#\ All\ pairs\ of\ events}$$
$$= \frac{Total\ Positives}{Total\ Positives\ +\ Total\ Negatives} \tag{9}$$
$$= \frac{TP\ +\ FN}{TP\ +\ FN\ +\ FP\ +\ TN} = \frac{TP}{TP\ +\ FN\ +\ FP\ +\ TN}$$

Hypothesis 1 (Causality spread hypothesis). *The confidence in the predictions of the Bloom clock as measured by precision, accuracy, and* fpr *increases as the causality spread α of the application's set of relevant events increases.*

A higher α signifies more (fraction of) event pairs being related by causality, which are correctly classified as true positives, thereby increasing TP (say, by a), decreasing FP, decreasing TN, and decreasing FP + TN (by a). Theoretically, we expect precision and accuracy will improve (as per some non-linear functions), while the impact on *fpr* depends on the factors by which its numerator FP and its denominator FP + TN change.

This hypothesis is corroborated by our previously stated observation that increased message passing results in superior Bloom clock predictions. In order to quantify this hypothesis, we took a sample of executions from both the decentralized experiment and the client-server experiment and computed α. We observed that precision and accuracy increase and *fpr* decreases as α increases,

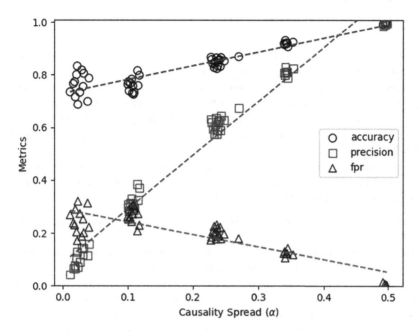

Fig. 5. A plot of metrics vs. *causality spread*

for $0 < \alpha < 0.5$, empirically confirming our hypothesis. A graph showing the increase in metrics as a function of causality spread is shown in Fig. 5.

An important note about causality spread is that it will range between 0 and 0.5 in our experiment because we check for causality between all pairs of events. An extreme case where $\alpha = 0$ would be each process executing only one event. Another extreme case where $\alpha = 0.5$ would be a linear chain of events. In the client-server experiment, α is near 0.5 due to the nature of transmission of causal relationships because of the server behavior. In the complete graph configuration with a high pr_i, the large number of timestamped internal events in the set of relevant events significantly increases the number of pairs of concurrent events and hence decreases α considerably, resulting in poor prediction by Bloom clocks.

We performed an experiment for multicast/broadcast messages to check if it conforms to our causality spread hypothesis. In the broadcast experiment, each process broadcasts a message to all $n-1$ processes and waits to receive $n-1$ broadcast messages from the other processes. Here, causality does not spread much because there is only one message send event followed by many receive events for each process. Here the receive events act as internal events that are timestamped (akin to high pr_i), and in effect there are many pairs of events that are concurrent and hence not related by causality, thereby resulting in a low α. In the experiment, $\alpha = 0.005$, precision $= 0.014$, accuracy $= 0.661$, and fpr $= 0.341$. The poor performance of Bloom clock in this experiment can be attributed to a low α as per the hypothesis.

8   Conclusions

Detecting the causality relationship between a pair of events in a distributed execution is a fundamental problem. To address this problem in a scalable way, this paper gave the formal Bloom clock protocol, and derived the expression for the probability of false positives, given two events' Bloom timestamps. We ran experiments to calculate the accuracy, precision, and *fpr* for a slice of the execution. We also ran experiments to calculate the probability of a false positive prediction based on the Bloom timestamps of two events. Based on the experiments, we made suggestions for the number of hash functions and size of Bloom clocks and identified conditions under which it is advantageous to use Bloom clocks over vector clocks. The findings are summarized as follows.

1. Bloom clocks can perform well for small size m and small number of hash functions k.
2. Bloom clocks perform well when the number of internal events considered is low compared to the number of send events (low pr_i).
3. Bloom clocks perform increasingly better as the system size n increases.
4. We also postulated the *causality spread hypothesis* from the application's perspective to determine whether Bloom clocks would give good performance (precision, accuracy, and *fpr*) for the application, and validated it through experiments. A high α indicates good performance.

Thus, Bloom clocks are seen to provide a viable space-, time-, and message-space-efficient alternative to vector clocks for the class of applications which meet the properties summarized above, when some false positives can be tolerated. It would be interesting to study the applicability of Bloom clocks to some practical applications.

References

1. Bloom, B.: Space/time tradeoffs in hash coding with allowable errors. Commun. ACM **13**(7), 422–426 (1970)
2. Broder, A.Z., Mitzenmacher, M.: Survey: network applications of bloom filters: a survey. Internet Math. **1**(4), 485–509 (2003). https://doi.org/10.1080/15427951.2004.10129096
3. Charron-Bost, B.: Concerning the size of logical clocks in distributed systems. Inf. Process. Lett. **39**(1), 11–16 (1991). https://doi.org/10.1016/0020-0190(91)90055-M
4. Couvreur, J., Francez, N., Gouda, M.G.: Asynchronous unison (extended abstract). In: Proceedings of the 12th International Conference on Distributed Computing Systems, Yokohama, Japan, 9–12 June 1992, pp. 486–493 (1992). https://doi.org/10.1109/ICDCS.1992.235005
5. Fidge, C.J.: Logical time in distributed computing systems. IEEE Comput. **24**(8), 28–33 (1991). https://doi.org/10.1109/2.84874
6. Kshemkalyani, A.D., Khokhar, A.A., Shen, M.: Encoded vector clock: using primes to characterize causality in distributed systems. In: Proceedings of the 19th International Conference on Distributed Computing and Networking, ICDCN 2018, Varanasi, India, 4–7 January 2018, pp. 12:1–12:8 (2018). https://doi.org/10.1145/3154273.3154305

7. Kshemkalyani, A.D., Misra, A.: The bloom clock to characterize causality in distributed systems. In: Barolli, L., Li, K.F., Enokido, T., Takizawa, M. (eds.) NBiS 2020. AISC, vol. 1264, pp. 269–279. Springer, Cham (2021). https://doi.org/10.1007/978-3-030-57811-4_25

8. Kshemkalyani, A.D., Shen, M., Voleti, B.: Prime clock: encoded vector clock to characterize causality in distributed systems. J. Parallel Distrib. Comput. **140**, 37–51 (2020). https://doi.org/10.1016/j.jpdc.2020.02.008

9. Kshemkalyani, A.D., Singhal, M.: Distributed Computing: Principles, Algorithms, and Systems. Cambridge University Press, Cambridge (2011). https://doi.org/10.1017/CBO9780511805318

10. Lamport, L.: Time, clocks, and the ordering of events in a distributed system. Commun. ACM **21**(7), 558–565 (1978)

11. Mattern, F.: Virtual time and global states of distributed systems. In: Proceedings of the Parallel and Distributed Algorithms Conference, pp. 215–226 (1988)

12. Meldal, S., Sankar, S., Vera, J.: Exploiting locality in maintaining potential causality. In: Proceedings of the Tenth Annual ACM Symposium on Principles of Distributed Computing, PODC 1991, pp. 231–239. ACM, New York (1991). https://doi.org/10.1145/112600.112620

13. Misra, J.: Phase synchronization. Inf. Process. Lett. **38**(2), 101–105 (1991). https://doi.org/10.1016/0020-0190(91)90229-B

14. Pozzetti, T.: Resettable Encoded Vector Clock for Causality Analysis with an Application to Dynamic Race Detection. M.S. Thesis, University of Illinois at Chicago (2019)

15. Pozzetti, T., Kshemkalyani, A.D.: Resettable encoded vector clock for causality analysis with an application to dynamic race detection. IEEE Trans. Parallel Distrib. Syst. **32**(4), 772–785 (2021). https://doi.org/10.1109/TPDS.2020.3032293

16. Ramabaja, L.: The bloom clock. CoRR (2019). http://arxiv.org/abs/1905.13064

17. Schwarz, R., Mattern, F.: Detecting causal relationships in distributed computations: in search of the holy grail. Distrib. Comput. **7**(3), 149–174 (1994). https://doi.org/10.1007/BF02277859

18. Singhal, M., Kshemkalyani, A.D.: An efficient implementation of vector clocks. Inf. Process. Lett. **43**(1), 47–52 (1992). https://doi.org/10.1016/0020-0190(92)90028-T

19. Tarkoma, S., Rothenberg, C.E., Lagerspetz, E.: Theory and practice of bloom filters for distributed systems. IEEE Commun. Surv. Tutor. **14**(1), 131–155 (2012). https://doi.org/10.1109/SURV.2011.031611.00024

20. Torres-Rojas, F.J., Ahamad, M.: Plausible clocks: constant size logical clocks for distributed systems. Distrib. Comput. **12**(4), 179–195 (1999). https://doi.org/10.1007/s004460050065

Model Development in the Tool USE: Explorative, Consolidating and Analytic Steps for UML and OCL Models

Martin Gogolla[(✉)] [ID]

Database Systems Group, University of Bremen, 28334 Bremen, Germany
`gogolla@informatik.uni-bremen.de`

Abstract. This contribution concentrates on the development process for descriptive and prescriptive UML and OCL models. We have decided to concentrate on three not necessarily disjoint techniques that we have labeled *explorative, consolidating* and *analytic*. We assume an imaginary, prototypical development process in that (1) informal ideas and requirements are first realized by *exploring* initial formal descriptions through interaction with a modeling tool, (2) stated ideas are *consolidated* with more detailed descriptions for structural and behavioral specifications, and (3) achieved descriptions are *analyzed* with respect to questions about stakeholder expectations. The contribution uses a running example for demonstration purposes.

Keywords: UML · OCL · Software development

1 Introduction

Building models is part of our everyday life, although we are not always aware of it. Thus naturally, modeling is part of software development. Even a program may be regarded as an executable model. "Engineering models aim to reduce risk by helping us better understand both a complex problem and its potential solutions before undertaking the expense and effort of a full implementation" (Bran Selic) [34].

In recent years, modeling with the visual Unified Modeling Language (UML) [33] and its textual extension Object Constraint Language (OCL) [37] has received much attention. With UML and OCL one can build descriptive and prescriptive models, and one can describe structural and behavioral aspects in a visual or textual style.

The aim of the tool UML-based Specification Environment (USE) was and is to support the design process for a textual UML and OCL model. The tool offers a graphical and shell-based user interface (GUI, CLI). It may be regarded as an interpreter for a subset of UML and for full OCL. It supports descriptive and prescriptive modeling with focus on model execution, validation, and verification. Starting from a textual model, it allows the developer to visualize aspects with class, object, sequence, communication and state diagrams.

© Springer Nature Switzerland AG 2021
D. Goswami and T. A. Hoang (Eds.): ICDCIT 2021, LNCS 12582, pp. 24–43, 2021.
https://doi.org/10.1007/978-3-030-65621-8_2

USE was developed over a number of years. Milestones in the tool development with accompanying publications were: basic UML features as UML class, object and sequence diagrams and full OCL support [18], the language ASSL (A Snapshot Sequence Language) [16] for model validation, an evaluation browser for debugging OCL expressions [6], the language SOIL serving for imperative model execution of the basis of OCL [7], behavior models in form of UML protocol state machines [23], behavior visualization with UML communication diagrams [19], the USE model validator [26] for automatic object model construction including use cases as invariant independence and constraint deduction [22] as well as classifying terms for systematically constructing diverse object models [24], and advanced support for object diagram features as hide-show-grayOut for objects and links and automatic layout options [20,21].

The rest of this contribution is structured as follows. Section 2 gives an overview on the considered model development steps. Section 3 discusses explorative methods within USE, Sect. 4 treats consolidating steps, and Sect. 5 shows methods for analyzing models. Related work is handled in Sect. 6. The contribution ends with conclusions and future work in Sect. 7.

2   Overview on Discussed Development Steps

This contribution concentrates on the development process for descriptive and prescriptive UML and OCL models. Modeling occurs typically in the early development phases, but when one regards a program as an efficiently executable model also in later phases modeling occurs. In all phases, validation and verification must happen, for example, in form of construction of test scenarios or a formal proof of a particular property. The different tasks in the different phases call for different techniques. We have decided to concentrate here on three not necessarily disjoint techniques that we have labeled *explorative, consolidating* and *analytic*. The terms come from an imaginary, prototypical development process in that (1) informal ideas and requirements for a project are first realized by *exploring* initial formal descriptions through interaction with a modeling tool using easy-to-apply methods that give quick results and feedback, (2) stated ideas are manifested and *consolidated* with more detailed descriptions for structure and in particular for behavior specifications, e.g., in form of state machines and operation implementations, and (3) achieved descriptions are *analyzed*, e.g., with respect to questions about informal stakeholder expectations or formal properties like consistency or constraint independence. We do not assume that the mentioned steps are complete or that they have to occur in the stated sequential order. All steps will typically be applied iteratively in a flexible development process. The overall aim is that the underlying model develops and changes in such a way that stakeholder requirements are met.

The aim of this contribution is to demonstrate how such development steps having an explorative, consolidating or analytic nature can be realized in the UML and OCL modeling tool USE (UML-based Specification Environment). We want to show how central tasks in these steps are supported by tool features.

For demonstration purposes, the contribution will use a running example, namely the development of a social network model.

3   Explorative Steps

By an *explorative step* we refer to development actions that start with somewhat diffuse ideas, possibly arising from a brainstorming step, and that try to formalize these ideas in terms of models. It might well be the case that inconsistencies in notions or in formal properties are detected. This step ideally ends up in an intermediate model that tries to be consistent, but not necessarily is so.

In the social network model, users with a first and last name as well as an identifying user name should be represented by Profile objects. Users should be enabled to establish Friendships with other users. The status of a Friendship may change from pending (after Friendship initiation by an inviter) to accepted or declined (after response by the invitee). Users may be interested in particular Topics (like Sports or Soccer) described by a tag. Topics can be arranged in an ontology-like structure with more general concepts and more special entities. For example, the Topic Pet (being the concept) could be detailed by the Topics Dog and Cat (being the entities); the Topic Dog in turn could be detailed by Lassie and Fang.

In Fig. 1, we get a first impression on how exploring USE models works. On the left, an underlying textual UML model with classes and associations is displayed in a project browser that allows the developer to select model elements and to zoom on their details in the lower window. Menus and buttons on the top give the option to execute particular functionalities as displaying a class diagram or an object diagram with a system state instantiating classes and associations with objects and links. The evaluation of an OCL query in the system state is shown as well as the command sequence that lead to the system state. The system state has been constructed interactively on the GUI by selecting classes from the browser, drawing them into the object diagram and by this creating objects for the selected class. The displayed command sequence has been reconstructed from the GUI actions and can be saved textually for repeated execution on the USE CLI (Command Line Interface). Attributes of created objects can be manipulated by selecting the objects and interactively setting the attribute values. Binary links can be constructed by selecting two objects in the object diagram and by choosing one option from the offered options in the right-click context menu. In the example, the selected objects Profile2 and Profile3 can be inserted as Friendship links either as (inviter:Profile3, invitee:Profile2) or as (inviter:Profile2, invitee:Profile3). The order for the role names comes from the textual model file and is also displayed in the project browser.

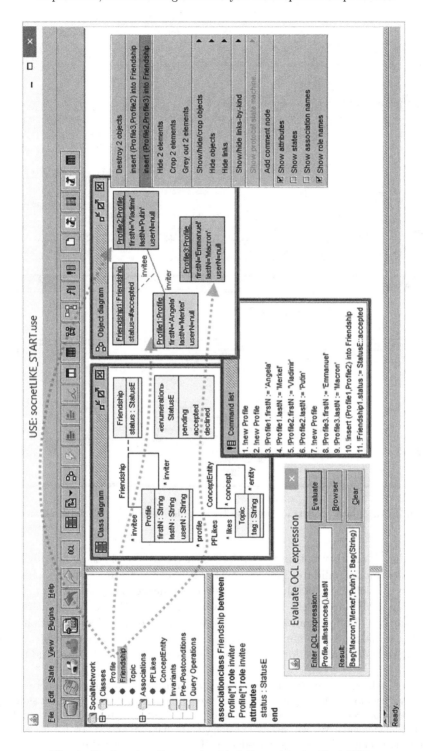

Fig. 1. Explorative, Interactive Modeling with the Tool USE.

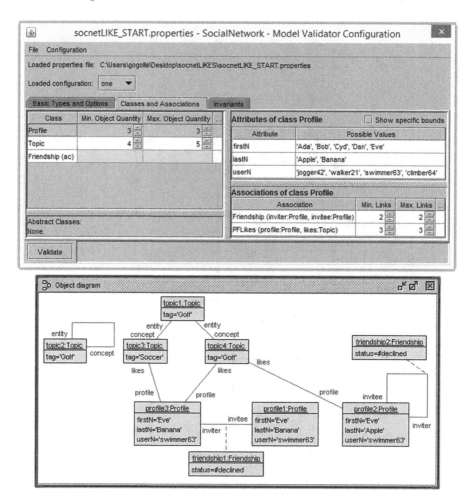

Fig. 2. Automatic Construction of an Object Model with the Model Validator.

In Fig. 2, another option for exploring the class model[1] is shown. In USE, a so-called model validator (for short MV; roughly speaking, a model checker) for class models is available that offers to automatically construct an object model. In UML, an object model is always finite in the sense that there is a finite number of objects and links. The MV needs a so-called configuration that specifies in particular a mandatory upper bound for the number of objects per class. Optionally and in addition, (1) lower class bounds and (2) lower and upper

---

[1] Sort of pedantic, we distinguish between a diagram and a model. A model reflects general principles. One model may be represented by two different diagrams showing different concrete model representations, e.g., left-right and upside-down orientation of model elements. We will use the notions 'class diagram' and 'class model' as well as 'object diagram' and 'object model' (with synonym 'system state').

bounds for the number of links per association, and (3) possible attribute values may be specified in a configuration. The displayed configuration requires, for example, four or five Topic objects, exactly two Friendship linkobjects to be present, and user names to look like 'jogger42' or 'swimmer63'.

The lower part of Fig. 2 displays the automatically and partially randomly constructed object diagram. The diagram appearance was basically determined automatically through a 'swimlane' layout method and few manual adjustments for better readability. The object model gives the opportunity to reflect on whether this currently allowed model is adequate for the desired purpose of the class model. For example, there are (1) different Topic objects with the same tag value, (2) cycles in the ConceptEntity ontology, and (3) a Profile object that refuses (declines) to have a Friendship connection with itself[2]. Such oddities call for further restriction of the class model with an additional description mechanism to be realized as textual constraints in form of OCL class invariants.

4   Consolidating Steps

By a *consolidating step* we refer to development actions that take up an intermediate model in which open questions are present and that try to solve the open issues. It might well be the case that more details are added, or conflicting model parts are identified before the conflicts are tried to be solved.

Figure 3 shows a model that is further developed consolidating a slightly changed and augmented structural UML class model with added OCL invariants and operations and a behavioral model in form of a UML protocol state machine (PSM) specifying the order in that Friendship operations are allowed to occur.

The structural class model has changed in comparison to the previous one in Fig. 1 in that the association class Friendship is now realized as an ordinary class with two associations to the class Profile. Previously, a Friendship linkobject has had two inviter and invitee connections to class Profile through its nature as an association class, now this is represented by a Friendship object with two separate inviter and invitee links both having a single-valued multiplicity. The reason for this change is that we have decided that this second model should be closer to concepts available in a programming language as association classes are not present there. Furthermore, this class model is augmented by OCL invariants that partly remove the discussed oddities from the previous class model: (a) the invariant userNUnique guarantees that the attribute userN is unique among all Profile objects; (b) invariant inviterInviteeUnique realizes something similar for Friendship objects, however not through attributes, but through the role names inviter and invitee and the requirement that no other Friendship is allowed to exist with the same inviter and invitee role combination; (c) invariant asymmetricFriendship requires that between two given Profile objects only one Friendship object exists (not allowed are two symmetric connections (1) inviter 'ada' and invitee 'bob' *and* (2) inviter 'bob' and invitee 'ada'); (d) invariant tagUnique

---

[2] Groucho Marx would be happy to see this is possible.

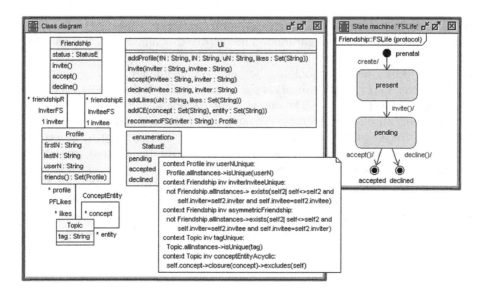

Fig. 3. Class model, OCL invariants and PSM for Social Network Example.

requires uniqueness of the attribute tag in the class Topic (analogously to userN for class Profile); (e) invariant conceptEntityAcyclic demands that the graph consisting of Topic objects as nodes and directed edges going into the 'concept' direction is acyclic. The two uniqueness and the acyclicity requirements would be violated in the object model from Fig. 2.

The class model in Fig. 3 shows behavioral aspects in form of operation declarations in the classes Friendship and UI (User Interface) and the protocol state machine (PSM) for class Friendship. The Friendship PSM restricts the operation call lifecycle of a Friendship object insofar that basically only two lifecycles are possible: (1) create; invite(); accept(); (2) create; invite(); decline(). The seven operations in class UI provide means to manipulate object models in a consolidated way. With 'consolidated', we refer to the fact that the UI operations in general work on objects from different classes in such a way that each single operation realizes a coherent and meaningful, complex functionality: (1) addProfile adds a new Profile with first, last and user name and guarantees that PFLikes links between the new Profile and Topic objects identified by the parameter likes are present; (2) invite establishes a new pending Friendship between an inviter and an invitee; (3,4) accept and decline change an existing pending Friendship into accepted or declined, respectively; (5) addLikes guarantees that PFLikes links identified by the parameter likes are present for the Profile object identified by the parameter uN; (6) addCE guarantees that ConceptEntity links between the Topic objects identified by the parameter concept and the Topic objects identified by the parameter entity are present; (7) recommendFS (recommend Friendship) recommends a new Friendship for the Profile identified by the parameter inviter based on the existing PFLikes links; the recommended Profile should 'somehow' like the same Topics as the potential inviter.

Behavior is further detailed with operation implementations formulated on the modeling level in the language SOIL (Simple OCL-like Imperative Language). Figure 4 prototypically pictures the implementation of the operation addProfile and an example of its execution. The sequence diagram with the top-most call addProfile('Bob', '', 'bob', Set{'Cat', 'Dog'}) shows how the left object model is transformed into the right object model. Basically, this call adds a new Profile object ('bob') with appropriate attribute values determined by the actual parameters, checks that one existing required Topic object ('Cat') can be reused and newly introduces another Topic object ('Dog'). The textual SOIL code in the UML comment node details how this is achieved in a generic way utilizing operation parameters, OCL expressions for checks and variable assignments, basic commands for object creation (new), attribute manipulation (:=), association manipulation (insert) and control flow commands for conditional (if) and iterative (for) execution.

There are five basic SOIL commands for object creation (new), object destruction (destroy), attribute manipulation (:=), link insertion (insert) and link destruction (delete). For the running example, we only show in detail one operation implementation as the other operations are implemented analogously. Operations may be connected optionally to operation contracts in form of declarative OCL pre- and postconditions, a feature that we do not have employed in the running example.

It might be interesting to see a scenario with operation calls where all operations are called at least once, as the one displayed below.[3]

```
create ui:UI
ui.addProfile('Ada','','ada',Set{'Dog'});
ui.addProfile('Bob','','bob',Set{'Dog'});
ui.addProfile('Cyd','','cyd',Set{'Jogging'});
BIDDER:=ui.recommendFS('ada');
ui.invite('ada',BIDDER.userN);
ui.accept(BIDDER.userN,'ada');
ui.addCE(Set{'Pet'},Set{'Dog','Cat'});
ui.addLikes('ada',Set{'Smoking'});
ui.invite('ada','cyd');
ui.decline('cyd','ada');
```

Because both an accept() and a decline() have to happen, at least three Profile objects including three addProfile() and two invite() calls must be present, leading to ten calls. The operation recommendFS() has a return value which is saved in the local, undeclared variable BIDDER. The resulting object model is displayed as an object diagram in Fig. 5.

---

[3] The scenario may be labeled 'Joggers do not like smoking dog owners'.

32   M. Gogolla

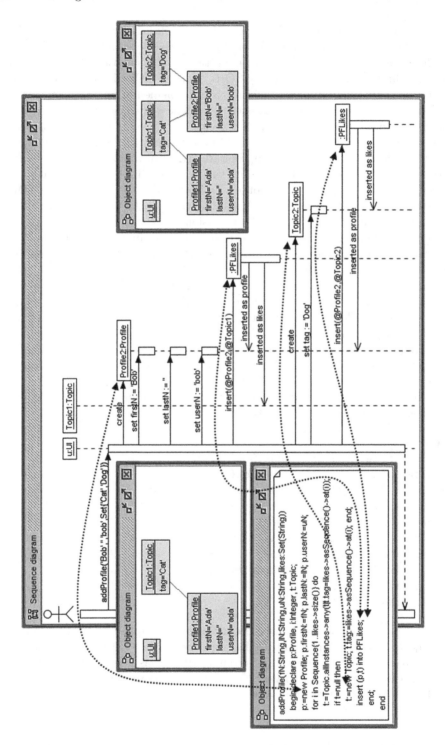

Fig. 4. SOIL operation with effects in object and sequence diagrams.

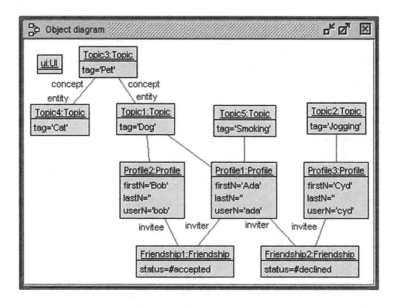

Fig. 5. Object model after scenario execution with all operations.

5   Analytic Steps

By an *analytic step* we refer to development actions that rely on an intermediate, temporarily completed model. This model is then analyzed w.r.t. some expectations of stakeholders to what extent the expectations are met, or the analysis tries to deduce some property of the model that is not explicitly present in it.

A first example of an analytic development step is presented in Fig. 6. This step is applicable in Fig. 2 in which an object model was shown that violates the later introduced invariant requiring acyclicity of the ConceptEntity association. The constraint corresponds to the OCL expression in Fig. 6 which evaluates to false. It would be interesting to find the objects that lead to the constraint violation. By clicking on the 'Browser' button in the OCL expression window, the 'Evaluation Browser' window in the bottom would open. This window can be configured to show the pictured display. The display clearly indicates that there is exactly one violating object for which the body of the OCL expression evaluates to false, namely the object topic2. Thus the 'Evaluation Browser' option is a means to analyze failure of an OCL invariant and to detect the objects leading to constraint violation.

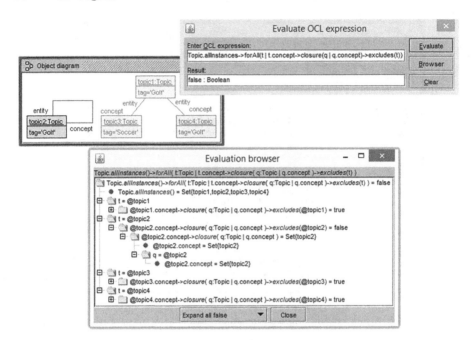

Fig. 6. Evaluation Browser Used for Analyzing Constraint Violation.

Figure 7 analyses the five present invariants. It checks whether there are dependencies among them. There is a dependency between invariants A and B given that: if invariant A is stronger than invariant B; in formal terms, A implies B, i.e., if all object models satisfying A also satisfy B; or the dependency could also be the other way round, i.e., B is stronger than A.

A and B dependent: $\forall o \in ObjectModelSet : (o \models A) \Rightarrow (o \models B)$ or
$\forall o \in ObjectModelSet : (o \models B) \Rightarrow (o \models A)$
A and B independent: $\exists o \in ObjectModelSet : \neg(o \models A) \wedge (o \models B)$ and
$\exists o \in ObjectModelSet : (o \models A) \wedge \neg(o \models B)$

In other words, A and B are independent, if there is an object model that satisfies B, but that does not satisfy A, i.e., validity of A does not necessarily imply the validity of B; and, validity of B does not necessarily imply the validity of A. As our model validator is able to find object models satisfying also a given set of invariants or its negations, one can systematically negate each single invariant and look for object models that satisfy all invariants except the chosen, negated one. In addition to checking this kind of invariant independence, this method exposes to the developer a number of object models that may be regarded as negative test cases demonstrating illegal situations that are ruled out by the invariants.

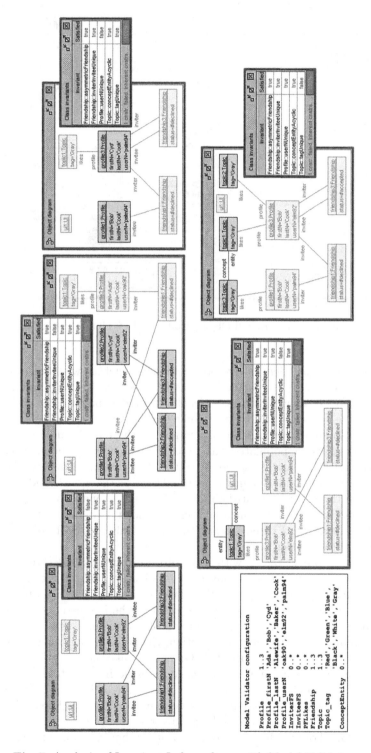

Fig. 7. Analysis of Invariant Independence with Model Validator.

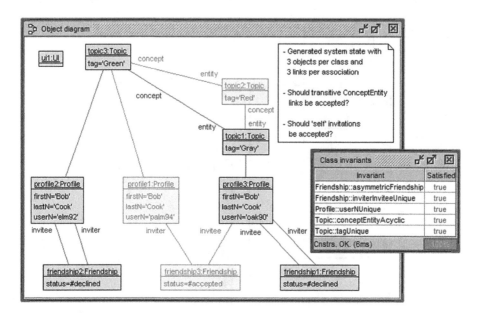

Fig. 8. Automatically Constructed Object Model for Revealing Missing Constraints.

In Fig. 7, one can identify five object models together with the evaluation status of the invariants. In each object model, one invariant is negated. These five object models show that the invariants are independent from each other, and contribute to model validation insofar that negative test cases are shown. The figure also shows the used configuration for the model validator in which basically all classes are populated with up to three objects, the population of the associations is left open, and appropriate attribute values are provided. Designing the 'right' configuration is a highly non-trivial task, as the model validator might respond with the answer 'unsatisfiable'. For example, if one would require three Profile objects to be present, but would only provide two values for the attribute userN which is required to be unique, the model validator will not be able to find a valid object model.

In Fig. 8, an object model with three objects per class and three links per association was constructed by our model validator. The object model contributes to model analysis insofar that links constellations that are admissible under the current invariants are shown, but these constellations need to be reflected and to be discussed. As previously possible, self invitations that are declined are still admissible. In addition, the object model shows transitive links for the association ConceptEntity. One might take the viewpoint, that such transitive connections are always implicitly available in an ontology-like structure and should not be presented explicitly in order to keep the fundamental information as simple as possible. Thus both phenomena, declined self invitations and transitive ConceptEntity links, give rise to a reflection whether these should be allowed or whether additional invariants should be introduced in order to forbid them.

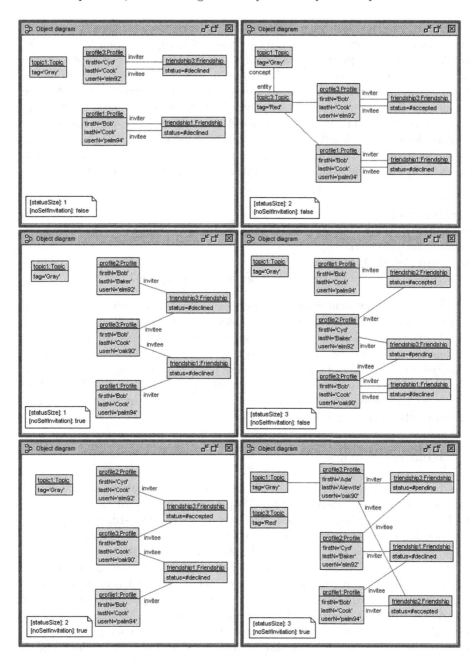

Fig. 9. Classifying Terms for Generating Diverse Object Models.

Figure 9 displays another analytic option in USE. So-called classifying terms, i.e., closed OCL query terms, are used for generating object models by the model validator that show properties determined by the OCL terms of type Boolean or Integer. The used configuration is the same as in shown Fig. 7. The aim is so see a collection of diverse object models in which each two object models are essentially different, e.g., two structurally isomorphic object models with only first names 'Ada' and 'Bob' changed to 'Adam' and 'Ben' would typically not be considered as 'essentially different'. The diversity and difference is controlled by the OCL query terms. In each two generated object models at least one OCL query term has to be evaluated to a different result. For our running example two considered classifying terms are defined as follows.

```
[statusSize]
Friendship.allInstances->collect(p|p.status)->asSet()->size()
[noSelfInvitation]
not(Profile.allInstances->
  exists(p | p.friendshipR.invitee->includes(p)))
```

The first Integer term statusSize counts the number of occurring Friendship status values in the respective object model. The second Boolean term checks whether no self invitation is present. Figure 9 shows six different generated object models (in the order the MV generates them) and the result of evaluating the classifying terms. Each of the object models has a unique value pair for the two classifying terms. Classifying terms help analyzing the UML and OCL model by systematically constructing object models with given properties that are determined by the classifying terms.

6   Related Work

The transformation of UML and OCL into formal specifications for validation and verification is a widely considered topic. In [35], a translation from UML to UML-B is presented und used for the validation and verification of models, focusing on consistency and checking safety properties. The approach in [4] presents a translation of UML and OCL into first-order predicate logic to reason about models utilizing theorem provers. Similarly, *OCL2MSFOL*, a tool recently introduced in [12], can automatically reason about UML/OCL models through a mapping from UML/OCL to many-sorted first-order logic. The tool can check satisfiability of OCL invariants by applying SMT solvers. There are also other tools that validate model instances against UML and OCL constraints directly, like *DresdenOCL* [13]. Another similar tool is *UML-RSDS* [27], which allows for the validation of UML class diagrams. Several approaches rely on different technological cornerstones like logic programming and constraint solving [10], relational logic and Alloy [2], term rewriting with Maude [32] or graph transformations [14]. In contrast to the tool used in this work, which is based on the transformation of UML and OCL into relational logic [26], these approaches either do not support full OCL (e.g., higher-order associations [2] or recursive operation definitions [10] are not supported) or do not facilitate full OCL syntax checks [32]. Also, the feature to automatically scroll through several valid object models from one verification task is not possible in all of the above approaches. (Semi)-automatic proving approaches for UML class properties have been put forward on the basis of description logics [31], on the basis of relational logic and pure Alloy [2] using a subset of OCL, and in [36] focusing on model inconsistencies by employing Kodkod. A classification of model checkers with respect to verification tasks can be found in [15].

Verification tools use such transformations to reason about models and verify test objectives. *UMLtoCSP* [9] is able to automatically check correctness properties for UML class diagrams enhanced with OCL constraints based on Constraint Logic Programming. The approach operates on a bounded search space similar to the model validator. In [2], *UML2Alloy* is presented. A transformation of UML and OCL into Alloy [25] is used to be able to automatically test models for consistency with the help of the *Alloy Analizer*. Another approach based on Alloy is presented in [28]. In particular, limitations of the previous transformation are eliminated by introducing new Alloy constructs to allow for a transformation of more UML features, e.g., multiple inheritance. In [38], OCL expressions are transformed into graph constraints and instance validation is performed by checking models against the graph constraints. Additionally, in [8], a transformation of OCL pre- and postconditions is presented for graph transformations.

The work in [5] describes an approach for test generation based on a transformation of UML and OCL into higher-order logic (HOL). With the *HOL-TestGen* tool, test cases (model instances) are generated and validated. In [30], a transformation of UML and OCL into first-order logic is described and test methods for models are shown, e.g., *class liveliness* (consistency) and *integrity of invariants* (constraint independence). A different approach is presented in [11]. The authors suggest to use Alloy for the early modeling phase of development due to its better suitability for validation and verification. Additionally, FOML, an F-logic based language, is introduced in [3] as an approach for modeling, analyzing and reasoning about models.

UML together with OCL have been successfully used for system modeling in numerous industrial and academic projects. Here, we refer to only three example projects trying to indicate the wide spectrum of application options. In our own early work [39], we have specified safety properties of a train system in the context of the well-known BART case study (Bay Area Rapid Transit, San Fransisco). In [1], central aspects of an industrial video conferencing system developed by Cisco have been studied. In [29], UML and OCL are employed for the specification of the UML itself by introducing the so-called UML metamodel in which fundamental well-formedness rules of UML are expressed as OCL constraints.

Finally, the USE model validator is to a certain degree the successor of *ASSL* (A Snapshot Specification Language) [16]. ASSL allows the specification of generation procedures for objects and links of each class and association. ASSL searches for a valid system state by iterating through all combinations defined by the procedures. In comparison, the USE model validator translates all model constraints into a SAT formula allowing for a more efficient generation of a system state, due to detecting bad combinations earlier. However, use cases like invariant independence have been discussed employing ASSL in earlier work [17]. But ASSL has, in comparison to the model validator, the advantage that Strings can be handled as composed entities and operations like substring() can be used, and not only simple checks for equality. The substring() operation is not supported in the more efficient model validator as Strings are atomic there.

7   Conclusion and Future Work

Our aim in this contribution was to demonstrate that the design tool USE for UML and OCL models can be employed in the software development process in a flexible manner for a number of tasks, namely explorative, consolidating, and analytic tasks. These tasks have to be combined in an adjustable way that meet stakeholder requirements, in particular for customers and developers.

Although USE has reached some degree of maturity, more work remains to be done. Systematically keeping track of model development steps, model versioning and carrying over test scenarios from early to later development phases is needed. The support for transformation into executable models and programs must be improved. Enhancing validation and verification options in the model validator would offer more possibilities. Improving and harmonizing the user interface in various corners of USE, e.g., between GUI and CLI, is necessary. Last but not least, assistance for imperfect, partial models as well as for runtime models and temporal and deontic constraints, as has already been initiated with first steps, should be worked on.

Acknowledgments. USE is not the result of the work of the author, but of numerous colleagues that have contributed significantly to its success (mentioned in order of appearance): Mark Richters, Jörn Bohling, Paul Ziemann, Mirco Kuhlmann, Lars Hamann, Duc-Hanh Dang, Frank Hilken, Khanh-Hoang Doan, Nisha Desai. Furthermore numerous students have added value through their final theses. Thank you very much. It was a pleasure for the author to work with you.

References

1. Ali, S., Iqbal, M.Z.Z., Arcuri, A., Briand, L.: A search-based OCL constraint solver for model-based test data generation. In: Núñez, M., Hierons, R.M., Merayo, M.G. (eds.) Proceedings of 11th International Conference on Quality Software QSIC, pp. 41–50. IEEE (2011)
2. Anastasakis, K., Bordbar, B., Georg, G., Ray, I.: On challenges of model transformation from UML to Alloy. Softw. Syst. Model. **9**(1), 69–86 (2010). https://doi.org/10.1007/s10270-008-0110-3
3. Balaban, M., Kifer, M.: Logic-based model-level software development with F-OML. In: Whittle, J., Clark, T., Kühne, T. (eds.) MODELS 2011. LNCS, vol. 6981, pp. 517–532. Springer, Heidelberg (2011). https://doi.org/10.1007/978-3-642-24485-8_38

4. Beckert, B., Keller, U., Schmitt, P.: Translating the object constraint language into first-order predicate logic. In: Proceedings of 2nd Verification WS: VERIFY, vol. 2, pp. 2–7 (2002)

5. Brucker, A.D., Krieger, M.P., Longuet, D., Wolff, B.: A specification-based test case generation method for UML/OCL. In: Dingel, J., Solberg, A. (eds.) MODELS 2010. LNCS, vol. 6627, pp. 334–348. Springer, Heidelberg (2011). https://doi.org/10.1007/978-3-642-21210-9_33

6. Brüning, J., Gogolla, M., Hamann, L., Kuhlmann, M.: Evaluating and debugging OCL expressions in UML models. In: Brucker, A.D., Julliand, J. (eds.) TAP 2012. LNCS, vol. 7305, pp. 156–162. Springer, Heidelberg (2012). https://doi.org/10.1007/978-3-642-30473-6_13

7. Büttner, F., Gogolla, M.: On OCL-based imperative languages. J. Sci. Comput. Program. **92**, 162–178 (2014)

8. Cabot, J., Clarisó, R., Guerra, E., de Lara, J.: Synthesis of OCL pre-conditions for graph transformation rules. In: Tratt, L., Gogolla, M. (eds.) ICMT 2010. LNCS, vol. 6142, pp. 45–60. Springer, Heidelberg (2010). https://doi.org/10.1007/978-3-642-13688-7_4

9. Cabot, J., Clarisó, R., Riera, D.: On the verification of UML/OCL class diagrams using constraint programming. J. Syst. Softw. **93**, 1–23 (2014)

10. Cabot, J., Clarisó, R., Riera, D.: UMLtoCSP: a tool for the formal verification of UML/OCL models using constraint programming. In: Proceedings of ASE 2007, pp. 547–548 (2007)

11. Cunha, A., Garis, A.G., Riesco, D.: Translating between alloy specifications and UML class diagrams annotated with OCL. SoSyM **14**(1), 5–25 (2015). https://doi.org/10.1007/s10270-013-0353-5

12. Dania, C., Clavel, M.: OCL2MSFOL: a mapping to many-sorted first-order logic for efficiently checking the satisfiability of OCL constraints. In: Proceedings of ACM/IEEE 19th International Conference on Model Driven Engineering Languages and Systems, MODELS 2016, pp. 65–75. ACM (2016)

13. Demuth, B., Wilke, C.: Model and object verification by using Dresden OCL. In: Proceedings of Russian-German WS Innovation Information Technologies: Theory and Practice, pp. 687–690 (2009)

14. Ehrig, K., Küster, J.M., Taentzer, G.: Generating instance models from meta models. Softw. Syst. Model. **8**, 479–500 (2009). https://doi.org/10.1007/s10270-008-0095-y

15. Gabmeyer, S., Brosch, P., Seidl, M.: A classification of model checking-based verification approaches for software models. In: Proceedings of the 1st VOLT Workshop (2013)

16. Gogolla, M., Bohling, J., Richters, M.: Validating UML and OCL models in USE by automatic snapshot generation. Softw. Syst. Model. **4**(4), 386–398 (2005). https://doi.org/10.1007/s10270-005-0089-y

17. Gogolla, M., Kuhlmann, M., Hamann, L.: Consistency, independence and consequences in UML and OCL models. In: Dubois, C. (ed.) TAP 2009. LNCS, vol. 5668, pp. 90–104. Springer, Heidelberg (2009). https://doi.org/10.1007/978-3-642-02949-3_8

18. Gogolla, M., Büttner, F., Richters, M.: USE: a UML-based specification environment for validating UML and OCL. J. Sci. Comput. Program. **69**, 27–34 (2007)

19. Gogolla, M., Hamann, L., Hilken, F., Sedlmeier, M.: Modeling behavior with interaction diagrams in a UML and OCL tool. In: Roubtsova, E., McNeile, A., Kindler, E., Gerth, C. (eds.) Behavior Modeling – Foundations and Applications. LNCS, vol. 6368, pp. 31–58. Springer, Cham (2015). https://doi.org/10.1007/978-3-319-21912-7_2

20. Gogolla, M., Hamann, L., Xu, J., Zhang, J.: Exploring (Meta-)model snapshots by combining visual and textual techniques. In: Gadducci, F., Mariani, L. (eds.) Proceedings of Workshop Graph Transformation and Visual Modeling Techniques (GTVMT 2011), ECEASST, Electronic Communications (2011). https://journal.ub.tu-berlin.de/eceasst/issue/view/95

21. Gogolla, M., Havakili, H., Schipke, C.: Advanced features for model visualization in the UML and OCL tool USE. In: Michael, J., et al. (eds.) Companion Proceedings Modellierung 2020, CEUR, vol. 2542, pp. 203–207. CEUR-WS.org (2020)

22. Gogolla, M., Hilken, F., Doan, K.H.: Achieving model quality through model validation, verification and exploration. J. Comput. Lang. Syst. Struct. **54**, 474–511 (2018)

23. Hamann, L., Hofrichter, O., Gogolla, M.: Towards integrated structure and behavior modeling with OCL. In: France, R., Kazmeier, J., Breu, R., Atkinson, C. (eds.) Proceedings of 15th International Conference on Model Driven Engineering Languages and Systems (MoDELS 2012), LNCS 7590, pp. 235–251. Springer, Berlin (2012)

24. Hilken, F., Gogolla, M., Burgueno, L., Vallecillo, A.: Testing models and model transformations using classifying terms. J. Softw. Syst. Model. **17**(3), 885–912 (2018). https://doi.org/10.1007/s10270-016-0568-3

25. Jackson, D.: Software Abstractions - Logic, Language, and Analysis. MIT Press, Cambridge (2006)

26. Kuhlmann, M., Gogolla, M.: From UML and OCL to relational logic and back. In: France, R.B., Kazmeier, J., Breu, R., Atkinson, C. (eds.) MODELS 2012. LNCS, vol. 7590, pp. 415–431. Springer, Heidelberg (2012). https://doi.org/10.1007/978-3-642-33666-9_27

27. Lano, K., Kolahdouz-Rahimi, S.: Specification and verification of model transformations using UML-RSDS. In: Méry, D., Merz, S. (eds.) IFM 2010. LNCS, vol. 6396, pp. 199–214. Springer, Heidelberg (2010). https://doi.org/10.1007/978-3-642-16265-7_15

28. Maoz, S., Ringert, J.O., Rumpe, B.: CD2Alloy: Class diagrams analysis using alloy revisited. In: Whittle, J., Clark, T., Kühne, T. (eds.) MODELS 2011. LNCS, vol. 6981, pp. 592–607. Springer, Heidelberg (2011). https://doi.org/10.1007/978-3-642-24485-8_44

29. OMG - Object Management Group: Unified Modeling Language Specification, Version 2.5, June 2015

30. Queralt, A., Teniente, E.: Reasoning on UML class diagrams with OCL constraints. In: Embley, D.W., Olivé, A., Ram, S. (eds.) ER 2006. LNCS, vol. 4215, pp. 497–512. Springer, Heidelberg (2006). https://doi.org/10.1007/11901181_37

31. Queralt, A., Artale, A., Calvanese, D., Teniente, E.: OCL-Lite: finite reasoning on UML/OCL conceptual schemas. Data Knowl. Eng. **73**, 1–22 (2012)

32. Roldán, M., Durán, F.: Dynamic validation of OCL constraints with mOdCL. ECEASST **44** (2011)

33. Rumbaugh, J., Jacobson, I., Booch, G.: The Unified Modeling Language Reference Manual, 2nd edn. Addison-Wesley, Boston (2004)

34. Selic, B.: The pragmatics of model-driven development. IEEE Softw. **20**(5), 19–25 (2003)

35. Snook, C., Savicks, V., Butler, M.: Verification of UML models by translation to UML-B. In: Aichernig, B.K., de Boer, F.S., Bonsangue, M.M. (eds.) FMCO 2010. LNCS, vol. 6957, pp. 251–266. Springer, Heidelberg (2011). https://doi.org/10.1007/978-3-642-25271-6_13

36. Straeten, R.V.D., Puissant, J.P., Mens, T.: Assessing the kodkod model finder for resolving model inconsistencies. In: ECMFA, pp. 69–84 (2011)

37. Warmer, J., Kleppe, A.: The Object Constraint Language: Getting Your Models Ready for MDA, 2nd edn. Addison-Wesley, Boston (2004)

38. Winkelmann, J., Taentzer, G., Ehrig, K., Küster, J.M.: Translation of restricted OCL constraints into graph constraints for generating meta model instances by graph grammars. ENTCS **211**, 159–170 (2008)

39. Ziemann, P., Gogolla, M.: Validating OCL specifications with the USE tool: an example based on the BART case study. ENTCS **80**, 157–169 (2003)

ReLink: Open Information Extraction by Linking Phrases and Its Applications

Xuan-Chien Tran and Le-Minh Nguyen[✉]

Japan Advanced Institute of Science and Technology, Nomi, Japan
chientranx@gmail.com, nguyenml@jaist.ac.jp

Abstract. Recently, many Open IE systems have been developed based on using deep linguistic features such as dependency-parse features to overcome the limitations presented in older Open IE systems which use only shallow information like part-of-speech or chunking. Even though these newer systems have some clear advantages in their extractions, they also possess several issues which do not exist in old systems. In this paper, we analyze the outputs from several popular Open IE systems to find out their strength and weaknesses. Then we introduce RELINK, a novel Open IE system for extracting binary relations from open-domain text. Its working model is based on identifying correct phrases and linking them in the most proper way to reflect their relationship in a sentence. After establishing connections, it can easily extract relations by using several pre-defined patterns. Despite using only shallow linguistic features for extraction, it does not have the same weakness that existed in older systems, and it can also avoid many similar issues arising in recent Open IE systems. Our experiments show that RELINK achieves larger Area Under Precision-Recall Curve compared with REVERB and OLLIE, two well-known Open IE systems.

Keywords: Open information extraction · Relink

1 Introduction

Since the COVID-19 pandemic, the number of documents written about it has become explosive and overwhelming. The problem of extraction information about this issue becomes very important. Information extraction (IE) is a task to extract required information from unstructured data such as raw text. The extracted information can be events, facts, entities, or relationship between entities in the text. These extracted data enable computers to perform computation or logical inference on it, a difficult task if we just work with raw text. Traditional methods for IE are based on pre-defined target relations and they usually work on a specific domain [10,21]. Because of this, these IE methods do not scale very well on an open-domain and large corpora such as Web text.

Open IE is proposed to solve this problem. It provides a different way of extraction in which all potential relations are extracted without requiring any target relations or human input [1]. Therefore it can work and scale really well

D. Goswami and T. A. Hoang (Eds.): ICDCIT 2021, LNCS 12582, pp. 44–62, 2021.
https://doi.org/10.1007/978-3-030-65621-8_3

with open-domain corpora, especially Web text. Open IE provides a simple way to transform unstructured data into a relational data which is used to support other tasks like question-answering system [7,15], text summarization [3,11,18], textual entailment [2,17], or some semantic tasks [16,19].

Many Open IE systems focus on extracting binary relations from the text. Those binary relations are in the form

(*argument 1*; *relation phrase*; *argument 2*)

in which *argument 1* and *argument 2* are two noun phrases and *relation phrase* represents the relationship between those noun phrases in the sentence. For example, given the sentence *"Barrack Obama was born in the United States"*, we want to extract the following relation:

(Barrack Obama; was born in; the United States)

In this relation, *"Barrack Obama"* and *"the United States"* are two entities in this sentence and *"was born in"* describes their relationship. A relation can also be called as a *triple* or *tuple*, and the relation phrase can be called *predicate*.

Open IE systems can be categorized into two groups depending on what information they use for extraction. The first group includes systems like REVERB [6] or TEXTRUNNER [1] in which they use only shallow linguistic features (POS tags or chunks) to extract relations. These features have flat structure and thus prevent the above systems from capturing long-range dependencies between words or phrases in a sentence. The second group includes systems like DEPOE [9], OLLIE [14] or STANFORDOPENIE [8]. These systems utilize deep linguistic features of a sentence for extractions. Specifically, they use dependency-parse features to resolve the issues of long-range dependencies that existed in the first group's system. As a result, these systems were reported to extract relations more accurately.

Interestingly, we found that using deeper linguistic features also has a limitation. Systems which tightly depend on the deep parsing features can produce incorrect relations due to a small error on the parsing output. Table 1 gives an example of this situation. REVERB uses only shallow linguistic information but it correctly identifies two relations meanwhile OLLIE only discovers one and STAN-FORDOPENIE yields no extractions. This raises the question of whether we can avoid using deep linguistic features but still manage to achieve long-range dependencies. In this paper, we introduce a novel system called RELINK to answer this question. In particular, our system uses shallow linguistic information but can deal with the long-range dependencies. This allows us to overcome several issues that existed in REVERB and at the same time avoid the issues caused by bad dependency-parsing output.

The rest of this paper is organized as follows. Section 2 presents some related work in this research topic. Section 3 introduces the method we use to deal with two important elements in extracting a relation: Verb Phrases and Noun Phrases. Section 4 describes in details RELINK, our proposed Open IE system. We present our experimental results in Sect. 5 and finally, we give a conclusion and some words about our future work in Sect. 6.

Table 1. Extractions of ReVerb, Ollie and StanfordOpenIE for the sentence *"Einstein, who was born in Germany, is a scientist."*

Einstein, who was born in Germany, is a scientist.	
ReVerb	(Einstein; was born in; Germany)
	(Einstein; is; a scientist)
Ollie	(Einstein; is; a scientist)
StanfordOpenIE	No extractions

2 Related Work

The first Open IE system is TextRunner [1]. This system uses a self-trained classifier to decide when to extract the relationship between two noun phrases. Its features for the classifier are extracted from the POS tags and chunks. When comparing with another IE system called KnowItAll [5], TextRunner achieved competitive accuracy with lower error rate.

Later, a new Open IE called WOE [22] is proposed which dramatically improved precision and recall comparing to TextRunner. Its idea is to use information from Wikipedia to train the extractor. It also supports using dependency-parse features to further improve the system performance.

Fader et.al. [6] observed several issues presented in TextRunner and WOE, and proposed a system called ReVerb to solve these issues. The authors listed out two main types of incorrect relations extracted by previous systems: *incoherent* (a relation has no meaningful interpretation) and *uninformative* (a relation misses critical information). Hence, they defined two types of constraints to reduce these errors: *syntactic constraint* and *lexical constraint*. Syntactic constraint is basically a token-based regular expression used to capture the correct predicate appearing in the sentence. It requires the relation phrase to be a contiguous sequence or words, start with a verb and end with a preposition. *Lexical constraint* is built from a large dictionary, and it is used to filter out overspecific relations.

The main problem of ReVerb is that it is unable to capture the long-distance relationship between predicate and arguments. Most of the incorrect extractions from ReVerb are due to its wrong argument identification. Its argument-finding heuristics often return the closest noun phrase on the left side of the predicate as Argument 1 and therefore unable to output a correct triple if arguments and predicate are far apart. Thus many researchers started using a richer linguistic information to overcome this limitation. Ollie [14], which is considered as the next version of ReVerb, resolves ReVerb's issue by supporting a wider syntactic range via its *open pattern templates*. These templates are applied directly on the dependency-parsing output to find valid relations. Ollie also has the ability to provide context information for a relation and extract relations mediated by nouns or adjectives.

Another Open IE system which uses dependency parser for extraction is DepOE [9]. This system is multilingual and achieves better performance than ReVerb in their evaluation. It relies on DepPattern, a multilingual dependency parser[1], to parse a sentence and then apply a list of pre-defined rules on the parse output to extract relations.

Some recent Open IE systems take another further step in using the dependency-parsing output for their extraction, that is they divide the sentences into multiple clauses before extraction. A system called ClauseIE [4] follows this approach. From dependency-parsing output, the system extract relations by identifying different types of *useful* clauses. Each clause can result in multiple relations. This system achieved higher precision than previous extractors in all of their experiment datasets.

Lastly, a new clause-based Open IE system is also implemented as a part of Stanford CoreNLP [13], which leverages the linguistic structure of the sentence for extraction[8]. This system works by first extracting self-contained clauses in a sentence and then running a logic inference on these clauses to find the correct arguments for each triple. They reported a better performance than OLLIE on the end-to-end TAC-KBP 2013 Slot Filling task [20].

Our work is partly inherited from REVERB and inspired by newer systems. We adopt a similar method as REVERB for identifying phrases in a sentence, but we use a novel linking mechanism to build the relationship between phrases to capture long-range dependencies. We also define a list of patterns, but they are used for extracting relations from the connected phrases, not for identifying clause type like ClauseIE.

3   Verb Phrases and Noun Phrases

In Open IE, one important step is to recognize correct Verb Phrases (VP) and Noun Phrases (NP) in the sentence. In this section, we describe how we adopt the mechanism used in REVERB and extend it to use in our system.

3.1   Verb Groups

The information of a VP can determine the position of its subject and object in the sentence. Based on this idea, we treat VP differently depending on their POS information. In particular, we categorize VP into four groups:

- *A-VP*: if their POS tags start with MD, VB, VBZ or VBD.
- *P-VP*: if their POS tags start with VBN.
- *G-VP*: if their POS tags start with VBG.
- *T-VP*: if their POS tags start with TO followed by a VB tag.

Table 2 shows some example sentences with their corresponding POS tags in each verb group. Notice that even though a VP can contain multiple words, we only look at the POS tag of its first word to categorize.

The reason for categorizing VP into different groups is because they can affect the way we extract a relation from a sentence. For example, given the sentence:

---

[1] https://gramatica.usc.es/pln/tools/deppattern.html.

Table 2. Some examples of Verb Groups

Verb Group	Example sentence
A-VP	He *is walking* on the street PRP *VBZ VBG* IN DT NN
P-VP	Mary likes the photo *posted* by Peter NNP VBZ DT NN *VBN* IN NNP
G-VP	People *making* this statement are rich NNS *VBG* DT NN VBP JJ
T-VP	I want him *to stay* here tonight PRP VBP PRP' *TO VB* RB RB

*A smart guy **living** in this house **invented** a new machine **to do** the task **assigned** by his boss.*

There are four VPs presented in this sentence: *"living"* is a G-VP, *"invented"* is an A-VP, *"to do"* is a T-VP and *"assigned"* is a P-VP. With G-VP and P-VP, it is likely that their subjects stay right before them in a sentence and therefore we can extract the following relations with high confidence:

0: (A smart guy; be living in; this house)
1: (the task; be assigned by; his boss)

This, however, might not be true for an A-VP because *"this house"* should not be the subject of the verb *"invented"*, its correct argument should be *"A smart guy"* as in the following relation:

2: (A smart guy; invented; a new machine)

T-VP, on the other hand, cannot take its preceding NP as its first argument and should be combined with other phrases to build a coherent relation like this:

3: (A smart guy; invented a new machine to do; the task)

REVERB is unable to extract any of above relations from the example sentence, its only extraction is an incoherent relation: *(this house; invented; a new machine)*. OLLIE can extract relation 1 and 2, but its third relation is a bit controversial: *(A smart guy living in this house; invented; a new machine to do the task)*. In our opinion, arguments should not contain too much information which can be considered as an extra relation.

Table 3. Regular expression for recognizing VP.

Verb Group	Expression
A-VP	prefix [MD|VB|VBZ|VBD|VBP] suffix
P-VP	prefix VBN suffix
G-VP	prefix VBG suffix
T-VP	prefix TO prefix VB suffix
prefix	(adv|particle)*
suffix	(adv|particle|vp-chunk)*

For recognizing these VPs from their POS tags and Chunks, we adopt the token-based regular expression used in REVERB. Here, each verb group has its own expression as shown in Table 3. As can be seen, these expressions are able to recognize other components such as adverbs or particles around the main verb. It is worth noting that we also utilize chunking information (I-VP tags) to recognize VP because this information is useful in the case some adverbs or verbs are mistagged by the POS tagger but correctly tagged by the chunker.

If there are multiple adjacent VPs, we merge all of them into a single VP with verb group is the same as the left-most VP. Besides, our VP expansion also deals with two special cases:

1. If a VP is followed by a preposition and a G-VP, we should merge them into the VP. Some example phrases are *"aim at hurting"*, *"look forward to seeing"*. Both of these phrases are considered as a single VP.
2. If a VP is followed by multiple prepositions, we merge all prepositions except the last one into the VP. This is a small correction for the case when POS tagger incorrectly identifies a particle as a preposition. Example phrases are: *"come out of"*, *"look forward to"*.

3.2 Noun Phrases

We can easily get all base NPs from the sentence based on chunking information, but we also want to group related NP together to form a bigger NP if necessary. For example, phrases like *"a president of the United States"* should be viewed as a single NP even though they are recognized as two NPs by the chunker.

For this purpose, we define three cases for grouping multiple NPs into a single NP:

1. An NP followed by a possessive NP.
2. Two NPs separated by the lexical token *"of"*.
3. Two NPs separated by the lexical token *"and"* and: (i) the second NP is not followed by a VP, or (ii) the first NP is right after an SBAR chunk.

REVERB also supports expanding NP by following the first two cases, but we think the third case is also necessary, especially when the chunker is unable to tag them properly as a single phrase.

3.3 Disputed Noun Phrases

On analyzing the output from REVERB, we have realized that there are two common cases where an NP can be incorrectly identified as an argument of a relation phrase: (i) an NP that stays exactly between two A-VP phrases, or (ii) an NP that follows a PP and stays before an A-VP. We call those NPs as *disputed NPs*. In Table 4, we give two sentences containing disputed NP and corresponding extractions from REVERB. In the first sentence, the NP *"the man"* is between two A-VPs *"said"* and *"had"*. REVERB does not take this into account and blindly extract the first relation even though it is incoherent.

Table 4. Extractions from ReVerb on sentences with disputed NP.

He said ***the man*** was a criminal.
(He; said; the man)
(the man; was; a criminal)

The students in ***the classroom*** are second language learners.
(the classroom; are; second language learners)

In the second case, the phrase *"the classroom"* is a disputed NP because it is between the PP *"in"* and the A-VP *"are"*. With this sentence, ReVerb yields the relation *"(the classroom; are; second language learners)"*. This relation is clearly incoherent because the first argument should be *"the students"*. In ReLink, we explicitly handle these disputed NPs to let the extractor know which NP should be selected for a certain predicate and thus we can avoid incoherent relations.

4 ReLink

This section describes the algorithm of ReLink for extracting binary relations. First, it starts by chunking and identifying phrases in a sentence using the methods described in Sect. 3. Then it employs a new method for building the relationship between phrases by iterating through each phrase and create left and right connections. Finally, relations are extracted using several pre-defined patterns. Figure 1 shows the steps performed in ReLink to extract relations from an input sentence.

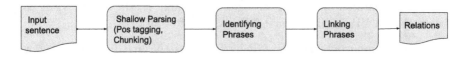

Fig. 1. Procedure of ReLink to extract relations from a sentence.

4.1 Phrase Identification

In this step, we use Apache OpenNLP[2] for POS tagging and chunking the sentence. From the chunked sentence, we construct four groups of phrases: VP, NP, PP and O. VP and NP are identified using the methods described in Sect. 3, PP is directly captured from chunking information, and all other tokens are converted to O phrases. The process of phrase identification is illustrated in Fig. 2. As can be seen from the example, we successfully capture the long noun phrase

---

[2] https://opennlp.apache.org/.

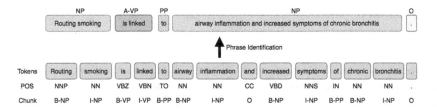

Fig. 2. An example of Phrase Identification for the sentence *"Routing smoking is linked to airway inflammation and increased symptoms of chronic bronchitis."*

"airway inflammation and increased symptoms of chronic bronchitis" by grouping several NPs together. This is achieved thanks to the patterns we described in Sect. 3.2.

4.2   Phrase Linking

This is a crucial step to decide which phrases should go together to form a valid extraction. In RELINK, we go through each phrase from left to right and decide which phrases should be linked to reflect the relationship of phrases in the most proper way. Specifically, each phrase is assigned a number of *available_slots*, i.e. the maximum number of connections a phrase can have with other phrases in the sentence. Whenever a connection is established between two phrases, their *available_slots* is decreased 1. A phrase with no available slots can not connect with any other phrases. The value of *available_slots* varies depending on the phrase type as follows:

- NP: has 1 *available slot* by default. In our assumption, an NP is either a subject or an object of a clause but not both. Exceptional cases are handled separately.
- VP: has 2 *available slots*, 1 slot for the connection on the left side and another slot for the connection on the right side. We give 2 slots to a VP based on an assumption that a VP always has 1 subject and 1 object.
- PP: has 2 *available slots* similar to VP. PP here should play a role of connecting its preceding phrase and its succeeding phrase.
- O: does not have any available slots. We do not want them to connect with any other phrases.

Before iterating through each phrase, we perform two pre-linking tasks to deal with some special cases:

1. We add 1 additional slot to the NPs that are followed by a WH-modifier because they are likely the argument of many relations.
2. We identify and mark disputed NPs as described in Sect. 3.3. These NPs will be processed differently in our algorithm.

After this preparation, we start processing each phrase one by one from left to right. NPs will play a passive role in our algorithm, they stay waiting for connections from phrases of other types. Because of this, we only focus on how to create connections from VP and PP.

Connections from VP. From each VP, we will try to create two connections with other phrases, one connection on its left side and the other connection on the right side.

It is simple to create a connection on the right side, we only need to make sure the succeeding phrase is an NP or PP. This is because, in our observation, the phrase follows a VP is usually directly related to that VP. Of course this will be wrong if the succeeding phrase is a disputed NP. This problem will be handled by the VP staying right after the disputed NP when it tries to create a left connection.

It is, however, more complicated to create a connection with a phrase on the left side. The detailed algorithm to look for proper phrase and create a left connection is shown in Algorithm 1. First of all, we deal with a special case where the word *"and"* stays in front of the VP. In that case, the current VP is likely to be an extension of another existing clause. Thus we look for the first VP of the same group and try to connect the left phrase of that VP to the current phrase (using the function `getArg1OfVerbGroup`).

If the previous phrase is not *"and"*, we will look for candidate phrase depending on the group of the current VP. In case of A-VP, there are three cases as follows:

- If its immediate preceding phrase is an available NP, we directly create a connection between it and the current VP. This is actually the normal case in simple sentences like *"Donald Trump is the new president of the United States."*, there is no confusion to establish the connection between *"is"* and *"Donald Trump"*.
- If its previous phrase is not available, we have to search until the beginning of the sentence to find an available NP (using the function `getAvailableNP`).
- If no available NP is found and the previous phrase is a disputed NP, we remove current connections from this disputed NP and connect it with the current VP.

The function `getAvailableNP` starts searching on phrases within the specified range from right to left. An available NP is returned if it has *available_slots* > 0 and satisfies one of the following conditions:

- It has a right-side connection with another VP.
- It has no right-side connections with another VP but we have not seen any verbs on the way to reach this NP.

These conditions are mainly used to prevent an irrelevant NP which is far away from current VP to be selected as a candidate for connection.

Lastly, if current VP is not an A-VP and the previous phrase is an NP, we simply increase previous NP's *available_slots* by 1 and create a connection between this NP and the current VP.

Algorithm 1: Creating a left connection from a VP. *idx* is index of the current phrase.

```
if prevPhrase.token == 'and' then
    leftNp = getArg1OfVerbGroup(0, idx-2, phrase.verbGroup)
    if leftNp != null then
        leftNp.increaseAvailableSlots()
        connect(leftNp, phrase)
    end
else
    if phrase is A-VP then
        if prevPhrase.isAvailableNP then
            connect(prevPhrase, phrase)
        else
            leftNp = getAvailableNP(0, idx-2)
            if leftNp != null then
                connect(leftNp, phrase)
            else if prevPhrase.isDisputeNP then
                prevPhrase.removeLeftConnection()
                connect(prevPhrase, phrase)
            end
        end
    else if prevPhrase.isNP then
        prevPhrase.increaseAvailableSlots()
        connect(prevPhrase, phrase)
    end
end
```

Connections from PP. For a PP node, we simply create connections with its left and right phrases if they are NP. We do not check if the previous phrase is VP because it has already been handled by that VP. Algorithm 2 shows how we create connections with its left and right phrases from a PP.

Quote and Comma Characters. When linking phrases, we temporarily ignore O phrases which contain only quote characters. This mean that if immediate preceding phrase of the current phrase is a quote, we simply move one step further to the left to get the correct preceding phrase. The same thing applies for getting the succeeding phrase.

Algorithm 2: Creating left and right connection from a PP.

```
if prevPhrase is NP then
    prevPhrase.increaseAvailableSlots() connect(prevPhrase, phrase)
end
if nextPhrase is NP then
    connect(phrase, nextPhrase)
end
```

4.3   Relation Extraction

After setting up connections between phrases, the final step is to detect valid verb-based relations and extract their arguments accordingly. Unlike REVERB in which the relation phrase is extracted before identifying two arguments, in RELINK we extract a relation in the following order:

1. Identify phrases belonging to A-VP, P-VP or G-VP group which have both left and right connection.
2. Extract Argument 1 from its left connection.
3. Extract Predicate and Argument 2 simultaneously from its right connection using predefined patterns.

Extracting Argument 1. Because of the way we build connections between phrases, a connection on the left side of a VP (if any) is always an NP and this should be extracted as the Argument 1 of a relation. But we also consider the case when this NP has a connection to another NP through PP, if so then we follow the NP's right connection to build a full argument.

Extracting Predicate and Argument 2. We do not merely use the identified VP as Predicate and extract the closest NP to the right of the relation phrase as Argument 2. Instead, we obtain Predicate and Argument 2 simultaneously because they are mutually related in a relation. For example, in a sentence like *"He bought a new car as a present"*, we observe that there are two relations:

1: *(He; bought; a new car)*
2: *(He; bought a new car as; a present)*

The phrase *"a new car"* can both be Argument 2 and a part of Predicate name in this case. Which parts to include in the Predicate will affect the decision to extract the Argument 2. Therefore we need to be able to recognize them in our connected phrases for extraction. We do this by defining several patterns for matching against the connected phrase list. Whenever we find a list of connected phrases that matches the pattern, we extract them out as a relation. The last NP will be selected as the Argument 2 and all other phrases are grouped to become the Predicate. We combine these with the Argument 1 already extracted previously to have a complete relation.

5   Experiments

We compare RELINK with two well-known systems in different categories: one system uses shallow linguistic feature and one system use deep linguistic feature.

- REVERB: This Open IE system is considered as state-of-the-art in terms of using only shallow linguistic features for extracting relations. Because our system also uses similar information, this is a good baseline for comparison.

– OLLIE: This system extracts relations by using templates learned from seed training data. These templates work against the output of a dependency parser. In this research, we run OLLIE using the default Malt parser shipped in its package.

For testing, we collected 200 random sentences from news articles of CNN[3]. These sentences are fed to each system to get a list of binary relations. Two human judges were asked to independently evaluate each relation as correct or incorrect. We got an agreement of 82.9% on the extractions, agreement score $\kappa = 0.63$. We compute precision-recall on the subset of extractions where evaluations from both judges are the same. Similar to the experiments performed in [6], we calculate the total of correct relations using relations marked as correct by both judges. Duplicate relations are treated as a single relation. In ReLink, we do not design a separate confidence score model but instead, we use the logistic regression model available in ReVerb for assigning confidence score. The precision-recall curve is drawn by varying the confidence score from 0 to 1.

5.1 Results

Figure 3 shows the Area Under Precision-Recall Curve (AUC) of each system. As we can see, ReLink gets the highest AUC (≈ 0.554), both OLLIE and ReVerb get AUC about 30% smaller than ReLink, 0.375 and 0.324 respectively. It is interesting to see that OLLIE does not work very well in our experiment even though it uses dependency parser to support the extraction process.

Figure 4 shows Precision-Recall curves of three systems. ReLink achieves a stable precision of nearly 0.8 in almost all levels of recall. It also gets higher precision than ReVerb when recall increases to higher than around 0.08. OLLIE curve is quite interesting. It gets the highest precision at the beginning of the curve but starts to decrease as recall increases. When recall reaches around 0.2, OLLIE starts to get lower precision than ReLink; and at the end of the curve, OLLIE precision drops to lower than ReVerb. An explanation for this is that OLLIE depends entirely on the result from the dependency parser to extract the relations. Because of this, only a minor error in the dependency parsing can also confuse the extractor and make it produce uninformative or incoherent relations. ReVerb and ReLink, on the other hand, use only the shallow syntax of the sentence and therefore are not sensitively prone to errors. In English, shallow parsing is also considered more robust than deep parsing [12].

In our view, ReVerb gets low precision because its model is quite simple and cannot handle complex cases in a sentence. This prevents it from detecting valid relations as well as extracting correct arguments from the text. OLLIE is able to extract more relations from text but many are incorrect because it relies completely on the result of dependency parsing, and just a small error can also lead to all incorrect relations. With ReLink, even though it uses similar information as ReVerb, its model allows it to deal with multiple sentence forms

---

[3] https://edition.cnn.com.

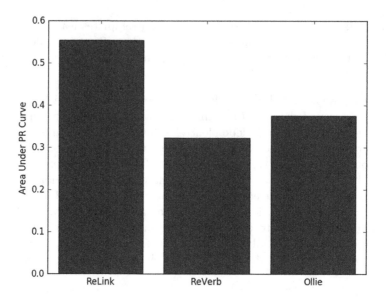

Fig. 3. Area Under Precision-Recall Curve

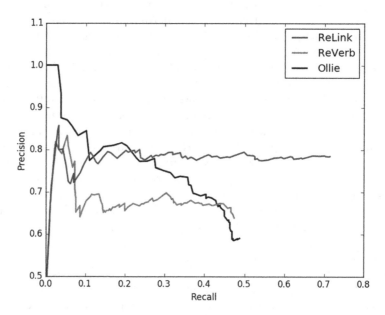

Fig. 4. Precision-Recall curve.

and produce better relations. For example, given a sentence like *"I took a flight from New York"*, REVERB can extract only one relation: *(I; took a flight from; New York)*. However, we believe that the relation *(I; took; a flight)* also contains important information and should be extracted as well. This is, in fact, similar to the approach taken by newer Open IE systems like OLLIE or STANFORDOPENIE. In RELINK, we follow the same approach and extract both relations. That is another reason why the precision of RELINK is higher than REVERB most of the time.

Another contribution to high precision in RELINK is the way we handle T-VP in a sentence. As can be seen from our defined patterns, we consider T-VP not as an independent relation phrase but as a part of a bigger relation phrase. Our approach led to results different from REVERB and OLLIE.

5.2   Evaluation on Other Datasets

For a fair comparison, we also conducted an experiment on the datasets used for evaluating CLAUSEIE[4]. These datasets consist of:

- 500 sentences from ReVerb data.
- 200 sentences from Wikipedia.
- 200 sentences from New York Times.

Each dataset contains the original sentences, the extractions from three systems (REVERB, OLLIE, CLAUSIE), and the annotated labels. Normally, a common approach will be to re-annotate all these extractions, then compute the precision and recall like we did in the previous experiment. However, this process is time-consuming considering the number of extractions in these datasets. We, therefore, took another approach which utilizes the available annotations for comparison. To be more specific, we fed these sentences to RELINK to get a list of extractions and set the label of each RELINK extraction to be the same with the annotated extraction. For those extractions which do not exist in the original annotation, we ask two human judges from our side to annotate (similar to how we did on the custom dataset). By doing this, we significantly reduce the number of extractions needed to be annotated while still having a fair comparison. Two judges got an agreement of 71% with $\kappa = 0.38$. Table 5 shows the statistics of each system based on the original annotated data, and Table 6 shows the result of our annotation on *out-of-db* extractions. Correct extractions are those which marked as *correct* by both annotators.

We calculate the Precision, Recall and F1 scores for each system with the new annotated data. The final set of correct extractions is the union of correct extractions in the CLAUSIE data and correct extractions in our *out-of-db* annotation. We present the results in Table 7 and visually plot the F1 score in Fig. 5.

---

[4] https://www.mpi-inf.mpg.de/departments/databases-and-information-systems/ software/clausie/.

Table 5. Statistics of extractions from each system on different dataset. *#out-of-db* column indicates the number of extractions which do not exist in the annotated data.

	#correct	#incorrect	#out-of-db
ReVerb data			
ReVerb	384	343	
Ollie	556	686	
ClausIE	1692	1283	
ReLink	465	231	310
Wiki data			
ReVerb	164	85	
Ollie	235	330	
ClausIE	597	404	
ReLink	181	72	162
NYT data			
ReVerb	152	119	
Ollie	216	281	
ClausIE	685	618	
ReLink	152	78	174

Table 6. Statistics of *out-of-db* extractions after annotating.

	#correct	#incorrect
ReVerb data	147	163
Wiki data	98	64
NYT data	95	79

As we can see from the results, our system achieves better scores than ReVerb and Ollie on all three datasets. This is consistent with the results we got on the custom data, and it shows the stable performance of ReLink. But ReLink gets lower F1 score than ClausIE even though it achieves higher Precision. This is mainly due to that fact that the number of extractions from ClausIE is significantly more than all other methods, making its Recall is quite high. This shows that the process of splitting the sentence into clauses before extracting the relations in ClausIE is effective in this case. Perhaps breaking the sentence into multiple clauses makes the dependency-parsing error less severe than treating the sentence as a whole. More investigation into this matter can be done in future work.

Table 7. Precision, Recall and F1 score calculated on the new annotated data.

	Precision	Recall	F1
ReVerb data			
ReVerb	0.53	0.13	0.20
Ollie	0.45	0.18	0.26
ClausIE	0.57	0.56	0.56
ReLink	0.62	0.23	0.33
Wiki data			
ReVerb	0.66	0.16	0.26
Ollie	0.42	0.23	0.30
ClausIE	0.60	0.58	0.59
ReLink	0.71	0.32	0.44
NYT data			
ReVerb	0.56	0.14	0.22
Ollie	0.43	0.19	0.27
ClausIE	0.53	0.61	0.57
ReLink	0.65	0.26	0.37

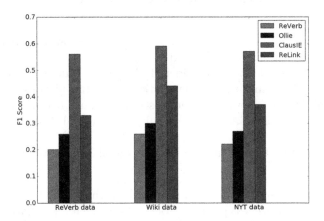

Fig. 5. Comparison of F1 score between four OpenIE systems on new annotated data.

5.3 Application of ReLink for COVID-19 Data

As stated at the beginning, when COVID-19 data increase rapidly, current machine learning models could not deal with the change of data. Therefore, unsupervised model as open information extraction is expected. Figure 6 shows the use of our system performing on COVID-19 data. As results, the relations we obtained are useful for users in terms of understanding about MERS-COV and H1N1. In our future work, we would like to exploit our tools for large-scale of COVID-19 data.

arg_1	rel	arg_2
[MERS-CoV]$_{GGP}$	include	[fever]$_{DISEASE}$, [chills/rigors]$_{DISEASE}$, [headache]$_{DISEASE}$, non-productive [cough]$_{DISEASE}$
[MERS-CoV]$_{GGP}$	is responsible for causing	lower [respiratory infections]$_{DISEASE}$ with [fever]$_{DISEASE}$ and [cough]$_{DISEASE}$

Fig. 6. Example of relations presented in COVID-19 papers.

We extend our work to perform an information retrieval system to search either "entities" or "relation" when we extracted from the large-scale of data.

6 Conclusion and Future Work

This paper introduced RELINK - a novel Open IE system which uses only shallow linguistic feature including POS and Chunking for extractions. Our main contributions in this paper are:

- We analyzed several notable Open IE systems and showed their drawbacks on extracting relations from free text.
- We proposed a simple method to identify VP and NP more accurately, then we proposed a mechanism to extract relations by linking phrases in a sentence. Experimental results showed that our system performed better than REVERB and OLLIE in terms of AUC. The results were also the same on different datasets.
- We implemented RELINK and published it on Github for the research community in this field[5].

In our future work, we want to firstly explore the possibility of extending this model to extract other types of relations (N-ary relations, relational nouns, etc). In addition, we also consider applying a machine learning technique to deal with the case where some words are incorrectly tagged by Apache OpenNLP.

Acknowledgments. This work was supported by JST CREST Grant Number JPMJCR1513 and in part by the Asian Office of Aerospace R&D (AOARD), Air Force Office of Scientific Research (Grant no. FA2386-19-1-4041).

---

[5] https://github.com/linktorepository.

References

1. Banko, M., Cafarella, M.J., Soderland, S., Broadhead, M., Etzioni, O.: Open information extraction from the web. In: IJCAI, vol. 7, pp. 2670–2676 (2007)
2. Berant, J., Dagan, I., Goldberger, J.: Global learning of typed entailment rules. In: Proceedings of the 49th Annual Meeting of the Association for Computational Linguistics: Human Language Technologies, vol. 1, pp. 610–619. Association for Computational Linguistics (2011)
3. Christensen, J., Mausam, S.S., Soderland, S., Etzioni, O.: Towards coherent multi-document summarization. In: HLT-NAACL, pp. 1163–1173. Citeseer (2013)
4. Del Corro, L., Gemulla, R.: Clausie: Clause-based open information extraction. In: Proceedings of the 22nd International Conference on World Wide Web, pp. 355–366. ACM (2013)
5. Etzioni, O., et al.: Unsupervised named-entity extraction from the web: an experimental study. Artif. Intell. **165**(1), 91–134 (2005)
6. Fader, A., Soderland, S., Etzioni, O.: Identifying relations for open information extraction. In: Proceedings of the Conference of Empirical Methods in Natural Language Processing (EMNLP 2011), Edinburgh, Scotland, UK, 27–31 July 2011 (2011)
7. Fader, A., Zettlemoyer, L., Etzioni, O.: Open question answering over curated and extracted knowledge bases. In: Proceedings of the 20th ACM SIGKDD International Conference on Knowledge Discovery and Data Mining, pp. 1156–1165. ACM (2014)
8. Gabor Angeli, M.J.P., Manning, C.D.: Leveraging linguistic structure for open domain information extraction. In: Proceedings of the Association of Computational Linguistics (ACL) (2015)
9. Gamallo, P., Garcia, M., Fernández-Lanza, S.: Dependency-based open information extraction. In: Proceedings of the Joint Workshop on Unsupervised and Semi-Supervised Learning in NLP, pp. 10–18. Association for Computational Linguistics (2012)
10. Kim, J.T., Moldovan, D.I.: Acquisition of semantic patterns for information extraction from corpora. In: Proceedings of Ninth Conference on Artificial Intelligence for Applications, pp. 171–176. IEEE (1993)
11. Li, P., Cai, W., Huang, H.: Weakly supervised natural language processing framework for abstractive multi-document summarization: weakly supervised abstractive multi-document summarization. In: Proceedings of the 24th ACM International on Conference on Information and Knowledge Management, pp. 1401–1410. ACM (2015)
12. Li, X., Roth, D.: Exploring evidence for shallow parsing. In: Proceedings of the 2001 Workshop on Computational Natural Language Learning, vol. 7, p. 6. Association for Computational Linguistics (2001)
13. Manning, C.D., Surdeanu, M., Bauer, J., Finkel, J., Bethard, S.J., McClosky, D.: The Stanford CoreNLP natural language processing toolkit. In: Association for Computational Linguistics (ACL) System Demonstrations, pp. 55–60 (2014). http://www.aclweb.org/anthology/P/P14/P14-5010
14. Mausam, Schmitz, M., Bart, R., Soderland, S., Etzioni, O.: Open language learning for information extraction. In: Proceedings of Conference on Empirical Methods in Natural Language Processing and Computational Natural Language Learning (EMNLP-CONLL) (2012)

15. Reddy, S., Lapata, M., Steedman, M.: Large-scale semantic parsing without question-answer pairs. Trans. Assoc. Comput. Linguist. **2**, 377–392 (2014)
16. Ruppert, E.: Unsupervised conceptualization and semantic text indexing for information extraction. In: Sack, H., Blomqvist, E., d'Aquin, M., Ghidini, C., Ponzetto, S.P., Lange, C. (eds.) ESWC 2016. LNCS, vol. 9678, pp. 853–862. Springer, Cham (2016). https://doi.org/10.1007/978-3-319-34129-3_54
17. Schoenmackers, S., Etzioni, O., Weld, D.S., Davis, J.: Learning first-order horn clauses from web text. In: Proceedings of the 2010 Conference on Empirical Methods in Natural Language Processing, pp. 1088–1098. Association for Computational Linguistics (2010)
18. Soderland, J.C.S., Mausam, G.B.: Hierarchical summarization: scaling up multi-document summarization. In: Proceedings of the 52nd Annual Meeting of the Association for Computlational Linguistics, pp. 902–912 (2014)
19. Stanovsky, G., Mausam, I.D.: Open IE as an intermediate structure for semantic tasks (2015)
20. Surdeanu, M.: Overview of the TAC2013 knowledge base population evaluation: English slot filling and temporal slot filling. In: Sixth Text Analysis Conference (2013)
21. Vo, D.T., Bagheri, E.: Open information extraction. arXiv preprint arXiv:1607.02784 (2016)
22. Wu, F., Weld, D.S.: Open information extraction using Wikipedia. In: Proceedings of the 48th Annual Meeting of the Association for Computational Linguistics, pp. 118–127. Association for Computational Linguistics (2010)

Cloud Computing and Networks

Energy-Efficient Scheduling of Deadline-Sensitive and Budget-Constrained Workflows in the Cloud

Anurina Tarafdar[✉], Kamalesh Karmakar, Sunirmal Khatua,
and Rajib K. Das

Department of Computer Science and Engineering, University of Calcutta,
Kolkata, India
anurinatarafdar@gmail.com, k.karmakar.ju@gmail.com,
skhatuacomp@caluniv.ac.in, rajib.k.das@ieee.org

Abstract. Due to the rapid advancement of Cloud computing, more and more users are running their scientific and business workflow applications in the Cloud. The energy consumption of these workflows is high, which negatively affects the environment and also increases the operational costs of the Cloud providers. Moreover, most of the workflows are associated with budget constraints and deadlines prescribed by Cloud users. Thus, one of the main challenges of workflow scheduling is to make it energy-efficient for Cloud providers. At the same time, it should prevent budget and deadline violations for Cloud users. To address these issues, we consider a heterogeneous Cloud environment and propose an energy-efficient scheduling algorithm for deadline-sensitive workflows with budget constraints. Our algorithm ensures that the workflow is scheduled within the budget while reducing energy consumption and deadline violation. It utilizes Dynamic Voltage and Frequency Scaling (DVFS) to adjust the voltage and frequency of the virtual machines (VMs) executing tasks of the workflow. These adjustments help to achieve significant energy savings. Extensive simulation using real-world workflows and comparison with some state-of-art approaches validate the effectiveness of our proposed algorithm.

Keywords: Workflow scheduling · Cloud computing ·
Energy-efficiency · Budget constraints · Deadline

1 Introduction

A workflow comprises of a set of interdependent tasks executed in the specified order. Workflows are useful tools to model complex scientific and business applications that require large-scale computation and storage. Cloud computing is an in-demand technology in which Cloud Service Providers (CSPs) deliver resources

© Springer Nature Switzerland AG 2021
D. Goswami and T. A. Hoang (Eds.): ICDCIT 2021, LNCS 12582, pp. 65–80, 2021.
https://doi.org/10.1007/978-3-030-65621-8_4

and services to the Cloud users in a pay-per-use manner over the internet. Due to several advantages of Cloud computing, such as elasticity, cost-effectiveness, reliability, numerous workflow applications are being submitted by users for execution in the Cloud. The tasks of these workflows run in the virtual machines (VMs) deployed in the hosts or servers of a Cloud data center.

The scheduling of workflow applications in the Cloud is quite challenging. Large-scale virtualized Cloud data centers consume a large amount of energy, and that harms the environment [1]. Moreover, the high energy costs of the data center affect the profit margin of the CSPs. Thus, it is necessary to develop an energy-efficient workflow scheduling approach to reduce the energy consumption of the Cloud.

The CSPs offer several types of VMs having different resource capacities and prices, and charge the users in a pay-per-use policy. In a heterogeneous Cloud environment, creating a cost-effective schedule of the workflows is quite challenging. Moreover, many workflow applications are associated with budget constraints and deadlines mentioned by the users. In such a situation, it is critical to schedule the workflow within the prescribed budget and minimize deadline violation at the same time.

Although in the recent past, a significant number of research works have investigated workflow scheduling in Cloud, many of them consider a homogeneous environment [6,7,14]. In some research works [2,11], the authors perform scheduling of budget-constrained workflows in a heterogeneous Cloud environment. However, they do not consider energy-efficiency as a scheduling objective. On the other hand, works like [4,13] aim to minimize the energy consumption of workflows having deadline constraints, but do not take into account the monetary cost due to the execution of the workflows. Workflow scheduling in the Cloud must be energy-efficient to promote green computing and reduce the operational costs of the CSPs. At the same time, the scheduling approach must generate a schedule that is within the budget and deadline prescribed by the Cloud user. Consideration of all these aspects simultaneously makes the scheduling problem very challenging. To address this issue, we consider a heterogeneous Cloud environment and propose an energy-efficient scheduling approach for deadline-sensitive workflows with budget constraints.

The rest of the paper is organized as follows: Section 2 consists of a brief discussion on the related works, followed by the description of the system models in Sect. 3. Our proposed scheduling algorithm appears in Sect. 4. Section 5 presents the performance evaluation and Sect. 6 concludes the paper with some future directions.

2   Related Work

In the recent past, a large number of research works have focused on workflow scheduling in the Cloud environment. A workflow is scheduled by considering different objectives like- minimizing the makespan, increasing energy efficiency, reducing monetary cost, and so on. Some of the works in the literature have scheduled workflow considering a single objective, whereas some others have proposed multi-objective workflow scheduling.

In [9], the authors aim to generate a shorter makespan for the workflow through effective scheduling, while in [2], the authors have considered budget satisfaction as their principal objective. On the contrary, Rizvi et al. [11] have proposed a fair scheduling policy that aims to minimize the makespan of the schedule and satisfies the budget constraints at the same time. An evolutionary multi-objective optimization (EMO) technique presented in [15] optimizes cost as well as makespan. Tang et al. [13] have proposed an energy-aware workflow scheduling algorithm based on Dynamic Voltage and Frequency Scaling (DVFS) that tries to schedule the workflow within a given deadline. In [4], the authors have presented a workflow scheduling algorithm that aims to improve resource utilization, reduce energy consumption, and satisfy the given deadline. Li et al. [8] have presented a cost and energy-aware scheduling algorithm for scientific workflows. However, [4,13] do not consider the monetary cost of workflow execution. Works like [2,9,11,15], though consider budget and makespan, do not take into account the energy consumption of the workflows. Unlike the works mentioned above, we propose a scheduling heuristic that ensures the completion of the workflow within the given budget while reducing energy consumption and deadline violation.

3   System Models

In this section, we describe the system models: Cloud data center model, workflow model, and energy model. We also define the budget constraint of the workflow.

3.1   Cloud Data Center Model

We consider a Cloud data center with n heterogeneous VMs, $V = \{v_1, v_2, \ldots, v_n\}$. Each VM v_k has some characteristics like processing speed p_k represented in million instructions per scond (MIPS), and cost per unit time c_k. We assume the data center offers x types of VM, $V_{type} = \{\tau_1, \tau_2, \ldots, \tau_x\}$. Each VM in V belongs to a particular type in V_{type} and VMs of same type have the same characteristics.

3.2   Workflow Model

A workflow application W is represented by a directed acyclic graph $G(T, E)$ where $T = \{t_1, t_2, \ldots, t_m\}$ is the set of tasks in the workflow, and E is the set of directed edges between the tasks. Each task t_i has length l_i represented in million instructions(MI). The directed edges of $G(T, E)$ indicate the dependencies between the tasks. If there exists an edge from task t_i to task t_j, then t_i is considered to be an immediate predecessor of t_j and t_j as an immediate successor of t_i. The sets $pre(t_i)$ and $suc(t_i)$ denote all immediate predecessors and all immediate successors of task t_i respectively. The data transmission time between two tasks t_i and t_j where t_i is an immediate predecessor of t_j is denoted by TT_{ij}. It depends on the size of the data transmitted from t_i to t_j, and the internal network bandwidth of the data center. TT_{ij} is considered to be zero if t_i and t_j are assigned to the same VM. T_{entry} denotes the set of entry tasks of the workflow having no predecessor, whereas T_{exit} is the set of exit tasks of the workflow having no successor.

The execution time of task t_i when executed on a VM v_k is denoted by $ET(t_i, v_k)$, and is defined as:

$$ET(t_i, v_k) = \frac{l_i}{p_k} \tag{1}$$

where l_i is the length of t_i in million instructions(MI) and p_k is the processing speed of v_k in million instructions per scond (MIPS).

The earliest start time $EST(t_i)$, and earliest finish time $EFT(t_i)$ of task t_i can be recursively calculated using the following equations where $f(t_i)$ and $f(t_p)$ indicate the index of the VMs on which tasks t_i and t_p are assigned respectively.

$$EST(t_i) = \begin{cases} 0, & \text{if } t_i \in T_{entry} \\ \max_{t_p \in pre(t_i)} \{EST(t_p) + ET(t_p, v_{f(t_p)}) + TT_{pi}\}, & \text{otherwise} \end{cases} \tag{2}$$

$$EFT(t_i) = EST(t_i) + ET(t_i, v_{f(t_i)}) \tag{3}$$

The latest start time $LST(t_i)$ and latest finish time $LFT(t_i)$ are similarly calculated according to the following equations where W_m^e denotes the estimated makespan of the workflow and is calculated as: $W_m^e = \max_{t_i \in T_{exit}} \{EFT(t_i)\}$.

$$LST(t_i) = \begin{cases} W_m^e - ET(t_i, v_{f(t_i)}), & \text{if } t_i \in T_{exit} \\ \min_{t_j \in suc(t_i)} \{LST(t_j) - TT_{ij} - ET(t_i, v_{f(t_i)})\}, & \text{otherwise} \end{cases} \tag{4}$$

$$LFT(t_i) = LST(t_i) + ET(t_i, v_{f(t_i)}) \tag{5}$$

The W_m^e value obtained assuming all tasks are scheduled on VMs of the fastest type can be considered as the minimum makespan of the workflow W_m^{min}. Thus the deadline W_D of the workflow can be defined using the following equation:

$$W_D = \alpha \cdot W_m^{min}, \tag{6}$$

where α is the deadline factor specified by the Cloud user, and $\alpha \geq 1$.

3.3   Energy Model

For the energy model used in this paper, we assume that the physical machines (hosts) of the Cloud infrastructure support dynamic voltage and frequency scaling technique (DVFS). Also, each VM is assigned a virtual CPU (vCPU) that corresponds to a single core of a physical machine. Thus a VM $v_k \in V$ can operate at some distinct CPU frequencies in the range $[f_k^{min}, f_k^{max}]$ by varying the voltage levels in the range $[V_k^{min}, V_k^{max}]$. The dynamic power consumption of VM v_k is expressed as [13]:

$$P_k = K \cdot (V_k^l)^2 \cdot f_k^l, \tag{7}$$

where K is a constant parameter related to the dynamic power, V_k^l is the supply voltage of VM v_k at level l, and f_k^l is the CPU frequency of VM v_k corresponding to voltage V_k^l. The energy consumption E due to execution of a task t_i on VM v_k is determined as: $E = P_k \cdot ET(t_i, v_k)$. Thus the total energy consumption of the workflow W comprising of m tasks is calculated as follows [10]:

$$E_W = \sum_{i=1}^{m} P_{f(t_i)} \cdot ET(t_i, v_{f(t_i)}), \tag{8}$$

where $f(t_i)$ is the index of the VM on which task t_i is assigned.

The processing speed p_k of VM v_k depends on its voltage and frequency, and lies in the range $[p_k^{min}, p_k^{max}]$. p_k^l represents the processing speed of VM v_k operating at (V_k^l, f_k^l) voltage-frequency combination. Though VMs generally operate at their maximum voltage level when they are busy [10], using DVFS, one can dynamically set the voltage and frequency, and thus improve energy-efficiency.

3.4   Budget Constraint of the Workflow

The monetary cost of execution of task t_i on VM v_k is determined as:

$$c(t_i, v_k) = \lceil ET(t_i, v_k) \rceil \cdot c_k, \tag{9}$$

where c_k is the cost per unit time of VM v_k. The unit of time can be hour-based or second-based depending upon the CSP and the type of VM. The VM will be charged/billed for an integral unit of time, even if the task completes early. As all VMs are in the same data center, data transfer costs are ignorable. Thus, the total cost of scheduling the workflow is:

$$C_W = \sum_{i=1}^{m} c(t_i, v_{f(t_i)}), \tag{10}$$

where $f(t_i)$ is the index of the VM on which task t_i is assigned.

As discussed in Sect. 3.1, the data center offers x types of VM, $V_{type} = \{\tau_1, \tau_2, \ldots, \tau_x\}$. We consider that c_{τ_q}, $p_{\tau_q}^{min}$ and $p_{\tau_q}^{max}$ represent the cost per unit time, minimum processing speed and maximum processing speed of a VM of type τ_q. VMs of different types may have different cost per unit time and processing speed ranges. However, all VMs of a particular type have identical cost per unit time and processing speed range. That is, for each VM v_k of type τ_q, the cost per unit time c_k is equal to c_{τ_q} and the processing speed range $[p_k^{min}, p_k^{max}]$ is equal to $[p_{\tau_q}^{min}, p_{\tau_q}^{max}]$.

For each VM type τ_q, we calculate the value $\frac{c_{\tau_q}}{p_{\tau_q}}$. The lowest cost of workflow scheduling C_l is obtained by considering all tasks to be executed on VMs of the type τ_q that has the least value of $\frac{c_{\tau_q}}{p_{\tau_q}^{max}}$. Likewise, the highest cost of workflow scheduling C_h is obtained by selecting VMs of the type τ_q that has the highest value of $\frac{c_{\tau_q}}{p_{\tau_q}^{max}}$, for every task in the workflow. As in [10], the budget of the workflow is represented by Eq. (11) stated below:

$$Bu_W = C_l + \beta \cdot (C_h - C_l), \tag{11}$$

where β is the budget factor such that $\beta \in [0, 1)$. The Cloud user sets the budget of the workflow by specifying the budget factor.

The budget constraint of the workflow implies that the cost of workflow scheduling must be within the given budget, i.e., $C_W \leq Bu_W$.

4   Workflow Scheduling Strategy

While scheduling the tasks of a workflow, our objective is to reduce energy consumption and deadline violation of the workflow and also ensure that the budget constraint is satisfied. Workflow scheduling is NP-hard in nature [10,13]. Thus, we propose a heuristic for effective scheduling of workflow in the Cloud environment. We assume that at a given time, only one task can be executed on a VM to prevent contention for resources.

4.1   Deadline, Priority and Budget of a Task

Before describing our proposed scheduling algorithm, we define the deadline, priority, and budget of a task in the workflow.

Assuming each task is scheduled on VMs of the fastest type, we calculate the latest start time $LST(t_i)$ and latest finish time $LFT(t_i)$ of a task t_i using Eq. (4) and Eq. (5) respectively. Thereafter, we determine the deadline $D(t_i)$ of task t_i by extending its $LFT(t_i)$ proportionately as follows [8]:

$$D(t_i) = \alpha \cdot LFT(t_i), \tag{12}$$

where α is the deadline factor specified by the Cloud user. It is logical that if each task is completed within its deadline, then the entire workflow will also be completed within the deadline W_D.

In workflow scheduling, the tasks of a workflow have to be selected one at a time and allocated to suitable VMs. To perform task selection, we assign priority to each task [10]. The priority $Pr(t_i)$ of task t_i is calculated as:

$$Pr(t_i) = ET_{avg}(t_i) + \max_{t_j \in suc(t_i)} \{TT_{ij} + Pr(t_j)\}, \tag{13}$$

where $ET_{avg}(t_i)$ is the average execution time of t_i over all types of VMs in the data center. Priority $Pr(t_i)$ denotes the length of the longest path from task t_i to an exit task.

As in [10,11], we divide the budget Bu_W among all the tasks in the workflow. To determine the budget of each task, we consider the parameter Surplus Budget of Workflow (SBW). Initially SBW is set to $Bu_W - C_l$ where C_l denotes the lowest cost of workflow scheduling as discussed in Sect. 3.4. Let $c_{min}(t_i)$ denote the minimum cost of executing t_i. Then, for the first task t_i which is scheduled, its budget $Bu(t_i)$ is given by:

$$Bu(t_i) = SBW + c_{min}(t_i), \tag{14}$$

A suitable VM v_k has to be selected for task t_i such that the cost of execution of t_i on v_k expressed as $c(t_i, v_k)$ lies within $Bu(t_i)$. Once the task t_i is scheduled, SBW is updated as:

$$SBW = SBW - (c(t_i, v_k) - c_{min}(t_i)) \tag{15}$$

In this way, after scheduling every task, we update SBW, and determine the budget of the next task from the new SBW.

4.2 Proposed Approach

Our proposed workflow scheduling approach- Energy-efficient Scheduling of Deadline sensitive Workflow with Budget constraint (ESDWB), has been presented in Algorithm 1. In this Algorithm, each task t_i of the workflow is selected priority wise, and assigned to a suitable VM. Since each task t_i is scheduled within its budget $Bu(t_i)$, the cost of the workflow remains within its budget Bu_W. Here $AST(t_i, v_k)$ and $AFT(t_i, v_k)$ denotes the actual start time and actual finish time of task t_i on VM v_k respectively. To determine $AST(t_i, v_k)$, we introduce a term $PST(t_i)$ indicating the possible start time of task t_i. It is defined below:

$$PST(t_i) = \begin{cases} 0, & \text{if } t_i \in T_{entry} \\ \max_{t_p \in pre(t_i)} \{AST(t_p, v_{f(t_p)}) + ET(t_p, v_{f(t_p)}) + TT_{pi}\}, & \text{otherwise} \end{cases} \tag{16}$$

This implies that it is possible to start execution of task t_i only after all its predecessor tasks have completed execution and have transferred necessary data

---

Algorithm 1: Energy-efficient Scheduling of Deadline-sensitive Workflow with Budget constraint (ESDWB)

Input: Workflow W, Deadline W_D, Budget Bu_W

Output: Schedule of the workflow S_W

1 Determine deadline $D(t_i)$ of each task t_i in task set T of W using Eq. (12);

2 Calculate priority $Pr(t_i)$ of each task using Eq. (13);

3 Sort the tasks in T in descending order of their priorities;

4 $SBW \leftarrow Bu_W - C_l$; $S_W \leftarrow \phi$;

5 **foreach** $t_i \in T$ **do**

6      $v_{f(t_i)} \leftarrow null$;   // $v_{f(t_i)}$ indicates the VM on which t_i will be assigned

7   Calculate $Bu(t_i)$ using Eq. (14);

8   **if** $(pre(t_i) \neq \phi)$ **then**

9   Sort the tasks in $pre(t_i)$ in descending order of the data size to be transferred to t_i;

10   **foreach** $t_p \in pre(t_i)$ **do**

11              $v_k \leftarrow v_{f(t_p)}$;   // $v_{f(t_p)}$ indicates the VM on which t_p is assigned

12   **if** $((AFT(t_i, v_k) \leq D(t_i))$ **and** $(c(t_i, v_k) \leq Bu(t_i)))$ **then**

13                  $v_{f(t_i)} \leftarrow v_k$; $S_W \leftarrow S_W \cup \langle t_i, v_{f(t_i)} \rangle$;

14   Update SBW using Eq. (15) ;

15   **break**;

16   **end**

17   **end**

18   **end**

19   **if** $((pre(t_i) = \phi)$ **or** $(v_{f(t_i)} = null))$ **then**

20   Compute $ps(t_i)$ using Eq. (21);

21          $Q \leftarrow \{\tau_q \mid \tau_q \in V_{type} \wedge (p_{\tau_q}^{max} \geq ps(t_i))\}$;

22   Sort the VM types in set Q in ascending order of their $p_{\tau_q}^{max}$ values;

23   **foreach** $\tau_q \in Q$ **do**

24   Consider an idle or new VM v_k of type τ_q;

25   **if** $(c(t_i, v_k) \leq Bu(t_i))$ **then**

26                  $v_{f(t_i)} \leftarrow v_k$; $S_W \leftarrow S_W \cup \langle t_i, v_{f(t_i)} \rangle$;

27   Update SBW using Eq. (15) ;

28   **break**;

29   **end**

30   **end**

31   **if** $(v_{f(t_i)} = null)$ **then**

32              $G \leftarrow \{\tau_g \mid \tau_g \in V_{type} \wedge (\frac{l_i}{p_{\tau_g}^{max}} \cdot c_{\tau_g} \leq Bu(t_i))\}$;

33              $\tau_b \leftarrow \{\tau_g \mid \tau_g \in G \wedge (p_{\tau_g}^{max} \geq p_{\tau_y}^{max} \ \ \forall \tau_y \in G)\}$;

34   Consider an idle or new VM v_k of type τ_b;

35               $v_{f(t_i)} \leftarrow v_k$; $S_W \leftarrow S_W \cup \langle t_i, v_{f(t_i)} \rangle$;

36   Update SBW using Eq. (15);

37   **end**

38   **end**

39 **end**

40 Calculate actual makespan of workflow W_m^a using Eq. (19);

41 $S_W \leftarrow \text{ERT}(S_W, W_m^a)$;   //***Algorithm 2***

42 Calculate energy E_W and cost C_W using Eq. (8) and Eq. (10) respectively;

43 Calculate Deadline violation DV using Eq. (20);

44 **return** S_W

to it. $AST(t_i, v_k)$ and $AFT(t_i, v_k)$ is defined in Eq. (17) and Eq. (18) respectively as follows:

$$AST(t_i, v_k) = \begin{cases} PST(t_i), & \text{if } T_k^i = \phi \\ \max\{PST(t_i), AFT(t_b, v_k)\}, & \text{if } T_k^i \neq \phi \end{cases} \quad (17)$$

where T_k^i represents the set of tasks of the workflow scheduled on VM v_k before task t_i, and t_b is the task scheduled on v_k just before t_i.

$$AFT(t_i, v_k) = AST(t_i, v_k) + ET(t_i, v_k) \quad (18)$$

Thus the actual makespan of the workflow W_m^a and the percentage of deadline violation of the workflow DV can be calculated using Eq. (19) and Eq. (20) respectively as:

$$W_m^a = \max_{t_i \in T_{exit}} \{AFT(t_i, v_{f(t_i)})\} \quad (19)$$

$$DV = \begin{cases} \frac{(W_m^a - W_D)}{W_D} \cdot 100\%, & \text{if } W_m^a > W_D \\ 0, & \text{otherwise} \end{cases} \quad (20)$$

Algorithm ESDWB: Algorithm 1 first tries to allocate a task t_i to a VM executing one of its predecessor tasks (lines 8 to 18 of Algorithm 1) to avoid the data transmission time and thus reduce the actual finish time of t_i. It would help to reduce the actual makespan of the workflow W_m^a and the percentage of deadline violation of the workflow DV. If the task t_i does not have a predecessor, or if it is not possible to allocate it to a VM executing one of its predecessor tasks due to deadline violation or budget constraint, then a VM of a suitable type is selected for it (lines 19 to 38 of Algorithm 1). For this, we compute the minimum processing speed $ps(t_i)$ needed to complete t_i before its deadline using the following equation:

$$ps(t_i) = \frac{l_i}{D(t_i) - PST(t_i)} \quad (21)$$

where l_i is the length of t_i in million instructions(MI).

After calculating $ps(t_i)$, the set Q is determined (line 21 of Algorithm 1) which contains the types of VM that can complete t_i before its deadline. $p_{\tau_q}^{max}$ represents the maximum processing speed of a VM of type τ_q. Algorithm 1 tries to allocate t_i to a VM by choosing the VM types in Q in ascending order of their processing speeds. Lower processing speed corresponds to lower voltage and frequency and thus lower power consumption. If the VM types in Q do not permit the execution of the task within its budget, we need to pick a VM type that will violate the task's deadline. But while doing so, we choose the fastest VM available within its budget (lines 31 to 37 of Algorithm 1) so that there is less chance of deadline violation of the workflow. In Algorithm 1, G represents the set of VM types that can schedule t_i within its budget $Bu(t_i)$, and τ_b is a member of G with the highest processing speed. In this way, all tasks are scheduled and the actual makespan of the workflow W_m^a is determined.

Algorithm 2: Energy Reduction of Tasks (ERT)

Input: Schedule of the workflow S_W, actual makespan of the workflow W_m^a
Output: Schedule S_W after updation

1 **foreach** $t_i \in T$ **do**
2 $\quad$ $v_k \leftarrow v_{f(t_i)}$; $\quad // v_{f(t_i)}$ indicates the VM on which task t_i is assigned
3 $\quad$ Calculate $ExFT(t_i)$ using Eq. (22);
4 $\quad$ **if** $(ExFT(t_i) > AFT(t_i, v_k))$ **then**
5 $\quad\quad$ Determine $PExFT(t_i, v_k)$ using Eq. (23);
6 $\quad\quad$ Calculate $p_{min}(t_i, v_k)$ using Eq. (24);
7 $\quad\quad$ $PS \leftarrow \{p_k^l \mid p_k^l \in [p_k^{min}, p_k^{max}] \wedge (p_k^l \geq p_{min}(t_i, v_k))\}$;
8 $\quad\quad$ $p_k^l \leftarrow \min(PS)$; $f_k^l \leftarrow$ frequency corresponding to p_k^l
9 $\quad\quad$ **if** $p_k^l < p_k^{max}$ **then**
10 $\quad\quad\quad$ Update the frequency of VM v_k from f_k^{max} to f_k^l for task t_i;
11 $\quad\quad\quad$ Update $ET(t_i, v_k)$ and $AFT(t_i, v_k)$ in the schedule S_W;
12 $\quad\quad$ **end**
13 $\quad$ **end**
14 **end**
15 **return** S_W

Algorithm 2 uses DVFS to reduce the energy consumption of the tasks by extending their finish times without affecting the actual makespan and budget of the workflow. Here $ExFT(t_i)$ represents the extended finish time of a task t_i in the workflow. It is defined below:

$$ExFT(t_i) = \begin{cases} W_m^a, & \text{if } t_i \in T_{exit} \\ \min_{t_j \in suc(t_i)} \{AST(t_j, v_{f(t_j)}) - TT_{ij}\}, & \text{otherwise} \end{cases} \quad (22)$$

The above equation implies that extension in finish time of a task t_i must not affect the makespan of the workflow and the actual start time of the successor tasks.

A task t_i is said to have some slack time if $ExFT(t_i)$ is greater than $AFT(t_i)$. The finish time of such a task t_i assigned to a VM v_k can be extended to its possible extended finish time $PExFT(t_i, v_k)$ formulated as:

$$PExFT(t_i, v_k) = \begin{cases} \min\{ExFT(t_i), AST(t_a, v_k), \{AST(t_i, v_k) + \lceil \frac{l_i}{p_k^{max}} \rceil \}\}, & case\ 1 \\ \min\{ExFT(t_i), \{AST(t_i, v_k) + \lceil \frac{l_i}{p_k^{max}} \rceil \}\}, & case\ 2 \end{cases}$$
$$(23)$$

Two cases can occur while determining the possible extended finish time of task t_i on VM v_k. They are:

– **Case 1:** This situation occurs if another task t_a is scheduled for execution on VM v_k after t_i. It is possible to extend the finish time of t_i till $ExFT(t_i)$, or $AST(t_a, v_k)$, or till the end of the billing period, whichever is earliest. This is because extension of t_i beyond $AST(t_a, v_k)$ would delay the start of task

t_a and extension of t_i beyond $\{AST(t_i, v_k) + \lceil \frac{l_i}{p_k^{max}} \rceil\}$ would lead to increase in cost of scheduling t_i.

- **Case 2:** This situation occurs if no other tasks are scheduled for execution on v_k after t_i.

The minimum processing speed $p_{min}(t_i, v_k)$ required to complete task t_i on VM v_k within its possible extended finish time $PExFT(t_i, v_k)$ is calculated as:

$$p_{min}(t_i, v_k) = \frac{l_i}{PExFT(t_i, v_k) - AST(t_i, v_k)} \tag{24}$$

where l_i is the length of t_i in million instructions(MI).

Algorithm 2 finds an allowable set of processing speeds PS of v_k greater than or equal to $p_{min}(t_i, v_k)$. The processing speed $p_k^l = \min(PS)$ will cause lowest energy consumption as explained below. The energy consumption E of VM v_k due to execution of task t_i is :

$$E = \left(K \cdot (V_k^l)^2 \cdot f_k^l\right) \cdot \left(\frac{l_i}{p_k^l}\right), \tag{25}$$

where V_k^l, f_k^l, p_k^l are the voltage, frequency and processing speed of VM v_k, and l_i is length of task t_i. As processing speed is proportional to the frequency, energy consumption $E \propto (V_k^l)^2$. From Table 1, it is observed that for a given VM type, lower voltage corresponds to lower frequency and thus lower processing speed. Hence we determine the minimum processing speed in the set PS and accordingly update the frequency of the VM (lines 8 to 12 of Algorithm 2). This helps to reduce the energy consumption.

5   Performance Evaluation

To evaluate the performance of our proposed approach ESDWB, we compare it with two existing workflow scheduling algorithms- FBCWS [11] and DEWTS [13]. FBCWS tries to minimize the makespan of the workflow while satisfying the user-defined budget. On the other hand, DEWTS tries to reduce the energy consumption of the workflow while keeping its makespan within the deadline.

5.1   Performance Metrics

We evaluate and compare our proposed algorithm with respect to the following performance metrics-

(i) Normalized Energy Consumption: The Normalized Energy Consumption (NE) of scheduling a workflow W by an algorithm is defined as follows:

$$NE = \frac{E_W}{E_W^{min}}, \tag{26}$$

where E_W is the energy consumption of the workflow W obtained using Eq. (8), and E_W^{min} is the minimum energy consumption value obtained among all the algorithms under comparison.

(ii) Normalized Makespan: The Normalized Makespan (NM) of a workflow W is defined as follows:

$$NM = \frac{W_m^a}{W_D},\tag{27}$$

where W_m^a is the actual makespan of the workflow W obtained using Eq. (19), and W_D is the deadline of the workflow. If the value of NM becomes greater than 1, then it indicates that the deadline has been violated.

(iii) Normalized Cost: The Normalized Cost (NC) of scheduling workflow W is defined as follows:

$$NC = \frac{C_W}{Bu_W},\tag{28}$$

where C_W is the monetary cost of scheduling the workflow W calculated using Eq. (10), and Bu_W is the budget of the workflow. If the value of NC becomes greater than 1, then it indicates that the cost of scheduling has exceeded the budget.

5.2   Experimental Setup

We have used WorkflowSim [5], a well-accepted and widely used workflow simulator, to simulate a Cloud data center. The VMs in the simulated data center are of three types- Type 1, Type 2, and Type 3. The VMs of Type 1, 2, and 3 are modeled to run on AMD Turion MT-34 processor, AMD Opteron 2218 processor, and Intel Xeon E5450 processor respectively. The voltage-frequency pairs of these real-world processors are shown in Table 1 [12,13]. The price of each VM

Table 1. Voltage-frequency pairs of different processors.

Level	AMD Turion MT-34		AMD Opteron 2218		Intel Xeon E5450	
	Voltage (V)	Frequency (GHz)	Voltage (V)	Frequency (GHz)	Voltage (V)	Frequency (GHz)
0	1.20	1.80	1.30	2.60	1.35	3.00
1	1.15	1.60	1.25	2.40	1.17	2.67
2	1.10	1.40	1.20	2.20	1.00	2.33
3	1.05	1.20	1.15	2.00	0.85	2.00
4	1.00	1.00	1.10	1.80		
5	0.90	0.80	1.05	1.00		

of Type 1, Type 2, and Type 3 are respectively $0.0058 per hour, $0.0116 per hour, and $0.023 per hour. These values correspond to the price of Amazon EC2 on-demand VM instances having one vCPU and Linux OS. Similar to CSPs like Google and Amazon, we consider a per-second billing model with a minimum billing period of 1 min. That is, if a VM runs for 75.2 s, the charge will be for 76 s, but if a VM runs for 35 s, the same will be for 1 min. We assume that the average bandwidth between the VMs is 1 Gbps.

We have experimented with four real scientific workflows- CyberShake, Epigenomics, SIPHT, and Montage. The structure and characteristics of these workflows appear in detail in [3]. We have conducted experiments for different combinations of α and β. It is noteworthy that the deadline factor α, and budget factor β significantly affects the deadline satisfaction of a workflow. For a particular value of β, a high α increases the chance of deadline satisfaction. Again, for a given α, a higher β leads to a greater chance of deadline satisfaction. Thus by varying the α and β parameters, the users can suitably adjust the deadline and budget depending upon the relative importance of the makespan and monetary cost of the workflow. After trying with different values of α and β, we have finally settled on $\alpha = 1.3$, $\beta = 0.6$, and plotted the normalized energy, makespan, and cost.

5.3   Experimental Results and Analysis

Figures. 1, 2 and 3 show the simulation results. From the figures, it is clear that FBCWS keeps the scheduling cost within the budget and tries to reduce the makespan. However, it leads to high energy consumption. DEWTS reduces energy consumption and satisfies the deadline of the workflow, but significantly increases the cost of scheduling which exceeds the budget. Our proposed approach ESDWB effectively schedules the workflow within its budget and tries to lessen deadline violation and energy consumption at the same time. The makespan for our approach mostly lies within the deadline, and when it does not, it exceeds the deadline by a small amount keeping the cost within budget. In workflows like CyberShake and Epigenomics, where there is a significant amount of data transfer between tasks of the workflow, the makespan generated by our approach is lesser than that of FBCWS and DEWTS. Our approach

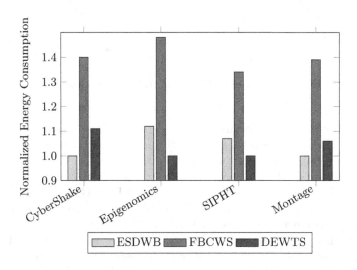

Fig. 1. Energy consumption of scheduling different workflows.

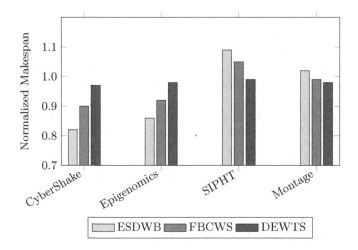

Fig. 2. Makespan of different workflows.

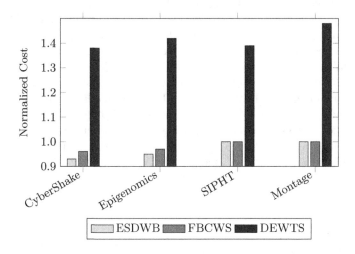

Fig. 3. Monetary cost of workflow scheduling.

gives a smaller makespan because it tries to allocate the predecessor and successor tasks of the workflow that have high data transfer between them, in the same VM, and thus reduces the data transmission time.

Our algorithm ESDWB achieves significant energy savings by adjusting the voltage and frequency of the VMs using the DVFS technique. Although the energy consumption value generated by ESDWB is sometimes more than that of DEWTS, it is much lesser than that of FBCWS. Moreover, unlike DEWTS, the cost of scheduling in our approach ESDWB never exceeds the budget. Our proposed method outperforms the other algorithms under comparison, by considering all three scheduling parameters- energy, makespan, and cost.

6   Conclusion and Future Work

In this paper, we have proposed an energy-efficient scheduling algorithm for deadline-sensitive and budget-constrained workflows in the Cloud environment. Our approach ensures that the schedule is within the user-defined budget. It also reduces energy consumption by assigning tasks to VMs having comparatively lower processing speeds, without violating the deadline of the tasks. It further promotes energy efficiency by reducing the frequency of the VMs using the DVFS technique. Our proposed approach tries to schedule the workflow such that deadline violation is prevented as far as possible. In case the deadline violation cannot be avoided due to insufficient budget, the algorithm assigns tasks to VMs of the fastest type available within the budget to minimize the makespan. Experimental results validate the efficacy of our approach in comparison to other state-of-art workflow scheduling techniques. As future work, we would like to explore the workflow scheduling problem by considering the data transfer costs between the tasks of the workflow. We also intend to investigate workflow scheduling in the multi-cloud environment.

Acknowledgment. We acknowledge the contribution of UGC-NET Junior Research Fellowship (UGC-Ref. No.: 3610/(NET-NOV 2017)) provided by the University Grants Commission, Government of India to the first author for research work. We would also like to thank the Visvesvaraya PhD Scheme of Ministry of Electronics & Information Technology, Government of India (Ref. No. MLA/MUM/GA/10(37)C) for their support.

References

1. How to stop data centres from gobbling up the world's electricity (2018). https://www.nature.com/articles/d41586-018-06610-y. Accessed 6 Jul 2020
2. Arabnejad, H., Barbosa, J.G.: A budget constrained scheduling algorithm for workflow applications. J. Grid Comput. **12**(4), 665–679 (2014)
3. Bharathi, S., Chervenak, A., Deelman, E., Mehta, G., Su, M.H., Vahi, K.: Characterization of scientific workflows. In: 2008 3rd Workshop on Workflows in Support of Large-Scale Science, pp. 1–10. IEEE (2008)
4. Chen, H., Zhu, X., Qiu, D., Guo, H., Yang, L.T., Lu, P.: EONS: minimizing energy consumption for executing real-time workflows in virtualized cloud data centers. In: 2016 45th International Conference on Parallel Processing Workshops (ICPPW), pp. 385–392. IEEE (2016)
5. Chen, W., Deelman, E.: WorkflowSim: a toolkit for simulating scientific workflows in distributed environments. In: 2012 IEEE 8th International Conference on E-science, pp. 1–8. IEEE (2012)
6. Karmakar, K., Das, R.K., Khatua, S.: Resource scheduling of workflow tasks in cloud environment. In: 2019 IEEE International Conference on Advanced Networks and Telecommunications Systems (ANTS), pp. 1–6. IEEE (2019)
7. Karmakar, K., Das, R.K., Khatua, S.: Resource scheduling for tasks of a workflow in cloud environment. In: Hung, D.V., D'Souza, M. (eds.) ICDCIT 2020. LNCS, vol. 11969, pp. 214–226. Springer, Cham (2020). https://doi.org/10.1007/978-3-030-36987-3_13

8. Li, Z., Ge, J., Hu, H., Song, W., Hu, H., Luo, B.: Cost and energy aware scheduling algorithm for scientific workflows with deadline constraint in clouds. IEEE Trans. Serv. Comput. **11**(4), 713–726 (2015)

9. Mathew, T., Sekaran, K.C., Jose, J.: Study and analysis of various task scheduling algorithms in the cloud computing environment. In: 2014 International Conference on Advances in Computing, Communications and Informatics (ICACCI), pp. 658–664. IEEE (2014)

10. Qin, Y., Wang, H., Yi, S., Li, X., Zhai, L.: An energy-aware scheduling algorithm for budget-constrained scientific workflows based on multi-objective reinforcement learning. J. Supercomput. **76**(1), 455–480 (2019). https://doi.org/10.1007/s11227-019-03033-y

11. Rizvi, N., Ramesh, D.: Fair budget constrained workflow scheduling approach for heterogeneous clouds. Clust. Comput. **23**(4), 3185–3201 (2020). https://doi.org/10.1007/s10586-020-03079-1

12. Stavrinides, G.L., Karatza, H.D.: An energy-efficient, QoS-aware and cost-effective scheduling approach for real-time workflow applications in cloud computing systems utilizing DVFs and approximate computations. Fut. Gener. Comput. Syst. **96**, 216–226 (2019)

13. Tang, Z., Qi, L., Cheng, Z., Li, K., Khan, S.U., Li, K.: An energy-efficient task scheduling algorithm in DVFs-enabled cloud environment. J. Grid Comput. **14**(1), 55–74 (2016)

14. Wu, C.Q., Lin, X., Yu, D., Xu, W., Li, L.: End-to-end delay minimization for scientific workflows in clouds under budget constraint. IEEE Trans. Cloud Comput. **3**(2), 169–181 (2014)

15. Zhu, Z., Zhang, G., Li, M., Liu, X.: Evolutionary multi-objective workflow scheduling in cloud. IEEE Trans. Parallel Distrib. Syst. **27**(5), 1344–1357 (2015)

An Efficient Renewable Energy-Based Scheduling Algorithm for Cloud Computing

Sanjib Kumar Nayak[1], Sanjaya Kumar Panda[2(✉)], Satyabrata Das[1], and Sohan Kumar Pande[1]

[1] Veer Surendra Sai University of Technology, Burla 768018, Odisha, India
fortunatesanjib@gmail.com, teacher.satya@gmail.com, ersohanpande@gmail.com
[2] National Institute of Technology, Warangal 506004, Telangana, India
sanjayauce@gmail.com

Abstract. The global growth of cloud computing services is witnessing a continuous surge, starting from storing data to sharing information with others. It makes cloud service providers (CSPs) efficiently utilize the existing resources of datacenters to increase adaptability and minimize the unexpected expansion of datacenters. These datacenters consume enormous amounts of energy generated using fossil fuels (i.e., non-renewable energy (NRE) sources), and emit a substantial amount of carbon footprint and heat. It drastically impacts the environment. As a result, CSPs are pledged to decarbonize the datacenters by adopting renewable energy (RE) sources, such as solar, wind, hydro and biomass. However, these CSPs have not completely ditched fossil fuels as RE sources are subjected to inconsistent atmospheric conditions. Recent studies have suggested using both NRE and RE sources by the CSPs to meet user requirements. However, these studies have not considered flexible duration, nodes and utilization of the user requests (URs) with respect to datacenters. Therefore, we consider these URs' properties and propose a RE-based scheduling algorithm (RESA) to efficiently assign the URs to the datacenters. The proposed algorithm determines both the earliest completion time and energy cost, and takes their linear combination to decide a suitable datacenter for the URs. We conduct extensive simulations by taking 1000 to 16000 URs and 20 to 60 datacenters. Our simulation results are compared with other algorithms, namely round-robin (RR) and random, which show that RESA is able to reduce the overall completion time (i.e., makespan (M)), energy consumption (EC), overall cost (OC) and the number of used RE ($|URE|$) resources.

Keywords: Cloud computing · Renewable energy · Non-renewable energy · Scheduling algorithm · Datacenters · Coronavirus disease

1 Introduction

Over the last few years, many companies, such as Netflix, Instagram, Apple and many more, have moved to the cloud [1]. These companies are looking for part or all of their information technology (IT) solutions, starting from storing

© Springer Nature Switzerland AG 2021
D. Goswami and T. A. Hoang (Eds.): ICDCIT 2021, LNCS 12582, pp. 81–97, 2021.
https://doi.org/10.1007/978-3-030-65621-8_5

data to sharing information with others [2–5]. The cloud-based services enable them to meet the spike in demand and depletion in activity without owning any infrastructure and upfront commitment. According to the MarketsandMarkets report [6], the market of global cloud computing is expected to increase at a compound annual growth rate of 17.5% (i.e., \$832.1 billion by 2025 from \$371.4 billion in 2020) and its adoption is drastically increasing due to Coronavirus Disease (COVID)-19 pandemic. The continuous surge of cloud computing creates enormous challenges for the CSPs. One such challenge is to efficiently utilize the existing resources of datacenters, so that new users' applications can be deployed without increasing the physical infrastructure [7,8]. Moreover, efficient resource management and monitoring minimize the unexpected expansion of datacenters.

The electricity use of global datacenters is rapidly increasing day by day. It is generated using fossil fuels (NRE resources), such as coal, petroleum, gas and oils. Due to the high demand for electricity, the cost of fossil fuels is also increasing. These fuels adversely affect the environment by emitting a huge amount of carbon dioxide (i.e., CO_2) and heat. For instance, streaming a 30-min Netflix video generates 0.028 to 0.057 kg CO_2, which is the same as 200 m driving as reported in International Energy Agency [9]. As a result, CSPs are pledged to decarbonize the datacenters by adopting RE sources, such as solar, wind, hydro, tidal, geothermal and biomass [10,11]. Many CSPs like Amazon, Google and Microsoft claim that datacenters' resources are 100% powered by RE resources, as reported in an American magazine [12]. However, these CSPs have not completely ditched NRE sources as RE sources are reliant on the atmospheric conditions. Recent studies have suggested that the CSPs use both NRE and RE sources for addressing the user requirements [10,11,13–15]. These studies present the user requirements, such as start time, nodes and duration in the form of URs, and they are assigned to the datacenters based on the availability of RE resources, energy cost, specific ordering and randomly. However, these studies have not considered flexible duration, nodes and utilization of the URs on the datacenters. This phenomenon inspired us to think of the URs' properties and introduce a new scheduling problem in the RE-based cloud computing environment.

In this paper, we address the following scheduling problem. Given a set of n URs and a set of m datacenters with their resources, the problem is to assign the URs to the datacenters, so that M, EC and OC are minimized, and $|URE|$ resources is maximized. We propose a three-phase algorithm, called RESA to efficiently assign the URs to the datacenters. The proposed algorithm estimates the earliest completion time (CT) and energy cost (CO) of the URs in all the datacenters, and takes their linear combination to select a suitable datacenter for the URs. The performance of the RESA is carried out through simulation runs by taking 1000 to 16000 URs and 20 to 60 datacenters. The results of simulation runs are compared with two algorithms, namely RR [10] and random [16] in terms of four performance metrics, namely M, EC, OC and $|URE|$ resources to show the effectiveness of the RESA. Note that existing scheduling algorithms do not model the URs in flexible duration, nodes and utilization; hence, those algorithms are not directly comparable to the proposed algorithm. Therefore, we compare with RR and random as compared in [10,15–17].

The rest of this paper is organized as follows. In Sect. 2, we survey the task consolidation and scheduling algorithms with their pros and cons. In Sect. 3, we discuss the cloud, cost and energy models, and formulate the scheduling problem. The proposed algorithm is presented in Sect. 4 with an illustration. Simulation results of the proposed and existing algorithms are given in Sect. 5. The paper concludes in Sect. 6 with some possible future works.

2   Related Work

RE-based scheduling algorithms are commonly focused on minimizing the OC [10,11,13,15] and maximizing the green power utilization [10,11,14,15,18]. These scheduling algorithms have modeled the URs in the start time, nodes and duration without considering utilization. Moreover, these algorithms have assigned the URs to the resources of datacenters without considering heterogeneity.

Beloglazov et al. [19] have proposed an energy-aware resource allocation algorithm by considering CPU utilization. They have shown a significant reduction of energy in the cloud datacenters using experimentation. However, they have considered mapping virtual machines (VMs) to hosts without looking into the URs. Consequently, Esfandiarpoor et al. [20] have improved the algorithm proposed in [19] by taking the structural advantage of datacenters. Like [19], the mapping of URs to VMs is not focused on their algorithm. Lee et al. [16] have suggested considering resource utilization in scheduling algorithm to improve the energy efficiency and proposed two energy-conscious task consolidation algorithms. But, the relationship between resource utilization and energy consumption is considered as a linear one. Later, Hsu et al. [21] have stated that the relationship is not linear. As a result, they have presented an energy-aware task consolidation by limiting the CPU usage to a specified threshold (i.e., 70%). The rationality behind this threshold is that energy consumption is drastically increased beyond this threshold. Panda and Jana [17] have addressed the demerits associated with task consolidation and scheduling, and proposed an energy-efficient task scheduling without considering nodes. In the above works, the RE-based sources are not used to reduce energy consumption.

Rajeev and Ashok [18] have presented a dynamic load shifting program for cloud computing. This program locally computes the generation and demand in each time frame and determine the possibility of RE sources for the customer. However, they have not considered inconsistent atmospheric conditions in their program. Grange et al. [13] have proposed an attractiveness-based blind scheduling algorithm for scheduling the jobs to the machines. However, the cost associated with powering machines is not well-studied in their algorithm. Xu et al. [14] have presented a workload shifting algorithm to reduce NRE resources and carbon dioxide emissions. They have performed workload sharing among the datacenters to properly utilizing their RE resources. They have suggested that the workload execution can be delayed, if allowed, to maximize RE resources usage. The above works have not considered resource utilization, which significantly reduces energy consumption.

Toosi and Buyya [10] have proposed an algorithm for geographical load balancing to minimize cost and maximize RE utilization. They have considered future-aware best fit (FABEF), RR and highest available renewable first (HAREF) benchmark algorithms in their study. FABEF performs better in overall cost, whereas HAREF performs better in green power utilization. However, they have assumed that URs can be assigned to any datacenter with identical time and nodes. Nayak et al. [15] have presented a RE-based task consolidation algorithm by considering the resource utilization. They have also assigned the URs by taking identical time, nodes and utilization on the datacenters. The proposed algorithm is different in various aspects in comparison with other algorithms. (1) Unlike [10,13,15–17,21], the RESA considers different flexible duration, nodes and utilization of URs on the datacenters to make it a realistic one. (2) The RESA takes a linear combination of the earliest CT and CO to select a suitable datacenter in contrast to OC or $|URE|$ resources as used in [10,15]. (3) We evaluate the RESA using M and EC in addition to OC and $|URE|$ resources as used in [10,15].

3   Models and Problem Statement

3.1   Cloud System Model

Consider a cloud system that consists of a set of geographically distributed datacenters. Each datacenter houses a set of servers/resources and is connected to both NRE and RE sources. Here, we assume that the resources are powered with RE and NRE sources based on their availability. On the other hand, there is a CSP portal's user interface to submit the URs and keep track of the URs and the resources. These URs are placed in a global queue and served in the order of their arrival without any interruption. It is noteworthy to mention that multiple URs can be assigned to a single resource without any interference, as stated in [16,17,21]. The data transfer time between the portal and datacenters' resources, including resource mapping, is assumed to be negligible.

3.2   Cost and Energy Model

The cost and energy model is based on the utilization of resources and duration of UR as used in [16,17]. As a resource can be powered with NRE or RE source, the relationship between resource utilization and power consumption depends on the energy source type. If the energy source is NRE, then the relationship is considered as linear one up to a certain utilization (UT) (say, $\tau\%$) and non-linear one beyond that utilization as considered in [21]. Here, we consider that the CO is associated with utilization and it is calculated for NRE resource as follows.

$$CO = \begin{cases} COST_{jkl} \times 2 & \text{if } UT \geq \tau\% \\ COST_{jkl} & \text{Otherwise} \end{cases} \tag{1}$$

Table 1. p_{max} and p_{min} values

Resource	Utilization	p_{max}	p_{min}
NRE	0 to $< \tau\%$	25	20
	$\geq \tau\%$ to 100%	30	20
RE	0 to 100%	25	20

where $COST_{jkl}$ is the cost of kth resource of jth datacenter at time instance l. Similarly, we calculate the EC for NRE resource as follows.

$$EC = (p_{max} - p_{min}) \times UT + p_{min} \tag{2}$$

where p_{max} (100% utilization) and p_{min} (1% utilization) values are set as per Table 1, where 20, 25 and 30 values represent 200 W, 250 W and 300 W, respectively as suggested in [16]. On the other hand, the relationship between resource utilization and power consumption is a linear one irrespective of utilization in RE source. Therefore, the CO is calculated as follows.

$$CO = COST_{jkl} \tag{3}$$

The EC for RE resource is calculated using Eq. (2), where p_{max} and p_{min} values are set as mentioned in Table 1.

3.3   Problem Statement

Consider a global queue Q, which keeps a set of n URs, $U = \{U_1, U_2, U_3,\ldots, U_n\}$, in which each UR U_i, $1 \leq i \leq n$, is represented in the form of 3-tuple, i.e., $<D, N, UT>$, where D is the flexible duration, N is the number of nodes and UT is the utilization. Here, flexible duration means that there is no specific start and end time. On the other hand, consider a set of m datacenters, $DC = \{DC_1, DC_2, DC_3,\ldots, DC_m\}$, in which each datacenter DC_j, $1 \leq j \leq m$, consists of a set of p resources/nodes, $R_j = \{R_{j1}, R_{j2}, R_{j3},\ldots, R_{jp}\}$. Each resource $R_{jk} \in DC_j$, $1 \leq j \leq m$, $1 \leq k \leq p$, consists of a set of o resource slots/time window, $S_{jk} = \{S_{jk1}, S_{jk2}, S_{jk3},\ldots, S_{jko}\}$. Each resource slot $S_{jkl} \in R_{jk}$, $1 \leq j \leq m$, $1 \leq k \leq p$, $1 \leq l \leq o$, can be run using NRE (brown) or RE (green) energy source with a given time l. If a resource slot S_{jkl} is running using NRE source, then the cost is variable, identifiable and pre-determined up to o resource slots. On the contrary, if a resource slot S_{jkl} is running using RE source, then the cost is fixed, identifiable and pre-determined up to o resource slots as stated in [10,11].

Given a D matrix, N matrix and UT matrix between the URs and the datacenters, the problem is to find an efficient mapping function f between U and DC (i.e., $f: U \rightarrow DC$), such that M, EC and OC are minimized and $|URE|$ resources is maximized.

$$D = \begin{array}{c} \\ U_1 \\ U_2 \\ \vdots \\ U_n \end{array} \overset{DC_1 \ DC_2 \ \cdots \ DC_m}{\left\{\begin{array}{ccccc} D_{11} & D_{12} & \cdots & D_{1m} \\ D_{21} & D_{22} & \cdots & D_{2m} \\ \vdots & \vdots & \vdots & \vdots \\ D_{n1} & D_{n2} & \cdots & D_{nm} \end{array}\right\}} \quad (4) \qquad N = \begin{array}{c} \\ U_1 \\ U_2 \\ \vdots \\ U_n \end{array} \overset{DC_1 \ DC_2 \ \cdots \ DC_m}{\left\{\begin{array}{ccccc} N_{11} & N_{12} & \cdots & N_{1m} \\ N_{21} & N_{22} & \cdots & N_{2m} \\ \vdots & \vdots & \vdots & \vdots \\ N_{n1} & N_{n2} & \cdots & N_{nm} \end{array}\right\}} \quad (5)$$

$$UT = \begin{array}{c} \\ U_1 \\ U_2 \\ \vdots \\ U_n \end{array} \overset{DC_1 \ DC_2 \ \cdots \ DC_m}{\left\{\begin{array}{ccccc} UT_{11} & UT_{12} & \cdots & UT_{1m} \\ UT_{21} & UT_{22} & \cdots & UT_{2m} \\ \vdots & \vdots & \vdots & \vdots \\ UT_{n1} & UT_{n2} & \cdots & UT_{nm} \end{array}\right\}} \quad (6)$$

where D_{ij}, N_{ij} and UT_{ij}, $1 \le i \le n$, $1 \le j \le m$, represent the flexible duration, nodes and utilization of UR U_i on datacenter DC_j, respectively. The problem is restricted to the following constraints.

1. $UT[S_{jkl}] + UT_{ij} \le 100\%$, $1 \le i \le n$, $1 \le j \le m$, $1 \le k \le p$, $1 \le l \le o$
2. $\sum_{j=1}^{m} I_{ij} = 1, \forall U_i \in U$

$$\text{where } I_{ij} = \begin{cases} 1 & \text{if UR } U_i \text{ is assigned to datacenter } DC_j \\ 0 & \text{Otherwise} \end{cases} \quad (7)$$

3. $\sum_{i=1}^{n} G_{ij} \ge 1, \forall DC_j \in DC$

$$\text{where } G_{ij} = \begin{cases} 1 & \text{if datacenter } DC_j \text{ is executing UR } U_i \\ 0 & \text{Otherwise} \end{cases} \quad (8)$$

4 Proposed Algorithm

The proposed algorithm RESA is an on-line algorithm for cloud computing and the pseudo code for RESA is shown in Algorithm 1. It aims to minimize the M, EC and OC, and maximize the $|URE|$ resources. The RESA consists of three phases, namely estimation, selection, and assignment and execution. In the first phase, RESA finds the earliest CT and CO of the URs on the datacenters (Line 3 to Line 43 of Algorithm 1). In the second phase, it selects a datacenter by finding the fitness value of the URs on the datacenters followed by finding the minimum fitness value (Line 44, and Line 1 to Line 5 of Procedure 1). Finally, it assigns the URs to their selected datacenter and executes in the resources of the datacenters (Line 45, and Line 1 to Line 28 of Procedure 2).

4.1   Phase 1: Estimation

In this phase, RESA finds the earliest CT and CO of a UR on the datacenters. For this, it finds the available resource slots in the datacenter by taking the flexible duration, nodes and utilization of that UR. If the sum of the utilization of the resource slot by early arrived URs and utilization of that UR does not exceed the maximum utilization of the resource slot, i.e., 100% (Line 9 of Algorithm 1), then the resource slot can be selected for that UR. However, this process continues until the nodes of that UR is completely satisfied for the given duration (9 to Line 15). If the number of nodes is not sufficient (Line 17), then it skips the resource for that particular time. Otherwise, it finds the cost for that UR by checking whether that resource slot is powered with NRE source or not (Line 19 and Line 20). If it is an NRE source, then it finds the utilization of that resource slot (Line 21). Note that the utilization is zero iff there are no early arrived URs. It then checks whether the UR's utilization is greater than or equal to the threshold $\tau\%$ or not (Line 22). If it is so, then the cost is doubled by following the proposed cost and energy model (Line 23). Otherwise, the normal cost is taken for using that resource slot (Line 24 and Line 25). On the other hand, if the early arrived URs occupy the resource slot, then the sum of the utilization of early arrived URs and the current UR is determined. If it is greater than or equal to the threshold, then the normal cost is taken for using that resource slot (Line 28 to Line 30). On the contrary, the normal cost is taken for the resource slot powered with RE source irrespective of the value of utilization (Line 33 to Line 35). This process continues until the duration of that UR is satisfied (Line 38 to Line 41). Note that the CT is the end time of the duration of the UR.

4.2   Phase 2: Selection

In this phase, RESA selects a datacenter by finding the UR's fitness value on the datacenters. For this, it normalizes the CT and CO of that UR on the datacenters (Line 1 of Procedure 1) and takes their linear combination (Line 3). Finally, it finds the minimum fitness value and the corresponding datacenter (Line 4 and Line 5). The rationality behind this is that the CT and CO need to be minimized. Therefore, its linear combination also needs to be minimized. Note that EC and $|URE|$ resources are associated with the cost; hence, these are not explicitly shown here.

4.3   Phase 3: Assignment and Execution

In this phase, RESA assigns a UR to the selected datacenter of phase 2 and executes it in the resources of that datacenter. For this, it first finds the start time of the UR from the CT (Line 1 of Procedure 2). Then it assigns the resource slots between the start time and the CT as per the nodes of that UR. If the sum of the resource slot utilization and utilization of that UR does not exceed 100%, then that resource slot is assigned to the UR (Line 4). Like phase 1, this process continues until the nodes of that UR is completely satisfied for the given

Algorithm 1. Pseudo code for RESA

Input: 1-D matrices: Q, n, m, p, o, τ and $\lambda \in (0, 1)$
2-D/3-D matrices: D, N, UT, S and $COST$
Output: M, EC, OC and $|URE|$ resources

1: Set $OC = 0$
2: **while** $Q \neq$ NULL **do**
3:　　**for** $i = 1, 2, 3, \ldots, n$ **do**
4:　　　　**for** $j = 1, 2, 3, \ldots, m$ **do**
5:　　　　　　Set $CO_{ij} = 0$, $tempd = 0$
6:　　　　　　**for** $l = 1, 2, 3, \ldots, o$ **do**
7:　　　　　　　　Set $ncount = 0$, $tempn = N_{ij}$
8:　　　　　　　　**for** $k = 1, 2, 3, \ldots, p$ **do**
9:　　　　　　　　　　**if** $(UT[S_{jkl}] + UT_{ij}) \leq 100\%$ **then**　　　　　▷ Constraint 1
10:　　　　　　　　　　　　$ncount += 1$
11:　　　　　　　　　　　　**if** $ncount == tempn$ **then**
12:　　　　　　　　　　　　　　$tempd += 1$
13:　　　　　　　　　　　　　　Break
14:　　　　　　　　　　　　**end if**
15:　　　　　　　　　　**end if**
16:　　　　　　　　**end for**
17:　　　　　　　　**if** $ncount < tempn$ **then**
18:　　　　　　　　　　Set $tempd = 0$
19:　　　　　　　　**else**
20:　　　　　　　　　　**if** $S_{jkl} == 1$ **then**　　　　　　　　　　▷ NRE Resource
21:　　　　　　　　　　　　**if** $UT[S_{jkl}] == 0\%$ **then**
22:　　　　　　　　　　　　　　**if** $UT_{ij} \geq \tau\%$ **then**
23:　　　　　　　　　　　　　　　　$CO_{ij} += COST_{jkl} \times 2$
24:　　　　　　　　　　　　　　**else**
25:　　　　　　　　　　　　　　　　$CO_{ij} += COST_{jkl}$
26:　　　　　　　　　　　　　　**end if**
27:　　　　　　　　　　　　**else**
28:　　　　　　　　　　　　　　**if** $(UT[S_{jkl}] + UT_{ij}) \geq \tau\%$ **then**
29:　　　　　　　　　　　　　　　　$CO_{ij} += COST_{jkl}$
30:　　　　　　　　　　　　　　**end if**
31:　　　　　　　　　　　　**end if**
32:　　　　　　　　　　**else**　　　　　　　　　　　　　　▷ RE Resource
33:　　　　　　　　　　　　**if** $UT[S_{jkl}] == 0\%$ **then**
34:　　　　　　　　　　　　　　$CO_{ij} += COST_{jkl}$
35:　　　　　　　　　　　　**end if**
36:　　　　　　　　　　**end if**
37:　　　　　　　　**end if**
38:　　　　　　　　**if** $D_{ij} == tempd$ **then**
39:　　　　　　　　　　Set $CT_{ij} = l$
40:　　　　　　　　　　Break
41:　　　　　　　　**end if**
42:　　　　　　**end for**
43:　　　　**end for**
44:　　　　Procedure 1 $SELECT\text{-}DATACENTER\text{-}UR(i, m, \lambda, CT, CO)$　　▷ Constraint 2
45:　　　　Procedure 2 $ASSIGN\text{-}UR\text{-}DATACENTER(i, j', p, \tau, D, N, UT, S, COST, CT,$
　　　$OC)$　　　　　　　　　　　　　　　　　　　　　　　▷ Constraint 3
46:　　**end for**
47: **end while**
48: Calculate the M, EC, OC and $|URE|$ resources

Procedure 1. $SELECT\text{-}DATACENTER\text{-}UR(i, m, \lambda, CT, CO)$

1: Find $norm(CO_{ij})$ and $norm(CT_{ij})$, $1 \leq j \leq m$　　　　▷ norm is a function to perform
　normalization of all the values.
2: **for** $j = 1, 2, 3, \ldots, m$ **do**
3:　　$F_{ij} = \lambda \times norm(CT_{ij}) + (1 - \lambda) \times norm(CO_{ij})$
4: **end for**
5: Find $min(F_{ij})$ and determine the datacenter j' that holds $min(F_{ij})$　　▷ min is a function to
　find the minimum of all the values.

duration. Next, it finds the OC for that UR by checking whether that resource slot is powered with NRE or RE source and the utilization, as discussed in phase 1 (Line 6 to Line 22). This process continues from the start time to the CT of that UR.

Procedure 2 $ASSIGN\text{-}UR\text{-}DATACENTER(i, j', p, \tau, D, N, UT, S, COST, CT, OC)$

```
 1: for l = (CT_{ij'} - D_{ij'} + 1), (CT_{ij'} - D_{ij'} + 2), (CT_{ij'} - D_{ij'} + 3),..., CT_{ij'} do
 2:     Set ncount = 0
 3:     for k = 1, 2, 3,..., p do
 4:         if (UT[S_{j'kl}] + UT_{ij'}) ≤ 100% then
 5:             ncount += 1
 6:             if S_{j'kl} == 1 then                              ▷ NRE Resource
 7:                 if UT[S_{j'kl}] == 0% then
 8:                     if UT_{ij'} ≥ τ% then
 9:                         OC_{ij'} += COST_{j'kl} × 2
10:                     else
11:                         OC_{ij'} += COST_{j'kl}
12:                     end if
13:                 else
14:                     if (UT[S_{j'kl}] + UT_{ij'}) ≥ τ% then
15:                         OC_{ij'} += COST_{j'kl}
16:                     end if
17:                 end if
18:             else                                              ▷ RE Resource
19:                 if UT[S_{j'kl}] == 0% then
20:                     OC_{ij'} += COST_{j'kl}
21:                 end if
22:             end if
23:         end if
24:         if ncount == N_{ij} then
25:             Break
26:         end if
27:     end for
28: end for
```

4.4 An Illustration

Let us illustrate the proposed algorithm using ten URs, U_1 to U_{10} and three datacenters, DC_1 to DC_3. The properties of the URs, such as D, N and UT, are shown in Table 2. Each datacenter contains three resources/nodes in which NRE (RE) resource slots are represented in gray (white) color, as shown in Table 3. The $COST$ of using the NRE resource slots is represented in the first row of the respective datacenters and the $COST$ of using the RE resource slots is fixed as 1 irrespective of time l. The $COST$ and resource slots are identifiable and pre-determined up to a time window of 9 and the threshold is fixed at 70%.

Initially, the Q contains ten URs in the order of U_1 to U_{10} and there is no URs assigned to the datacenters as shown in Table 3. In the first phase, UR U_1 is selected from Q, and its D, N and UT on three datacenters are 4, 5, 2; 3, 2, 1 and 59, 19, 50, respectively. If UR U_1 is assigned to datacenter DC_1, then

Table 2. A set of ten URs with their properties

User Request	Duration			Nodes Datacenter			Utilization		
	D_1	D_2	D_3	D_1	D_2	D_3	D_1	D_2	D_3
U_1	4	5	2	3	2	1	59	19	50
U_2	2	2	5	1	2	3	65	69	12
U_3	3	5	3	1	3	2	17	68	61
U_4	4	2	3	1	3	1	65	39	66
U_5	5	5	5	1	1	1	48	58	51
U_6	5	2	2	3	2	2	15	18	56
U_7	3	1	4	3	2	3	26	35	55
U_8	1	2	4	1	2	2	43	65	33
U_9	1	4	2	3	3	2	68	58	49
U_{10}	2	3	3	1	3	1	68	68	20

Table 3. A set of three datacenters with their NRE and RE resources

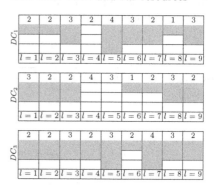

CT and CO is 4 and 18 (i.e., $1 \times 8 + 2 + 2 + 3 + 3$), respectively. Similarly, if it is assigned to datacenter DC_2 and DC_3, then CT is 5 and 2, and CO is 14 (i.e., $1 \times 7 + 3 + 2 + 2$) and 2, respectively. In the second phase, the CTs are normalized as 0.80, 1.00 and 0.40, and the COs are normalized as 1.00, 0.78 and 0.11 on three datacenters, respectively. Then the fitness value (F) is calculated as 0.90, 0.89 and 0.26 on the datacenters by taking the λ value as 0.50. As the minimum F is achieved on datacenter DC_3, UR U_1 is assigned to datacenter DC_3 in the third phase. The OC of datacenter DC_3 is updated to 2 and the CT of UR U_1 is set to 2.

Next, UR U_2 is selected from Q, and its D, N and UT on three datacenters are 2, 2, 5; 1, 2, 3 and 65, 69, 12, respectively. If UR U_2 is assigned to datacenter DC_1, then CT and CO is 2 and 2, respectively. Similarly, if it is assigned to datacenter DC_2 and DC_3, then CT is 2 and 5, and CO is 7 and 29, respectively. In the second phase, the CTs are normalized as 0.40, 0.40 and 1.00, and the COs are normalized as 0.07, 0.24 and 1.00 on three datacenters, respectively. Then the F is calculated as 0.23, 0.32 and 1.00 on the datacenters. As the minimum F is achieved on datacenter DC_1, UR U_2 is assigned to datacenter DC_1 in the third phase. The OC of datacenter DC_1 is updated to 2 and the CT of UR U_2 is set to 2. In the similar fashion, URs U_3 to U_{10} are assigned to datacenters DC_1, DC_3, DC_2, DC_2, DC_2, DC_1, DC_3 and DC_1, respectively, as shown in Table 4. The summary of step by step process for RESA is shown in Table 5.

We also produce the Gantt chart for RR and random algorithms by following [10,16] in Table 6 and Table 7, respectively. The comparison of the proposed and existing algorithms in terms of four performance metrics is shown in Table 8. The comparison results show the superiority of the proposed algorithm over the existing algorithms.

Theorem 1. *The overall time complexity of RESA (Algorithm 1) is $O(Knmpo)$.*

Proof. The phase 1 of Algorithm 1 finds the CT and CO, which takes $O(nmpo)$ time. Then it calls the Procedure 1 to select a suitable datacenter, which takes

Table 4. Gantt chart for RESA algorithm

Table 5. Summary of step by step process for RESA algorithm

		U_1	U_2	U_3	U_4	U_5	U_6	U_7	U_8	U_9	U_{10}
	DC_1	4	2	3	4	5	5	5	1	3	2
CT	DC_2	5	2	5	2	5	2	1	3	9	8
	DC_3	2	5	3	3	5	4	7	4	2	3
	DC_1	18	2	1	3	7	27	21	1	6	3
CO	DC_2	14	7	23	12	5	5	3	8	19	14
	DC_3	2	29	12	5	11	9	30	10	4	4
	DC_1	0.90	0.23	0.32	0.63	0.82	1.00	0.71	0.18	0.32	0.23
F	DC_2	0.89	0.32	1.00	0.75	0.73	0.29	0.12	0.78	1.00	1.00
	DC_3	0.26	1.00	0.56	0.58	1.00	0.57	1.00	1.00	0.22	0.33
$min(F)$		0.26	0.23	0.32	0.58	0.73	0.29	0.12	0.18	0.22	0.23
Datacenter		DC_3	DC_1	DC_1	DC_3	DC_2	DC_2	DC_2	DC_1	DC_3	DC_1

Table 6. Gantt chart for RR algorithm

Table 7. Gantt chart for random algorithm

$O(m)$ time. Next, it calls the Procedure 2 to assign and execute the UR on the selected datacenter, which takes $O(po)$ time in the worst case. However, Algorithm 1 is invoked K times (say). Therefore, the overall time complexity is

$$\underbrace{[K \times O(nmpo)]}_{\text{Phase 1}} + \underbrace{[K \times n \times O(m)]}_{\text{Phase 2}} + \underbrace{[K \times O(po)]}_{\text{Phase 3}} = O(Knmpo).$$

Lemma 1. *The mapping function $f: U \rightarrow DC$ is surjective.*

Proof. RESA assigns a UR to a datacenter by checking that the sum of the resource slot's utilization and the utilization of the UR does not exceed the maximum utilization. Here, utilization of the UR is between 1% to 100% and it varies with respect to the datacenters. As $|U| >> |DC|$ or $n >> m$, every datacenter is assigned with some URs and these URs may share the same resource slot of the datacenter subjected to maximum utilization. As a result, there is no datacenter left out without URs. Therefore, the mapping function $f: U \rightarrow DC$ is surjective.

Table 8. Comparison of four performance metrics for RESA, RR and random algorithms

Algorithm	M (in time units)	EC (in energy units)	OC (in cost units)	$|URE|$
RESA	5	6850	31	13
RR	8	17350	92	24
Random	9	18565	98	24

Lemma 2. *The mapping between the URs to the resource slots of the datacenter is injective iff the utilization of the URs in any datacenter exceeds 50%.*

Proof. RESA can assign two URs, $U_{i'}$ and $U_{i''}$, $1 \leq i',\ i'' \leq n$, $i' \neq i''$, to the same resource slot of the datacenter DC_j, $1 \leq j \leq m$ iff $UT_{i'j} + UT_{i''j} \leq 100\%$. It is given that $UT_{i'j} > 50\%$ or $UT_{i''j} > 50\%$. Therefore, these URs cannot be assigned to the same resource slot of the datacenter. Alternatively, each resource slot cannot be accommodated with more than one URs. Therefore, the mapping between the URs to the resource slots of the datacenter is injective.

Lemma 3. *If a UR is estimated to complete in two different datacenters simultaneously, then the datacenter with the lowest cost is selected for that UR.*

Proof. Let us assume that UR U_i is completed in datacenter $DC_{j'}$ at $CT_{ij'}$ and datacenter $DC_{j''}$ at $CT_{ij''}$. It is given that $CT_{ij'} = CT_{ij''}$. The fitness value of UR U_i on datacenter $DC_{j'}$ is calculated as follows.

$F_{ij'} = \lambda \times norm(CT_{ij'}) + (1 - \lambda) \times norm(CO_{ij'})$

Similarly, the fitness value of UR U_i on datacenter $DC_{j''}$ is calculated as follows.

$F_{ij''} = \lambda \times norm(CT_{ij''}) + (1 - \lambda) \times norm(CO_{ij''})$

If $F_{ij'} > F_{ij''}$, then UR U_i is assigned to datacenter $DC_{j''}$. Otherwise, it is assigned to datacenter $DC_{j'}$. It can be simplified as follows.

$F_{ij'} > F_{ij''}$

$\Rightarrow \lambda \times norm(CT_{ij'}) + (1-\lambda) \times norm(CO_{ij'}) > \lambda \times norm(CT_{ij''}) + (1-\lambda) \times norm(CO_{ij''})$

$\Rightarrow \lambda \times norm(CO_{ij'}) > \lambda \times norm(CO_{ij''})$ $\qquad \because CT_{ij'} = CT_{ij''}$

$\Rightarrow norm(CO_{ij'}) > norm(CO_{ij''}) \Rightarrow CO_{ij'} > CO_{ij''}$

Therefore, UR U_i is assigned to datacenter $DC_{j''}$, which results in the lowest cost.

Lemma 4. *If a UR is estimated to take same cost in two different datacenters, then the datacenter with the earliest CT is selected for that UR.*

Proof. The proof is the same as Lemma 3.

Lemma 5. *If a datacenter takes the earliest CT and CO for a UR, then that datacenter is selected irrespective of the value of λ.*

Proof. Let datacenter $DC_{j'}$ takes $CT_{ij'}$ and $CO_{ij'}$ for UR U_i in comparison to another datacenter $DC_{j''}$, which takes $CT_{ij''}$ and $CO_{ij''}$. It is given that

$CT_{ij'} < CT_{ij''}$ and $CO_{ij'} < CO_{ij''}$

$\Rightarrow norm(CT_{ij'}) < norm(CT_{ij''})$ and $norm(CO_{ij'}) < norm(CO_{ij''})$

$\Rightarrow \lambda \times norm(CT_{ij'}) < \lambda \times norm(CT_{ij''})$ and $(1 - \lambda) \times norm(CO_{ij'}) < (1 - \lambda) \times norm(CO_{ij''})$

$\Rightarrow \lambda \times norm(CT_{ij'}) + (1 - \lambda) \times norm(CO_{ij'}) < \lambda \times norm(CT_{ij''}) + (1 - \lambda) \times norm(CO_{ij''}) \Rightarrow F_{ij'} < F_{ij''}$

Therefore, UR U_i is assigned to datacenter $DC_{j'}$.

5 Performance Metrics, Datasets and Simulation Results

This section presents four performance metrics, the generation of five different datasets and simulation results.

5.1 Performance Metrics

We use four performance metrics, namely M, EC, OC and $|URE|$ resources to compare the proposed and existing algorithms. These metrics are defined as follows. The M of a datacenter DC_j (i.e., M_j), $1 \leq j \leq m$, is the maximum CT of the URs that are assigned to that datacenter. However, overall M is the maximum of all the CTs of the datacenters. Mathematically, $M = max(M_j)$, $1 \leq j \leq m$. The EC is the total amount of energy required to execute all the URs in the datacenters' resources and it is calculated as described in Sect. 3.2. The OC is the total cost gained by the CSPs for executing the URs and it is calculated as described in Sect. 3.2. Alternatively, it is the sum of the cost of using NRE and RE resource slots. The $|URE|$ resources is the total number of RE resource slots of the datacenters used to execute all the URs.

5.2 Datasets

We generated five datasets in which each dataset contains three different instances. These datasets are generated by the pre-defined function, *randi*, of MATLAB R2017a. This function returns a 2-D integer array using the discrete uniform distribution on the given interval. The rows and columns of the array represent URs and datacenters, respectively, and the array is represented by URs × datacenters. To select a wide variety of URs, datacenters and intervals, we follow the well-known Monte Carlo method [22] as follows.

Table 9. Comparison of M, EC, OC and $|URE|$ for RESA, RR and random algorithms

Dataset	Instance	M			EC			OC			|URE|		
		RESA	RR	Random	RESA	RR	Random	RESA	RR	Random	RESA	RR	Random
1000 × 20	i1	181	1254	1533	74428905	444813335	439204225	773562	4228062	4158470	70241	492015	480342
	i2	162	1217	1358	73577120	443654830	453793255	755997	4168973	4281804	70394	489694	495545
	i3	178	1320	1499	74849105	446569175	460535005	754474	4236899	4360274	71167	497864	500565
2000 × 30	i1	174	1643	1674	126319995	891023145	896693565	1333253	8548678	8539553	116501	941808	951647
	i2	168	1608	1845	126759150	870422385	888788650	1327548	8302101	8386787	116358	935279	962645
	i3	169	1491	1612	124661385	882644790	879682715	1305842	8379219	8395016	115401	927865	936648
4000 × 40	i1	216	2578	2317	224425155	1805839200	1781000940	2374636	17076916	16976451	197795	1847563	1826773
	i2	216	2295	2563	224685435	1760172230	1767916780	2368048	16775597	16775991	201938	1827420	1822893
	i3	211	2341	2416	220132700	1774122800	1758765700	2329875	16865780	16720189	197352	1841633	1808720
8000 × 50	i1	299	3280	3274	408465360	3591663065	3593372040	4393962	34308194	34182230	355171	3534790	3517949
	i2	294	3479	3501	405928155	3588989840	3603123675	4356600	34231837	34198062	352187	3504015	3541726
	i3	292	3561	3538	405147270	3581061730	3632697640	4382475	34122022	34479219	351375	3526839	3600477
16000 × 60	i1	450	5437	5445	767065705	7322619235	7370971110	8378616	70167828	70691777	648829	6902719	7007246
	i2	446	5513	5783	765533565	7386703120	7303789235	8284972	70633870	69974505	656224	6991771	6918273
	i3	450	5293	5293	767302105	7257734730	7410603900	8280241	69280800	70537691	653569	6838319	6995578

Step 1: We choose the number of URs as 1000, 2000, 4000, 8000 and 16000, and the number of datacenters as 20, 30, 40, 50 and 60, respectively, for five different datasets. Similarly, we choose the interval of D, N and UT datasets as [10–100], [10–50] and [10–70], respectively. The maximum number of resources is set as 50 in which NRE and RE resources are generated randomly. The cost of using NRE and RE resource slots is set as [2–10] and 1, respectively.

Step 2: We generate three instances of each dataset by taking the same intervals, as discussed in Step 1.

Step 3: We apply the proposed algorithm on the generated instances of datasets. We consider $\tau = 70\%$ for RESA, RR and random as adopted in [21].

Step 4: We find the results in terms of four performance metrics and average the results of three instances of the datasets.

5.3   Simulation Results

We apply the existing algorithms, RR and random, on the generated instances of datasets to obtain the results. Then we compare the results of the proposed and existing algorithms using four performance metrics, namely M, EC, OC and $|URE|$ resources, as shown in Table 9. The visual comparisons are also carried out separately in Fig. 1 to Fig. 4 for easy visualization of results. The results demonstrate that the proposed algorithm RESA outperforms the RR and random in terms of four performance metrics. The rationality behind this better performance is that the URs are assigned to datacenters' resources by calculating the minimum F, which is the linear combination of CT and CO. As CO is associated with resource utilization and $|URE|$ resources, the RESA also takes care of these metrics while assigning the UR to the datacenters.

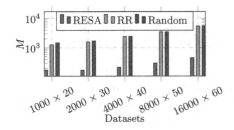

Fig. 1. Comparison of M.

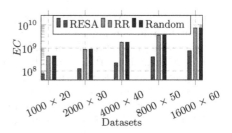

Fig. 2. Comparison of EC.

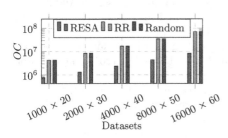

Fig. 3. Comparison of OC.

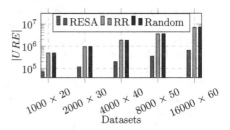

Fig. 4. Comparison of $|URE|$.

6   Conclusion

In this paper, we have presented a scheduling algorithm, RESA, for cloud computing. This algorithm iterates through a three-phase process, and is shown to require $O(Knmpo)$ time for n URs, m datacenters, p resources, o slots and K iterations. The simulation results of the proposed and existing algorithms have been carried out using five datasets and compared using four performance metrics, namely M, EC, OC and $|URE|$ resources. The comparison results demonstrate the efficacy of the proposed algorithm over the existing algorithms. However, we have considered an equal number of resources per datacenter in this scheduling problem. In our future work, we will extend this problem by taking a different number of resources, as seen in small, medium and large datacenters. Moreover, we have assumed that there are no outages during the scheduling process. In practice, the datacenter faces various outages, such as human error, cooling failure, hardware failure, software failure and many more. It can be addressed to make the proposed algorithm a more practical one.

References

1. Khayer, A., Talukder, M.S., Bao, Y., Hossain, M.N.: Cloud computing adoption and its impact on SMEs' performance for cloud supported operations: a dual-stage analytical approach. Technol. Soc. **60**, 101225 (2020)
2. Gill, S.S., et al.: Holistic resource management for sustainable and reliable cloud computing: an innovative solution to global challenge. J. Syst. Softw. **155**, 104–129 (2019)

3. Gholipour, N., Arianyan, E., Buyya, R.: A novel energy-aware resource management technique using joint VM and container consolidation approach for green computing in cloud data centers. Simul. Model. Pract. Theor. **104**, 102127 (2020)
4. Panda, S.K., Jana, P.K.: Normalization-based task scheduling algorithms for heterogeneous multi-cloud environment. Inf. Syst. Front. **20**(2), 373–399 (2018)
5. Panda, S.K., Jana, P.K.: An efficient request-based virtual machine placement algorithm for cloud computing. In: Krishnan, P., Radha Krishna, P., Parida, L. (eds.) ICDCIT 2017. LNCS, vol. 10109, pp. 129–143. Springer, Cham (2017). https://doi.org/10.1007/978-3-319-50472-8_11
6. MarketsandMarkets: Cloud computing market. https://www.marketsandmarkets.com/Market-Reports/cloud-computing-market-234.html. Accessed 6 Aug 2020
7. Qiu, C., Shen, H.: Dynamic demand prediction and allocation in cloud service brokerage. IEEE Trans. Cloud Comput. (2019)
8. Panda, S.K., Jana, P.K.: Efficient task scheduling algorithms for heterogeneous multi-cloud environment. J. Supercomput. **71**(4), 1505–1533 (2015). https://doi.org/10.1007/s11227-014-1376-6
9. Kamiya, G.: The carbon footprint of streaming video. https://www.iea.org/commentaries/the-carbon-footprint-of-streaming-video-fact-checking-the-headlines. Accessed 6 Aug 2020
10. Toosi, A.N., Buyya, R.: A fuzzy logic-based controller for cost and energy efficient load balancing in geo-distributed data centers. In: Proceedings of the 8th International Conference on Utility and Cloud Computing, pp. 186–194. IEEE Press (2015)
11. Nayak, S.K., Panda, S.K., Das, S.: Renewable energy-based resource management in cloud computing: a review. In: Tripathy, A.K., Sarkar, M., Sahoo, J.P., Li, K.-C., Chinara, S. (eds.) Advances in Distributed Computing and Machine Learning. LNNS, vol. 127, pp. 45–56. Springer, Singapore (2021). https://doi.org/10.1007/978-981-15-4218-3_5
12. Oberhaus, D.: Amazon, Google, Microsoft: Here's who has the greenest cloud. https://www.wired.com/story/amazon-google-microsoft-green-clouds-and-hyperscale-data-centers/. Accessed 11 Apr 2020
13. Grange, L., Da Costa, G., Stolf, P.: Green it scheduling for data center powered with renewable energy. Fut. Gener. Comput. Syst. **86**, 99–120 (2018)
14. Minxian, X., Buyya, R.: Managing renewable energy and carbon footprint in multi-cloud computing environments. J. Parallel Distrib. Comput. **135**, 191–202 (2020)
15. Nayak, S.K., Panda, S.K., Das, S, Pande, S.K.: A renewable energy-based task consolidation algorithm for cloud computing. In: Electric Power and Renewable Energy Conference, pp. 1–10. Springer (2020)
16. Lee, Y.C., Zomaya, A.Y.: Energy efficient utilization of resources in cloud computing systems. J. Supercomput. **60**(2), 268–280 (2012)
17. Panda, S.K., Jana, P.K.: An energy-efficient task scheduling algorithm for heterogeneous cloud computing systems. Clust. Comput. **22**(2), 509–527 (2018). https://doi.org/10.1007/s10586-018-2858-8
18. Rajeev, T., Ashok, S.: Dynamic load-shifting program based on a cloud computing framework to support the integration of renewable energy sources. Appl. Energy **146**, 141–149 (2015)
19. Beloglazov, A., Abawajy, J., Buyya, R.: Energy-aware resource allocation heuristics for efficient management of data centers for cloud computing. Future Gener. Comput. Syst. **28**(5), 755–768 (2012)

20. Esfandiarpoor, S., Pahlavan, A., Goudarzi, M.: Structure-aware online virtual machine consolidation for datacenter energy improvement in cloud computing. Comput. Electr. Eng. **42**, 74–89 (2015)
21. Hsu, C.-H., Slagter, K.D., Chen, S.-C., Chung, Y.-C.: Optimizing energy consumption with task consolidation in clouds. Inf. Sci. **258**, 452–462 (2014)
22. Cunha, Jr., A., Nasser, R., Sampaio, R., Lopes, H., Breitman, K.: Uncertainty quantification through the Monte Carlo method in a cloud computing setting. Comput. Phys. Commun. **185**(5), 1355–1363 (2014)

A Revenue-Based Service Management Algorithm for Vehicular Cloud Computing

Sohan Kumar Pande[1], Sanjaya Kumar Panda[2(✉)], and Satyabrata Das[1]

[1] Veer Surendra Sai University of Technology, Burla 768018, Odisha, India
ersohanpande@gmail.com, teacher.satya@gmail.com
[2] National Institute of Technology, Warangal 506004, Telangana, India
sanjayauce@gmail.com

Abstract. Vehicular cloud computing (VCC) is an emerging research area among business and academic communities due to its dynamic computing capacity, on-road assistance, infotainment services, emergency and traffic services. It can mitigate the hindrance faced in the existing infrastructure, relying on the cellular networks, using roadside units (RSUs). Moreover, the existing cellular networks cannot provide better quality services due to the influx of vehicles. In the VCC, RSUs can prefetch the content and data required by the vehicles, and provide them in terms of services when vehicles are residing within the communication range of RSUs. However, RSUs suffer from their limited communication range and data rate. Therefore, it is quite challenging for the RSUs to select suitable vehicles to provide services, such that its revenue can be maximized. In this paper, we propose a revenue-based service management (RBSM) algorithm to tackle the above-discussed challenges. RBSM is a two-phase algorithm that finds data rate zones of the vehicles and selects a suitable vehicle at each time slot to maximize the total revenue of the RSUs, the total download by the vehicles and the total number of completed requests. We assess the performance of RBSM and compare it with an existing algorithm, namely RSU resource scheduling (RRS), by considering various traffic scenarios. The comparison results show that RBSM performs 87%, 90% and 170% better than RRS in terms of total revenue, download and number of completed requests.

Keywords: Vehicular cloud computing · Revenue-based service management · Roadside unit · Resource scheduling · Cellular networks

1 Introduction

Innovation and research in technologies for smart cities urged the information technology (IT) industries, professionals and researchers to explore the features of VCC [1–5]. VCC is the integration of cloud computing, wireless networks, and smart vehicles to provide better on-demand solutions and expand the capabilities of existing infrastructure [6–8]. It offers numerous services in the form

© Springer Nature Switzerland AG 2021
D. Goswami and T. A. Hoang (Eds.): ICDCIT 2021, LNCS 12582, pp. 98–113, 2021.
https://doi.org/10.1007/978-3-030-65621-8_6

of Network as a Service (NaaS), STorage as a Service (STaaS), Computing as a Service (CaaS), COoperation as a Service (COaaS), INformation as a Service (INaaS), ENtertainment as a Service (ENaaS), Traffic Safety as a Service (TSaaS) and many more [3–5]. Nowadays, maximum smart vehicles are facilitated with the modern onboard unit (OBU), which comprises various resources, such as communication systems, storage devices, computing processors, cognitive radios, programmable sensors, global positioning systems and other advanced things [2,3,5]. These highly sophisticated resources remain idle for a considerable amount of time when the vehicles are at the parking lot, roadways or traffic. These underutilized resources can be used by the RSUs to deliver various services offered by the cloud service provider (CSP). It can be performed by creating an infrastructure in which services are provisioned by creating virtual machines (VMs) [4,9]. This infrastructure enables three types of communications, namely vehicle to vehicle (V2V), vehicle to infrastructure (V2I) and infrastructure to vehicle (I2V) [4,5].

Generally, vehicles on the move request various services, such as information, video, entertainment and many more, from the CSP through cellular networks [1,10]. Recent studies reveal that video content contributes to 70% of data traffic [11]. With the increasing demand for video content by smart vehicles, the existing cellular networks cannot provide better quality services [1,10,11]. Therefore, RSUs can augment the cellular networks by prefetching the content and data required by the vehicles [1] and deliver them when vehicles are residing within the communication range of RSUs. Here, RSUs can make a significant amount of revenue by providing better quality services [1,10]. However, the main challenging issues are the coverage and data rate of RSUs, which are maximum up 1 km and 28 MBPS, respectively [12]. On the other hand, RSUs cannot provide content and data to all the vehicles. Therefore, it is quite challenging for the RSUs to select suitable vehicles to provide content and data, such that its revenue can be maximized.

To tackle the above-discussed challenges, we propose a novel algorithm, called RBSM, to maximize the total revenue of the RSUs. RBSM comprises of two phases. In the first phase, it finds the data rate zones of the vehicles. The second phase selects a suitable vehicle at each time slot to download the content from the RSU. For this, it considers the arrival time, velocity, revenue and requested content size of the vehicles. We compare RBSM with an existing algorithm, called RRS [1], using three performance metrics, namely total revenue (TR), total download (TD) by the vehicles and total number of completed requests (TCR). The comparison is performed by simulating both the algorithms in a virtual environment. The results show that RBSM outperforms RRS in all the performance metrics. The significant contributions of our work are as follows.

- Development of a novel algorithm, RBSM, to maximize the revenue of the RSUs.
- RBSM considers arrival time, velocity, revenue and requested content size of the vehicles for selecting a suitable vehicle, which results in the maximum revenue.

- Extensive simulation is carried out to compare RBSM and RRS by considering various traffic scenarios with twenty-five instances of five datasets.

The organization of this paper is as follows. Section 2 discusses scope of VCC and its related problems, followed by the VCC model and problem statement in Sect. 3. Section 4 presents the proposed algorithm and Sect. 5 discusses performance metrics used to evaluate the algorithms. Simulation results and concluding remarks are presented in Sect. 6 and Sect. 7, respectively.

2   Related Work

VCC has gained a remarkable attraction among IT industries, professionals, researchers in today's technology-driven world due to its broad area of services [2,3,5]. It unfolds a set of problems and challenges along with the services [1,4]. In VCC, V2V, V2I and I2V, communications enable the smart vehicles to sublet their underutilized resources to the CSP through the RSUs [4]. RSUs make revenue by delivering various services, such as displaying advertisements, providing navigation facilities, producing video and game content, and many more [1,13–15]. Here, smart vehicles lease their resources through the RSUs for providing services to needy vehicles and gain enormous revenue. Therefore, many researchers have proposed different models and algorithms to maximize the total revenue by providing better quality services.

Einziger et al. [13] have explored that RSUs can act as brokers to manage and send the advertisements to the vehicles intelligently. Moreover, RSUs can earn revenue from advertisers. Fux et al. [16] have suggested that the owners of the physical resources can sell their content to the vehicles. They have proposed a game model to improve the quality and stabilize the price war among the RSUs owners. In [14], the cooperation and competition between parked vehicles and RSUs are studied, and a game-theoretic approach is proposed to increase individual profit. Wang et al. [17] have proposed a distributed game theoretical framework to improve the performance and efficiency of the network infrastructure.

Some researchers have focused on data and video delivery by the RSUs to earn incentives. Researchers in [1,11] have discussed that the percentage of video content requested by vehicles is approximately 70% and around 90% of the 5G data traffic by 2028. Han et al. [11] have discussed and identified the different types of obstacles and challenges present in the network that degrades the performance of content delivery. Some other models and strategies are proposed by Sun et al. [15] and Xu et al. [18] to improve the process of data delivery. Zhou et al. [19] have proposed an innovative data delivery scheme that detects optimal relay nodes to improve performance and security with the help of k-nearest neighbors-based machine learning system.

Researchers have discussed that existing infrastructure cannot cope with the rapid demand for data and video services in real-time [1,10]. A minor delay of 2 s can cause high degradation in QoS and it can ultimately lead to customer dissatisfaction [11]. Zhao et al. [20] have discussed content prefetching to solve the delay problems associated with the vehicular ad-hoc networks. They have proposed a module that predicts the vehicle mobility to select RSU and suitable time for prefetching the respective content. Yao et al. [21] have proposed a solution, which downloads popular content into vehicles that are going to visit different hot spot regions shortly. They have discussed that vehicles staying at the hot spot region can provide more services to others for a longer time. Al-Hilo et al. [1] have proposed a revenue-driven video delivery model to select a vehicle for delivering content, which gives the highest profit in each time slot.

Most of the above-discussed works do not consider the vehicles' arrival time and velocity to design an incentive model for the RSUs. Our proposed algorithm RBSM is somehow different from others, as it takes advantage of the heterogeneity of the content in terms of arrival time, velocity, revenue and requested content size of the vehicles. RBSM selects suitable vehicles for providing content, such that the revenue of RSUs is maximized.

3   Vehicular Cloud Model and Problem Statement

3.1   Vehicular Cloud Model

We consider a heterogeneous vehicular cloud environment over a geographical area or grid. This area consists of cellular network, multi-way lanes, RSU, traffic junctions, parking lot and vehicles, as shown in Fig. 1. Vehicles spend a significant amount of time in the parking lot of airports, shopping malls and hospitals. These vehicles are equipped with different types of modern resources, which are generally underutilized and idle for a considerable amount of time. VMs can be formed using these underutilized resources of vehicles to expand the CSP capabilities and provide various services. Here, these vehicles are connected to the RSUs and the RSUs are connected to the CSP with high-speed Internet facilities.

Besides the vehicles present at the grid, many vehicles also cross the grid at different times. Vehicles on the move or the grid request various services, such as traffic information, video content, live streaming, gaming services, infotainment services and many more. Previously, these services were delivered to the vehicles from the CSP using the cellular networks. With an increase in the number of vehicles and the size of requests, the cellular network cannot provide real-time services. Here, RSUs play a significant role by co-operating with cellular networks.

Whenever a vehicle enters a grid, it broadcasts a beacon beam containing detailed information, such as arrival time, residing time, velocity, revenue and path, which are received and processed by the RSU. In this scenario, if the RSU gets the information from the CSP regarding the requested content by the respective vehicle, then it can download or pre-fetch the content before the arrival of the vehicle to the grid. After downloading the requested content, RSU may save it locally or by incorporating the vehicles present in the parking lot. Consequently, when the vehicle reaches the communication range of the RSU, it can download the content directly from the RSU. RSU can earn revenue from the

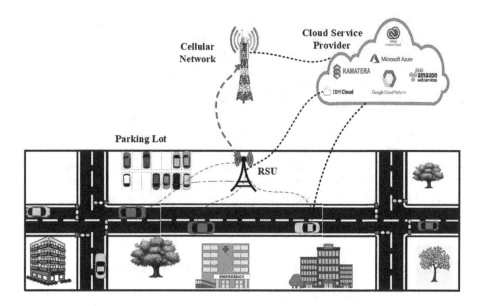

Fig. 1. A vehicular cloud model.

vehicle user through the cellular network for providing services to that vehicle. It encourages the RSU owner for active involvement in delivering services.

Consider another scenario in which some vehicles may get part of the content from the RSU and rest part from the cellular networks, as the RSU communication range is limited. Alternatively, the vehicle on the move can be out of the communication range of the RSU. The requested content of the vehicles is of different size and revenue, so it is essential for the RSU to select an appropriate vehicle to provide service in order to generate maximum revenue. Here, RSU uses information, such as arrival time, velocity and revenue of the vehicles to deliver the services.

3.2   Problem Statement

Consider a geographical area, which is covered with a set of r RSUs, $RSU = \{RSU_1, RSU_2, RSU_3,\ldots, RSU_r\}$, and a set of multi-way lanes. The coverage of RSU_o, $1 \le o \le r$, is X_o. The downlink data rate from RSU to vehicle depends on the distance between them. Therefore, the coverage of each RSU is divided into a set of n data rate zones, $R = \{R_0, R_1, R_2, \ldots, R_n\}$. Each data rate zone R_s, $1 \le s \le n$, has a downlink data rate of d_s, which is calculated as follows [22].

$$d_s = \beta \log_2(1 + SNR_s), 1 \le s \le n \tag{1}$$

where β is the bandwidth of RSU and SNR_s is the signal to noise ratio in data rate zone R_s. Consider a set of m vehicles, $V = \{V_1, V_2, V_3,\ldots, V_m\}$, that crosses the RSU_o, $1 \le o \le r$. Each vehicle, V_k, $1 \le k \le m$, is represented with

5-tuple, i.e., $<VID_k, VAT_k, VS_k, VRDS_k, VRDP_k>$. Here, VID, VAT and VS denote vehicle id, arrival time and velocity, respectively. The revenue per MB and requested content size are denoted by $VRDP$ and $VRDS$.

The problem is to select suitable vehicles for receiving various services, such that the RSUs can generate maximum revenue. This problem is divided into two sub-problems. The first sub-problem finds the position of the vehicles, V_k, $1 \leq k \leq m$, in the data rate zones R_s, $1 \leq s \leq n$. The second sub-problem selects suitable vehicles to get desired services from the RSUs. These sub-problems are subjected to the following constraints.

1. A vehicle V_k, $1 \leq k \leq m$, can only download the content at time t from the data rate zone R_s, $1 \leq s \leq n$, of RSU_o, $1 \leq o \leq r$, (i.e., $F[k, t, s]$), as follows.

$$F[k, t, s] = \begin{cases} 1, & \text{if } R[s, START] \leq X_o \times \frac{t}{VS_k} \leq R[s, END] \\ 0, & \text{otherwise} \end{cases} \qquad (2)$$

where $R[s, START]$ and $R[s, END]$ define the boundary of R_s, $1 \leq s \leq n$, X_o defines the coverage of RSU_o, $1 \leq o \leq r$, and $T_k = \frac{X_o}{VS_k}$.

2. The total download by the vehicle V_k, $1 \leq k \leq m$, from RSU_o is $DD[k, o] = \sum_{t=1}^{T_k} F[k, t, s] \times d_s$. Here, T_k is the time required by vehicle V_k to cover X_o.
3. The total download by the vehicle V_k, $1 \leq k \leq m$, is always less than or equal to the requested content size. Mathematically, $DD[k, o] \leq VRDS_k$.
4. At time t, only one vehicle V_k, $1 \leq k \leq m$ can download its content from the RSU_o, $1 \leq o \leq r$. Mathematically, $\sum_{k=1}^{m} F[k, t, s] = 1$, $1 \leq t \leq max(T_k)$, $1 \leq s \leq n$.

4   Proposed Algorithm

The proposed algorithm RBSM is an online algorithm in a vehicular cloud environment that selects different vehicles to receive content from the RSUs, such that the revenue is maximized. RBSM is divided into two phases, as follows. (1) Finding the data rate zone of a vehicle at a particular time (2) Selection of the vehicle to receive the content. The pseudocode for the proposed algorithm RBSM is shown in Algorithm 1, Procedures 1 and 2, respectively. Table 1 represents the mathematical notations and their definitions used in the pseudocode.

Firstly, RBSM maintains all the upcoming vehicles in a global queue, Q, to provide content (Line 1, Algorithm 1). Then travel time and exit time are calculated for each vehicle (Lines 2–5). Let us explore the same with an example for clear understanding. We consider that three vehicles, V_1, V_2, V_3, have requested content to the RSU and their details are shown in Table 2. We also consider an RSU with seven data rate zones, namely R_1, R_2, R_3, R_4, R_5, R_6, R_7 and their downlink data rate 2 MBPS, 3 MBPS, 4 MBPS, 5 MBPS, 4 MBPS, 3 MBPS, 2 MBPS, respectively. The covering range of the RSU is considered as 100 m.

For vehicle V_1, travel time ($TTIME[1]$) is calculated as $3\,\text{s}$ (i.e., $\frac{100}{33} = 3.03 \approx 3$) and exit time ($VET[1]$) is calculated as $3\,\text{s}$ (i.e., $VAT[1] + TTIME[1] - 1 = 1 + 3 - 1 = 3$). In the similar manner, $TTIME[2]$ and $TTIME[3]$ are calculated as $4\,\text{s}$ and $7\,\text{s}$, respectively, and $VET[2]$ and $VET[3]$ are calculated as $5\,\text{s}$ and $9\,\text{s}$, respectively.

Table 1. Mathematical notations and their definitions

Notation	Definition
Q	Global queue
X	Covering range of RSU
m	Numbers of vehicles
n	Number of data rate zones
V	Set of vehicles
$R[s]$	Data rate zone s (in MBPS)
$VID[k]$	ID of vehicle k
$VAT[k]$	Arrival time of vehicle k (in seconds)
$VS[k]$	Velocity/Speed of vehicle k (in meters/seconds)
$VRDP[k]$	Requested content revenue per MB of vehicle k
$VRDS[k]$	Requested content size of vehicle k
$TTIME[k]$	Travel time of vehicle k (in seconds)
$VET[k]$	Exit time of vehicle k (in seconds)
$VPRZ[k,t]$	Data rate zone of vehicle k at time t
$ASSIGN[t]$	Selected vehicle to provide content at time t
TR	Total revenue of the RSUs
TD	Total download by the vehicles
TCR	Total numbers of completed requests

Next, RBSM calls Procedure 1 to find the data rate zones of each vehicle (Line 6, Algorithm 1). Procedure 1 finds the duration of a vehicle in each data rate zone (Line 4, Procedure 1). Then the vehicles are assigned to the data rate zones according to time slots (Lines 5–7). This process is repeated for all the vehicles in Q (Lines 1–10). Let us explain this procedure with the earlier discussed example. For vehicle V_1, $TTIME[1]$ is $3\,\text{s}$. Therefore, $temp2$ is calculated as 0 (i.e., $round(\frac{3}{7} \times 1) = 0$) for $s = 1$. As a result, there is no assignment in the data rate zone $R[1]$. For $s = 2$, $temp2$ is calculated as 1 (i.e., $round(\frac{3}{7} \times 2) = 1$). Therefore, $VPRZ[1,1]$ is updated to $R[2] = 3\,\text{MBPS}$ at $t = 1\,\text{s}$. In the similar manner, $VPRZ[1,2]$ and $VPRZ[1,3]$ are calculated as $5\,\text{MBPS}$ and $3\,\text{MBPS}$, respectively. The same procedure is repeated for vehicles, V_2 and V_3, and the assignment of data rate zones of three vehicles are shown in Table 3.

Next, RBSM calls Procedure 2 to select suitable vehicles that can download their requested content (Line 7, Algorithm 1). In Procedure 2, all the vehicles, in

---

Algorithm 1. Pseudocode for RBSM

Input: $Q, X, R, n, m, VID, VAT, VS, VRDP, VRDS$
Output: TR, TD, TCR

1: **while** $Q \neq 0$ **do**
2:     **for** $k = 1, 2, 3, \ldots, m$ **do**
3:         $TTIME[k] = round(\frac{X}{VS[k]})$ ▷ *round* is a function to return a rounded number.
4:         $VET[k] = VAT[k] + TTIME[k]$ - 1
5:     **end for**
6:     Call $FIND\text{-}VEHICLE\text{-}DATA\_RATE\_ZONE(R, n, m, VAT, TTIME, VET)$

7:     Call $SELECT\text{-}VEHICLE(n, m, VAT, VRDP, VRDS, VET, VPRZ)$
8: **end while**

Procedure 1. $FIND\text{-}VEHICLE\text{-}DATA\_RATE\_ZONE(R, n, m, VAT, TTIME, VET)$

1: **for** $k = 1, 2, 3, \ldots, m$ **do**
2:     $temp1 = 1$
3:     **for** $s = 1, 2, 3, \ldots, n$ **do**
4:         $temp2 = round(\frac{TTIME[k]}{n} \times s)$
5:         **for** $t = temp1, temp1 + 1, temp1 + 2, \ldots, temp2$ **do**
6:             $VPRZ[k, VAT[k] + t - 1] = R[s]$
7:         **end for**
8:         $temp1 = temp2 + 1$
9:     **end for**
10: **end for**

Table 2. Specification of three vehicles

Vehicle	AT	VS (in m/s)	$VRDP$ (in Rs.)	$VRDS$ (in MB)
V_1	01	33	10	08
V_2	02	25	30	10
V_3	03	15	05	22

the Q, are sorted in the descending order of $VRDP$ (Line 2 of Procedure 2). Then the vehicle with the highest value of $VRDP$ is selected for further processing (Line 4). Now, the procedure assigns the time slots to the vehicle based on the exit time (Lines 5–25). However, before assigning the time slots, it checks whether the RSU is available to provide content or not (Line 7). This process continues until the vehicle downloads the entire content or there are no more available time slots (Lines 7–19). Finally, TR and TD are calculated (Lines 11–12 and Lines 14–16) followed by task completion status and TCR are updated (Line 21 and Line 22).

Procedure 2. $SELECT\text{-}VEHICLE(n, m, VAT, VRDP, VRDS, VET, VPRZ)$

1: $ASSIGN[] = 0, TASK\_COMP[] = 0, TR = 0, TD = 0, TCR = 0$
2: $VEH\_SORT = sortdes(VRDP)$ ▷ $sortdes$ is a function to sort the elements in
   descending order.
3: **for** $k = 1, 2, 3, \ldots, m$ **do**
4:    $veh = VEH\_SORT[k]$
5:    $rdw = VRDS[veh], temp3 = VET[veh]$
6:    **while** $rdw \neq 0$ **and** $temp3 \geq VAT[veh]$ **do**
7:      **if** $ASSIGN[temp3] == 0$ **then**
8:        $temp4 = VPRZ[veh, temp3]$
9:        **if** $rdw < temp4$ **then**
10:            $TR += (rdw \times VRDP[veh])$
11:            $TD += rdw$
12:            $rdw = 0$
13:        **else**
14:            $TR += (temp4 \times VRDP[veh])$
15:            $TD += temp4$
16:            $rdw -= temp4$
17:        **end if**
18:        $ASSIGN[temp4] = veh$
19:      **end if**
20:      **if** $rdw == 0$ **then**
21:            $TASK\_COMP[k] = 1$
22:            $TCR += 1$
23:      **end if**
24:      $temp3 -= 1$
25:    **end while**
26: **end for**

Let us discuss Procedure 2 with the earlier discussed example. Here, vehicles, V_1, V_2 and V_3, are sorted in the descending order of $VRDP$, which results vehicles, V_2, V_1, V_3, respectively. As vehicle V_2 contains highest $VRDP$ (i.e., $VRDP[2] = 30$), it is selected for further processing. The VET of vehicle V_2 is 5 s. As a result, the assignment of time slots starts from 5 s. At $t = 5$ s, the data rate zone of vehicle V_2 is 2 MBPS. Therefore, vehicle V_2 is able to download 2 MB of data from RSU. However, the required download (rdw) of vehicle V_2 is 10 MB. As a result, rdw is updated to 8 MB. Then TR and TD are updated to Rs. 60 and 2 MB, respectively. At $t = 4$ s, the data rate zone of vehicle V_2 is 4 MBPS. In this time slot, vehicle V_2 is able to download 4 MB of data. Therefore, rdw, TR and TD are updated to 4 MB, Rs. 180 and 6 MB, respectively. Similarly, at $t = 3$ s, vehicle V_2 is able to download 4 MB of data. Here, rdw of vehicle V_2 is updated to 0. It indicates that vehicle V_2 has downloaded its desired content from the RSU. In the similar fashion, other vehicles, V_1 and V_3 are processed. Table 4 shows the assignment of vehicles to RSU at different time slots.

We compare the proposed algorithm, RBSM, with an existing algorithm, RRS [1]. RRS tries to maximize the revenue at each time slot. Therefore, it selects a vehicle from the group of vehicles present in the communication range

Table 3. Movement of vehicles in seven data rate zones

Time	2 MBPS	3 MBPS	4 MBPS	5 MBPS	4 MBPS	3 MBPS	2 MBPS
$t = 1$		V_1					
$t = 2$	V_2			V_1			
$t = 3$	V_3		V_2			V_1	
$t = 4$		V_3			V_2		
$t = 5$			V_3				V_2
$t = 6$				V_3			
$t = 7$					V_3		
$t = 8$						V_3	
$t = 9$							V_3

Table 4. Assignment of vehicles to RSU using RBSM

Time	$t=1$	$t=2$	$t=3$	$t=4$	$t=5$	$t=6$	$t=7$	$t=8$	$t=9$
Selected Vehicle	V_1	V_1	V_2	V_2	V_2	V_3	V_3	V_3	V_3

Table 5. Assignment of vehicles to RSU using RRS

Time	$t=1$	$t=2$	$t=3$	$t=4$	$t=5$	$t=6$	$t=7$	$t=8$	$t=9$
Selected Vehicle	V_1	V_2	V_2	V_2	V_3	V_3	V_3	V_3	V_3

of RSU and provides content that gives maximum revenue at each time slot. The assignment of vehicles to RSU by RRS is shown in Table 5. We compare RBSM and RRS in terms of three performance metrics, namely TR, TD and TCR, respectively, as shown in Table 6. The comparison results clearly show that RBSM performs better than RRS in terms of all the performance metrics.

Table 6. Comparison of RBSM and RRS algorithms

	TR (in Rs.)	TD (in MB)	TCR (in Nos.)
RBSM	450	32	2
RRS	420	31	1

Lemma 1. *If two vehicles are entering a grid at different times with the same speed and their travel times in the grid overlapping, then each vehicle can get a chance to download its content irrespective of $VRDP$ and $VRDS$.*

Proof. Let us assume that two vehicles, $V_{k'}$ and $V_{k''}$, are moving at the same speed and their arrival times, $VAT_{k'}$ and $VAT_{k''}$, respectively, in the grid. We know that $VAT_{k'} \neq VAT_{k''}$. There are two cases. Case 1: If $VAT_{k''} > VAT_{k'}$, then $VRDP[k'']$ is compared with $VRDP[k']$. If $VRDP[k''] > VRDP[k']$ (or $VRDP[k''] < VRDP[k']$), then vehicle $V_{k''}$ (or $V_{k'}$) is selected first and the assignment of time slots start from $VET[k'']$ (or $VET[k']$). If $VRDS[k'']$

(or $VRDS[k']$) is huge in size by considering the worst case, then vehicle $V_{k''}$ (or $V_{k'}$) is assigned with all the time slots during its existence in the grid. In this scenario, vehicle $V_{k'}$ (or $V_{k''}$) can only download its content from $VAT_{k'}$ ($VET_{k'}$) to $VAT_{k''}$ ($VET_{k''}$). Case 2: If $VAT_{k''} < VAT_{k'}$, then $VRDP[k'']$ is compared with $VRDP[k']$. If $VRDP[k''] > VRDP[k']$ (or $VRDP[k''] < VRDP[k']$), then vehicle $V_{k''}$ (or $V_{k'}$) is selected first and the assignment of time slots start from $VET[k'']$ (or $VET[k']$). If $VRDS[k'']$ (or $VRDS[k']$) is huge in size by considering the worst case, then vehicle $V_{k''}$ (or $V_{k'}$) is assigned with all the time slots during its existence in the grid. In this scenario, vehicle $V_{k'}$ (or $V_{k''}$) can only download its content from $VET_{k''}$ ($VAT_{k''}$) to $VET_{k'}$ ($VAT_{k'}$). Therefore, each vehicle can get a chance to download its content irrespective of $VRDP$ and $VRDS$.

Lemma 2. *If two vehicles are entering a grid at the same time and speed, then the vehicle requested content with the least cost can get a chance to download its content at a higher data rate.*

Proof. Let us assume that vehicle $V_{k'}$ is requested content with a higher revenue than vehicle $V_{k''}$, i.e., $VRDP[k'] > VRDP[k'']$. Then vehicle $V_{k'}$ is selected first and assigned time slots between $VET[k']$ to $(VET[k'] - \gamma)$ (say). The downlink data rate is increasing from $VET[k']$ to $VET[k'] - \gamma$. If $VRDS[k']$ is smaller in size, then vehicle $V_{k'}$ downloads its content prior to $VET[k'] - \gamma$ (say, ζ). Therefore, vehicle $V_{k''}$ can download its content from ζ. As the data rate at ζ is higher than the data rate at $VET[k'']$, the vehicle $V_{k''}$ downloads its content at a higher data rate.

Lemma 3. *If two vehicles are entering a grid at the same time with different speeds, then the vehicle requested content with the least cost can get a chance to download its content.*

Proof. Let us assume that vehicle $V_{k'}$ is requested content with a higher revenue than vehicle $V_{k''}$, i.e., $VRDP[k'] > VRDP[k'']$ and $VS[k'] > VS[k'']$. Then vehicle $V_{k'}$ is selected first and assigned time slots from $VET[k']$. As $VS[k'] > VS[k'']$, $VET[k''] > VET[k']$. As a result, vehicle $V_{k'}$ is out of the grid (the range of RSU) after time slot $VET[k']$. Therefore, vehicle $V_{k''}$ downloads its content from $VET[k']$ to $VET[k'']$.

5   Performance Metrics

In this section, we discuss three performance metrics to compare the proposed algorithm with the existing algorithm.

5.1 Total Revenue

The total revenue (TR) is defined as the total amount of revenue paid by the vehicles to the RSUs for downloading their respective contents. Mathematically, it can be written as follows.

$$TR = \sum_{t=1}^{max(VET)} VPRZ[ASSIGN[t], t] \times VRDP[ASSIGN[t]] \quad (3)$$

5.2 Total Download

The total download (TD) is defined as the total amount of content downloaded by all the vehicles from the RSUs. Mathematically, it can be defined as follows.

$$TD = \sum_{t=1}^{max(VET)} VPRZ[ASSIGN[t], t] \quad (4)$$

5.3 Total Number of Completed Requests

The total number of completed requests (TCR) is defined as the number of requested content by the vehicles, which are downloaded completely from the RSUs. Mathematically, it is stated as follows.

$$TCR = \sum_{k=1}^{m} COM[k] \quad (5)$$

where $COM[k] = \begin{cases} 1 & \text{if } VRDS[k] == \sum_{t=VAT[k]}^{VET[k]} VPRZ[k,t] \text{ and } ASSIGN[t] == k \\ 0 & \text{Otherwise} \end{cases}$

6 Simulation Results

We simulated the proposed algorithm, RBSM, and the existing algorithm, RRS, in a virtual environment created on a system with Intel(R) Core(TM) i5-4210U CPU @ 1.70 GHz 1.70 GHz, 8.00 GB of primary memory and Windows 10 64-bit operating system and installed with MATLAB R2017a. It is important to note that the simulation, evaluation and performance comparison of RBSM and RRS are independent of the virtual environment. The performance of RBSM and RRS are compared using the performance metrics discussed in Sect. 5.

To perform the extensive simulation of RBSM and RRS, we used five different datasets. The traffic density is different in each dataset and represented as $\frac{XX \text{ vehicles}}{1000 \, textm}$. Here, XX represents 10, 20, 30, 40 and 50. Each dataset contains five distinct instances, namely i1 to i5. We considered that vehicles' arrival followed the Poisson distribution. We used the truncated normal distribution to calculate the vehicles' velocity. For the datasets' generation, we followed the Monte Carlo simulation process, as used in [23–25]. Here, we assume that only one vehicle can download its content from the RSU at a particular time. Table 7 shows the values of the parameters used for the simulation of RBSM and RRS.

The proposed algorithm, RBSM and the existing algorithm RRS are simulated, and their results are shown in Table 8. For better comparison, we generated the bar chart diagrams by taking the average of five results of each dataset, as shown in Figs. 2, 3, and 4, respectively. From the comparison, it is clear that RBSM performs better than RRS. It is wise to mention that RBSM performs 87%, 90% and 170% better than RRS in terms of TR, TD, and TCR, respectively. The reason behind the better performance of RBSM is that we consider the vehicle's arrival time and velocity in the selection process to deliver content from RSUs.

Table 7. Parameters and their values

Parameters	Values
X	1000 m
Number of data rate zones	7
Traffic density	(10, 20, 30, 40 or 50) vehicles/1000 m
VAT	10–50 s
VS	10–40 m/s
$VRDP$	Rs. 10–100
$VRDS$	20–100 MB

Table 8. Simulation results of RBSM and RRS algorithms

Density (vehicles/meters)	Instance	RBSM			RRS		
		TR	TD	TCR	TR	TD	TCR
10	$i1$	14620	276	04	07179	102	00
	$i2$	17965	419	06	16154	331	06
	$i3$	18533	387	05	13567	273	03
	$i4$	17986	365	04	14516	294	04
	$i5$	19006	367	05	07752	131	02
20	$i1$	19101	394	11	09451	165	01
	$i2$	17266	335	11	06586	105	01
	$i3$	17730	351	09	07689	130	01
	$i4$	16535	282	07	09418	183	05
	$i5$	15717	332	10	09128	178	02
30	$i1$	17948	310	18	07580	132	05
	$i2$	17607	331	22	07394	110	05
	$i3$	16954	320	18	06152	091	01
	$i4$	16702	354	24	12188	261	12
	$i5$	16064	337	18	08587	150	06

(*continued*)

Table 8. (*continued*)

Density (vehicles/meters)	Instance	RBSM			RRS		
		TR	TD	TCR	TR	TD	TCR
40	$i1$	15482	173	21	05097	068	05
	$i2$	16547	199	19	10645	147	06
	$i3$	13445	167	20	06297	081	04
	$i4$	14948	181	20	08930	118	10
	$i5$	14388	169	23	06510	085	04
50	$i1$	11597	148	27	05293	071	07
	$i2$	12643	161	29	05131	080	12
	$i3$	11294	140	29	10251	138	26
	$i4$	11885	156	27	05157	086	10
	$i5$	12592	158	28	05041	070	09

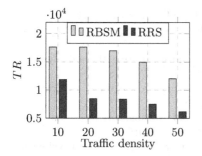

Fig. 2. Pictorial comparison of TR for RBSM and RRS algorithms.

Fig. 3. Pictorial comparison of TD for RBSM and RRS algorithms.

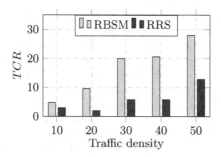

Fig. 4. Pictorial comparison of TCR for RBSM and RRS algorithms.

7 Conclusion

In this paper, we have proposed the RBSM algorithm for the vehicular cloud environment, which maximizes the total revenue of the RSUs by providing content to the vehicles. RBSM consists of two phases, namely finding data rate zones of the vehicles and selecting a suitable vehicle at each time slot. The comparison of RBSM and RRS algorithms has been performed by conducting simulation on different datasets with different traffic density. It has been observed that RBSM performs better than RRS and generates 87% more revenue than RRS. Moreover, in RBSM, vehicles download 90% more content and 170% more completed requests than RRS. However, we have considered that only one vehicle can download content at a particular time. In our future work, we will try to improve the algorithm, such that more numbers of vehicles can get content simultaneously.

References

1. Al-Hilo, A., Ebrahimi, D., Sharafeddine, S., Assi, C.: Revenue-driven video delivery in vehicular networks with optimal resource scheduling. Veh. Commun. **23**, 100215 (2020)
2. Ashok, A., Steenkiste, P., Bai, F.: Vehicular cloud computing through dynamic computation offloading. Comput. Commun. **120**, 125–137 (2018)
3. Boukerche, A., Robson, E.: Vehicular cloud computing: architectures, applications, and mobility. Comput. Netw. **135**, 171–189 (2018)
4. Refaat, T.K., Kantarci, B., Mouftah, H.T.: Virtual machine migration and management for vehicular clouds. Veh. Commun. **4**, 47–56 (2016)
5. Whaiduzzaman, Md, Sookhak, M., Gani, A., Buyya, R.: A survey on vehicular cloud computing. J. Netw. Comput. Appl. **40**, 325–344 (2014)
6. Ridhawi, I.A., Aloqaily, M., Kantarci, B., Jararweh, Y., Mouftah, H.T.: A continuous diversified vehicular cloud service availability framework for smart cities. Comput. Netw. **145**, 207–218 (2018)
7. Hagenauer, F., Higuchi, T., Altintas, O., Dressler, F.: Efficient data handling in vehicular micro clouds. Ad Hoc Netw. **91**, 101871 (2019)
8. Midya, S., Roy, A., Majumder, K., Phadikar, S.: Multi-objective optimization technique for resource allocation and task scheduling in vehicular cloud architecture: a hybrid adaptive nature inspired approach. J. Netw. Comput. Appl **103**, 58–84 (2018)
9. Al-Rashed, E., Al-Rousan, M., Al-Ibrahim, N.: Performance evaluation of widespread assignment schemes in a vehicular cloud. Veh. Commun. **9**, 144–153 (2017)
10. Guo, H., Rui, L., Gao, Z.: A zone-based content pre-caching strategy in vehicular edge networks. Future Gener. Comput. Syst. **106**, 22–33 (2020)
11. Han, T., Ansari, N., Mingquan, W., Heather, Y.: On accelerating content delivery in mobile networks. IEEE Commun. Surv. Tutor. **15**(3), 1314–1333 (2012)
12. Teixeira, F.A., Silva, V.F., Leoni, J.L., Macedo, D.F., Nogueira, J.M.S.: Vehicular networks using the IEEE 802.11 p standard: an experimental analysis. Veh. Commun. **1**(2), 91–96 (2014)
13. Einziger, G., Chiasserini, C.F., Malandrino, F.: Scheduling advertisement delivery in vehicular networks. IEEE Trans. Mob. Comput. **17**(12), 2882–2897 (2018)

14. Zhou, S., Qichao, X., Hui, Y., Wen, M., Guo, S.: A game theoretic approach to parked vehicle assisted content delivery in vehicular Ad Hoc networks. IEEE Trans. Veh. Technol. **66**(7), 6461–6474 (2016)
15. Sun, Y., Le, X., Tang, Y., Zhuang, W.: Traffic offloading for online video service in vehicular networks: a cooperative approach. IEEE Trans. Veh. Technol. **67**(8), 7630–7642 (2018)
16. Fux, V., Maillé, P., Cesana, M.: Price competition between road side units operators in vehicular networks. In: 2014 IFIP Networking Conference, pp. 1–9. IEEE (2014)
17. Wang, B., Han, Z., Liu, K.R.: Distributed relay selection and power control for multiuser cooperative communication networks using Stackelberg game. IEEE Trans. Mob. Comput. **8**(7), 975–990 (2008)
18. Xu, C., Quan, W., Vasilakos, A.V., Zhang, H., Muntean, G.M.: Information-centric cost-efficient optimization for multimedia content delivery in mobile vehicular networks. Comput. Commun. **99**, 93–106 (2017)
19. Zhou, Y., Li, H., Shi, C., Ning, L., Cheng, N.: A fuzzy-rule based data delivery scheme in VANETs with intelligent speed prediction and relay selection. Wirel. Commun. Mob. Comput. **2018** (2018)
20. Zhao, Z., Guardalben, L., Karimzadeh, M., Silva, J., Braun, T., Sargento, S.: Mobility prediction-assisted over-the-top edge prefetching for hierarchical VANETs. IEEE J. Sel. Areas Commun. **36**(8), 1786–1801 (2018)
21. Yao, L., Chen, A., Deng, J., Wang, J., Guowei, W.: A cooperative caching scheme based on mobility prediction in vehicular content centric networks. IEEE Trans. Veh. Technol. **67**(6), 5435–5444 (2017)
22. Shannon: Shannon channel capacity. Accessed 2 Aug 2020
23. Pande, S.K., Panda, S.K., Das, S.: Dynamic service migration and resource management for vehicular clouds. J. Ambient Intell. Humanized Comput., 1–21 (2020). https://doi.org/10.1007/s12652-020-02166-w
24. Pande, S.K., et al.: A smart cloud service management algorithm for vehicular clouds. IEEE Trans. Intell. Transp. Syst., 1–12 (2020)
25. Panda, S.K., Jana, P.K.: An efficient request-based virtual machine placement algorithm for cloud computing. In: Krishnan, P., Radha Krishna, P., Parida, L. (eds.) ICDCIT 2017. LNCS, vol. 10109, pp. 129–143. Springer, Cham (2017). https://doi.org/10.1007/978-3-319-50472-8_11

Interference Reduction in Directional Wireless Networks

Manjanna Basappa[1]($\boxtimes$) and Sudeepta Mishra[2]

[1] Department of Computer Science and Information Systems, Birla Institute of
Technology and Science Pilani, Hyderabad Campus, Shameerpet 500078, India
manjanna@hyderabad.bits-pilani.ac.in
[2] Department of Computer Science and Engineering, Indian Institute of Technology
Ropar, Nangal Road, Rupnagar 140001, India
sudeepta@iitrpr.ac.in

Abstract. In a wireless network using directional transmitters, a typical
problem is to schedule a set of directional links to cover all the receivers
in a region, such that an adequate data rate and coverage are maintained while minimizing interference. We can model the coverage area of
a directional transmitter as an unit triangle and the receiver as a point
in the plane. Motivated by this, we first consider a *minimum ply covering
(MPC)* problem. We propose a 2-approximation algorithm for the *MPC*
problem in $O((opt+n)m^{14opt+1}(\log opt))$ time, where m is the number of
transmitters and n is the number of receivers given in the plane, and opt
is the maximum number of triangles, in the optimal solution, covering
a point in the plane. We also show that the *MPC* problem is NP-hard,
and is not $(2 - \epsilon)$-approximable for any $\epsilon > 0$ unless P = NP. We also
study channel allocation in directional wireless networks by posing it
as a colorable covering problem, namely, *3-colorable unit triangle cover
(3CUTC)*. We propose a simple 4-approximation algorithm in $O(m^{30}n^2)$
time, for this problem.

Keywords: Unit triangles · Approximation algorithm · Minimum ply
cover · Interference

1 Introduction

Directional communication technologies are considered to enhance or mitigate
problems experienced in omni-directional technologies. Directional communication links such as mmWave, free-space optics, and visible light communication
are being exploited in various wireless networks such as vehicular ad-hoc networks and cellular networks. The capacity, coverage, and interference characteristics of these networks are very different than that of existing omni-directional
wireless networks. This is because the slightest change in the beam orientation of the transmitter and/or the receiver results in a drastic change in the
coverage and interference characteristics of these networks. Typically, a directional transmitter has high gain toward one direction, which helps reduce energy

D. Goswami and T. A. Hoang (Eds.): ICDCIT 2021, LNCS 12582, pp. 114–126, 2021.
https://doi.org/10.1007/978-3-030-65621-8_7

consumption when the receiver actively receives or transmits packets. In addition, this will also reduce undesired interference when compared to using an omni-directional transmitter because the transmitted signal is directed toward its intended recipient. Furthermore, unlike omni-directional transmitters, the directional transmitter has a narrow coverage area directed toward its recipient. Due to this, a frequency channel the receiver uses will be available in the areas of the network not covered by the directional transmitter. In this paper, we model the narrow coverage areas of directional transmitters as unit triangles (all sides are of unit length) and receivers as points in the 2-dimensional plane. We then consider a combinatorial optimization problem, namely, *minimum ply coverage (MPC)* problem, as follows. Given a set P of n points and a set T of m y-parallel unit triangles in the plane, our objective is to choose a set $T^* \subseteq T$ such that $P \subset \cup_{t \in T^*} t$ and every point in the plane (not only points of P) is covered by a minimum number of triangles in T^*, where by y-parallel unit triangles we mean one of the three sides of every triangle $t \in T$ is parallel to y-axis.

Motivated by further reduction of interference and usage of minimum number of channels in directional wireless networks, we define a variant of the *MPC* problem, namely, *3-colorable unit triangle cover (3CUTC)* problem as follows. Given a set P of n points and a set T of m unit triangles, we wish to select a set $T^* \subseteq T$ of triangles, whose union covers all points in P such that $T^* = T_1 \cup T_2 \cup T_3$ and triangles within each T_a are pairwise disjoint for $a \in \{1,2,3\}$, i.e., the triangles in T^* are 3-colorable while achieving coverage of all points in P. Achieving 3-colorable covering of receivers by transmitters is motivated by the fact that usage of three channels is a common practise in frequency channel assignment in wireless networks [2].

2   Related Work

In cellular communication systems, interference has been recognized as a major bottleneck in achieving good quality of service. Motivated by this important challenge of minimizing interference in cellular networks, Kuhn et al. [8] formulated a combinatorial optimization problem, namely, the *minimum membership set cover (MMSC)* problem. In the *MMSC* problem, we are given a set X of n elements, and a family F of subsets of X, the objective is to compute a set $F' \subseteq F$ such that $X \subseteq \cup_{f \in F'} f$ and the maximum membership of an element $x \in X$ with respect to F', i.e., the number of sets in F' that contains x, is minimized. Kuhn et al. [8] proved that the *MMSC* problem is NP-complete, and can not be approximated better than $\ln n$ factor unless NP$\subset TIME(n^{O(\log \log n)})$. They also proposed an $O(\ln n)$-approximation algorithm for the MMSC problem. A geometric version of the *MMSC* problem is called the *geometric minimum membership set cover (GMMSC)* problem. In the *GMMSC* problem, we have a set of points P and geometric objects Q in the plane, we wish to choose a set $Q^* \subseteq Q$ such that (i) every point in P is covered by at least one object in Q^*, and (ii) a maximum number of objects of Q^* covering a point in P is minimized. Erlebach and van Leeuwen [7] proved that the *GMMSC* problem is NP-hard and can not be approximated with a factor smaller than 2 unless P = NP, when the geometric objects are unit disks and unit squares. For the unit squares, they presented a 5-approximation algorithm in polynomial time if the cost of an optimal solution is constant. At times when minimizing interference in cellular networks, it is required to compute a cover of P with the goal of not only minimizing the membership of every point of P, but also of every point in the plane containing P. Biedl et al. [1] coined this as the *minimum ply covering of points*, and studied two variants of the problem, namely, the *minimum ply covering of points by unit disks (MPCUD)* and *by unit squares (MPCUS)*. They proved that both the *MPCUD* and *MPCUS* problems are NP-hard and can not be approximated better than the factor 2, and presented 2-approximation algorithms for both of them if the cost of an optimal solution is constant. They also solved the problem in dimension one optimally in polynomial time, in which case unit disks or unit squares are just intervals on the real line. Directional transmitter such as mmWave transmitter mounted on a Unmanned aerial vehicle(UAV) is used for achieving coverage in UAV-enabled cellular network [9]. In [9], the authors have studied optimal resource allocation problem by formulating the problem as a mixed-integer non-convex programming problem. There are other works in the literature which consider the problem of increasing the lifetime of omni-directional networks by reducing interference (for example, [3–5]).

3 Minimum Ply Covering Problem

In this section we present an approximation algorithm for the *minimum ply covering of points by y-parallel unit triangles (MPC)* problem.

3.1 Preliminaries

Let a and b be two points on a straight line ℓ (see Fig. 1). We use $[a, b]$ to denote the closed interval on ℓ, when ℓ is considered to be a real line. If ℓ is an integer line, i.e., when we are interested in only the integer points on ℓ, then $[a, b]$ includes only the points that represent integers within the interval on ℓ. In the geometric context, we use $[a, b]$ to denote either a vertical slab or a horizontal slab when a and b represent a pair of parallel lines. We refer to the y-axis aligned side of a triangle t as the y-side of t, i.e., a side of t that is parallel to y-axis. Assume that the x-coordinates of y-side and the vertex opposite to y-side of all triangles $t \in T$ and all points $p \in P$ are distinct. Similarly, assume that the y-coordinates of the vertex opposite to y-side of all triangles $t \in T$ and all points

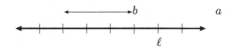

Fig. 1. Illustrating closed interval on integer/real line

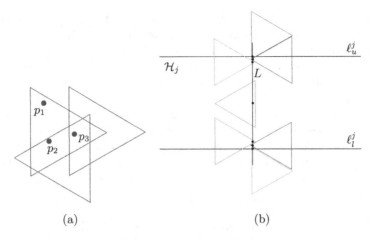

Fig. 2. (a) The plies of p_1, p_2 and p_3 are 1, 2 and 3 respectively, (b) Illustrating the proof of Lemma 1

$p \in P$ are distinct. Let $mid(y\text{-side}(t))$ be the midpoint of y-side of a triangle t. Let $x(p)$ (resp. $y(p)$) be the x-coordinate (resp. y-coordinate) of any point p in the plane. Given any two arbitrary points p_1 and p_2 in the plane, let $dist(p_1, p_2)$ denote the Euclidean distance between p_1 and p_2. Given an arbitrary straight line ℓ, the minimum distance between an arbitrary point p and ℓ, denoted by $dist(p, \ell)$, is the distance from p to its closest point on ℓ.

3.2   Problem Description

Given a set T of m triangles in the plane, the ply of any point p in the plane with respect to the set T is defined to be the maximum number k of triangles in T such that the point p lies in the common intersection region between these k triangles, where k is an integer $0 \le k \le m$ (see Fig. 2(a)). Thus, we say that any set $T' \subseteq T$ has ply equal to the maximum number of triangles in T' that have nonempty common intersection region.

Formally, the *MPC* problem is defined as follows:

MPC: Given a set P of n points and a set T of m y-parallel unit triangles in the plane, our objective is to compute a set $T^* \subseteq T$ such that T^* covers all points of P and has minimum ply.

3.3   Algorithm

In order to solve *MPC*, we have taken ideas from [1] to develop an approximation algorithm which finds a cover $T' \subseteq T$ of points in P such that T' has minimum ply. We describe the algorithm as follows. Firstly, we partition the plane into horizontal strips of two units height. Assume that no point of P lies on the boundary of any strip. Let us label these horizontal strips as $\mathcal{H}_1$, $\mathcal{H}_2$, ..., $\mathcal{H}_r$, from bottom to top, where $\mathcal{H}_r$ is the topmost strip containing at least one point from P. Let P_j be the set containing all points of P lying within the strip $\mathcal{H}_j$, and T_j be the set of triangles from T intersecting with $\mathcal{H}_j$, for every $j = 1, 2, \ldots, r$. Let α be an upper bound on the minimum ply of a cover of the given instance of the MPC problem. As a standard practice in most of the geometric covering problems, in order to solve the MPC problem we first solve the MPC problem restricted to strip $\mathcal{H}_j$ separately for $j = 1, 2, \ldots, r$. Now observe that if for some $\mathcal{H}_j$, there is no subset $T'_j \subset T_j$ that covers all points P_j and has minimum ply at most α, then the original point set P can not have any covering with minimum ply at most α. Hence, we have a cover $T'_j \subset T_j$ with ply at most α, that covers all points P_j lying within the strip $\mathcal{H}_j$, for every $j = 1, 2, \ldots, r$. Then $T' = \bigcup\limits_{j=1}^{r} T'_j$ will cover all points P and have ply at most 2α since a triangle in T can participate in covering of points in two consecutive strips. We approximate the minimum value of α by using doubling technique and bisection method on the integer line $\mathbb{Z}^+$.

Now we describe an algorithm for computing a cover T'_j with ply at most α for the points lying in the strip $\mathcal{H}_j$. Given an integer α, points P_j, triangles T_j, and that there is a cover of points P_j with ply at most α, we do the following to compute T'_j. Let $\ell_1, \ell_2, \ldots, \ell_{k-1}$ be the vertical lines, passing through y-sides and vertices opposite to y-sides of triangles in T_j, in the increasing order of their x-coordinates. We can view these vertical lines as forming vertical strips $[\ell_i, \ell_{i+1}]$ for $i = 0, 1, \ldots, k-1$, where ℓ_0 and ℓ_k are two dummy vertical lines to be explained later. Since $|T_j| \leq m$, $k \leq 2m$.

Lemma 1. *If we have a solution T'_j covering all points P_j and having ply at most α, then there are at most 7α unit triangles of T'_j intersecting with any vertical strip $[\ell_i, \ell_{i+1}]$ for $i = 0, 1, \ldots, k-1$.*

Proof. For the sake of contradiction assume that there are more than 7α y-parallel unit triangles intersecting with some vertical slab $[\ell_i, \ell_{i+1}]$. Consider an arbitrarily placed vertical line L, but passing through this vertical slab $[\ell_i, \ell_{i+1}]$. Let the seven points $p_1, p_2, \ldots, p_7$ be marked on $L \cap \mathcal{H}_j$ such that p_4 is at a point equidistant from both upper and lower boundary lines ℓ^j_u and ℓ^j_l defining the strip $\mathcal{H}_j$ i.e., $dist(p_4, \ell^j_u) = dist(p_4, \ell^j_l)$, the points $p_1, p_2,$ and p_3 are placed closed to the upper boundary line ℓ^j_u of $\mathcal{H}_j$ separated by very small distance from one another, and similarly, the points $p_5, p_6,$ and p_7 are placed closed to the lower boundary line ℓ^j_l of $\mathcal{H}_j$ separated by very small distance from one another (see Fig. 2(b)). Let us suppose that there are seven disjoint y-parallel unit triangles covering $p_1, p_2, \ldots, p_7$ respectively. Observe that no more y-parallel unit triangle disjoint from the above seven triangles can be placed covering a new point p_8 on $L \cap \mathcal{H}_j$ (in fact, lying anywhere on $[\ell_i, \ell_{i+1}] \cap \mathcal{H}_j$). Now we can replace the above seven triangles with seven groups of almost coinciding α triangles respectively by still maintaining the above pairwise disjointness property between these groups, and covering their respective seven points. Hence, if there are more than 7α y-parallel unit triangles intersecting with the vertical slab $[\ell_i, \ell_{i+1}]$, then one of the seven points p_1, p_2, ..., p_7, is covered by more than α triangles. Therefore, the ply of T'_j is more than α, a contradiction.

Based on Lemma 1 we define a *pair* $([\ell_i, \ell_{i+1}], R)$ for $i \in \{1, 2, \ldots, k-1\}$ as follows: for every vertical strip $[\ell_i, \ell_{i+1}]$ a subset $R \subseteq T_j$ is any set consisting of at most 7α unit triangles intersecting with $[\ell_i, \ell_{i+1}]$ such that $\bigcup_{t \in R} t$ covers all points in $[\ell_i, \ell_{i+1}] \cap P_j$ and the ply of R is at most α. Now given any pair $([\ell_i, \ell_{i+1}], R)$, a *pair* $([\ell_{i+1}, \ell_{i+2}], R')$ is said to be a *successor* of the $([\ell_i, \ell_{i+1}], R)$ if and only if $|R'| \leq 7\alpha$, $\bigcup_{t \in R'} t$ covers all points in $[\ell_{i+1}, \ell_{i+2}] \cap P_j$, the ply of R' is at most α, and $|R \triangle R'| \leq 1$, where $\triangle$ denotes symmetric difference of two sets.

Observe that R and R' differ by at most one triangle, y-side or vertex opposite to y-side of which lies on the line ℓ_{i+1}. Let us introduce two dummy triangles T_{dummy_l} and T_{dummy_r} to cover two dummy points in $\mathcal{H}_j$, placed lying to the left and right of all triangles of T_j respectively. Let ℓ_0 and ℓ_k be the vertical lines through the y-side or vertex opposite to y-side of T_{dummy_l} and the y-side or vertex opposite to y-side of T_{dummy_r} respectively. Based on the above definitions we construct a directed acyclic graph $G = (V, E)$ as follows: for $i = 1, 2, \ldots, k-1$, consider all possible *pairs* $([\ell_i, \ell_{i+1}], R)$ and define a vertex $v(R)$ corresponding to each such *pair*. Let the set V_i contain vertices corresponding to all possible pairs $([\ell_i, \ell_{i+1}], R)$ for the vertical strip $[\ell_i, \ell_{i+1}]$. Let $V = \bigcup_{i=1}^{k} V_i$. We add an edge $e = (v, v')$ to the set E, where e is a directed edge from a vertex $v(R) \in V_i$ to a vertex $v'(R') \in V_{i+1}$ if and only if the *pair* $([\ell_{i+1}, \ell_{i+2}], R')$ is a *successor* of the *pair* $([\ell_i, \ell_{i+1}], R)$. Finally, we add the edges from the dummy vertex $v(\{T_{dummy_l}\})$ to all vertices in V_1 and edges from all vertices in V_{k-1} to the dummy vertex $v(\{T_{dummy_r}\})$, to the set E. We argue below that any path from $v(\{T_{dummy_r}\})$ to $v(\{T_{dummy_r}\})$ in G corresponds to a cover of P_j with ply at most α.

Lemma 2. *Given an instance (T_j, P_j) of the MPC problem on the strip H_j, then there is a cover $T'_j \subseteq T_j$ of all points in P_j, with ply at most α, if and only if there is a path ρ, corresponding to T'_j, from vertex $v(\{T_{dummy_l}\})$ to $v(\{T_{dummy_r}\})$ in G.*

Proof. First consider a solution $T^*_j \subseteq T_j$ with ply at most α, by Lemma 1 there can be at most 7α triangles in T^*_j covering points in each vertical slab $[\ell_i, \ell_{i+1}]$, $i = 1, 2, \ldots, k-1$. Because the boundaries of vertical slabs $[\ell_i, \ell_{i+1}]$ are formed by y-sides or vertex opposite to y-sides of triangles, we can associate a vertex with each such group of at most 7α triangles, and an edge between two such groups of at most 7α triangles provided they differ in at most one triangle. These vertices form a path ρ corresponding to T^*_j, of length at most $2m + 1$. Next, if we have a path ρ from $v(\{T_{dummy_l}\})$ to $v(\{T_{dummy_r}\})$ in G, then because of the way in which the graph G is constructed, the union of all collections of at most 7α triangles, corresponding to all vertices in ρ, will cover all points in P_j and have ply at most α. Thus the lemma follows. □

Lemma 3. *The algorithm for the MPC problem on the strip H_j runs in $O((\alpha + |P_j|)|T_j|^{7\alpha+1})$ time.*

Proof. Recall that there is a set of at most 7α triangles corresponding to each vertex in G, and there are at most three directed edges from each vertex to its *successor* vertices in G. The time required to verify that triangles corresponding to each vertex cover all the points in the corresponding vertical slab and identifying its *successors* is $O((\alpha + |P_j|)|T_j|)$. Hence, the construction of G takes $O((\alpha + |P_j|)|T_j|^{7\alpha+1})$ time. We can run a DFS algorithm starting from $v(\{T_{dummy_l}\})$ to find a path ρ in $O(|T_j|^{7\alpha})$ time. Therefore, the overall running time of the algorithm is dominated by the time needed for the construction of G. ∎

In order to compute a cover of all the points P, we repeat the algorithm of Lemma 3 for all strips $\mathcal{H}_j$, $j = 1, 2, \ldots, r$. Then set $T' = \bigcup_{j=1}^{r} T'_j$. Since a triangle can participate in the covering of points in two consecutive strips and the ply of each T'_j is at most α, the ply of T' is at most 2α.

To find the minimum value of α, we solve the *MPC* problem repeatedly for $\alpha = 2^i$, $i = 0, 1, 2, \ldots$, until the above algorithm succeeds in finding T'_j for every strip $\mathcal{H}_j$, $j = 1, 2, \ldots, r$, where T'_j is a cover of points P_j and has ply at most α. Let that value of α be 2^τ. Then we know that the algorithm has failed to compute T'_j for some strip $\mathcal{H}_j$ when $\alpha = 2^{\tau-1}$. Hence the minimum ply *opt* lies in the interval $[2^{\tau-1}, 2^\tau]$ for the given point set P and unit triangle set T. We can now do a standard binary search in the interval $[2^{\tau-1}, 2^\tau]$, which would need only τ bisection steps, where $\tau \leq \log opt + 1$ Finally, the ply of the cover T' returned by the last invocation of the algorithm for the *MPC* problem is at most *opt*. Hence, we have the following theorem.

Theorem 1. *We have a 2-approximation algorithm for the MPC problem in $O((opt + n)m^{14opt+1}(\log opt))$, where opt is the maximum number of triangles of T, in the optimal solution, covering a point in the plane.*

Proof. Given an upper bound α on the minimum ply, the algorithm of Lemma 3 computes a cover T'_j of points P_j, with ply at most α, in the strip H_j. Since a triangle can participate in the covering of points in only two consecutive strips $\mathcal{H}_j$ and $\mathcal{H}_{j+1}$ ($j = 1, 2, \ldots, r - 1$) and the ply of each T'_j is at most α, the ply of $T' = \bigcup_{i=1}^{r} T'_j$ is at most 2α. In solving the *MPC* problem on each strip $\mathcal{H}_j$ for $j = 1, 2, \ldots, r$, the algorithm of Lemma 3 is invoked at most $\log 2opt$ times and at most $\log opt + 1$ times due to doubling technique and standard binary search respectively. During this bisection process, the algorithm may get called for a value of α that is almost twice as large as *opt*. Therefore, the overall running time for computing the cover T' is $\sum_{i=0}^{2\log opt+2} (\sum_{j=1}^{r} (\alpha + |P_j|)|T_j|^{7\cdot\alpha+1}) \leq$

$\sum_{i=0}^{2\log opt+2} (\sum_{j=1}^{r} (2opt + |P_j|)|T_j|^{7\cdot2opt+1}) = O((opt + n)m^{14opt+1}(\log opt))$. Since the bisection process and the repeated calling of the algorithm ensure that the value of α is ultimately at most *opt* for each $\mathcal{H}_j$, the overall cover T' will have ply at most $2opt$. Thus, the theorem follows. □

Remark 1. In the approximation algorithm for the *MPC* problem, we have used only the properties that for each element $t \in T$, the length of y-side of t is unit and t is a triangle. Hence, the algorithms can be extended to work even when T consists of y-parallel isosceles triangles with unit length y-side.

3.4 NP-Hardness of *MPC* Problem

In this subsection we show that the *MPC* problem is NP-hard. Biedl et al., [1] proved that the *minimum ply covering of points by unit disks (MPCUD)* and the *minimum ply covering of points by unit squares (MPCUS)* are both NP-hard by reducing from the NP-complete planar graph 3-coloring problem. As with Biedl et al., [1] we prove that the *minimum ply covering of points by unit triangles (MPC)* is also NP-hard, in particular, by modifying gadgets in the reduction of Biedl et al. [1] and introducing gadgets as required. As it is argued in [1] that because of ply being an integer, the *MPCUS* and *MPCUD* problems can not be approximated with a factor smaller than 2, *MPC* is also not $(2-\epsilon)$-approximable, for any $\epsilon > 0$.

In the decision version of planar graph 3-coloring problem, we are given a planar graph $G(V, E)$, and our aim is to answer the question: is G 3-colorable? i.e., whether all vertices in V can be colored with three distinct colors such that adjacent vertices receive different colors, or not. Given a planar graph $G(V, E)$, we describe the construction of an instance (P_G, T_G) of the *MPC* problem as follows. The vertex gadget in Fig. 3(a) will be constructed corresponding to each vertex $v \in V(G)$. Depending on which of the three colors is used to color the vertex v, one of the three triangles t_0, t_1, and t_2 is selected to cover the point p_v. The selected color can be carried over by the transport gadget as shown in Fig. 3(b). When a vertex v has degree $d(v)$ more than 2, using as many copies of the duplicate gadget, as shown in Fig. 3(c), as the degree $d(v)$, we can carry over the selected color/triangle of the point p_v along all those edges incident on v. In the construction, whenever we want to change the orientation of triangles in the transport gadget, we can then insert the orientation change gadget there, as shown in Fig. 3(d). In between every pair of adjacent vertices u and v in G, we introduce the color-conflict avoidance gadget (Fig. 4) to avoid that these two vertices receive the same color, i.e., to avoid that the corresponding points p_u and p_v are covered by the same labeled triangles among the triples t_0, t_1, and t_2. Let P_G and T_G consist of all those points and triangles respectively, thus constructed.

Theorem 2. *A planar graph $G(V, E)$ is 3-colorable if and only if the instance (P_G, T_G) of the MPC problem has a solution with ply 1.*

Proof. Now, if all the vertices in $V(G)$ can be colored with three distinct colors, then the corresponding triangles of T_G to the chosen colors cover all the points

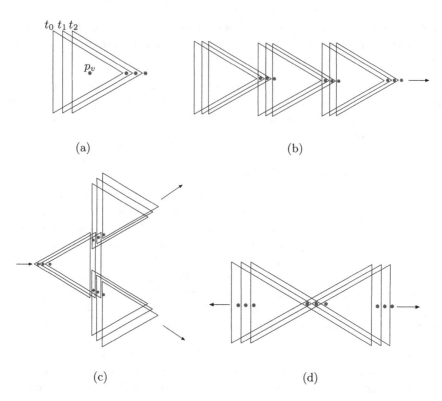

Fig. 3. Hardness of *MPC* problem: (*a*) vertex gadget, (*b*) transport gadget, (*c*) duplicate gadget, and (*d*) orientation change gadget

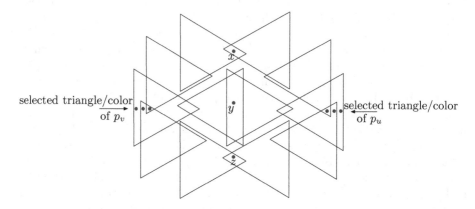

Fig. 4. Color conflict avoidance gadget

in P_G, and no two triangles overlap anywhere. Hence, there exists a set $T_G^* \subseteq T_G$ covering all the points in P_G and having ply 1. On the other hand, if we have a solution $T_G' \subseteq T_G$, with ply 1, which covers all the points in P_G, then by the construction of G, the colors corresponding to the triangles in T_G' result in 3-coloring of G. Thus, the theorem follows.   □

4   Channel Allocation in Directional Wireless Networks

In this section, we study the channel allocation in wireless networks with directional transmitters. In particular, we investigate the *3-colorable unit triangle cover (3CUTC)* problem: given a set T of m y-parallel unit triangles (modelling transmission/interference regions of wireless directional transmitters) and a set P of n points (modelling receivers) in the plane, the objective is to compute a set $T^* \subseteq T$ such that T^* ensures coverage of all points in P (i.e., $P \subset \cup_{t \in T^*} t$) and at most three colors (i.e., channels) are sufficient to color all triangles in T^* (i.e, the set T^* can be split into T_1^*, T_2^* and T_3^* such that the triangles in T_a^* are pairwise disjoint for each $a \in \{1, 2, 3\}$). In other words, we need to compute 3-colorable cover of all points in P with unit triangles in T. The usage of three colors here is justified due to the constraints on channel selection in Wi-Fi networks [2,6]. The algorithm we describe next for this problem is based on the following observation.

Observation 1. *If we have a 3-colorable cover $T_\mathcal{R}$ of all points $P_\mathcal{R}$ lying within a rectangle $\mathcal{R}$ of dimension $1 \times \frac{\sqrt{3}}{2}$, then $|T_\mathcal{R}| \leq 30$.*

Proof. ince the horizontal length of $\mathcal{R}$ is $\frac{\sqrt{3}}{2}$, observe that at most ten sets of almost overlapping three triangles can cover the interior of $\mathcal{R}$ while all the triangles in these sets are 3-colorable (see Fig. 5). Therefore, in any 3-colorable cover of $P_\mathcal{R}$, there are at most 30 unit triangles from T participating. Thus the claim follows.   □

The algorithm for the above channel allocation problem proceeds as follows. First, place a rectangular grid of size $1 \times \frac{\sqrt{3}}{2}$ over the plane containing all points in P. For each rectangle $\mathcal{R}$ formed by this grid, for which $P \cap \mathcal{R} \neq \emptyset$, by exhaustively checking all subsets $T' \subseteq T$ of size at most 30, find that set $T_\mathcal{R}$ of size at most 30 that covers all points in $P_\mathcal{R}$ and is 3-colorable, where $P_\mathcal{R} = P \cap \mathcal{R}$. Let C_1, C_2, C_3 and C_4 be the four sets of three distinct colors. Triangles in any $T_\mathcal{R}$ thus computed can overlap with at most 8 adjacent rectangles. Now, consider the rectangular grid shown in Fig. 6. Let us assign the color set C_1 to the triangles in $T_\mathcal{R}$. Then the adjacent rectangles of $\mathcal{R}$ will get assigned the color sets C_2, C_3, and C_4 as shown in Fig. 6. Let $\mathcal{R}_l$, $\mathcal{R}_r$, $\mathcal{R}_t$, and $\mathcal{R}_b$ be the left, right, top, and bottom rectangles that share their edges with $\mathcal{R}$, and whose assigned colors are C_4, C_4, C_2 and C_3 respectively. Now the right side adjacent rectangle of $\mathcal{R}_l$ will get the color set C_1. Similarly, the left side adjacent rectangle of $\mathcal{R}_r$, top adjacent rectangle of $\mathcal{R}_t$, and bottom adjacent rectangle of $\mathcal{R}_b$ will also get the color set C_1. The same pattern then as shown in Fig. 6 will repeat. For a

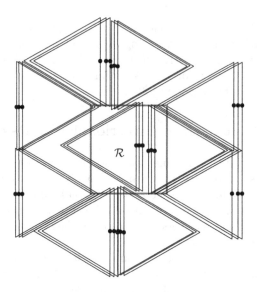

Fig. 5. (a) Illustrating observation 1

triangle t participating in the covering of points lying in more than one adjacent rectangles, we retain the color from the color set of the rectangle $\mathcal{R}$ for which the point $mid(y\text{-side}(t))$ lies in the interior of $\mathcal{R}$.

Theorem 3. *We have a 4-approximation algorithm for the 3CUTC problem, that runs in $O(m^{30}n^2)$ time.*

Proof. The approximation factor of the algorithm follows from the facts that we use four pairwise disjoint color sets, each containing three distinct colors, and there is vertical distance of at least one unit and horizontal distance of at least $\frac{\sqrt{3}}{2}$ units between any two rectangles with the same assigned color set. Because $|P| = n$, there are at most n nonempty rectangles $\mathcal{R}$, i.e., for which $\mathcal{R} \cap P \neq \emptyset$. For each rectangle $\mathcal{R}$, we invest $O(m^{30}n)$ time to compute the cover $T_{\mathcal{R}}$ which is 3-colorable (due to Observation 1). Therefore, the overall time of the algorithm is $O(m^{30}n^2)$. Thus, the theorem follows.   □

Remark 2. Since the triangles within each T_a for $a \in \{1,2,3\}$ are pairwise disjoint, the ply of T_a is 1. Hence, by pigeon hole principle the cover T^* $(= \bigcup_a T_a)$ has ply at most 3.

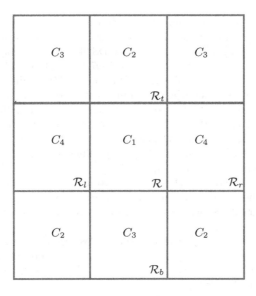

Fig. 6. Coloring triangles chosen to cover points in adjacent rectangles

5   Conclusion

In this paper we study some optimization issues pertained to directional wireless networks. We formulated these optimization issues related to coverage and interference as a geometric covering problem involving unit triangles with fixed orientations, and points, namely, the *minimum ply covering (MPC)* problem. The approximation algorithm that we have presented for the *MPC* problem in this paper has a running time that is polynomial in the input size, but unfortunately exponential in the size of optimal solution. However, in practice for a vehicular adhoc network utilizing directional transmitters, the number of candidate transmitters covering a single receiver is small. Furthermore, developing constant factor approximation algorithms for the above problems, that run in time polynomial in both input size and output size, is an important open problem.

References

1. Biedl, T., Biniaz, A., Lubiw, A.: Minimum ply covering of points with disks and squares. In: Proceedings of the 29th Canadian Conference on Computational Geometry, pp. 226–235 (2019)
2. Brass, A., Hurtado, F., Lafreniere, B.J., Lubiw, A.: A lower bound on the area of a 3-coloured disk packing. Int. J. Comput. Geom. Appl. **20**(3), 341–360 (2010)
3. Carrabs, F., Cerulli, R., D'Ambrosio, C., Raiconi, A.: Exact and heuristic approaches for the maximum lifetime problem in sensor networks with coverage and connectivity constraints. RAIRO-Oper. Res. **51**(3), 607–625 (2017)

4. Carrabs, F., Cerrone, C., D'Ambrosio, C., Raiconi, A.: Column generation embedding carousel greedy for the maximum network lifetime problem with interference constraints. In: Sforza, A., Sterle, C. (eds.) ODS 2017. SPMS, vol. 217, pp. 151–159. Springer, Cham (2017). https://doi.org/10.1007/978-3-319-67308-0_16
5. Carrabs, F., Cerulli, R., D'Ambrosio, C., Raiconi, A.: Prolonging lifetime in wireless sensor networks with interference constraints. In: Au, M.H.A., Castiglione, A., Choo, K.-K.R., Palmieri, F., Li, K.-C. (eds.) GPC 2017. LNCS, vol. 10232, pp. 285–297. Springer, Cham (2017). https://doi.org/10.1007/978-3-319-57186-7_22
6. Cisco Systems, Inc.: Channel Deployment Issues for 2.4-Ghz 802.11 WLANs. http://www.cisco.com/univercd/cc/td/doc/product/wireless/airo1200/accsspts/techref/channel.pdf. Accessed 15 Apr 2007
7. Erlebach, T., Van Leeuwen, E.J.: Approximating geometric coverage problems. In: Proceedings of the Nineteenth Annual ACM-SIAM Symposium on Discrete Algorithms, 20 January 2008, pp. 1267–1276. Society for Industrial and Applied Mathematics (2008)
8. Kuhn, F., von Rickenbach, P., Wattenhofer, R., Welzl, E., Zollinger, A.: Interference in cellular networks: the minimum membership set cover problem. In: Wang, L. (ed.) COCOON 2005. LNCS, vol. 3595, pp. 188–198. Springer, Heidelberg (2005). https://doi.org/10.1007/11533719_21
9. Kumar, S., Suman, S., De, S.: Dynamic resource allocation in UAV-enabled mmWave communication networks. IEEE Internet Things J. (2020)

Distributed Algorithms, Concurrency and Parallelism

Automated Deadlock Detection for Large Java Libraries

R. Rajesh Kumar$^{(\boxtimes)}$ ⓘ, Vivek Shanbhag, and K. V. Dinesha

International Institute of Information Technology,
Bangalore 560100, Karnataka, India
rajesh.kumar@iiitb.org
https://www.iiitb.ac.in

Abstract. Locating deadlock opportunities in large Java libraries is a subject of much research as the Java Execution Environment (JVM /JRE) does not provide means to predict or prevent deadlocks. Researchers have used static and dynamic approaches to analyze the problem.

Static approaches: With very large libraries, this analysis face typical accuracy/doability problem. If they employ a detailed modelling of the library, then the size of the analysis grows too large. Instead, if their model is coarse grained, then the results have too many false cases. Since they do not generate deadlocking test cases, manually creating deadlocking code based on the predictions is impractical for large libraries.

Dynamic approaches: Such analysis produces concrete results in the form of actual test cases to demonstrate the reachability of the identified deadlock. Unfortunately, for large libraries, generating the seed test execution paths covering all possible classes, to trigger the dynamic analysis becomes impractical.

In this work we combine a static approach (Stalemate) and a dynamic approach (Omen) to detect deadlocks in large Java libraries. We first run 'Stalemate' to generate a list of potential deadlocking classes. We feed this as input test case to Omen. In case of deadlock, details are logged for subsequent reproduction. This process is automated without the need for manual intervention.

We subjected the entire JRE v1.7.0_79 libraries (rt.jar) to our implementation of the above approach and successfully detected 113 deadlocks. We reported a few of them to Oracle as defects. They were accepted as bugs.

Keywords: Concurrency · Deadlock · Java · Static analysis · Dynamic analysis · Scalable

1 Introduction

The *synchronised* construct is provided in the Java Language to facilitate the development of code fragments that may run concurrently. When this happens in an uncoordinated manner it can give rise to *Lock Order Violations*. If such a lock

© Springer Nature Switzerland AG 2021
D. Goswami and T. A. Hoang (Eds.): ICDCIT 2021, LNCS 12582, pp. 129–144, 2021.
https://doi.org/10.1007/978-3-030-65621-8_8

order violation is realised during program execution it causes the executing JVM to deadlock. This problem has been widely investigated, and various researchers have tried different approaches to address it.

There have been numerous published research works for detecting deadlocks including both static and dynamic approaches [1,2,4–6,9,11–16] and some for preventing them [3,7,8].

Stalemate [1,2] is a static analysis approach that identifies lock order violations in large Java libraries, which have the possibility of being realised, during execution, in the form of a deadlock. However, its predictions include many false positives, since the analysis is at the *type* level while the contested locks are held on the actual objects. Consequently, one must develop a deadlocking test case by manual examination of the call cycles in the predictions. For a library as large as the entire JRE, it becomes impractical to apply this manual method to narrow down to realisable deadlocks. Other static approaches such as Jade [12,13] can scale well, produces notable results, however these methods also produce many false positives.

There are many dynamic analysis approaches to identify deadlocks such as Omen [4], Needlepoint [5] and Sherlock [6]. Omen, produces realisable deadlocks along with reproducible test cases. Such dynamic analysis, initiated using seed test cases, is limited to the execution traces realisable during the call flows of the seed test cases. For large libraries, the set of seed test cases would become substantial, and looking for lock cycles realisable in their execution traces would be impractical. The implementation Sherlock is suitable for large programs but not for libraries.

In this paper we address the problem of identifying reproducible deadlocks in large Java libraries without false positives, and produce deadlocking test cases for the detected deadlocks. Our approach combines a static approach Stalemate [1,2], as it can scale to analyze large libraries and a dynamic approach Omen [4] to detect real deadlocks along with deadlocking test cases.

We start by subjecting the library to Stalemate and from the lock order violations it reports, interleaving calls that could lead to deadlocks are extracted. Reading off classes/methods involved in such calls, we use Randoop to generate test cases that exercise these classes/methods. These tests are then subjected to dynamic analysis (Omen) narrowing down to reproducible deadlocks. In this way we eliminate the numerous false cases identified by static analysis. At the same time the attention of the dynamic analysis is directed to only those components in the library where there is a possibility of finding a deadlock. We have fully automated the process so that the complete analysis for the entire library can be completed with no manual intervention.

This paper is organized as follows: Sect. 2 states the problem we are attempting to address. Section 3 provides the solution overview and details the implementation, Sect. 4 summarizes the results, and Sect. 5 states the conclusions.

2   Problem Statement

Design an automated method to analyze large Java libraries to detect deadlocks by combining static and dynamic analysis approaches. For each of the lock order violations identified by the static analysis (Stalemate), create an automated process to detect any real deadlock associated with that violation using dynamic analysis (Omen). The process should also generate the deadlocking test cases to reproduce the deadlocks.

As an illustration, we have used the output of Stalemate [1] on the entire JRE v1.7.0_79 libraries (rt.jar) to generate a list of lock order violations (this number is more than 26,000) with many false positive cases. We have used the automated process described in this paper to generate a list of real deadlocks (number: 113) and test cases to reproduce the deadlocks.

3   Solution Details

The solution focuses on extracting the relevant details from the static analysis and targets the dynamic analysis only on those classes that have the potential to cause a deadlock. Given a lock order violation that is identified by the static analysis *Stalemate*, next, we want to develop single-threaded test programs that may individually realise each its thread stacks. For this purpose we use the *Randoop* tool, which synthesizes test cases for a given set of classes. The dynamic analysis tool *Omen* is then invoked by passing the generated test case as the seed test case. On completion of the analysis if deadlocks are found, Omen will synthesize a multi-threaded test case that will always deadlock.

The task is to use these tools, namely, *Stalemate*, *Randoop* and *Omen*, and devise an automated method to analyze large Java libraries to detect deadlocks and produce deadlocking test scenarios. The flow is designed to handle any exceptions and intermittent failures so that it is suitable to analyze large libraries and results in a truly automated solution.

3.1   Solution Steps

The process flow is represented in Fig. 1. Key steps of the automated analysis is described below.

1. **Static Analysis:** The jar file containing the libraries that are to be analyzed are subjected to the static analysis. This step produces the static analysis results (Sn), which contains the list of potential deadlocking scenarios containing the call flow details with the lock order violations involved in the synchronized functions calls, as represented in Fig. 2.

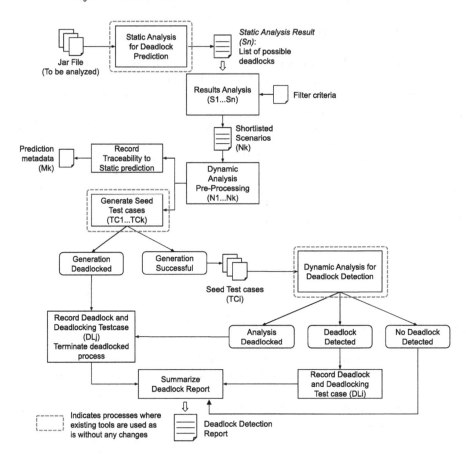

Fig. 1. Automated deadlock detection process flow

The result is interpreted as follows: the "Cycle-2" in its opening line means that is a lock order violation involving 2 locks. The class names of the locks are in the string that follows. This line is followed by a number of thread stacks enclosed within "Thread-i Option" descriptors. i ranging from 1 to n, the number of locks involved in the violation.

The example in Fig. 2, where $n = 2$, we refer to the "Thread-1" stacks as forward stacks, which acquire locks in the *forward order*, and the "Thread-2" stacks as reverse stacks, as they acquire them in the *reverse order*. If in a multi-threaded program, one thread were to realise one of the forward stacks, and another thread were to realise one of the reverse stacks, and if they were to do this concurrently, and if the two locks they are trying to acquire were to be the *same* two locks, then they could result in a deadlock.

```
<Cycle-2 java.util.logging.Logger.class java.util.logging.LogManager>

    <Thread-1 Option>
java.util.logging.Logger.getAnonymousLogger:()Ljava.util.logging.Logger;
java.util.logging.LogManager.getLogger:(Ljava.lang.String;)Ljava.util.logging.Logger;
    </Thread-1 Option>
<Thread-1 Option>
java.util.logging.Logger.getAnonymousLogger:(Ljava.lang.String;)Ljava.util.logging.Logger;
java.util.logging.LogManager.getLogger:(Ljava.lang.String;)Ljava.util.logging.Logger;
    </Thread-1 Option>
<Thread-1 Option>
java.util.logging.Logger.getLogger:(Ljava.lang.String;Ljava.lang.String;)Ljava.util.logging.Logger;
java.util.logging.LogManager.getLogger:(Ljava.lang.String;)Ljava.util.logging.Logger;
    </Thread-1 Option>
<Thread-1 Option>
java.util.logging.Logger.getLogger:(Ljava.lang.String;Ljava.lang.String;)Ljava.util.logging.Logger;
java.util.logging.LogManager.addLogger:(Ljava.util.logging.Logger;)Z
    </Thread-1 Option>
<Thread-1 Option>
java.util.logging.Logger.getLogger:(Ljava.lang.String;)Ljava.util.logging.Logger;
java.util.logging.LogManager.addLogger:(Ljava.util.logging.Logger;)Z
    </Thread-1 Option>
<Thread-1 Option>
java.util.logging.Logger.getLogger:(Ljava.lang.String;)Ljava.util.logging.Logger;
java.util.logging.LogManager.getLogger:(Ljava.lang.String;)Ljava.util.logging.Logger;
    </Thread-1 Option>

    <Thread-2 Option>
java.util.logging.LogManager.addLogger:(Ljava.util.logging.Logger;)Z
java.util.logging.Logger.getLogger:(Ljava.lang.String;)Ljava.util.logging.Logger;
    </Thread-2 Option>

</Cycle-2 java.util.logging.Logger.class java.util.logging.LogManager>
```

Fig. 2. Lock order violation output from static analysis

2. **Prediction Filtering and Data Preparation:** The results produced by Stalemate could be a very large data set. To narrow down the areas of focus, certain filters such as *Cycles*, *Call Depth* and *Call Density* are applied on the results (details of the filters are elaborated in Sect. 3.2). Each of the result nodes (S1 to Sn) are checked for the filter criteria and a subset Nk of the static analysis results ($Nk \subset Sn$) is produced. There is a possibility that this step could filter certain real deadlock candidates, however it helps to direct the analysis to the desired focus area. For each of the shortlisted nodes, the classes are extracted along with the metadata to trace back to the static analysis and it is referred as *Node Info*. An extract of a log created after the filtering exercise is shown in Fig. 3(a) and Node Info is shown in Fig. 3(b).

3. **Seed Test Case Generation:** Using the *Node Info* details collected during the data preparation step the seed test cases (TCk) are generated for each of the shortlisted predictions using the utility Randoop [10]. The test cases target specifically the classes involved in a lock order violation as detected by the static analysis. Example of a test case generated by Randoop is shown in Fig. 3(c).

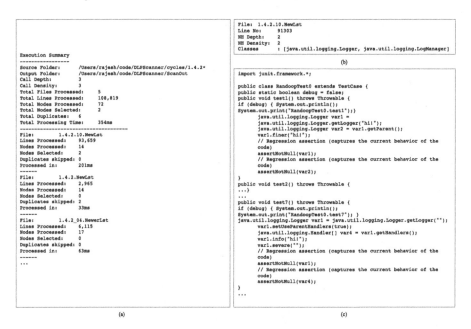

Fig. 3. (a) Execution summary (b) node info (c) test case generated by Randoop

4. **Dynamic Analysis for Deadlock Detection:** Post generation of the seed test cases, for each of the test cases (TC1 to TCk), the Dynamic Deadlock Analysis is initiated with Omen. The Dynamic Analysis starts by executing the seed test case and by tracing the lock dependency relations of the classes during the execution and recording them along with the invocation contexts. The presence of cyclic chains in the lock dependency relations are identified and potential deadlocking scenarios are synthesized. Multi-threaded tests are then generated by using the invocation details from the seed test case execution and by creating additional conditions that could result in a deadlock. At the end of the execution if any deadlocks are detected (DLj) successfully, they are recorded along with the deadlocking test cases. The class to be analyzed, seed test case, and the deadlocking test case generated by Omen are illustrated in Fig. 4 with a simple example. The flow continues by picking the next shortlisted result to be analyzed.

5. **Handling of Deadlocked Analysis:** It was observed that the execution of the analysis was getting deadlocked either during the generation of the seed test cases or during the dynamic analysis. It was observed that these deadlocking scenarios were occurring while processing specific set of classes. The stack traces of the deadlocked JVM revealed that these are indeed deadlocking scenarios as predicted by the static analysis and they were consistently occurring while processing those specific classes. The test case generation by Randoop is a multi-threaded process as it executes each test in a separate thread to speed up the generation. When the lock order violations occur in

the call flows of the classes for which the test cases are being generated, the possibility of deadlock occurs. Similarly, such scenarios occur during dynamic analysis as well. *JVM Monitoring Routine* was developed to watch the JVMs for such scenarios. Once a deadlocked JVM is detected then the stack traces were extracted and recorded along with the associated metadata so that it is traceable to the prediction. The hung JVM is then terminated by the routine so that the flow would continue to the next prediction to be analyzed. An extract of the JVM stack trace of such as scenario is shown in Fig. 5

```
public class Account {

int balance = 1000;

public void transfer(Account acc, int amount) {
    {
    synchronized(acc) { // To ensure atomicity
    if(acc != null && acc.debit(amount)) {
            credit(amount);
        }
    }
    }
}

public synchronized boolean debit(int amount) {
    if(balance < amount) return false;
    balance -= amount;
    return true;
}

public synchronized void credit(int amount) {
    balance += amount;
}

}
```

(a)

```
public class TestAccount {
    public static void main(String [] args) {
        Account user1, user2;
        user1 = new Account();
        user2 = new Account();
        // test credit
        user1.credit(200);
        // test debit
        user1.debit(100);
        // test transfer
        user1.transfer(user2,50);
    }
}
```

(b)

```
import java.util.*;
import java.io.*;
import omen.util.*;
public class TestDriver {

public static void cycle0() {
    Initializer.initialize(0);

    Thread thread0 = new Thread() {
    public void run() {
    List<Parameter> paramList =
        Initializer.collectedObjects.get(0);
    Account receiver =
        (Account)paramList.get(0).returnStored();
    Account par1 =
        (Account)paramList.get(1).returnStored();
    int par2 = (int)paramList.get(2).returnStoredInt();
    try {
        Thread.sleep(0);
        receiver.transfer(par1, par2);
    } catch (Exception e) {}
    }
};
Thread thread1 = new Thread() {
    public void run() {
    List<Parameter> paramList =
        Initializer.collectedObjects.get(1);
    Account receiver =
        (Account)paramList.get(0).returnStored();
    Account par1 =
        (Account)paramList.get(1).returnStored();
    int par2 =
        (int)paramList.get(2).returnStoredInt();
    try {
        Thread.sleep(1000);
        receiver.transfer(par1, par2);
    } catch (Exception e) {}
    }
};
//Start the threads
thread0.start();
thread1.start();
try {
    thread0.join();
    thread1.join();
} catch (Exception e) { }
}
/*
* Test all the cycles.
*/
public static void main(String args[]) {
        switch( Integer.parseInt(System.getenv()
                        .get("omen.errno"))) {
        case 0:
            cycle0();
            System.out.println("Printing cycle" +0);
            break;
        }

}
}
```

(c)

Fig. 4. Omen dynamic analysis example: (a) class to be analyzed (b) sequential seed test case to be subjected to the analysis (c) synthesized multi-threaded deadlocking test case generated by Omen

...

```
"Finalizer" daemon prio=5 tid=0x00007f8944813800 nid=0x3303 in
Object.wait() [0x0000700001e0e000]
    java.lang.Thread.State: WAITING (on object monitor)
        at java.lang.Object.wait(Native Method)
        - waiting on <0x0000000780004858> (a
java.lang.ref.ReferenceQueue$Lock)
        at java.lang.ref.ReferenceQueue.remove(ReferenceQueue.java:135)
        - locked <0x0000000780004858> (a
java.lang.ref.ReferenceQueue$Lock)
        at java.lang.ref.ReferenceQueue.remove(ReferenceQueue.java:151)
        at
java.lang.ref.Finalizer$FinalizerThread.run(Finalizer.java:209)

    ...

"main" prio=5 tid=0x00007f8944802800 nid=0x1b03 runnable
[0x00007000016f8000]
    java.lang.Thread.State: RUNNABLE
        at
java.util.logging.Logger.getEffectiveResourceBundleName(Logger.java:1703
)
        at java.util.logging.Logger.doLog(Logger.java:636)
        at java.util.logging.Logger.log(Logger.java:664)
        at java.util.logging.Logger.info(Logger.java:1182)
        at RandoopTest0.test7(RandoopTest0.java:109)
        at sun.reflect.NativeMethodAccessorImpl.invoke0(Native Method)
    ...
```

Fig. 5. Extract of JVM stack trace

6. **Data Collection and Report Creation:** Comprehensive reports of the analysis are generated based on the data collected when the execution concludes, resulting in a comprehensive Deadlock Detection Report.

3.2 Implementation

The implementation details of the solution is elaborated in this section. The complete source code for of this implementation is published in GitHub along with the test results of the executions.

Execution Flow. The end-to-end execution flow design is represented in the Fig. 6. The flow of the automated deadlock analyzer is as follows (refer Fig. 6, steps 1 to 7):

1. The *run cycles* are specified by providing the constraints that needs to be applied on the static analysis prediction output. The constraints specifies the output files that needs to be selected for analysis and the filter criteria that needs to be applied for each of the output files.
2. For each run, the *Prediction filter constraints* file is generated, which is the primary input for the *Static Analysis Prediction Scanner.*

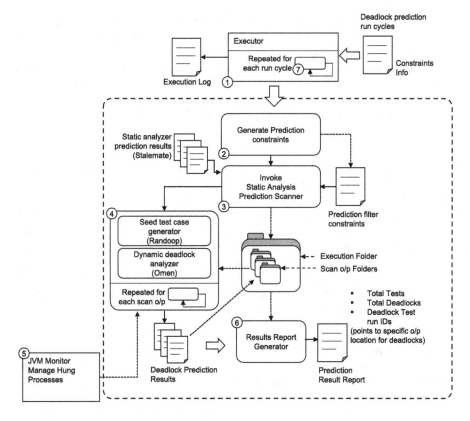

Fig. 6. Automated deadlock analyzer implementation design

3. The *Static Analysis Prediction Scanner* takes the generated Prediction filter constraints and scans each of the static analysis output files and selects the specific prediction nodes (the xml node that contain the lock order violations) along with the relevant metadata.

4. *Dynamic Deadlock Analyzer* is then invoked for each of the shortlisted node after generating the seed test cases for the classes involved in the potential deadlocks identified by the static analysis. The detected deadlocks are recorded in such a way that the corresponding static analysis prediction and the interleaving call details can be traced back.

5. During the execution of the dynamic analysis the *JVM Monitor* is invoked to monitor the execution for any hung scenarios. When such a scenario is detected, the monitor will extract the details for analysis and terminate the hung program so that the execution can continue. All the logs related to the deadlocking scenario are organized so that they can be seen in the context of the specific deadlock prediction.

6. After the completion of the analysis, the *Results Report Generator* is run to consolidate the complete execution results. The summary of each execution

is created in a master report file with the details of the constraints specified along with the results. With this information any detected deadlock can be consistently recreated.

7. The steps 2 through 6 are repeated for each of the run cycles specified in Step 1, thereby enabling the execution of a complete batch of automated analysis

The details of some of the key components of the implementation are described below:

Static Analysis Prediction Scanner. The static analysis prediction scanner is designed to shortlist the specific nodes from the output of the static analysis based on the constraints such as *Cycles*: Specifies the number of locks involved in a lock order violation, *Call Depth*: The number of function calls involved in a deadlock cycle that was predicted, *Call Density*: The number of classes involved in the prediction node resulting in a deadlocking cycle, and *Package Exclusions*: The list of packages that are to be excluded in the scan. All the necessary metadata required to target only the classes that could lead to a potential deadlock are collected at this stage. The Dynamic Deadlock Analysis is triggered after the completion of this scan.

Dynamic Deadlock Analysis. The first step of the process is to generate the sequential test cases that will act as the seed test cases for the dynamic analysis. Our aim is to target only the classes that are involved in a lock order violation, as predicted by the static analysis. The test cases corresponding to each of the selected prediction node from the static analysis are generated by the *Randoop* tool. *Omen*, is then invoked with the seed test case as input to initiate the dynamic analysis. The test cases are executed by Omen and the execution traces are scanned for cycles to detect the deadlocking scenarios. The detected deadlocks are then consolidated into a comprehensive report.

JVM Monitoring Routine. JVM Monitoring Routine was developed to handle the deadlocked analysis that happens either during *Randoop* execution or during *Omen* execution. JVM Monitor, once initiated is designed to run as long as there is an active JVM. As a first step, it fetches all the process identifiers (PIDs) of the java programs that are being executed in the JVM with a time delay. Then it checks if there are any identical processes between those time delays. If there are any identical processes, their respective stack traces are fetched. The stack traces are then compared to check the JNI global references held by the JVM. Analysis of the JNI global references is a predictable indicator to assess if the JVM is active or hung. If the JNI global references are identical across multiple snapshots with significant time delays, it predictably indicated a hung JVM. Once the hung state of the JVM is detected then logs are generated, and the details are collected in the reports. The processes that are hung are then terminated for the flow of the Dynamic Analyzer to progress ahead.

Report Generation. Following are the key reports generated during the execution:

1. **Test Runs Report:** Contains the execution status for each of the batches, along with the filter criteria applied for the analysis. This report provides an overview of the batch executions and enables to plan further batches for analysis.
2. **Execution Summary Report:** This report provides the summary of the execution results and helps to navigate to the specific deadlocking scenario. The metadata captured by this report enables to locate the specific Deadlock Report file along with the other details that indicates the number of tests executed and number of dead locking scenarios detected.
3. **Deadlock Report:** The Deadlock Report contains the log related to each of the nodes that were processed and which of the processed node resulted in a deadlock. If the dead locks are detected as a result of the hung JVM detected during test case generation or dynamic analysis, they are marked.

4   Results

The entire Java Runtime Libraries JRE v1.7.0_79 libraries (rt.jar) were subjected to Stalemate [1], the static analysis tool. The output files from the static analysis method were used as a starting point for the analysis. Table 1 lists the key details of the execution. We have been able to uncover deadlock in Java libraries that have not been demonstrated by other methods. We identified such cases and reported some of them to Oracle as bugs. Table 2 lists the bugs reported to Oracle.

Table 1. Summary of execution

Platform	MacOS High Sierra 17.3.0 Darwin Kernel Version 17.3.0, xnu-4570.31.3 1/RELEASE_X86_64 x86_6	
Java environment	java version "1.7.0_79", Java(TM) SE Runtime Environment (build 1.7.0_79-b15), Java HotSpot(TM) 64-bit server VM (build 24.79-b02, mixed mode)	
Execution summary	Total tests executed	1,563
	Total prediction nodes analyzed	26,728
	Duplicates eliminated	3,001
	Nodes filtered from static analysis	1,563
	Total deadlocking scenarios detected	**113**

Table 2. Bugs reported to Oracle

Deadlocking Java Library classes	Oracle JDK Bug ID
java.util.logging.Logger java.util.logging.LogManager	8194918
ava.awt.EventQueue sun.awt.AppContext javax.swing.plaf.basic.BasicDirectoryModel sun.awt.X11.XToolkit java.util.Vector	8194407
java.awt.EventQueue sun.awt.PostEventQueue java.awt.SentEvent sun.awt.SunToolkit	8194635
ava.awt.Component javax.swing.JFileChooser javax.swing.SwingUtilities java.awt.dnd.DropTarget javax.swing.JComponent	8194862
java.io.ObjectInputStream java.awt.KeyboardFocusManager java.awt.Component java.awt.Window java.awt.Frame	8194920
java.util.TimeZone java.util.Properties javax.naming.spi.DirectoryManager java.lang.SecurityManager java.util.Hashtable	8194919
java.awt.EventQueue java.awt.EventDispatchThread sun.awt.PostEventQueue	8194962
ava.awt.EventQueue sun.awt.AppContext javax.swing.plaf.basic.BasicDirectoryModel sun.awt.X11.XToolkit	8194983

Table 3. Examples: deadlocking call cycles

Calls between:	
`java.util.logging.Logger`	
`java.util.logging.LogManager`	
Forward calls	
`Logger.getAnonymousLogger()`	calls
`LogManager.getLogger(String)`	
`Logger.getLogger(String,String)`	calls
`LogManager.getLogger(String)`	
`Logger.getLogger(String)`	calls
`LogManager.addLogger(Logger)`	
Reverse calls	
`LogManager.addLogger(Logger)`	calls
`Logger.getLogger(String)`	
Calls between:	
`sun.awt.PostEventQueue`	
`java.awt.EventQueue`	
Forward calls	
`PostEventQueue.flush()`	calls
`EventQueue.postEventPrivate(AWTEvent)`	
Reverse calls	
`EventQueue.removeSourceEvents(Component)`	calls
`java.awt.SentEvent.dispose(AppContext,SentEvent)`	calls
`PostEventQueue.postEvent(SentEvent)`	
`EventQueue.push(EventQueue)`	calls
`EventQueue.getNextEvent()`	calls
`SunToolkit.flushPendingEvents()`	calls
`PostEventQueue.flush()`	
Calls between:	
`sun.rmi.server.Activation`	
`sun.rmi.server.Activation$GroupEntry`	
Forward calls	
`Activation.addLogRecord(Activation$LogRecord)`	calls
`Activation$ActivationSystemImpl.shutdown()`	calls
`Activation.checkShutdown()`	calls
`Activation$GroupEntry.restartServices()`	calls
`Activation$GroupEntry.getInstantiator(ActivationGroupID)`	
`Activation.addLogRecord(Activation$LogRecord)`	calls
`SystemImpl.shutdown()`	calls
`Activation$GroupEntry.unregisterGroup()`	
Reverse calls	
`Activation$GroupEntry.setActivationGroupDesc(ActivationGroupID)` calls	
`Activation.addLogRecord(Activation$LogRecord)`	

The results identified by our approach are reproducible. The static analysis [1] alone detected many thousands of potential deadlocks where one has to analyze the predictions manually to construct the deadlocking test cases, whereas we produce the deadlocking scenarios as output. The dynamic analysis [4] results are limited by the test cases that are subjected to it, hence it is not a viable tool in itself to analyze large libraries. Combining both together we have demonstrated an automated solution that is scalable for large libraries.

The Table 3 shows few examples of interleaving call details of the deadlocks detected by our method. For brevity the package names and return values of the methods are omitted while representing the call flows.

5   Conclusions

From the above results we assess that the method described was able to deal with the scale what it was intended for. It was successfully able to scan through tens of thousands of potential deadlocking scenarios and created over hundred reproducible deadlocking test cases without any false positives.

The approach was able to overcome the inherent limitation of the static approach of producing numerous 'potential' dead locking cases containing lot of false positives. Dynamic analysis on the other hand is effective in deadlock detection for programs for applications but not for libraries. It is limited by the coverage provided by the seed test case that is subjected to the analysis.

The presented approach provides an effective way to leverage both static and dynamic analysis methods to produce a viable automated way to detect deadlock in large java libraries.

Acknowledgements. We sincerely thank Dr. Murali Krishna Ramanathan for the discussion in formulating the problem. We also thank Malavika Samak and Dr. Murali Krishna Ramanathan for permitting us to use the program developed by them for dynamic deadlock detection.

References

1. Shanbhag, V.K.: Locating lock order violations in Java libraries - a scalable static analysis. Ph.D. dissertation. IIIT - Bangalore, Bangalore, Karnataka, India (2015). Reference [2] is the preliminary work of this thesis. Contact: IIIT-B Library (iiit-blibrary@iiitb.org) or Author (vivek.shanbag@gmail.com)
2. Shanbhag, V.K.: Deadlock-detection in Java-library using static-analysis. In: 2008 15th Asia-Pacific Software Engineering Conference, Beijing, 2008, pp. 361–368 (2008). https://doi.org/10.1109/APSEC.2008.68
3. Pandey, S., Bhat, S., Shanbhag, V.: Avoiding deadlocks using stalemate and Dimmunix. In: Companion Proceedings of the 36th International Conference on Software Engineering (ICSE Companion 2014), pp. 602–603. Association for Computing Machinery, New York (2014). https://doi.org/10.1145/2591062.2591136

4. Samak, M., Ramanathan, M.K.: Multithreaded test synthesis for deadlock detection. In: Proceedings of the 2014 ACM International Conference on Object Oriented Programming Systems Languages and Applications (OOPSLA 2014), pp. 473–489. Association for Computing Machinery, New York (2014). https://doi.org/10.1145/2660193.2660238

5. Nagarakatte, S., Burckhardt, S., Martin, M.M.K., Musuvathi, M.: Multicore acceleration of priority-based schedulers for concurrency bug detection. In: Proceedings of the 33rd ACM SIGPLAN Conference on Programming Language Design and Implementation (PLDI 2012), pp. 543–554. Association for Computing Machinery, New York (2012). https://doi.org/10.1145/2254064.2254128

6. Eslamimehr, M., Palsberg, J.: Sherlock: scalable deadlock detection for concurrent programs. In: Proceedings of the 22nd ACM SIGSOFT International Symposium on Foundations of Software Engineering (FSE 2014), pp. 353–365. Association for Computing Machinery, New York (2014). https://doi.org/10.1145/2635868.2635918

7. Jula, H., Tralamazza, D., Zamfir, C., Candea, G.: Deadlock immunity: enabling systems to defend against deadlocks. In: Proceedings of the 8th USENIX conference on Operating systems design and implementation (OSDI 2008), pp. 295–308. USENIX Association, USA (2008)

8. Jula, H., Tözün, P., Candea, G.: Communix: a framework for collaborative deadlock immunity. In: 2011 IEEE/IFIP 41st International Conference on Dependable Systems and Networks (DSN), Hong Kong, pp. 181–188 (2011). https://doi.org/10.1109/DSN.2011.5958217

9. Pradel, M., Gross, T.R.: Fully automatic and precise detection of thread safety violations. In: Proceedings of the 33rd ACM SIGPLAN Conference on Programming Language Design and Implementation (PLDI 2012), pp. 521–530. . Association for Computing Machinery, New York (2012). https://doi.org/10.1145/2254064.2254126

10. Pacheco, C., Ernst, M.D.: Randoop: feedback-directed random testing for Java. In: Companion to the 22nd ACM SIGPLAN Conference on Object-Oriented Programming Systems and Applications Companion (OOPSLA 2007), pp. 815–816. Association for Computing Machinery, New York (2007). https://doi.org/10.1145/1297846.1297902

11. Choudhary, A., Lu, S., Pradel, M.: Efficient detection of thread safety violations via coverage-guided generation of concurrent tests. In: 2017 IEEE/ACM 39th International Conference on Software Engineering (ICSE), Buenos Aires, pp. 266–277 (2017). https://doi.org/10.1109/ICSE.2017.32

12. Naik, M., Park, C.-S., Sen, K., Gay, D.: Effective static deadlock detection. In: Proceedings of the 31st International Conference on Software Engineering (ICSE 2009), pp. 386–396. IEEE Computer Society, USA (2009). https://doi.org/10.1109/ICSE.2009.5070538

13. Naik, M., Aiken, A., Whaley, J.: Effective static race detection for Java. In: Proceedings of the 27th ACM SIGPLAN Conference on Programming Language Design and Implementation (PLDI 2006), pp. 308–319. Association for Computing Machinery, New York (2006). https://doi.org/10.1145/1133981.1134018

14. Joshi, P., Park, C.-S., Sen, K., Naik, M.: A randomized dynamic program analysis technique for detecting real deadlocks. In: Proceedings of the 30th ACM SIGPLAN Conference on Programming Language Design and Implementation (PLDI 2009), pp. 110–120. Association for Computing Machinery, New York (2009). https://doi.org/10.1145/1542476.1542489

15. Williams, A., Thies, W., Ernst, M.D.: Static deadlock detection for Java libraries. In: Black, A.P. (ed.) ECOOP 2005. LNCS, vol. 3586, pp. 602–629. Springer, Heidelberg (2005). https://doi.org/10.1007/11531142_26
16. Cai, Y.: A dynamic deadlock prediction, confirmation and fixing frame- work for multithreaded programs. In: Doctoral Symposium of the 26th European Conference on Object-Oriented Programming (ECOOP 2012, DS) (2012)

DNet: An Efficient Privacy-Preserving Distributed Learning Framework for Healthcare Systems

Parth Parag Kulkarni$^{(\boxtimes)}$, Harsh Kasyap, and Somanath Tripathy

Department of Computer Science and Engineering, Indian Institute of Technology
Patna, Patna, India
{kulkarni.cs16,harsh_1921cs01,som}@iitp.ac.in

Abstract. Medical data held in silos by institutions, makes it challenging to predict new trends and gain insights, as, sharing individual data leaks user privacy and is restricted by law. Meanwhile, the Federated Learning framework [11] would solve this problem by facilitating on-device training while preserving privacy. However, the presence of a central server has its inherent problems, including a single point of failure and trust. Moreover, data may be prone to inference attacks. This paper presents a Distributed Net algorithm called DNet to address these issues posing its own set of challenges in terms of high communication latency, performance, and efficiency. Four different networks have been discussed and compared for computation, latency, and precision. Empirical analysis has been performed over Chest X-ray Images and COVID-19 dataset. The theoretical analysis proves our claim that the algorithm has a lower communication latency and provides an upper bound.

Keywords: Distributed learning · Federated Learning · Healthcare · Binary Tree Representation · Privacy

1 Introduction

The science of medicine has reached its advanced stage of research. New methodologies are taking shape, and efficient drugs are being developed. This research has been given wings, by the analysis of medical data using machine learning techniques. New deep learning methodologies have become the tool for gaining new insights without putting much of the domain knowledge. These techniques rely on training on a huge scale of data. However, the question is from where does this data come from and who holds access to it? How much sensitive information does the data leak? All these questions make the study challenging and demand new innovative ways of study.

In the age of sensors and devices spanning around us, data is continuously generated and has value to contribute to research. Three sources mainly possess healthcare data - the patients, hospitals and medical stores. A patient himself/herself owns his/her medical records. He/she keeps records prescribed from

© Springer Nature Switzerland AG 2021
D. Goswami and T. A. Hoang (Eds.): ICDCIT 2021, LNCS 12582, pp. 145–159, 2021.
https://doi.org/10.1007/978-3-030-65621-8_9

doctors, medical stores, and self-owned smart devices like fit-bits. Hospitals hold records of multiple patients and are significant repositories of data. Medical stores also own health/drug related data and statistics, which can infer many trends. However, sharing this data often reveals more than required. For example, if an institution is running cancer research; the data being studied should only tell how the tumor looks like rather revealing that a person has cancer. The institutions will come across patients with different symptoms and remedies working for them. As collaboration becomes indispensable, it becomes vital to exchange this information for developing the best cure. However, these sources owning data pose a high risk of losing sensitive data. There can be misuse of confidential personal information to gain benefits. Patients who own the data do not know what it has been used for.

In 2016, Google came with the Federated Learning framework that promised data security. Federated Learning keeps the data in-place and performs local model training. The training is iterated for thousands and millions of times for improving the model. These local models are sent to a central server and aggregated to obtain the global model. The global model is sent back to the devices for training in the next iteration. Though, Federated Learning improvises security and asserts privacy by keeping the data with the real owner. However, it becomes vulnerable to inference attacks by reverse engineering on the transmitted gradients. The presence of a trusted server is also questionable. It can be biased for some participants and may post malicious updates to others. It faces scalability issues for executing multiple tasks. It needs to instantiate individually for the operation of separate tasks. It also poses the risk of a single point of failure. As the central server reports to be down or broken, the complete system comes to a halt.

As discussed above, Federated Learning poses threats from a malicious central server and requires high communication overhead. It also violates being genuinely decentralized. However, health care institutions are demanding a privacy-preserving collaborative learning system to facilitate research advances. They would trust more on a peer-to-peer network that need not rely on any third party and also bear fault-tolerance, liveliness, and availability.

Keeping the above-discussed issues and requirements into consideration, we propose a communication-efficient decentralized variant of Federated Learning. The significant contributions are as follows.

- This paper presents a Distributed algorithm for in-place model training without the presence of central curator (DNet).
- Four variants of the algorithm are proposed, and analysis of their efficiency recommends Binary Tree Representation technique due to its optimal performance.
- This paper does an empirical and theoretical analysis of the algorithm and its variants, which shows our claim of communication efficiency.
- The proposed methods have been tested on real-world Pneumonia as well as recently released COVID-19 datasets.

The remainder of this paper is organized as follows. Section 2 discusses the background and related works. Section 3 summarizes some traditional frameworks. Section 4 discusses the DNet algorithm along with the proposed framework. Section 5 explains the training and experiment methodology. Section 6 lists the results and shows some empirical comparisons. Section 7 concludes and briefs the scope for future work.

2   Background and Related Work

This section briefs the concept of Federated Learning and its application in healthcare. It discusses the existing works in the same direction.

2.1   Federated Learning

Federated Learning is a collaborative learning paradigm by training across decentralized applications holding similar chunks of data. It involves multiple participants with a central server. The central server is responsible for delineating the computation rounds, selecting the devices for participation, and aggregating their respective model updates to build a global model. It is privacy-preserving in nature as it holds the data to the device itself. Previous approaches used to collect all these data to the central server and train, which induces a high data leak risk and violates various security principles and pacts. Federated Learning brings the model to the data while keeping the data to the device itself. It is an iterative process that involves significant communication overhead and a threat of a malicious server.

FedSGD (a variant of stochastic gradient descent (SGD)) is a widely used optimization and aggregation algorithm for federated averaging. SGD samples a subset of summand functions and updates the weight.

$$w := w - \eta \nabla Q_i(w) \tag{1}$$

SGD is effective and scalable for large training sets coupled with complex gradient calculation formulae. In FedSGD, each participant trains the model in-place with some random samples chosen in every iteration and sends the delta change in the gradient to the central aggregator.

$$w_{t+1} = w_t + \eta \frac{\sum_{k \in S_t} n_k \Delta w_t^k}{\sum_{k \in S_t} n_k} \tag{2}$$

The central aggregator sums up the weighted contributions of the delta updates received from all the participants and updates the global weight. Let the system has a total K number of users. In every iteration, a fraction of clients participates, some may drop out. The set comprising of participating clients be S_t and n_k be the number of samples held by client k with the server having a learning rate of η. Let w_t be the global weight of the previous iteration, server updates it, and evaluates w_{t+1} using distributed approximate Newton method [14].

Federated Learning can help the institutions and individuals owning data to come forward and share the inference over their information to build better predictive models and making research advances. It will also make way for the players involved in healthcare to collaborate. Sensors and devices in hospitals, laboratories, health metrics on smartwatches, and medical reports of individuals can help doctors, scientists, and institutions to learn and prepare better diagnosis.

2.2   Related Work

There have been independent studies citing the benefits of Federated Learning in healthcare and aggregator free learning. Researchers have discussed how multi-institutional secure learning infrastructure can be set up with the help of collaborative learning. For addressing issues of malicious server, various approaches involving cryptographic, distributed and decentralized-distributed techniques have been proposed [8,10,12].

Chen et al. [4] proposed a framework called Fedhealth, claiming to be the first federated transfer learning framework for wearable healthcare. They use existing deep learning techniques and additive homomorphic encryption for classification, distribution, and aggregation. In the proposed framework, the cloud works as a trusted central server, and the participants are present at remote locations. They claim to achieve an improvement of five to six percent accuracy. This work mainly focuses on the data islanding problem and aims to make personalized models for individuals. It lacks formal security analysis and privacy guarantees. Stephen et al. [16] demonstrated classification of positive and negative pneumonia data from a collection of chest X-ray images, relying heavily on the transfer learning approach using a Convolutional Neural Network (CNN) based model for the classification of the image data.

Brisimi et al. [3] proposed a decentralized computationally scalable methodology for large-scale machine learning problems in the healthcare domain. It aims to solve a binary supervised classification problem to predict hospitalizations for cardiac events using a distributed algorithm. They proposed an iterative cluster Primal-Dual Splitting (cPDS) algorithm to solve the problem in a decentralized fashion. They achieved higher convergence at the cost of expensive communication among the agents.

Liu et al. [9] proposed a new method called Federated-Autonomous Deep Learning (FADL) that relies upon training in a distributed manner across largely imbalanced scattered data. This work tried to handle the imbalance by training the first half of the neural globally using data collected from all sources. The second half is trained locally like traditional Federated Learning. They claimed to achieve similar performance to the conventional centralized and Federated Learning methods.

Lu et al. [10] took the communication problem of the distributed training into account and proposed an efficient framework with low latency over a fully decentralized network over the graph. They did the empirical analysis over a fully decentralized non-convex stochastic algorithm, which involves only local updates and communication among the participating nodes. They emphasized the local updates and considered to repeat it for the improved local model in each update. However, they did not talk about the network structure and how to improve the latency over it.

Xu et al. [18] discussed the challenges of incorporating Federated Learning in healthcare. They summarized solutions to system and statistical challenges as well as the privacy issues in Federated Learning. They also analyzed different frameworks[1][2][3] for experiments and simulation over the heterogeneous data available.

Shokri et al. [15] and Deist et al. [5] discussed about pre-federated distributed learning techniques. They proposed key technical innovations like selective sharing of model parameters during training and usage of Support Vector Machine (SVM), solved with Alternating Direction Method of Multipliers (ADMM). Ramaswamy et al. [13] shed light on working over large scale applications. Konevcny et al. [6], Wang et al. [17], Bonawitz et al. [2] and Agarwal et al. [1], made efforts for devising methods of distributed learning, for secure and communication efficient learning. They sketched different algorithms like PRLC, autotuned SecAgg, and cpSGD. Kuo et al. [7] proposed distributed learning using Blockchain technology, which assumes hierarchical network-of-networks.

3   Traditional Frameworks

Most discussed approaches of decentralized Federated Learning use Fully Connected networks. The other less discussed strategies are Pseudorandom, Random, and Cyclic. All of these approaches have their trade-offs like high latency, fault tolerance, and efficiency. We review all these variants in this section, and propose a Binary Tree Representation for the distributed network gaining high efficiency, in the next section, along with the DNet algorithm.

The three traditionally discussed frameworks for distributed networks could be described as follows. In the **Pseudorandom** framework, one node of the network is chosen randomly as root (n1 in Fig. 1a). It establishes connections with all the other nodes. Other nodes make a connection in the network with a probability of 40%. Figure 1a illustrates the Pseudorandom architecture. Figure 1b illustrates the **Cyclic** framework, where all nodes are connected to the next node in a cyclic fashion, i.e., one node is connected to two other adjacent nodes, making a cycle. In the **Fully Connected** framework, each node establishes a connection to the remaining nodes in the network. Figure 1c illustrates Fully Connected architecture.

---

[1] AI, W.: Federated ai technology enabler (2019), https://www.fedai.org/cn/.

[2] Google.: Tensorflow federated (2019), https://www.tensorflow.org/federate.

[3] OpenMined: Pysyft-tensorflow (2019), https://github.com/OpenMined/PySyft-TensorFlow.

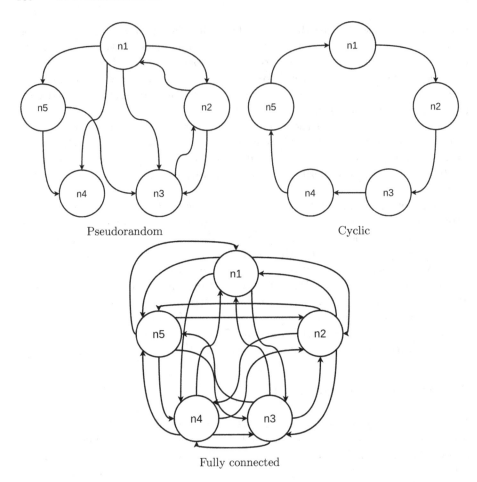

Fig. 1. Traditional distributed net structures (for 5 nodes)

4 Distributed Net

This section discusses the proposed algorithm, which is an aggregator-free Federated Learning approach. It presents an entirely distributed, decentralized system and addresses the existing communication and latency issues.

The basic system setup for Distributed Net architecture with N nodes in the network is as follows. The problem is formulated based on any participant's local data and model. The participant seeks collaboration for an improved global model (It is assumed that the participants are identified with the intersecting data and can contribute to the network). The datasets held by the participants are locally preprocessed, and the respective labels are one-hot encoded. For the purpose of running the experiments, out of $T_{\text{training}} + T_{\text{test}}$ samples of a dataset, each node is given T_{training}/N training samples and T_{test}/N test samples.

Each node trained on (V/V + 1) * (T_{training}/N) samples and validated on (1/V + 1) * (T_{training}/N) samples, where V:1 is train-validation split. Different distributed nets are trained till convergence, and test results are predicted according to the distributed net training algorithm (DNet).

4.1 Training Algorithm (DNet)

Algorithm 1 explains the DNet training algorithm. This algorithm can be used to train any framework (including the ones discussed in previous sections), only by changing the aggregation and propagation algorithms in steps 10 and 11 depending on the DNet variant.

Algorithm 1: Distributed Net Training Algorithm (DNet)

---

1 Train with local data, get $w_j^{ini}, \forall j \epsilon n(nodes)$
2 **while** $epochs(i)$ not complete **do**
3   **for** every node(j) in the net **do**
4   **for** every connection(c) from the node **do**
5   Send w_j^i from n_j to n_c
6              $w_c^i = federated\_average(w_j^i, w_c^i)$
7   Train n_c to get w_c^{i+1}
8   **end**
9   **end**
    /* Aggregation and propagation (Algorithm 2 for Binary Tree Representation). Varies as per the type of framework   */
10     $w_{root}^{i+1} = distributed\_average(w_j^{i+1} \forall j \epsilon n)$
11     $w_j^{i+1} = w_{root}^{i+1} \forall j \epsilon n$
12 **end**

First, all the nodes are trained locally once, to get the initial weights. After that, in every epoch, each node sends its weights to the nodes it is connected to. The receiver nodes take the federated average the incoming and local weights, and then train the model with those weights. Then all weights are aggregated, averaged and propagated, according to different strategies depending on the type of network (For an instance of our network, refer Algorithm 2). Thus, all the nodes have the trained weights at the end of each epoch.

4.2 Binary Tree Representation

This is the proposed architecture for the aggregator free and communication-efficient Federated Learning. Each node is connected to two other nodes like the Cyclic framework but rather form a binary tree instead of a cycle. It has minimum number of connections and ensures that each node is visited only once. Figure 2a and b illustrate the Binary Tree Representation and its tree view.

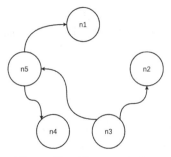

Binary Tree Representation

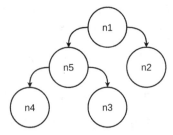

Binary Tree Representation
(Binary Tree View)

Fig. 2. Binary Tree Representation structures

Algorithm 2 lists down the steps involved in the aggregation and propagation of the final model weights in every epoch. The aggregation part, recursively sends the weights of each node to its parent, and sums them up. Eventually, the sum of all the weights reaches the root. At the root, it is divided by the number of nodes to get the average. The propagation part, simply recursively propagates the final weights from every parent node to its children, starting from the root and eventually reaching all the nodes. We can note that, aggregation and propagation happens only on the last step of every epoch, following the same path of Binary Tree, in reverse direction (from leaf to root) for aggregation, and in forward direction (from root to leaf), for propagation. Hence, the extent of privacy preservation is unchanged.

Algorithm 2: Aggregation and Propagation in Binary Tree Representation (Distributed Net)

---

1 **Function aggregation**(n_{root}, *connection matrix, n*):
2   sum = w_{root}
3   **for** *all connections from n_{root} to n_j* **do**
4   Send **aggregation**(n_j, *connection matrix, n*) from n_j to n_{root}
5   sum = sum + **aggregation**(n_j, *connection matrix, n*)
6   **end**
7   **return** sum
8 w_{root} = sum/no. of nodes
9 **Function Propagation**(n_{root}, *connection matrix, n*):
10   **for** *all connections from n_{root} to n_j* **do**
11   Send w_{root} from n_{root} to n_j
12   w_j = w_{root}
13   **Propagation**(n_j, *connection matrix, n*)
14   **end**

4.3   Theoretical Analysis

This provides proof for the claim of gaining communication efficiency in the decentralized Federated Learning using Binary Tree Representation. The system has N nodes connected in a Binary Tree Representation network (Fig. 2a). In every epoch of training, all nodes perform total $3(N-1)$ data transfers (First, weights are passed via the $(N-1)$ connections, which accounts for $(N-1)$ transfers. Aggregation of weights of all nodes to the root and propagation of average weights to all nodes, require $(N-1)$ transfers each. Adding all three, we get a total of $3(N-1)$ transfers per epoch). Let data transferred per epoch, per node, be d units. Hence, total data transferred per epoch by all the nodes would be Nd. Now, total data transferred per transfer, would be $\frac{\text{Total data transferred}}{\text{Total number of transfers}}$ which is $\frac{Nd}{3(N-1)}$.

The communication latency (L) can be seen as $L = L_s + L_r + L_{trans}$ where, L_s is latency at sender, L_r is latency at receiver and L_{trans} is the transmission latency. We are interested in calculating the upper bound for the communication bandwidth. We will calculate the value of γ and bound it to prove our claim.

$$\gamma = \frac{L}{L_{avg}}$$
$$= \frac{L_s + L_r + L_{trans}}{L_{s,avg} + L_{r,avg} + L_{trans,avg}}$$

Let port bandwidths for sender and receiver be B_s and B_r, respectively. Thus, the time required to transfer data would be $\mu_s = \frac{B_s}{d}$ and $\mu_r = \frac{B_r}{d}$ respectively. As per Queuing theory, latency at any node x can be represented as below, where λ is the arrival rate of updates at the device assuming Poisson process.

$$L_x = \frac{1}{\mu_x} + \frac{\lambda}{2\mu_x(\mu_x - d\lambda)}$$
$$= \frac{d}{B_x} + \frac{d\lambda}{2B_x(B_x - d\lambda)}$$

After substituting the values of latency at nodes (L_x) assuming it as sender and receiver respectively, γ can be expressed as:

$$\gamma = \frac{\frac{d}{B_s} + \frac{d\lambda}{2B_s(B_s - d\lambda)} + \frac{d}{B_r} + \frac{d\lambda}{2B_r(B_r - d\lambda)} + \frac{d}{B_{trans}}}{\frac{Nd}{3(N-1)}}{B_s} + \frac{\frac{Nd}{3(N-1)}\lambda}{2B_s(B_s - \frac{Nd}{3(N-1)}\lambda)} + \frac{\frac{Nd}{3(N-1)}}{B_r} + \frac{\frac{Nd}{3(N-1)}\lambda}{2B_r(B_r - \frac{Nd}{3(N-1)}\lambda)} + \frac{\frac{Nd}{3(N-1)}}{B_{trans}}}$$

$$\leq \frac{\frac{d}{B_s} + \frac{d}{B_r} + \frac{d}{B_{trans}} + \frac{d\lambda}{2B_s(B_s - d\lambda)} + \frac{d\lambda}{2B_r(B_r - d\lambda)}}{\frac{N}{3(N-1)}[\frac{d}{B_s} + \frac{d}{B_r} + \frac{d}{B_{trans}}] + \frac{N}{3(N-1)}[\frac{d\lambda}{2B_s(B_s - d\lambda)} + \frac{d\lambda}{2B_r(B_r - d\lambda)}]}$$

$$\gamma \leq \frac{3(N-1)}{N}$$

The above-stated proof states the upper bound as $\frac{3(N-1)}{N}$ for the Binary Tree Representation of DNet. For the other discussed networks, i.e., the Pseudorandom, Cyclic and Fully Connected, with a total number of transfers being

$\sim(0.4N + 2)(N - 1)$, $3N$ and $(N + 2)(N - 1)$ respectively, the bounds turn out to be $\frac{(0.4N + 2)(N - 1)}{N}$, 3 and $\frac{(N + 2)(N - 1)}{N}$. It justifies our claim of proposing an efficient communication framework for decentralized Federated Learning.

5   Experiments

We demonstrate experiments using Convolutional Neural Networks (CNNs) over two medical datasets with the proposed architecture. This section will discuss the dataset and the deep learning architecture used for training.

5.1   Datasets

Two datasets are primarily used for evaluating the proposed DNet algorithm with Binary Tree Representation and compared with other existing frameworks.

Chest X-ray Images (Pneumonia) Dataset[4]

- Number of samples: 5,840
- Sample desc: X-ray images (varying dimensions) of anterior-posterior chests, carefully chosen from retrospective pediatric patients between 1–5 years old.
- Number of classes: 2 (pneumonia (4,265), normal (1,575))
- Figure 3a and b plots some of the samples of this dataset

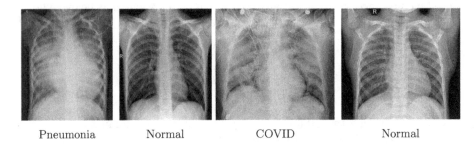

| Pneumonia | Normal | COVID | Normal |

Fig. 3. Examples from the datasets Pneumonia dataset: a and b | COVID-19 dataset: c and d

COVID-19 and Normal Posteroanterior (PA) X-rays Dataset[5]

- Number of samples: 280
- Sample desc: Posteroanterior chest X-ray images (varying dimensions)
- Number of classes: 2 (covid (140), normal (140))
- Figure 3c and d plots some of the samples of this dataset

---

[4] https://www.kaggle.com/paultimothymooney/chest-xray-pneumonia.
[5] https://www.kaggle.com/tarandeep97/covid19-normal-posteroanteriorpa-xrays.

5.2   Training

This section describes the training over both the datasets discussed above using the DNet algorithm with different architectures, with the Convolutional Neural Network (CNN) deep learning configuration as mentioned in Table 1.

Table 1. CNN configuration

Layer (type)	Output shape
Conv2D	(None, 198, 198, 32)
MaxPooling2	(None, 99, 99, 32)
Conv2D	(None, 97, 97, 64)
MaxPooling2	(None, 48, 48, 64)
Conv2D	(None, 46, 46, 128)
MaxPooling2	(None, 23, 23, 128)
Conv2D	(None, 21, 21, 128)
MaxPooling2	(None, 10, 10, 128)
Flatten	(None, 12800)
Dropout	(None, 12800)
Dense	(None, 512)
Dense	(None, 2)

First, we carried the experiment over the Chest X-ray (Pneumonia) dataset. It is a comprehensive dataset with 5840 X-ray images of pneumonia patients and healthy people, thus being a binary classification candidate. The algorithm's effectiveness was tested on a domain problem in this experiment. The dataset was split into a 75:25(3:1) train:test set, implying 4380 training images and 1460 test images. The base classifier was trained on the complete training set (with a 4:1 train:validation split) and tested on 1460 samples. It simulates the scenario where the data from all nodes is pooled, for ground values without federated setup. The complete training ran for 10 epochs. In the federated experiment, the training was conducted in an environment with 5 nodes. The number of local training epochs for each was set to be 10. The number of global iterations to converge the training was set to 2. We implemented all the code in Keras 2.2.4. The optimizer used was Adam and the loss function used for training, was binary crossentropy.

The second experiment was conducted over the COVID-19 and Normal Posteroanterior (PA) X-rays dataset. We ran this experiment to verify our proposed method's performance for a minimal amount of data. It ran with precisely the same configuration, parameters, and hyperparameters as of the first experiment.

6   Results and Discussion

This section discusses the empirical results of all the different experiments performed. It also shows the comparison among the different architectures used with DNet.

The results for both the experiments carried out, i.e., over the Chest X-ray (Pneumonia) dataset and over the small COVID 19 dataset, for five nodes with all the variants of the DNet algorithm are compiled in Table 2. We can infer that the proposed Binary Tree Representation architecture achieves similar performance in less than half the number of computations compared to the Fully Connected variant. The Binary Tree Representation outperforms the traditional variants with the least number of computations.

Table 2. Results of the experiments

DNet architecture	Dataset	n1	n2	n3	n4	n5	Average	Computations per epoch
Base classifier	Pneumonia	-	-	-	-	-	94.66	-
	COVID 19	-	-	-	-	-	95.29	
Pseudorandom	Pneumonia	97.6	95.21	96.58	94.18	95.55	95.824	17
	COVID 19	100	92.86	100	100	100	98.57	
Cyclic	Pneumonia	96.92	95.55	95.55	93.49	92.81	94.864	15
	COVID 19	92.86	100	92.86	92.86	85.71	92.86	
Fully Connected	Pneumonia	96.23	95.55	97.6	95.89	95.2	96.092	28
	COVID 19	85.71	85.71	100	100	78.57	90	
Binary Tree Representation	Pneumonia	93.49	92.12	94.86	95.21	94.86	94.108	12
	COVID 19	100	100	100	100	92.86	98.57	

From the results of the experiments conducted, we can conclude the following about DNet:

– DNet performs well on Image data, which is evident from the results of both the experiments
– DNet handles a real-world healthcare task of image classification, very efficiently. This is made clear by the results of the main experiment.
– DNet also passed the test of performing in the scenario of very less data to train. This is made clear by the results of the second experiment.

All the variants of DNet are on par with the Base classifier in terms of accuracy, while being much more secure and privacy-preserving. The main experiment with the Chest X-ray data showed that this model is feasible to be applied in the healthcare domain and thus, the model established itself. The results show that the DNet was on par with the base classifier and hence, the experiment was a success.

The second experiment was in a different setting, with very less amount of data. Empirically, the results show that the model does perform well in that scenario too. In the case of a very small number of data points, the results tend to depend on particular data points, which means that the results can change drastically due to even one misclassification by the model. Thus some random erratic behavior, for e.g. lower accuracy in node n5, is observed. But overall, the performance of the model was satisfactory.

Comparing the DNet frameworks with each other, we see that all four tend to perform similarly, as results show that all of them are on par with the base classifier, and show about equivalent accuracy measure, in all cases. The main difference comes in the efficiency part. As we can see from Table 2, the Cyclic and Binary Tree Representation frameworks achieve similar accuracy to the other nets, but in very few numbers of computations in comparison. The rate at which the number of computations increases with the number of nodes is as shown in Fig. 4.

We see that Fully Connected framework has a very high rate of increase in the number of computations as the number of nodes increase. The Pseudorandom framework follows with a considerably high rate of increase. Meanwhile, Cyclic and Binary Tree Representation frameworks show a linear increase rate, thus being much more efficient than the other two. (Binary being slightly better, as a number of computations for N nodes, 3N for Cyclic and $3(N-1)$ for Binary Tree Representation). In Fig. 4, due to scale, lines representing Cyclic and Binary Tree Representation networks are very close to each other, Cyclic being slightly above.

As far as robustness is concerned, the proposed Binary Tree Representation framework outclasses the Cyclic one. The collapse of even one node in the Cyclic framework would completely shut down the training procedure. While, in case of Binary Tree Representation network, the part of the tree below the malfunctioned node would get cut off from the training, but this won't stop the process altogether. Thus, considering factors of performance, efficiency, and robustness, the proposed Binary Tree Representation framework is the best option among the four DNet variants we have studied.

There are also certain limitations, a far as the DNet and the Binary Tree Representation are concerned. In case of the DNet as a whole, the training procedure is slow, as compared to a traditional Federated Learning scheme. The absence of a central server, gives rise to more non-simultaneous transfers between nodes, thus increasing the training time, at the benefit of increase in privacy. The proposed Binary Tree Representation framework is very rigid, and thus cannot incorporate nodes entering and exiting while the training is in progress. The number of nodes needs to be fixed beforehand. Also, the framework lacks differential privacy. These are some problems which could be addressed in the future.

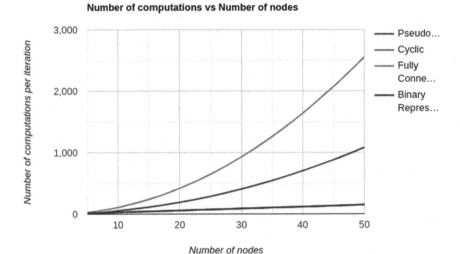

Fig. 4. Rate of increase in the number of computations

7   Conclusion and Future Work

This paper proposed the DNet algorithm with Binary Tree Representation and compared it with the existing frameworks. It aims to set up a decentralized Federated Learning system with low communication latency. It achieved slightly less accuracy by 2% compared to a Fully Connected framework by reducing communication by more than half. We theoretically proved that the communication latency of the Binary Tree Representation has the lower upper bound as compared to the Pseudorandom, Cyclic, and Fully Connected networks. The network is privacy-preserving in nature but prone to inference and poisoning attacks. Many works are already going in this direction and should be incorporated to make this model more secure. There is also scope for research to integrate Multimodality, Selective Parameter Sharing, Transfer Learning, Interoperability, and local compensation for making the network more robust.

References

1. Agarwal, N., Suresh, A.T., Yu, F.X.X., Kumar, S., McMahan, B.: cpSGD: communication-efficient and differentially-private distributed SGD. In: Advances in Neural Information Processing Systems, pp. 7564–7575 (2018)
2. Bonawitz, K., Salehi, F., Konečnỳ, J., McMahan, B., Gruteser, M.: Federated learning with autotuned communication-efficient secure aggregation. arXiv preprint arXiv:1912.00131 (2019)
3. Brisimi, T.S., Chen, R., Mela, T., Olshevsky, A., Paschalidis, I.C., Shi, W.: Federated learning of predictive models from federated electronic health records. Int. J. Med. Inform. **112**, 59–67 (2018)

4. Chen, Y., Qin, X., Wang, J., Yu, C., Gao, W.: Fedhealth: a federated transfer learning framework for wearable healthcare. IEEE Intell. Syst. **35**, 83–93 (2020)
5. Deist, T.M., et al.: Infrastructure and distributed learning methodology for privacy-preserving multi-centric rapid learning health care: euroCAT. Clin. Transl. Radiat. Oncol. **4**, 24–31 (2017)
6. Konečný, J., McMahan, H.B., Yu, F.X., Richtárik, P., Suresh, A.T., Bacon, D.: Federated learning: strategies for improving communication efficiency. arXiv preprint arXiv:1610.05492 (2016)
7. Kuo, T.T., Kim, J., Gabriel, R.A.: Privacy-preserving model learning on a blockchain network-of-networks. J. Am. Med. Inform. Assoc. **27**, 343–354 (2020)
8. Lalitha, A., Kilinc, O.C., Javidi, T., Koushanfar, F.: Peer-to-peer federated learning on graphs (2019)
9. Liu, D., Miller, T., Sayeed, R., Mandl, K.D.: FADL: federated-autonomous deep learning for distributed electronic health record. arXiv preprint arXiv:1811.11400 (2018)
10. Lu, S., Zhang, Y., Wang, Y., Mack, C.: Learn electronic health records by fully decentralized federated learning (2019)
11. McMahan, H.B., Moore, E., Ramage, D., Arcas, B.A.: Federated learning of deep networks using model averaging. CoRR abs/1602.05629 (2016). http://arxiv.org/abs/1602.05629
12. Ramanan, P., Nakayama, K.: BAFFLE: blockchain based aggregator free federated learning (2019)
13. Ramaswamy, S., Mathews, R., Rao, K., Beaufays, F.: Federated learning for emoji prediction in a mobile keyboard. arXiv preprint arXiv:1906.04329 (2019)
14. Shamir, O., Srebro, N., Zhang, T.: Communication efficient distributed optimization using an approximate newton-type method. CoRR abs/1312.7853 (2013). http://arxiv.org/abs/1312.7853
15. Shokri, R., Shmatikov, V.: Privacy-preserving deep learning. In: Proceedings of the 22nd ACM SIGSAC Conference on Computer and Communications Security, pp. 1310–1321 (2015)
16. Stephen, O., Sain, M., Maduh, U.J., Jeong, D.U.: An efficient deep learning approach to pneumonia classification in healthcare. J. Healthc. Eng. **2019** (2019)
17. Wang, H., Qu, Z., Guo, S., Gao, X., Li, R., Ye, B.: Intermittent pulling with local compensation for communication-efficient federated learning. arXiv preprint arXiv:2001.08277 (2020)
18. Xu, J., Wang, F.: Federated learning for healthcare informatics. arXiv preprint arXiv:1911.06270 (2019)

Memory Optimized Dynamic Matrix Chain Multiplication Using Shared Memory in GPU

Girish Biswas$^{(\boxtimes)}$ and Nandini Mukherjee

Department of Computer Science and Engineering, Jadavpur University, Kolkata, IN, India
girishbiswas@gmail.com, nmukherjee@cse.jdvu.ac.in

Abstract. Number of multiplications needed for Matrix Chain Multiplication of n matrices depends not only on the dimensions but also on the order to multiply the chain. The problem is to find the optimal order of multiplication. Dynamic programming takes $O\left(n^3\right)$ time, along with $O\left(n^2\right)$ space in memory for solving this problem. Now-a-days, Graphics Processing Unit (GPU) is very useful to the developers for parallel programming using CUDA computing architecture. The main contribution of this paper is to recommend a new memory optimized technique to solve the Matrix Chain Multiplication problem in parallel using GPU, mapping diagonals of calculation tables $m[][]$ and $s[][]$ into a *single combined calculation table* of size $O\left(n^2\right)$, for better memory coalescing in the device. Besides optimizing the memory requirement, a versatile technique of *utilizing Shared Memory* in Blocks of threads is suggested to minimize time for accessing dimensions of matrices in GPU. Our experiment shows best ever Speedup as compared to sequential CPU implementation, run on large problem size.

Keywords: GPU · CUDA · Matrix chain · Memory mapping · Dynamic programming · Memory optimized technique

1 Introduction

Graphics Processing Unit (GPU) is a common architecture in today's machines that can provide high level of performance in graphical platform using many-core processors. Modern GPU offers the developers to use all cores of processors simultaneously to parallelize the general purpose computing. Many studies [2, 4, 6, 8, 9] have been carried out till date to implement parallel algorithms in CUDA for general computational problems. There are some Streaming Multiprocessors (SM) in a GPU device and each SM comprises of many cores (Fig. 1) which may be allocated to threads in parallel. The whole computation in the device is done over a Grid of some Blocks, where each Block is constituted of some number of threads. NVIDIA GPUs provide the parallel programming architecture, called CUDA (Compute Unified Device architecture) [5].

Using GPU architecture for solving the optimization problems with large number of combinations is challenging due to limited memory in the device and minimum dependency between different threads. The problem of Matrix Chain Multiplication arises in

© Springer Nature Switzerland AG 2021
D. Goswami and T. A. Hoang (Eds.): ICDCIT 2021, LNCS 12582, pp. 160–172, 2021.
https://doi.org/10.1007/978-3-030-65621-8_10

many real time applications such as image processing, modern physics and modelling etc. This optimization problem needs to find the optimal order of multiplication of the matrices.

Dynamic programming approach may be applied to find the optimal solution using GPU [2] with diagonal mapped matrices of calculation for assuring coalesced memory access. This approach uses two 2D calculation tables $m[][]$ and $s[][]$, each of n rows and n columns. So, $O(2 \cdot n^2)$ size memory space is required to be allocated in GPU device, which is made of limited space.

The main contribution of our paper is to suggest an efficient way of using only a single combined calculation table of size $O(n^2)$, to be allocated in the device, mapping diagonals of both of $m[][]$ and $s[][]$ into it (Fig. 3). Our memory optimized approach maintains memory coalescing and shows better results choosing proper Block-size in GPU (Sect. 4.B) for the varying number of elements in the diagonals of the tables. Also, a simple trick is taken in our study to use Shared Memory to store only the required dimensions of matrices (Fig. 4) in Blocks of threads executing in parallel in GPU to reduce the access time for accessing dimensions of matrices to enrich the Speedup even more, compared with sequential implementation run in CPU for large datasets. This paper presents the most effective technique with respect to both memory requirements and performance.

The paper is organized as follows, Sect. 2 illustrates the idea of CUDA programming architecture in GPU device. Section 3 provides the Dynamic Programming Techniques to solve the Matrix Chain Multiplication Problem in GPU. Section 4 discusses about our Proposed Approach. Section 5 discusses about the results. Section 6 concludes the paper.

1.1 Previous Works

As per our knowledge, very few studies have been made on Matrix Chain Multiplication optimization problem until now for parallelizing the problem especially through GPU. In 2011 Kazufumi Nishida, Yasuaki Ito and Koji Nakano [2] proposed an efficient technique of memory mapping to ensure coalesced memory access for accelerating the dynamic programming for the Matrix Chain Multiplication in GPU. The diagonals of $m[][]$ and $s[][]$ were mapped into rows of 2D arrays in a manner that all elements of a diagonal are consecutive in nature. They have passed all the diagonals of m and s tables to GPU one by one for computation of all elements of each diagonal by Blocks of threads in parallel. But, for a problem size of n matrices, this approach takes memory space of size $(2 \cdot n^2)$, where $O(n^2)$ size of memory is wasted. In addition, much time is wasted in accessing the array of dimensions from Global Memory of GPU by the threads of each Block which can be further accelerated with the help of Shared Memory.

Mohsin Altaf Wani and S.M.K Quadri [4] presented an accelerated dynamic programming on GPU in 2013. They have not used any mapping of m table, but simply used single Block of threads for the computation of a single diagonal of m where each thread independently calculates some elements of that diagonal in parallel. This approach suffers from non-coalesced memory access and does not use multiple Blocks of threads also.

2 GPU and CUDA

NVIDIA introduced CUDA^{TM}, a general purpose computing architecture in GPU in 2006. This massive parallel computing architecture can be applied to solve complex computational problems in highly efficient manner with respect to equivalent sequential solution implemented on CPU. Developers may use the high-level language, C in programming with CUDA [3].

2.1 GPU Architecture

GPU consists of several Streaming Multiprocessors (SM) with many cores and mainly two types of memory: *Global Memory, Shared Memory* (Fig. 1) [3]. Also, each SM has number of *registers* which are fastest and local to SM. Each SM has its own Shared Memory, which can be as fast as registers when bank conflict does not happen. Global Memory of higher memory capacity is potentially 150× slower than Shared Memory.

2.2 CUDA

In programming architecture of CUDA [3], parallelism is achieved with bunch of *threads* combined into a *Block* and multiple *Blocks* combined into a *Grid*. Each *Block* is always assigned to a single SM while the *threads* in a Block are scheduled to compute as a *warp* of 32 threads at a time. All threads of a Block can be synchronized within that Block and can access the Shared Memory of that assigned SM only. CUDA permits programmers to write C function, called *Kernel* for parallel computations in GPU using Blocks of threads.

2.3 Coalesced Memory Access

If access requests to Global Memory from multiple threads can be assembled into contiguous location accesses or same location access, this request can be performed at once which is known as *coalesced memory access* [3]. As a result of such memory coalescing, Global Memory works nearly as fast as register memory.

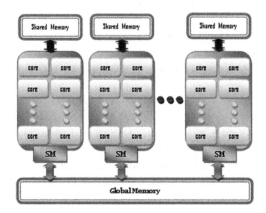

Fig. 1. GPU computing architecture in CUDA

2.4 Shared Memory and Memory Banks

Shared Memory [3, 10] is a collection of multiple banks of equal size which could be accessed simultaneously. Any memory accesses of n addresses from n distinct memory banks can effectively be serviced simultaneously. If multiple threads request to the same bank and to the same address, it is accessed only once and served to all those threads concurrently as multicast at once. However, multiple access requests to different addresses from same bank lead to *Bank Conflict*, which needs much time as requests are served serially [11]. For the GPU devices of compute capability $\geq 2.x$, there are 32 banks with each bank of 32-bits long whereas the warp size is of 32 threads. If multiple threads of a warp try to access data from the same memory address with same bank, there happens no bank conflict also which is termed as multicast. When used with 1Byte/2Byte long data in Shared Memory, each bank contains more than one data. In this case also there is no bank conflict if threads access these data from single bank, as this is taken as multicast [12] in GPU device with compute capability $\geq 2.x$. GPU devices of compute capability $= 2.x$ have the default settings of 48 KB Shared Memory/16 KB L1 cache.

3 Matrix Chain Multiplication Problem

Matrix Chain Multiplication or Matrix chain ordering problem requires to finding the best order for multiplying the given sequence of matrices so that the least number of multiplications are involved. This is merely an optimization problem using the associative property of matrix multiplication. Actually the solution is to provide the fully parenthesized chain of matrices through the optimal order of multiplication.

Provided the Matrix Chain, containing n matrices $\{A_1, A_2, \ldots . A_n\}$, is to be multiplied where $\{d_1, d_2, d_3, \ldots . d_n, d_{n+1}\}$ is the set of all dimensions of these matrices, described as follows:

$$A_1 : d_1 \times d_2$$
$$A_2 : d_2 \times d_3$$
$$\ldots \ldots \ldots \ldots \ldots$$
$$A_n : d_n \times d_{n+1}$$

Now, the problem is to find the order in which the computation of the product $A_1 \times A_2 \times \ldots . \times A_n$ needs the minimum number of multiplications and hence find the fully parenthesized chain denoting the optimal order of multiplication.

3.1 Solving Technique in Dynamic Programming

Dynamic programming is useful for storing the solutions of small sub-problems and reusing them step by step to combine into greater problems and finally finding the solution of the given problem in time efficient approach. Dynamic programming technique [1] makes it easy to solve the above Matrix Chain Multiplication problem with n matrices using a $m[][]$ table, where $m[i, j]$ denotes the minimum number of multiplications needed to compute the sub-problem <Ai x Ai + 1 x....x Aj> for 1 < i < j < n. Minimum cost $m[i, j]$ is calculated using the following recursion:

$$
\begin{cases}
0 & \text{if } i = j \\
\min_{i < k \le j} \{m[i, k] + m[k + 1, j] + d_i d_k d_{j+1} & \text{if } i < j
\end{cases}
\tag{1}
$$

Here "k" is stored in another table $s[][]$ at $s[i, j]$ when the minimum value for $m[i, j]$ is found. Thus $m[1, n]$ refers to the solution for the full problem and $s[][]$ table is used to determine the parenthesized solution of the chain.

Dynamic programming technique requires time of $O(n^3)$.

3.2 Accelerated Dynamic Programming in GPU

Dynamic Programming approach for solving Matrix Chain Multiplication problem can be easily parallelized by computing for the elements of each diagonal of $m[][]$ and $s[][]$ tables in GPU independently in different threads. But, this is inefficient and time-taking due to lack of coalescing in Global Memory access.

Kazufumi Nishida, Yasuaki Ito and Koji Nakano [2] innovated a technique of memory mapping of m and s to ensure coalesced memory access for accelerating the dynamic programming for the Matrix Chain Multiplication in GPU. m and s are mapped into arrays of $n \times n$ memory spaces in Global Memory of GPU along with the array of dimensions of matrices, $d[]$.

Let us take a problem sample of six matrices ($n = 6$):

$$A1 : 20 \times 25, A2 : 25 \times 50, A3 : 50 \times 35$$
$$A4 : 35 \times 10, A5 : 10 \times 40, A6 : 40 \times 30$$

Dynamic programming starts from the base case $m[i][j] = 0$ for $i = j$ i.e., the diagonal-1 (Fig. 2) of m. Then, $m[i][j]$ for each diagonal (upper) is to be computed using recursion (1) where the s table is needed to store values only in upper diagonals 2 to n. Required diagonals of m and s tables are mapped in row by row manner (Fig. 2). GPU kernel may be called for computation of diagonals one by one from diagonal-2 to diagonal-n of m and s, which ensures coalescing.

Here, m and s both table are implemented with an array of $n \times n$ elements of memory size $O(n^2)$. But, in computation we do not need the all locations. Say, the number of memory spaces wasted in m and s are W_m and W_s respectively.

Then, $W_m = \{(n - 1) + (n - 2) + \dots + 2 + 1\} = \sum_{i=1}^{n-1} i = \frac{n(n-1)}{2}$

$$W_s = \{n + (n - 1) + \dots + 2 + 1\} = \sum_{i=1}^{n} i = \frac{n(n + 1)}{2}$$

$$So, W_m + W_s = \frac{n(n - 1)}{2} + \frac{n(n + 1)}{2} = n^2$$

This technique suffers from memory wastage of size $\theta(n^2)$ (i.e. half of the spaces allocated) in GPU which is very limited in storage.

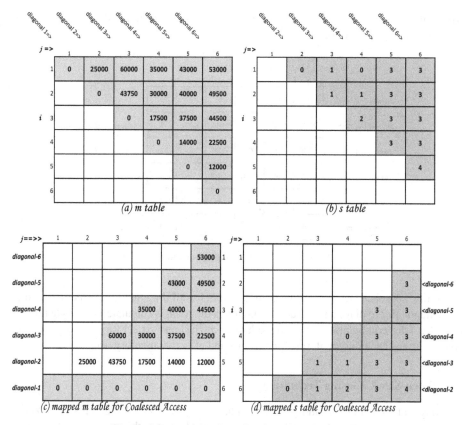

Fig. 2. Memory Mapping of *m* & *s* tables for n = 6

Recursion (1) shows that to compute $m[i][j]$, it needs to access $d_i, d_{i+1}, d_{i+2}, \ldots d_{j+1}$ from the array of dimensions $(d[])$ in Global Memory. All threads of a Block need to access the dimensions same way in GPU kernel for computation of a diagonal as shown in Fig. 4. Though this technique ensures the coalesced access of Global Memory from $d[]$ by the threads, this accessing time from Global Memory can rather be reduced much by our new efficient technique of using Shared Memory, which serves much faster with respect to Global Memory.

4 Proposed Approach

4.1 Combined *m* and *s* Table

The most significant thing in our approach is to optimize the memory spaces allocated in Global Memory of GPU device. Without taking two arrays, we have used only an array of $n \times n$ elements for containing *m* and *s* tables both combined (Fig. 3), using memory mapping [2, 8] for maintaining the coalesced memory access pattern for better efficiency. Our approach not only assures coalescing but also reduces the space complexity to half which offers to solve Matrix Chain Multiplication problem of larger datasets even with limited memory in GPU device.

		1	2	3	4	5	6	
diagonal 1 of m =>	1	0	0	0	0	0	0	
diagonal 2 of m =>	2	25000	43750	17500	14000	12000	3	<= diagonal 6 of S
diagonal 3 of m => i	3	60000	30000	37500	22500	3	3	<= diagonal 5 of S
diagonal 4 of m =>	4	35000	40000	44500	0	3	3	<= diagonal 4 of S
diagonal 5 of m =>	5	43000	49500	1	1	3	3	<= diagonal 3 of S
diagonal 6 of m =>	6	53000	0	1	2	3	4	<= diagonal 2 of S

Fig. 3. Combined table for Mapped m and s for $n = 6$

In this approach, we have done computations for all diagonal elements of m and s from diagonal-2 to diagonal-n. Each element in a diagonal is calculated by single thread in GPU. After computation, updating values of $m[i][j]$ and $s[i][j]$ for $i < j$ assures the coalescing for each diagonal, resulting in fast and effective memory access.

4.2 Block-Size Choosing Technique

l^{th} diagonal (upper) of m and s tables contains $e = n - l + 1$ elements [1]. When computation goes forward from 2nd diagonal to n^{th} diagonal, this number of elements (e) decreases from n to 1. Thus, if B threads/Block are assigned for each diagonal, then the diagonals with $e < B$ do not need the whole Block and some threads remain unutilized in computation. When, e becomes so less with respect to B, most of the threads in the Block are launched in vain.

In previous approach [2], a total Block or multiple Blocks of threads were assigned to the calculation of single element of a diagonal depending on the value of e. We have used a simple approach to assign varying number of threads per Block for e with less number of elements. We need to call the kernel with e/B number of Blocks while Block-size B denotes threads/Block. We have chosen a most suitable value of B provided that some value $\hat{B}$ is taken as threads/Block satisfying $\hat{B} \geq e$ and $\hat{B} mod 32 = 0$ when $e < B$. This technique saves our time, by not launching unnecessary threads for diagonals with few number of elements.

4.3 Using Shared Memory for $d[]$

Similar to m and s tables, $d[]$ array of dimensions of the Matrix Chain is copied to Global Memory in the device. While computation of $m[i][j]$ is done for l^{th} diagonal of m and s, $j = i + l - 1$ and i ranges from 1 to, where number of elements in the diagonal is $e = n - l + 1$ in dynamic programming technique [1]. For computation of $m[i][j]$, it is required to calculate all values of $d_i d_k d_{j+1}$ *for $i < k \leq j$* according to Recursion (1). In kernel, threads in a Block need to access the elements of $d[]$ array in coalesced manner as the threads are accessing contiguous memory locations in parallel (Fig. 4).

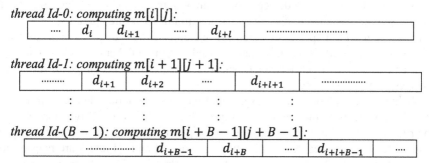

Fig. 4. Memory access patterns by the threads of a Block of Block-size B for l^{th} upper diagonal of m table. Here, $j = i + l - 1$ and $i = B \times b_x + 1$

GPU scheduler schedules Blocks one by one while all threads in that Block compute in parallel in warps of 32 threads at a time. If Block-size is B, then threads have thread-Id from 0 to $B - 1$ for any Block with Block-Id b_x, *where* $0 \leq b_x < e/B$ and e/B is total number of Blocks for l^{th} diagonal (Sect. 4.B). When, thread Id 0 of Block Id b_x is used to calculate the value of $m[i][j]$ (i^{th} element of the lth diagonal), it needs to access values of $d_i, d_{i+1} \ldots d_{j+1}$ i.e., $d_i, d_{i+1} \ldots d_{i+l}$ of $d[]$ as shown in Fig. 4 where $i = B \times b_x + 1$ and $j = i + l - 1$. Though this large number of Global Memory accesses can be arranged with coalesced access pattern, this time for memory accesses from Global Memory can be again reduced, as there is a scope to use Shared Memory to serve this purpose much rapidly.

We have used Shared Memory to reduce the access time and the number of Global Memory accesses. Though all threads run independently, they need to access only the elements of $d[]$ in a range and those values are to be used by multiple threads in that Block. This range is $d_i, d_{i+1} \ldots d_{i+l+B-1}$ (Fig. 4). Therefore, the total Block of threads uses only these $l + B$ elements of $d[]$ from Global Memory. Only these $l + B$ number elements of $d[]$ are copied to Shared Memory for each Block. Each thread of a Block can access Shared Memory of that Block in very fast and effective manner with no bank conflict. If we use 1Byte/2Byte long data for each element of $d[]$, the warp of 32 threads access distinct elements of $d[]$ and results in no bank conflict as discussed in Sect. 2.4 with the help of multicasting. Due to space limitation of Shared Memory, dimensions can be stored as 1Byte long data. We have used this approach along with the memory optimization technique (Sect. 4.1) and hence got very effective results.

5   Performance Evaluation

Tests have been carried out on the Matrix Chains containing different number of matrices whose dimensions are randomly generated in the range [1, 100]. Our experiment is made over a long range of Matrix Chain length (n) i.e. 1000 to 14000 number of matrices in the chain.

We have used NVIDIA GeForce GT 525 M graphics card of 1 *GB* for parallel computation using GPU and Intel Core i5 @2.5 GHz with 4 GB RAM for sequential processing in CPU. Our GPU device is of Fermi architecture [7] which has 16 SMs of 32 cores each, i.e. total 512 cores and allows maximum 1024 threads/Block.

While $e = n - l + 1$ specifies the number of elements in l th diagonal of m table, we obtained the best speed up when we have passed varying number of threads (multiple of 32) for $e < 768$ and 768 threads/Block for $e >= 768$ for l th diagonal for better occupancy in the GPU kernel.

In Table 1, we can compare the execution time (in sec.) of our Memory Optimized Approach in GPU with the Sequential Approach in CPU and other two approaches: Memory Unmapped Approach (diagonals of $m[]$ and $s[]$ tables are not mapped) and previous Memory Mapped Approach (diagonals of $m[]$ and $s[]$ tables are mapped to different arrays). Our Memory Optimized Approach using GPU shows increasingly better performance as the problem size increases in comparison to CPU according to Fig. 5, showing in logarithmic scale.

Table 1. Execution time (in sec.) of the Sequential Approach in CPU and different Approaches in GPU: Memory Unmapped Approach and Previous Technique of Memory Mapped Approach and our Memory Optimized Approach.

Matrix Chain length (n)	Sequential Approach in CPU (t_{seq})	Unmapped Approach in GPU (t_{pll})	Previous Memory Mapped Approach in GPU (t_{pll})	Our Memory Optimized Approach in GPU (t_{pll})
1000	1.2695	2.45833	0.312	0.3058
2000	13.1489	19.81633	1.33893	1.3018
3000	49.5611	66.682	3.96608	3.63
4000	152.9227	155.0192	7.79234	7.0868
5000	253.3594	297.1772	16.69396	13.9917
6000	449.1240	513.3569	26.90393	22.509
7000	793.9893	834.8231	44.34579	36.4512
8000	1441.5231	1243.0041	55.12547	47.5437
9000	1688.754	1761.305	91.98259	75.0826
10000	2295.8261	2411.3491	118.25785	96.9248
11000	3302.2165			137.9615
12000	4844.4406			149.7597
13000	5947.9613			221.5745
14000	9044.3004			254.0719

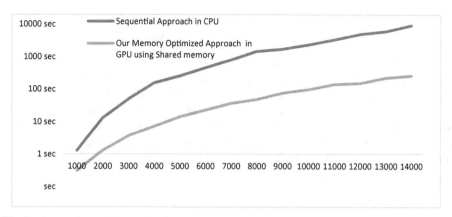

Fig. 5. Comparison of Execution time (in sec.) of Our Memory Optimized Approach in GPU vs. Sequential CPU implementation for $n = 1000\ to\ 14000$.

Speedup factors of the approaches in GPU over the CPU implementation (shown in Table 2) are computed as follows:

Table 2. Speedup achieved by different Approaches in GPU: Memory Unmapped Approach and Previous Technique of Memory Mapped Approach and our Memory Optimized Approach.

Matrix Chain length (n)	Unmapped Approach in GPU (t_{seq}/t_{pll})	Previous Memory Mapped Approach in GPU (t_{seq}/t_{pll})	Our Memory Optimized Approach in GPU (t_{seq}/t_{pll})
1000	0.52	4.07	4.15
2000	0.66	9.82	10.10
3000	0.74	12.50	13.65
4000	0.99	19.62	21.58
5000	0.85	15.18	18.11
6000	0.87	16.69	19.95
7000	0.95	17.90	21.78
8000	1.16	26.15	30.32
9000	0.96	18.36	22.49
10000	0.95	19.41	23.69
11000			23.94
12000			32.35
13000			26.84
14000			35.60

$$Speedup = \frac{Execution\ time\ in\ CPU\ Approach}{Execution\ time\ in\ GPU\ Approach}$$

Our approach acquired as much Speedup as 35.6 (Table 2) for the problem size (*n*) of 14000 matrices in the chain. Due to lack of available space in our GPU device (1 *GB*), other Approaches (Table 1) can be run over the datasets of Matrix Chain of length (*n*) only upto 10000 in our GPU device because of higher memory requirements, whereas our Memory Optimized Approach runs successfully upto Matrix Chain of length (*n*) upto 14000. Speedup factor our approach is compared with other GPU approaches in Fig. 6. It's quite clear that our technique not only requires much less memory in GPU device but also performs all time better.

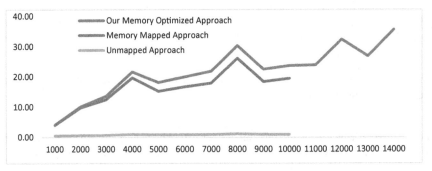

Fig. 6. Comparison of Speedup of Our Approach with other Approaches in GPU for *n* = 1000 *to* 14000.

We have used the Shared Memory to reduce Global Memory Access (Sect. 4.3), but the previous best Memory Mapped Approach used only Global Memory to access the array of Dimensions $d[]$. We have listed the total number of Memory Accesses from the array of Dimensions $d[]$ stored in Global Memory of GPU for Our Approach and the Memory Mapped Approach in Table 3. Our Approach needs much less number of Memory Accesses from $d[]$ as compared to the previous best Approach (Fig. 7). Our Approach is not only better in this access count, but also copies the required portion Global Memory of $d[]$ to Shared Memory in coalesced manner. For there is only 48 KB Shared Memory in our device, here, we took 1Byte space for each element of $d[]$ as it is in the range of [1, 100]. Thus, our Approach reduces the access time to a certain remarkable factor with the help of Shared Memory with no bank conflict.

Table 3. Number of Global Memory Accesses (in million) from the Dimension array $d[]$ in Our Approach and Previous Memory Mapped Approach in GPU

Matrix Chain length (n)	Previous Memory Mapped Approach in GPU (C_1)	Our Memory Optimized Approach (C_2)
1000	16767	103
2000	133733	487
3000	450900	1281
4000	1068266	2614
5000	2085833	4620
6000	3603599	7427
7000	5721566	11164
8000	8539732	15964
9000	12158099	21956
10000	16676666	29268

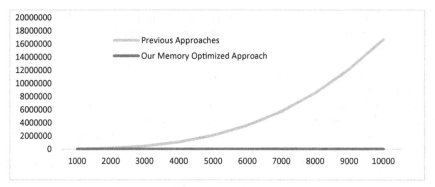

Fig. 7. Comparison of Number of Global Memory Accesses (in million) from the Dimension array $d[]$ between Our Approach and Previous Memory Mapped Approach in GPU for $n = 1000\ to\ 10000$.

6 Conclusion

In this paper, we have presented a new Dynamic Programming technique for parallel processing in CUDA enabled GPU to solve the problem of Matrix Chain Multiplication. All of the previous Approaches, known to us, needed two $n \times n$ size arrays ($O(2.n^2)$) to keep m and s tables which are required in Dynamic Programming to solve this problem. Here, we have suggested a technique to use only one $n \times n$ size array ($O(n^2)$) to which m and s both tables are to be mapped for minimizing the memory requirements in GPU. This allows us to solve problems of Matrix Chain with larger number of matrices in small sized memory in GPU device. Only with the GPU device of 1 *GB* memory, we have successfully run our Memory Optimized Technique upto matrix chain of length 14000, where the other approaches stuck at only 10000.

Another technique, we used, is to copy only the required elements of array of dimensions to Shared Memory. It reduces the memory access time and accelerates the execution of our Memory Optimized Approach. Our approach shows so vigorous results with nearly monotonously increasing speedup with respect to CPU on increasing the problem size and further proficient compared to other approaches. We have achieved the speedup factor of 35.6 over CPU-based approach for a randomly generated chain of 14000 matrices, which is unparalleled to other techniques. As a future scope, our approach could be run on the GPU device with much storage space and predictably, larger speedup could be achieved for larger Matrix Chain compared to other techniques. Hence, our paper proposes a new Memory Optimized and more efficient technique to solve Matrix Chain Multiplication problem using dynamic programming assisted with shared memory. ·

References

1. Cormen, T.H., Leiserson, C.E., Rivest, R.L., Stein, C.: Introduction to Algorithms, 3rd edn. MIT Press and PHI, New Delhi (2012)
2. Nishida, K., Ito, Y., Nakano, K.: Accelerating the dynamic programming for the matrix chain product on the GPU. In: Second International Conference on Networking and Computing, pp. 320–326 (2011)
3. NVIDIA, CUDA C Programming Guide Version 4.2 (2012). https://developer.download.nvidia.com/compute/DevZone/docs/html/C/doc/CUDA_C_Programming_Guide.pdf. Accessed 22 Jun 2020
4. Wani, M.A., Quadri, S.M.K.: Accelerated dynamic programming on gpu: a study of speed up and programming approach. In: Int. J. Comput. Appl., 0975–8887 (2013)
5. NVIDIA, CUDA ZONE. https://developer.nvidia.com/cuda-zone. Accessed 12 Jul 2020
6. Fauzia, N., Pouchet, L.N., Sadayappan, P.: Characterizing and enhancing global memory data coalescing on GPUs. In: IEEE/ACM International Symposium on Code Generation and Optimization (2015)
7. Whitepaper NVIDIA's Next Generation CUDA[TM] Compute Architecture: Fermi[TM]. https://www.nvidia.com/content/PDF/fermi_white_papers/NVIDIA_Fermi_Compute_Architecture_Whitepaper.pdf. Accessed 15 Jul 2020
8. Ito, Y., Nakano, K.: A GPU implementation of dynamic programming for the optimal polygon triangulation. IEICE Trans. Inf. Syst., **D**(12), 2596–2603 (2013)
9. Pimple, M.R., Sathe, S.R.: Analysis of resource utilization on GPU. Int. J. Adv. Comput. Sci. Appl., **10**(2) (2019)
10. Bergeron, J.P.: Programming of shared memory GPUs shared memory systems, University of Ottawa (2011)
11. NVIDIA, DEVELOPER ZONE. https://docs.nvidia.com/cuda/cuda-c-best-practices-guide/index.html#shared-memory. Accessed 26 Jul 2020
12. NVIDIA, Shared memory bank conflicts with byte arrays. https://forums.developer.nvidia.com/t/shared-memory-bank-conflicts-with-byte-arrays/20553/4. Accessed 26 Jul 2020

Graph Algorithms and Security

Parameterized Complexity of Defensive and Offensive Alliances in Graphs

Ajinkya Gaikwad, Soumen Maity$^{(\boxtimes)}$, and Shuvam Kant Tripathi

Indian Institute of Science Education and Research, Pune, India
{ajinkya.gaikwad,tripathi.shuvamkant}@students.iiserpune.ac.in,
soumen@iiserpune.ac.in

Abstract. In this paper we study the problem of finding small defensive and offensive alliances in a simple graph. Given a graph $G = (V, E)$ and a subset $S \subseteq V(G)$, we denote by $d_S(v)$ the degree of a vertex $v \in V$ in $G[S]$, the subgraph of G induced by S. A non-empty set $S \subseteq V$ is a defensive alliance in $G = (V, E)$ if $d_S(v) + 1 \geq d_{S^c}(v)$ for all $v \in S$. A non-empty set $S \subseteq V$ is an offensive alliance in G if $d_S(v) \geq d_{S^c}(v) + 1$ for all $v \in N(S)$. It is known that the problems of finding small defensive and offensive alliances are NP-complete. We enhance our understanding of the problems from the viewpoint of parameterized complexity by showing that (1) the problems are FPT when parameterized by neighbourhood diversity of the input graph, (2) the offensive alliance problem is FPT when parameterized by domino treewidth of the input graph, and (3) the defensive and offensive alliance problems are polynomial time solvable for graphs with bounded treewidth.

Keywords: Defensive and offensive alliance · Parameterized complexity · FPT · W[1]-hard · Treewidth

1 Introduction

In real life, an alliance is a collection of people, groups, or states such that the union is stronger than individual. The alliance can be either to achieve some common purpose, to protect against attack, or to assert collective will against others. This motivates the definitions of defensive and offensive alliances in graphs. The properties of alliances in graphs were first studied by Kristiansen, Hedetniemi, and Hedetniemi [16]. They introduced defensive, offensive and powerful alliances. An alliance is global if it is a dominating set. The alliance problems have been studied extensively during last fifteen years [4,11,20,22,23], and

A. Gaikwad—The first author gratefully acknowledges support from the Ministry of Human Resource Development, Government of India, under Prime Minister's Research Fellowship Scheme (No. MRF-192002-211).

S. Maity—The second author's research was supported in part by the Science and Engineering Research Board (SERB), Govt. of India, under Sanction Order No. MTR/2018/001025.

© Springer Nature Switzerland AG 2021
D. Goswami and T. A. Hoang (Eds.): ICDCIT 2021, LNCS 12582, pp. 175–187, 2021.
https://doi.org/10.1007/978-3-030-65621-8_11

generalizations called r-alliances are also studied [21]. Throughout this article, $G = (V, E)$ denotes a finite, simple and undirected graph of order $|V| = n$. The subgraph induced by $S \subseteq V(G)$ is denoted by $G[S]$. For a vertex $v \in V$, we use $N_G(v) = \{u : (u, v) \in E(G)\}$ to denote the (open) neighbourhood of vertex v in G, and $N_G[v] = N_G(v) \cup \{v\}$ to denote the closed neighbourhood of v. The degree $d_G(v)$ of a vertex $v \in V(G)$ is $|N_G(v)|$. For a subset $S \subseteq V(G)$, we define its closed neighbourhood as $N_G[S] = \bigcup_{v \in S} N_G[v]$ and its open neighbourhood as $N_G(S) = N_G[S] \setminus S$. For a non-empty subset $S \subseteq V$ and a vertex $v \in V(G)$, $N_S(v)$ denotes the set of neighbours of v in S, that is, $N_S(v) = \{u \in S : (u, v) \in E(G)\}$. We use $d_S(v) = |N_S(v)|$ to denote the degree of vertex v in $G[S]$. The complement of the vertex set S in V is denoted by S^c.

Definition 1. For an integer r, a non-empty set $S \subseteq V$ is a defensive r-alliance in G if for each $v \in S$, $d_S(v) \geq d_{S^c}(v) + r$. A set is a defensive alliance if it is a defensive (-1)-alliance.

A vertex $v \in S$ is said to be protected if $d_S(v) + 1 \geq d_{S^c}(v)$. A set $S \subseteq V$ is a defensive alliance if every vertex in S is protected.

Definition 2. For an integer r, a non-empty set $S \subseteq V$ is an offensive r-alliance in G if for each $v \in N(S)$, $d_S(v) \geq d_{S^c}(v) + r$. An offensive 1-alliance is called an offensive alliance.

Informally, given a graph $G = (V, E)$, we say a set S is an offensive alliance if every vertex that is adjacent to S is outgunned by S; more of its neighbours are in S than outside S.

In this paper, we consider DEFENSIVE ALLIANCE and OFFENSIVE ALLIANCE problems under structural parameters. We define these problems as follows:

DEFENSIVE ALLIANCE
Input: An undirected graph $G = (V, E)$ and an integer $1 \leq \ell \leq |V(G)|$.
Question: Is there a defensive alliance $S \subseteq V(G)$ such that $1 \leq |S| \leq \ell$?

OFFENSIVE ALLIANCE
Input: An undirected graph $G = (V, E)$ and an integer $1 \leq \ell \leq |V(G)|$.
Question: Is there an offensive alliance $S \subseteq V(G)$ such that $1 \leq |S| \leq \ell$?

A problem with input size n and parameter k is said to be 'fixed-parameter tractable (FPT)' if it has an algorithm that runs in time $\mathcal{O}(f(k)n^c)$, where f is some (usually computable) function, and c is a constant that does not depend on k or n. What makes the theory more interesting is a hierarchy of intractable parameterized problem classes above FPT which helps in distinguishing those problems that are not fixed parameter tractable. Closely related to fixed-parameter tractability is the notion of preprocessing. A reduction to a problem kernel, or equivalently, problem kernelization means to apply a data reduction process in polynomial time to an instance (x, k) such that for the reduced instance (x', k') it holds that (x', k') is equivalent to (x, k), $|x'| \leq g(k)$ and $k' \leq g(k)$ for some function g only depending on k. Such a reduced instance is called a problem kernel. We refer to [5] for further details on parameterized complexity.

Our results are as follows:

- DEFENSIVE ALLIANCE and OFFENSIVE ALLIANCE problems are FPT when parameterized by neighbourhood diversity of the input graph.
- OFFENSIVE ALLIANCE is FPT when parameterized by domino treewidth of the input graph.
- DEFENSIVE ALLIANCE and OFFENSIVE ALLIANCE problems are polynomial time solvable for graphs with bounded treewith.

Known Results: The decision version for several types of alliances have been shown to be NP-complete. The defensive r-alliance [21] and global defensive r-alliance problems [9] are NP-complete for any r. The defensive alliance problem is NP-complete even when restricted to split, chordal and bipartite graph [13]. Fernau et al. showed that the offensive r-alliance and global offensive r-alliance problems are NP-complete for any fixed r [10]. They also proved that for $r > 1$, r-offensive alliance is NP-hard, even when restricted to r-regular planar graphs. Fernau and Raible showed in [8] that the defensive, offensive and powerful alliance problems and their global variants are fixed parameter tractable when parameterized by solution size k. There are polynomial time algorithms for finding minimum alliances in trees [3,12,13]. A polynomial time algorithm for finding minimum defensive alliance in series parallel graph is presented in [12]. Enciso [6] proved that finding defensive and global defensive alliances is fixed parameter tractable when parameterized by domino treewidth. Bliem and Woltran [1] proved that defensive alliance problem is W[1]-hard when parameterized by treewidth of the input graph. This puts it among the few problems that are FPT when parameterized by solution size but not when parameterized by treewidth (unless FPT = W[1]).

2 FPT Algorithm Parameterized by Neighbourhood Diversity

In this section, we present FPT algorithms for DEFENSIVE ALLIANCE and OFFENSIVE ALLIANCE problems parameterized by neighbourhood diversity. It is known that the problems are fixed parameter tractable when parameterized by vertex cover number [15], which is larger than or equal to neighbourhood diversity. We prove that the problems remain fixed parameter tractable when parameterized by neighbourhood diversity. We say two vertices u and v have the same type if $N(u) \setminus \{v\} = N(v) \setminus \{u\}$. The relation of having the same type is an equivalence relation. The idea of neighbourhood diversity is based on this type structure.

Definition 3 [17]. The neighbourhood diversity of a graph $G = (V, E)$, denoted by $nd(G)$, is the least integer k for which we can partition the set V of vertices into k classes, such that all vertices in each class have the same type.

If neighbourhood diversity of a graph is bounded by an integer k, then there exists a partition $\{C_1, C_2, \ldots, C_k\}$ of $V(G)$ into k type classes. It is known that such a minimum partition can be found in linear time using fast modular decomposition algorithms [24]. Notice that each type class could either be a clique or an independent set by definition. For algorithmic purpose it is often useful to consider a *type graph* H of graph G, where each vertex of H is a type class in G, and two vertices C_i and C_j are adjacent if and only if there is complete bipartite clique between these type classes in G. It is not difficult to see that there will be either a complete bipartite clique or no edges between any two type classes. The key property of graphs of bounded neighbourhood diversity is that their type graphs have bounded size.

2.1 Defensive Alliance

In this subsection, we prove the following theorem:

Theorem 1. DEFENSIVE ALLIANCE *is fixed-parameter-tractable when parameterized by the neighbourhood diversity.*

Given a graph $G = (V, E)$ with neighbourhood diversity $nd(G) \le k$, we first find a partition of the vertices into at most k type classes $\{C_1, \ldots, C_k\}$. Next we guess a set of type classes C_i for which $C_i \cap S \ne \emptyset$, where S is a minimum defensive alliance. Let $\mathcal{P} \subseteq \{C_1, \ldots, C_k\}$ be a collection of type classes for which $C_i \cap S \ne \emptyset$. There are at most 2^k candidates for $\mathcal{P}$. Finally we reduce the problem of finding a minimum defensive alliance S to 2^k integer linear programming (ILP) optimizations with at most k variables in each ILP optimization. Since ILP optimization is fixed parameter tractable when parameterized by the number of variables [7], we conclude that our problem is fixed parameter tractable when parameterized by the neighbourhood diversity k.

ILP Formulation: Our goal here is to find a smallest defensive alliance S of G, with $C_i \cap S \ne \emptyset$ when $C_i \in \mathcal{P}$ and $C_i \cap S = \emptyset$ when $C_i \notin \mathcal{P}$, where $\mathcal{P}$ is given. For each C_i, we associate a variable x_i that indicates $|S \cap C_i| = x_i$. As the vertices in C_i have the same neighbourhood, the variables x_i determine S uniquely, up to isomorphism. The objective here is to minimize $\sum\limits_{C_i \in \mathcal{P}} x_i$ under the condition $x_i \in \{1, 2, \ldots, |C_i|\}$ for $i : C_i \in \mathcal{P}$ and the additional conditions given below. Note that S contains $x_i > 0$ vertices from class C_i if $C_i \in \mathcal{P}$ and contains no vertices from class C_i if $C_i \notin \mathcal{P}$. Let $\mathcal{C}$ be a subset of $\mathcal{P}$ consisting of all type classes which are cliques; $\mathcal{I} = \mathcal{P} \setminus \mathcal{C}$ and $\mathcal{R} = \{C_1, \ldots, C_k\} \setminus \mathcal{P}$. We consider two cases:

Case 1: Suppose $v \in C_j$ where $C_j \in \mathcal{I}$. Then the degree of v in S, that is,

$$d_S(v) = \sum_{C_i \in N_H(C_j) \cap \mathcal{P}} x_i \qquad (1)$$

Thus, including itself, v has $1 + \sum\limits_{C_i \in N_H(C_j) \cap \mathcal{P}} x_i$ defenders in G. Note that if $C_i \in \mathcal{P}$, then only x_i vertices of C_i are in S and the the remaining $n_i - x_i$ vertices of C_i are outside S. The number of neighbours of v outside S, that is,

$$d_{S^c}(v) = \sum_{C_i \in N_H(C_j) \cap \mathcal{P}} (n_i - x_i) + \sum_{C_i \in N_H(C_j) \cap \mathcal{R}} n_i \tag{2}$$

Therefore, a vertex v from an independent type class $C_j \in \mathcal{I}$ is protected if and only if $1 + \sum\limits_{C_i \in N_H(C_j) \cap \mathcal{P}} x_i \geq \sum\limits_{C_i \in N_H(C_j) \cap \mathcal{P}} (n_i - x_i) + \sum\limits_{C_i \in N_H(C_j) \cap \mathcal{R}} n_i$.

Case 2: Suppose $v \in C_j$ where $C_j \in \mathcal{C}$. The number of neighbours of v in S, that is,

$$d_S(v) = (x_j - 1) + \sum_{C_i \in N_H(C_j) \cap \mathcal{P}} x_i \tag{3}$$

This is to ensure that when v is picked in the solution it contributes to the x_j value and hence it itself can't be accounted as its own neighbour. The number of neighbours of v outside S, that is,

$$d_{S^c}(v) = \sum_{C_i \in N_H[C_j] \cap \mathcal{P}} (n_i - x_i) + \sum_{C_i \in N_H[C_j] \cap \mathcal{R}} n_i \tag{4}$$

Thus a vertex v from clique type class $C_j \in \mathcal{C}$ is protected if and only if $d_S(v) + 1 \geq d_{S^c}(v)$, that is, $\sum\limits_{C_i \in N_H[C_j] \cap \mathcal{P}} x_i \geq \sum\limits_{C_i \in N_H[C_j] \cap \mathcal{P}} (n_i - x_i) + \sum\limits_{C_i \in N_H[C_j] \cap \mathcal{R}} n_i$.

In the following, we present ILP formulation of defensive alliance problem, where $\mathcal{P} \subseteq \{C_1, \ldots, C_k\}$ is given:

Minimize $\sum\limits_{C_i \in \mathcal{P}} x_i$

Subject to

$$1 + \sum_{C_i \in N_H(C_j) \cap \mathcal{P}} 2x_i \geq \sum_{C_i \in N_H(C_j)} n_i, \quad \text{for all } C_j \in \mathcal{I},$$

$$\sum_{C_i \in N_H[C_j] \cap \mathcal{P}} 2x_i \geq \sum_{C_i \in N_H[C_j]} n_i, \quad \text{for all } C_j \in \mathcal{C},$$

$$x_i \in \{1, 2, \ldots, |C_i|\} \text{ for all } i \; : \; C_i \in \mathcal{P}.$$

Solving the ILP. Lenstra [18] showed that the feasibility version of p-ILP is FPT with running time doubly exponential in p, where p is the number of variables. Later, Kannan [14] proved an algorithm for p-ILP running in time $p^{O(p)}$. In our algorithm, we need the optimization version of p-ILP rather than the feasibility version. We state the minimization version of p-ILP as presented by Fellows et al. [7].

p-VARIABLE INTEGER LINEAR PROGRAMMING OPTIMIZATION (p-OPT-ILP): Let matrices $A \in Z^{m \times p}$, $b \in Z^{p \times 1}$ and $c \in Z^{1 \times p}$ be given. We want to find a vector $x \in Z^{p \times 1}$ that minimizes the objective function $c \cdot x$ and satisfies the m inequalities, that is, $A \cdot x \geq b$. The number of variables p is the parameter. Then they showed the following:

Proposition 1 [7]. p-OPT-ILP can be solved using $O(p^{2.5p+o(p)} \cdot L \cdot log(MN))$ arithmetic operations and space polynomial in L. Here L is the number of bits in the input, N is the maximum absolute value any variable can take, and M is an upper bound on the absolute value of the minimum taken by the objective function.

In the formulation for DEFENSIVE ALLIANCE problem, we have at most k variables. The value of objective function is bounded by n and the value of any variable in the integer linear programming is also bounded by n. The constraints can be represented using $O(k^2 \log n)$ bits. Proposition 1 implies that we can solve the problem with the guess $\mathcal{P}$ in FPT time. There are at most 2^k choices for $\mathcal{P}$, and the ILP formula for a guess can be solved in FPT time. Thus Theorem 1 holds.

2.2 Offensive Alliance

We also obtain the following result:

Theorem 2 ($\star^1$). OFFENSIVE ALLIANCE *is fixed-parameter-tractable when parameterized by the neighbourhood diversity.*

3   FPT Algorithm Parameterized by Domino Treewidth

It is known that defensive alliance problem is W[1]-hard when parameterized by treewidth of the input graph [1], thus we look at domino treewidth. Enciso [6] proved that finding defensive and global defensive alliances is fixed parameter tractable when parameterized by domino treewidth. In this section, we show that when parameterized by domino treewidth d, the problem of finding smallest offensive alliance is fixed parameter tractable. We now review the concept of a tree decomposition (introduced by Robertson and Seymour in [19]) and introduce some notations that we use in the paper.

Definition 4 [19]. A *tree decomposition* of a graph G is a pair $(T, \{X_t\}_{t \in V(T)})$, where T is a tree and each node t of the tree T is assigned a vertex subset $X_t \subseteq V(G)$, called a bag, such that the following conditions are satisfied:

1. Every vertex of G is in at least one bag.
2. For every edge $uv \in E(G)$, there exists a node $t \in T$ such that bag X_t contains both u and v.

---

1 Due to paucity of space, the proofs of statements marked with a $\star$ have been omitted.

3. For every $u \in V(G)$, the set $\{t \in V(T) \mid u \in X_t\}$ induces a connected subtree of T.

It is important to note that a graph may have several different tree decomposition. Similarly, the same tree decomposition can be valid for several different graphs. Every graph has a trivial tree decomposition for which T has only one vertex including all of V. However, this is not effective for the purpose of solving problems.

Definition 5 [2]. A tree decomposition $(T, \{X_t\}_{t \in V(T)})$ is a *domino tree decomposition* if for $i, j \in V(T)$ where $i \neq j$ and $(i, j) \notin E(T)$, then $X_i \cap X_j = \emptyset$. In other words, in a domino tree decomposition, every vertex of G appears in at most two bags in T.

The *width* of a tree decomposition is defined as $width(T) = max_{t \in V(T)} |X_t| - 1$ and the treewidth $tw(G)$ of a graph G is the minimum width among all possible tree decompositions of G. Similarly, domino treewidth $dtw(G)$ is defined for domino tree decomposition. Note that the number of nodes in a domino tree decomposition remains order n. Moreover, given a graph G with treewidth k and maximum degree Δ, the domino treewidth $dtw(G) \leq (9k+7)\Delta(\Delta+1)$, can be obtained in polynomial time [2].

Let $\tau = (T, \{X_t\}_{t \in V(T)})$ be a domino tree decomposition of the input n-vertex graph G that has width at most d. Suppose T is rooted at node r and $X_r = \emptyset$. For a node i of T, let V_i be the union of all bags present in the subtree of T rooted at i, including X_i. We denote by G_i the subgraph of G induced by V_i.

Let X_i be a non-leaf bag. Then a vertex $v \in X_i$ can be of three types. *Type 1*: v is also in one of the children of X_i; *Type 2*: v is also in the parent of X_i; *Type 3*: v is only in X_i.

For every bag i and every $S_i \subseteq X_i$, a *potential offensive alliance* (pOA) is a smallest set $\widehat{S}_i$ such that $S_i \subseteq \widehat{S}_i \subseteq V_i$, $\widehat{S}_i \cap X_i = S_i$, and $\widehat{S}_i$ protects the vertices of $N_{V_i}(\widehat{S}_i) - parent(X_i)$. We use $c[i, S_i]$ to denote the size of $\widehat{S}_i$. If no such set $\widehat{S}_i$ exists, then we put $c[i, S_i] = |\widehat{S}_i| = \infty$. We now move on to presenting how the values of $c[.,.]$ are computed. We compute the values of $c[.,.]$ at each node i based on the values computed for the children of i. We give a recursive formula for the computation of $c[.,.]$. The values of $c[.,.]$ for leaf node corresponds to the base case of the recurrence; whereas the values of $c[.,.]$ for a non-leaf node i depend on the values of $c[.,.]$ for the children of i. We finally compute $c[r, \emptyset]$ by applying the formulas in a bottom-up manner on T. Note that $c[r, \emptyset]$ is the size of minimum offensive alliance in G; this is due to the fact that $V_r = V(G)$ and $S_r = \emptyset$ (Fig. 1).

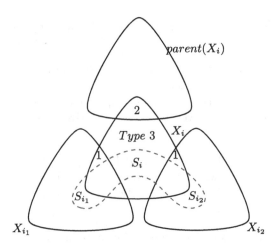

Fig. 1. Compatibility of S_i with S_{i_1} and S_{i_2}. Set S_i is the region bounded by the dotted line in X_i; S_{i_j} is the region bounded by the dotted line in X_{i_j} for $j = 1, 2$.

Leaf Node: If i is a leaf node, then for every $S_i \subseteq X_i \neq \emptyset$, we define $c[i, S_i]$ as follows:

$$c[i, S_i] = \begin{cases} |S_i| & \text{if } S_i \text{ is a non empty subset of } X_i \text{ and protects} \\ & \text{all vertices in } N_{X_i}(S_i) - parent(X_i) \\ \infty & \text{otherwise.} \end{cases}$$

Non Leaf Node: Suppose i is a non-leaf node with two children i_1 and i_2. We say that a set $S_i \subseteq X_i$ is compatible with $S_{i_1} \subseteq X_{i_1}, S_{i_2} \subseteq X_{i_2}$ if and only if

1. $X_i \cap X_{i_j} \cap S_i = X_i \cap X_{i_j} \cap S_{i_j}$ for $1 \leq j \leq 2$.
2. *Type 1* and *Type 3* vertices of $N_{X_i}(S_i \cup S_{i_1} \cup S_{i_1})$ are protected by $S_i \cup S_{i_1} \cup S_{i_2}$.

For $S_i \subseteq X_i$, if there does not exist any $S_{i_j} \subseteq X_{i_j}$ that is compatible with S_i for some j, then $c[i, S_i] = \infty$. Otherwise,

$$c[i, S_i] = |S_i| + min\left\{ \sum_{j=1}^{2} c[i_j, S_{i_j}] - |S_i \cap S_{i_j}| \ : \ S_{i_j} \subseteq X_{i_j}; \ S_{i_1}, S_{i_2} \text{ are compatible with } S_i \right\}.$$

Theorem 3 ($\star$). *For every node i in T and every $S_i \subseteq X_i$, $c[i, S_i]$ is the size of the smallest potential offensive alliance $\widehat{S}_i$ where $\widehat{S}_i \subseteq V_i$ and $\widehat{S}_i \cap X_i = S_i$. Further, the size of the minimum offensive alliance in G is $c[r, \emptyset]$, where T is rooted at node r.*

Note that the definition of compatibility and the above recurrence relation can be easily extended if a non-leaf node i has more than two children. At a non-leaf node we compute 2^{d+1} many $c[.,.]$ values and the time need to compute each of these values is $O(4^{d+1})$, assuming binary domino tree decomposition. As the number of nodes in domino tree decomposition is $O(n)$, the total running time of the algorithm is $O(8^d n)$.

4   Graphs of Bounded Treewidth

Bliem and Woltran [1] proved that DEFENSIVE ALLIANCE is W[1]-hard when parameterized by treewidth, which rules out FPT algorithms under common assumptions. This was surprising as DEFENSIVE ALLIANCE is a "subset problem" and FPT when parameterized by solution size, and "subset problems" that satisfy this property usually tend to be FPT for bounded treewidth as well. In this section we prove that DEFENSIVE ALLIANCE and OFFENSIVE ALLIANCE problems can be solved in polynomial time for graphs of bounded treewidth. In other words, this section presents XP-time algorithms for DEFENSIVE ALLIANCE and OFFENSIVE ALLIANCE problems parameterized by treewidth. We recall some necessary definitions.

Definition 6. A tree decomposition $(T, \{X_t\}_{t \in V(T)})$ is said to be *nice tree decomposition* if the following conditions are satisfied:

1. All bags correspond to leaves are empty. One of the leaves is considered as root node r. Thus $X_r = \emptyset$ and $X_l = \emptyset$ for each leaf l.
2. There are three types of non-leaf nodes:
   - **Introduce node:** a node t with exactly one child t' such that $X_t = X_{t'} \cup \{v\}$ for some $v \notin X_{t'}$; we say that v is *introduced* at t.
   - **Forget node:** a node t with exactly one child t' such that $X_t = X_{t'} \setminus \{w\}$ for some $w \in X_{t'}$; we say that w is *forgotten* at t.
   - **Join node:** a node with two children t_1 and t_2 such that $X_t = X_{t_1} = X_{t_2}$.

Note that, by the third property of tree decomposition, a vertex $v \in V(G)$ may be introduced several time, but each vertex is forgotten only once. Given a tree decomposition $(T, \{X_t\}_{t \in V(T)})$ of width at most k, one can compute a nice tree decomposition of G of width at most k that has at most $O(k|V(G)|)$ nodes.

4.1   Defensive Alliance

In this subsection, we prove the following theorem:

Theorem 4. *Given an n-vertex graph G and its nice tree decomposition T of width at most k, the size of a minimum defensive alliance of G can be computed in $O(2^k n^{2k+4})$ time.*

Let $(T, \{X_t\}_{t \in V(T)})$ be a nice tree decomposition rooted at node r of the input graph G. For a node t of T, let V_t be the union of all bags present in the subtree of T rooted at t, including X_t. We denote by G_t the subgraph of G induced by V_t. For each node t of T, we construct a table $dp_t(A, \mathbf{n}, a, \alpha) \in \{true, false\}$ where $A \subseteq X_t$, $\mathbf{n}$ is a vector of length n, and its ith coordinate is positive only if $v_i \in A$; a and α are integers between 0 and n. We set $dp_t(A, \mathbf{n}, a, \alpha) = true$ if and only if there exists a set $A_t \subseteq V_t$ such that:

1. $A_t \cap X_t = A$
2. $a = |A_t|$

3. the ith coordinate of vector $\mathbf{n}$ is

$$n(i) = \begin{cases} d_{A_t}(v_i) & \text{for } v_i \in A \\ 0 & \text{otherwise} \end{cases}$$

4. α is the number of vertices $v \in A_t$ that are protected, that is, $d_{A_t}(v) \geq \frac{d_G(v)-1}{2}$.

We compute all entries $dp_t(A, \mathbf{n}, a, \alpha)$ in a bottom-up manner. Since $tw(T) \leq k$, at most $2^k n^k (n+1)^2 = O(2^k n^{k+2})$ records are maintained at each node t. Thus, to prove Theorem 4, it suffices to show that each entry $dp_t(A, \mathbf{n}, a, \alpha)$ can be computed in $O(n^{k+2})$ time, assuming that the entries for the children of t are already computed.

Leaf Node: For leaf node t we have that $X_t = \emptyset$. Thus $dp_t(A, \mathbf{n}, a, \alpha)$ is true if and only if $A = \emptyset$, $\mathbf{n} = \mathbf{0}$, $a = 0$ and $\alpha = 0$. These conditions can be checked in $O(1)$ time.

Introduce Node: Suppose t is an introduction node with child t' such that $X_t = X_{t'} \cup \{v_i\}$ for some $v_i \notin X_{t'}$. Let A be any subset of X_t. We consider two cases:

Case (i): Let $v_i \notin A$. In this case $dp_t(A, \mathbf{n}, a, \alpha)$ is true if and only if $dp_{t'}(A, \mathbf{n}, a, \alpha)$ is true.

Case (ii): Let $v_i \in A$. Here $dp_t(A, \mathbf{n}, a, \alpha)$ is true if and only if there exist $A', \mathbf{n}', a'$, and α' such that $dp_{t'}(A', \mathbf{n}', a', \alpha')$=true, where

1. $A = A' \cup \{v_i\}$;
2. $n(j) = n'(j) + 1$, if $v_j \in N_A(v_i)$, $n(i) = d_A(v_i)$, and $n(j) = n'(j)$ if $v_j \in A \setminus N_A[v_i]$;
3. $a = a' + 1$;
4. $\alpha = \alpha' + \delta$; here δ is the cardinality of the set

$$\left\{ v_j \in A \mid n'(j) < \frac{d_G(v_j) - 1}{2}; n(j) \geq \frac{d_G(v_j) - 1}{2} \right\}.$$

That is, to compute α from α' we need to add the number δ of those vertices not satisfied in $(A', \mathbf{n}', a', \alpha')$ but satisfied in $(A, \mathbf{n}, a, \alpha)$.

For introduce node t, $dp_t(A, \mathbf{n}, a, \alpha)$ can be computed in $O(1)$ time. This follows from the fact that there is only one candidate of such tuple $(A', \mathbf{n}', a', \alpha')$.

Forget Node: Suppose t is a forget node with child t' such that $X_t = X_{t'} \setminus \{v_i\}$ for some $v_i \in X_{t'}$. Let A be any subset of X_t. Here $dp_t(A, \mathbf{n}, a, \alpha)$ is true if and only if either $dp_{t'}(A, \mathbf{n}, a, \alpha)$ is true (this corresponds to the case that A_t does not contain v_i) or $dp_{t'}(A', \mathbf{n}', a, \alpha)$=true for some $A', \mathbf{n}'$ with the following conditions:

1. $A = A' \setminus \{v_i\}$;
2. $n(j) = n'(j)$ for all $j \neq i$ and $n(i) = 0$;

(this corresponds to the case that A_t contains v_i). For forget node t, $dp_t(A, \mathbf{n}, a, \alpha)$ can be computed in $O(n)$ time. This follows from the fact that there are $O(n)$ candidates of such tuple $(A', \mathbf{n}', a, \alpha)$.

Join Node: Suppose t is a join node with children t_1 and t_2 such that $X_t = X_{t_1} = X_{t_2}$. Let A be any subset of X_t. Then $dp_t(A, \mathbf{n}, a, \alpha)$ is true if and only if there exist $(A_1, \mathbf{n_1}, a_1, \alpha_1)$ and $(A_2, \mathbf{n_2}, a_2, \alpha_2)$ such that $dp_{t_1}(A_1, \mathbf{n_1}, a_1, \alpha_1) = $ true and $dp_{t_2}(A_2, \mathbf{n_2}, a_2, \alpha_2) = $ true, where

1. $A = A_1 = A_2$;
2. $n(i) = n_1(i) + n_2(i) - d_A(v_i)$ for all $i \in A$, and $n(i) = 0$ if $i \notin A$;
3. $a = a_1 + a_2 - |A|$;
4. $\alpha = \alpha_1 + \alpha_2 - \gamma + \delta$; γ is the cardinality of the set

$$\left\{ v_j \in A \mid n_1(j) \geq \frac{d_G(v_i) - 1}{2}; \; n_2(j) \geq \frac{d_G(v_i) - 1}{2} \right\}$$

and δ is the cardinality of the set

$$\left\{ v_j \in A \mid n_1(j) < \frac{d_G(v_i) - 1}{2}; \; n_2(j) < \frac{d_G(v_i) - 1}{2}; \; n(j) \geq \frac{d_G(v_i) - 1}{2} \right\}.$$

To compute α from $\alpha_1 + \alpha_2$, we need to subtract the number of those v_j which are satisfied in both the branches and add the number of vertices v_j not satisfied in either of the branches t_1 and t_1 but satisfied in t.

For join node t, there are n^k possible pairs for $(\mathbf{n_1}, \mathbf{n_2})$ as $\mathbf{n_2}$ is uniquely determined by $\mathbf{n_1}$; $n+1$ possible pairs for (a_1, a_2); and $n+1$ possible pairs for (α_1, α_2). In total, there are $O(n^{k+2})$ candidates, and each of them can be checked in $O(1)$ time. Thus, for join node t, $dp_t(A, \mathbf{n}, a, \alpha)$ can be computed in $O(n^{k+2})$ time.

At the root node r, we look at all records such that $dp_r(\emptyset, \mathbf{n}, a, \alpha) = $ true, $a, \alpha > 0$ and $a = \alpha$. The size of a minimum defensive alliance is the minimum a satisfying $dp_r(\emptyset, \mathbf{n}, a, a) = $ true and $a > 0$.

4.2 Offensive Alliance

We also obtain the following result:

Theorem 5 ($\star$). *Given an n-vertex graph G and its nice tree decomposition T of width at most k, the size of a minimum offensive alliance of G can be computed in $O(2^k n^{2k+6})$ time.*

5 Conclusion

In this work we proved that DEFENSIVE ALLIANCE and OFFENSIVE ALLIANCE problems are FPT when parameterized by neighbourhood diversity; OFFENSIVE ALLIANCE is FPT when parameterized by domino treewidth; DEFENSIVE ALLIANCE and OFFENSIVE ALLIANCE problems are solvable in polynomial time on graphs of bounded treewidth. The paramererized complexity of different kinds of alliances such as offensive alliance or powerful alliance remains unsettled when parameterized by clique-width, treewidth or pathwidth.

Acknowledgement. We are grateful to the referees for thorough reading and comments that have made the paper better readable. We would like to thank Prof. Saket Saurabh, IMSc Chennai, for giving us the open problems on defensive and offensive alliances.

References

1. Bliem, B., Woltran, S.: Defensive alliances in graphs of bounded treewidth. Discret. Appl. Math. **251**, 334–339 (2018)
2. Bodlaender, H.L., Engelfriet, J.: Domino treewidth. J. Algorithms **24**(1), 94–123 (1997)
3. Chang, C.-W., Chia, M.-L., Hsu, C.-J., Kuo, D., Lai, L.-L., Wang, F.-H.: Global defensive alliances of trees and cartesian product of paths and cycles. Discret. Appl. Math. **160**(4), 479–487 (2012)
4. Chellali, M., Haynes, T.W.: Global alliances and independence in trees. Discuss. Math. Graph Theory **27**(1), 19–27 (2007)
5. Cygan, M., et al.: Parameterized Algorithms. Springer, Cham (2015). https://doi.org/10.1007/978-3-319-21275-3
6. Enciso, R.: Alliances in graphs: parameterized algorithms and on partitioning series-parallel graphs. Ph.D. thesis, USA (2009)
7. Fellows, M.R., Lokshtanov, D., Misra, N., Rosamond, F.A., Saurabh, S.: Graph layout problems parameterized by vertex cover. In: Hong, S.-H., Nagamochi, H., Fukunaga, T. (eds.) ISAAC 2008. LNCS, vol. 5369, pp. 294–305. Springer, Heidelberg (2008). https://doi.org/10.1007/978-3-540-92182-0_28
8. Fernau, H., Raible, D.: Alliances in graphs: a complexity-theoretic study. In: Proceeding Volume II of the 33rd International Conference on Current Trends in Theory and Practice of Computer Science (2007)
9. Fernau, H., Rodríguez-Velázquez, J.A., Sigarreta, J.M.: Global r-alliances and total domination. In: CTW (2008)
10. Fernau, H., Rodríguez, J.A., Sigarreta, J.M.: Offensive r-alliances in graphs. Discret. Appl. Math. **157**(1), 177–182 (2009)
11. Fricke, G., Lawson, L., Haynes, T., Hedetniemi, M., Hedetniemi, S.: A note on defensive alliances in graphs. Bull. Inst. Comb. Appl. **38**, 37–41 (2003)
12. Jamieson, L.H.: Algorithms and complexity for alliances and weighted alliances of various types. Ph.D. thesis, USA (2007)
13. Jamieson, L.H., Hedetniemi, S.T., McRae, A.A.: The algorithmic complexity of alliances in graphs. J. Comb. Math. Comb. Comput. **68**, 137–150 (2009)
14. Kannan, R.: Minkowski's convex body theorem and integer programming. Math. Oper. Res. **12**(3), 415–440 (1987)

15. Kiyomi, M., Otachi, Y.: Alliances in graphs of bounded clique-width. Discret. Appl. Math. **223**, 91–97 (2017)
16. Kristiansen, P., Hedetniemi, M., Hedetniemi, S.: Alliances in graphs. J. Comb. Math. Comb. Comput. **48**, 157–177 (2004)
17. Lampis, M.: Algorithmic meta-theorems for restrictions of treewidth. Algorithmica **64**, 19–37 (2012)
18. Lenstra, H.W.: Integer programming with a fixed number of variables. Math. Oper. Res. **8**(4), 538–548 (1983)
19. Robertson, N., Seymour, P.: Graph minors. III. Planar tree-width. J. Comb. Theory Ser. B **36**(1), 49–64 (1984)
20. Rodríguez-Velázquez, J., Sigarreta, J.: Global offensive alliances in graphs. Electron. Notes Discret. Math. **25**, 157–164 (2006)
21. Sigarreta, J., Bermudo, S., Fernau, H.: On the complement graph and defensive k-alliances. Discret. Appl. Math. **157**(8), 1687–1695 (2009)
22. Sigarreta, J., Rodríguez, J.: On defensive alliances and line graphs. Appl. Math. Lett. **19**(12), 1345–1350 (2006)
23. Sigarreta, J., Rodríguez, J.: On the global offensive alliance number of a graph. Discret. Appl. Math. **157**(2), 219–226 (2009)
24. Tedder, M., Corneil, D., Habib, M., Paul, C.: Simpler linear-time modular decomposition via recursive factorizing permutations. In: Aceto, L., Damgård, I., Goldberg, L.A., Halldórsson, M.M., Ingólfsdóttir, A., Walukiewicz, I. (eds.) ICALP 2008. LNCS, vol. 5125, pp. 634–645. Springer, Heidelberg (2008). https://doi.org/10.1007/978-3-540-70575-8_52

A Reconstructive Model for Identifying the Global Spread in a Pandemic

Debasish Pattanayak[1] , Dibakar Saha[2]([⊠]) , Debarati Mitra[3],
and Partha Sarathi Mandal[2]

[1] Cryptology and Security Research Unit, Indian Statistical Institute, Kolkata, India
drdebmath@gmail.com
[2] Department of Mathematics, Indian Institute of Technology Guwahati, Guwahati,
Assam, India
dibakar.saha10@gmail.com, psm@iitg.ac.in
[3] Department of Chemistry, Royal Global University, Guwahati, Assam, India
debarati.mitra@rgi.edu.in

Abstract. With existing tracing mechanisms, we can quickly identify potentially infected people with a virus by choosing everyone who has come in contact with an infected person. In the presence of abundant resources, that is the most sure-fire way to contain the viral spread. In the case of a new virus, the methods for testing and resources may not be readily available in ample quantity. We propose a method to determine the highly susceptible persons such that under limited testing capacity, we can identify the spread of the virus in a community. We determine highly suspected persons (represented as nodes in a graph) by choosing paths between the infected nodes in an underlying contact graph (acquired from location data). We vary parameters such as the *infection multiplier, false positive ratio,* and *false negative ratio.* We show the relationship between the parameters with the *test positivity ratio* (the number of infected nodes to the number of suspected nodes). We observe that our algorithm is robust enough to handle different infection multipliers and false results while producing suspected nodes. We show that the suspected nodes identified by the algorithm result in a high test positivity ratio compared to the real world. Based on the availability of the test kits, we can run our algorithm several times to get more suspected nodes. We also show that our algorithm takes a finite number of iterations to determine all the suspected nodes.

Keywords: Pandemic · Spread · Infection transmission tree · Location tracking · COVID-19

Dibakar Saha would like to acknowledge the Science and Engineering Research Board (SERB), Government of India, for financial support under the NPDF scheme (File Number: PDF/2018/000633).

D. Goswami and T. A. Hoang (Eds.): ICDCIT 2021, LNCS 12582, pp. 188–202, 2021.
https://doi.org/10.1007/978-3-030-65621-8_12

1 Introduction

In any pandemic, the infection grows fast worldwide. In the absence of a proper medicine or vaccine, to control the spreading; social distancing, self-quarantine, and wearing a face mask have been widely-used strategies for mitigation. In this context, mathematical models are required to estimate virus transmission, recovery, and deaths. A well known Susceptible-Infected-Removed (SIR) model provides a theoretical framework to investigate the spread of a virus in a pandemic. Cooper *et al.* [1] use the classical SIR model to study how the COVID-19 virus spreads within communities. The delivery of infection from asymptomatic carriers of COVID-19 in a familial cluster has been studied [2,3]. It is also the utmost requirement to find such asymptomatic carriers within a community or in a particular area such as a village, small town, to control the spreading of the disease. Hence, we propose a generalized model that can identify highly suspected persons and asymptomatic carriers efficiently.

In this model, we use an estimation of the length of the infectiousness of COVID-19. It takes 5 to 6 days on an average for a COVID-19 infected person to show symptoms [4]. He *et al.* [5] show that around 9% of transmission would occur three days before the onset of symptoms. Hence it is a reasonable estimate that we consider a person infected with the virus can spread the virus to other people after three days of infection [5,6]. Another marker is the duration of infectivity [7]. A person spreads the virus throughout the symptomatic period and stops spreading the virus after recovery from symptoms and develops immunity to the virus. Furthermore, all infected persons do not transmit the virus [7].

In any pandemic, the greatest challenge is identifying the infected people in an initial stage so that the probability of spreading the infection gets minimized. COVID-19, caused by the dreaded coronavirus, is an example of such a pandemic. Some companies, including Google, and Apple, along with many countries like India, China, and South Korea, are engaged in tracking the infected people by using the location data of their cell phones via apps. This tracking data can be used to construct a graph where each node represents a person. Now, if the nodes have been in contact with each other, then there exists an edge between two nodes. From location data, it can be determined whether a person has come within 2 m of range of another person or not. The resulting graph is a *contact graph*.

We may have a partial data of infected persons for k^{th} and $(k + i)^{th}$ days, where $i \geq 1$. With such data, we try to find the intermediate carriers responsible for spreading the infection. To find such intermediate nodes is very challenging where the infection proliferates over time. Let $G = (V, E)$ is the contact graph constructed, as discussed above. Since the most treacherous fact is that any person can transmit the virus unknowingly being asymptomatic, it is essential to determine the links to cease the spread.

Our Contributions. In this paper, we aim to identify the highly suspected persons infected with the virus in a pandemic so that those persons are to be tested or quarantined to prevent the spreading of the virus and make the following contributions. Our approach works by determining links that connect one infected

person to another in the underlying contact graph. We simulate our proposed
method on some ground-truth datasets assumed as the contact graph, such as
`Dolphin`, `Zachary karate club`, `Football`, and `Facebook ego`. The spread of
the virus is modeled as an infection transmission tree over the contact graph.

- We present an algorithm to determine a set of nodes that are highly suspected
  of having been infected.
- We show the robustness of our algorithm even with changing infection parameters as well as false positive and false negative results included.
- Our algorithm results in a high test positivity ratio (70%) compared to the
  real world (10%).
- The algorithm can be run multiple times to generate suspected nodes by
  including the results of previously identified suspected nodes to get a new set
  of suspected nodes. This is useful when the availability of test kits is limited.
- We show the number of times our algorithm needs to run before it terminates.
  Our algorithm determines more than 80% of the infected nodes on an average.

Outline. The rest of the paper is organized as follows: In Sect. 2, we present the
preliminaries and formulation of the problem. Section 3 describes the proposed
algorithms. Section 5 shows the performance evaluation of the proposed method.
Finally, Sect. 6 concludes the paper.

2 Preliminaries

In this section, we define the notations and describe the problem.

2.1 Notations

Given location data of persons, we construct a *contact graph* at time t, $G = (V, E)$ such that V is the set of persons, and each person is represented as a
node. There exists an edge between two nodes if the distance between any two
nodes has been less than $2\,m$ at some time $t' \leq t$. We define the set of symbols
used in Table 1.

Table 1. Notations

Notation	Description	Notation	Description
G	The contact graph	V	Set of nodes
E	Set of edges	λ	Infection multiplier
h	Maximum hop distance	T_i	i^{th} time interval
I_{T_i}	Infected node list at time T_i	S	Set of suspected nodes
S^+	Set of positive nodes	C	Set of carrier nodes
P	Set of paths	Δ	Maximum degree of the graph
Φ	Cutoff length of a path	ℓ	Number of paths
$|\cdot|$	Size of the set	$test\_results$	Test result of the nodes

2.2   Problem Formulation

Let $G(V, E)$ be an undirected unweighted graph, where V is a set of vertices or nodes, and E is a set of edges generated from the location data. Let $G' = (V', E')$ be a subgraph of G, where V' is a set of nodes infected with the virus, and E' represents a set of connections among the nodes in V'. G' can be considered the *infection transmission tree* of the virus on the graph G. The structure of G' is cycle-free because an infected node cannot be infected again, and since we consider the edge from the first node that infects another node. Hence, G' maybe a forest. We may not have the complete information of all the nodes with the virus. With tests performed on people with symptoms, we can determine a subset of V' with the virus by time T_j. Our objective is to determine the graph G', which represents the actual spread of the virus. This may not be possible due to the availability of partial information about the nodes carrying the virus. The available partial information is the positive test results that have been done in the past. We have two sets of nodes with confirmed positive test cases denoted as I_{T_i} and I_{T_j}, where $T_i < T_j$. So, we try to determine a set $C \subseteq V$, which is the set of suspected nodes. We have $I = C \cup I_{T_i} \cup I_{T_j}$, which should be very close to the set V'. The symmetric difference of two sets measures the closeness of two sets. If two sets are identical, then their symmetric difference is null. We have the following problem definition.

Problem Definition. Given a contact graph G, and two sets I_{T_i} and I_{T_j}, the target is to determine $I \subseteq V$ that minimizes the symmetric difference of V' and I, i.e., $minimize((V' \cup I) \setminus (V' \cap I))$.

3   Find Suspected Nodes from I_{T_i} and I_{T_j}

In this section, we describe Algorithm 1 (*Find_Infected_nodes*). The algorithm consists of Procedure 1 (*Find_suspected_nodes*) as a subroutine. We have a set I as an input that contains the day wise test results on $T = \{T_0, T_1, \ldots, T_t\}$. We determine I_{T_i} as the set of nodes infected before T_i and $I + T_j$ as the set of nodes infected between T_i and T_j. Given two sets of nodes I_{T_i} and I_{T_j} as input, Procedure 1 finds a set of nodes S as the output. To find the suspected node set S, we compute paths between nodes in I_{T_i} and I_{T_j}. To choose paths that are more likely to contain the infected nodes, we define infection parameters for the nodes. The infection parameter of a node depends on the hop distance from a known infected node, and the infection parameter of a path is the average of infection parameter of the nodes. Based on this, we determine the paths between nodes with high infection parameters. We choose the first ℓ paths in the decreasing order of the infection parameter. The suspected nodes S contains the intermediate nodes of these paths that are not present in I_{T_i} and I_{T_j}. Algorithm 1 runs with a feedback process. We can run the procedure once with I_{T_i} and I_{T_j}; and then we get S. Tests can be conducted for the nodes in S, and we determine S^+ as the set of nodes that tested positive. With this added input S^+, we can rerun Procedure 1 to find the next set of suspected nodes. We can continue this process until the number of tests available is exhausted. If we have sufficient test kits for the entire population, that is the best way to determine the spread of the virus. When a limited number of test kits available, it is better to test only the highly suspected nodes.

3.1 Infection Criteria

The COVID-19 virus has spread rapidly. Hence, testing and identification of the infected nodes are essential to prevent the spread. COVID-19 can infect people from another infected person. The virus can be spread from one person to another through small droplets from the nose or mouth, released when a person with COVID-19 coughs or exhales. These droplets land on objects and surfaces around the person. Other people may get infected when they touch those objects or surfaces, touching their eyes, nose, or mouth. People can also catch COVID-19 if they breathe in droplets from a person with COVID-19 who coughs out or exhales droplets that can travel up to $2\,m$ from an infected person with high concentration.

Infection Parameter for a Node. The COVID-19 virus can infect people from another infected person. Thus, we consider that a node may get infected by its infected neighbors, and the chance of infection depends on the hop distance from an infected node. Let λ_i be the infection parameter at hop distance i. Let k_i be the number of infected neighbors of a node u at a hop distance i. Here we define the infection parameter of a node u as

$$\mathcal{P}(u) = \sum_{i=1}^{h} \lambda_i k_i, \tag{1}$$

where h is the maximum hop distance considered.

Infection Parameter for a Path. Let u and v be two infected nodes with causal relation as u has been infected before v. By causal relation, there should be a transmission path of the virus from u to v. We can determine multiple paths from u to v. Now, we need to determine the most probable path that the virus has followed. If a path contains multiple nodes with suspected infection, it is a more likely path of virus transmission.

We determine the parameter of transmission along i^{th} path P_{uv}^i as the sum of the infection parameter of the path P_{uv}^i. Let $P_{uv}^i = (u, u_1, u_2, \ldots, u_l, v)$ be a path. The average infection parameter is

$$\mathcal{P}(P_{uv}^i) = \frac{1}{l} \sum_{j=1}^{l} \mathcal{P}(u_j) \tag{2}$$

3.2   Algorithm to Find Suspected Nodes

Initially, we are given a graph $G(V, E)$, which is a Geo-location-based network. We also have day wise test results, i.e., a set of time intervals $T = \{T_1, T_2, \ldots, T_t\}$, where for each $T_i \in T$, we have a list of infected nodes. We are given a graph G and two lists of infected nodes I_{T_i} and I_{T_j} corresponding to infected nodes before T_i and infected nodes between T_i and T_j, where $T_i < T_j$. We aim to propose an algorithm to find the intermediate nodes responsible for spreading the infection among the nodes in I_{T_j}. Thus, the algorithm can detect the carrier or infected nodes to be tested to prevent the infection's spreading. This algorithm executes the following steps.

Step-1: First, we compute the infection parameter $\mathcal{P}(u)$ of each node $u \in G(V)$.

Step-2: Next, for each pair of nodes $u \in I_{T_i}$ and $v \in I_{T_j}$, we explore all paths of length less than or equal to Φ. Let $P_{u,v} = \{P^1_{u,v}, P^2_{u,v}, \cdots, P^m_{u,v}\}$ be the set of paths from u to v in the graph G, where the ith path $P^i_{u,v} = \{u, u_1, u_2, \ldots, u_l, v\}$. Here, u_j, $j = 1, \ldots, l$, are the intermediate nodes in the path $P^i_{u,v} \in P_{u,v}$. We extract the first ℓ paths in the decreasing order of $\mathcal{P}(P_{u,v})$.

Step-3: Once we extracted all the paths $P = \{P_{u,v}, P_{u,v'}, \ldots\}$, we discard those paths having at least one intermediate node has tested report negative (not infected) or all intermediate nodes are tested positive. Hence, for each path $P_{u,v} \in P$, we check each of the intermediate nodes test reports. If at least one node has a negative report, then we discard that path from P. Here, only the positive or not tested cases are considered.

Step-4: Once we find all such paths, we report the updated P and all the intermediate nodes that are to be tested.

3.3   Example

In this example, we start with the **Zachary Karate club** network as the initial graph $G(V, E)$, as shown in Fig. 1(a). The corresponding underlying is shown in Fig. 1(b). In the infection transmission tree, all the nodes are infected.

- We first compute the infection parameter $\mathcal{P}(u)$, for each node $u \in G$. We get
$\mathcal{P} = \{1, 0.87, 0.87, 0.87, 1, 0.87, 0.87, 0.66, 0.66, 0.27, 1, 0.66, 0.66, 1, 0.18, 0.18, 0.27, 0.66, 0.18, 0.66, 0.18, 0.66, 0.18, 0.48, 0.69, 1, 0.18, 0.36, 0.57, 0.27, 0.27, 1, 0.57, 0.78\}$

- Let $I_{T_i} = \{0, 10\}$ and $I_{T_j} = \{4, 13, 25, 31\}$ be the two lists of infected nodes reported by day T_i and day T_j, respectively. All the nodes in I_{T_i} and I_{T_j} are represented by the red color in Fig. 1(c).

- Now, we compute all the paths of cutoff length $\Phi = 4$ between each pair of nodes u, v, where $u \in I_{T_i}$ and $v \in I_{T_j}$, and extracts the path having maximum infection parameter.

- We find the suspected node list $S = \{3, 5, 6, 33\}$. Each node in S is represented by orange color in the Fig. 1(c).

Procedure 1: $Find\_suspected\_nodes(G, I_{T_i}, I_{T_j}, \ell)$

Input: G, I_{T_i}, I_{T_j}
Output: P, S

1 **for** *each node* $v \in G$ **do**
2     $\mathcal{P}(v) \leftarrow$ Compute the infection parameter by Eq. 1;
    // $\mathcal{P}$ is the set containing all node probabilities.

    // Computing highest probability paths between (u, v) where $u \in I_{T_i}$ and $v \in I_{T_j}$

3 $\Phi \leftarrow (T_i - T_j)/3$;
4 **for** *each node* $u \in I_{T_i}$ **do**
5   **for** *each node* $v \in I_{T_j}$ **do**
6   Compute P_{uv};   // find all the paths from u to v using Iteratively deepening Depth-first Search with maximum length Φ
7   **for** *each path* $P_{uv}^i \in P_{uv}$ **do**
8   Compute the infection parameter of the path using Eq. 2 **if** P_{uv}^i *has nodes from* I_{T_i} *and* I_{T_j} **then**
9   discard the path
10   **if** P_{uv}^i *has a node with negative test result* **then**
11   discard the path
12   Take ℓ paths with highest infection parameter and add it to P

13 **for** *each path* $p \in P$ **do**
14     $S = S \cup$ intermediate nodes $\in p$
15 **return** P and S

Algorithm 1: $Find\_Infected\_nodes$

Input: $G, T, I_T, test\_results, \ell$
Output: Updated C

1 $I_{T_{j+1}} = I_{T_j}$;
2 $C = \{\}$;
3 **do**
4     $S = Find\_suspected\_nodes(G, I_{T_i}, I_{T_{j+1}} \cup C, \ell)$;   // Execute Procedure 1
5   Perform test for nodes in S and find positive nodes S^+;
6   Update $test\_results$;
7     $C = C \cup S^+$;
8 **while** $|S| > 0$;

We get all paths are:
$P_{0,31} : \{0, 13, 33, 31\}$
$P_{0,13} : \{0, 31, 33, 13\}$
$P_{0,4} : \{0, 5, 10, 4\}$
$P_{0,25} : \{0, 13, 33, 31, 25\}$

$P_{10,31} : \{10, 4, 6, 0, 31\}$
$P_{10,13} : \{10, 4, 0, 3, 13\}$
$P_{10,4} : \{10, 0, 6, 4\}$
$P_{10,25} : \{10, 5, 0, 31, 25\}$

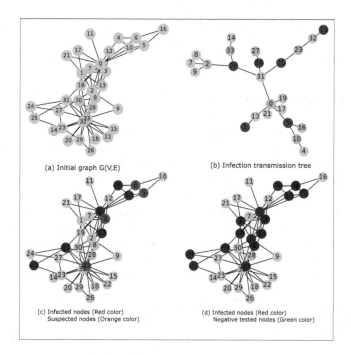

(a) Initial graph G(V,E)

(b) Infection transmission tree

(c) Infected nodes (Red color)
Suspected nodes (Orange color)

(d) Infected nodes (Red color)
Negative tested nodes (Green color)

Fig. 1. A sample run of the algorithm on a graph generated from Zachary Karate Club network (Color figure online)

- Next, we test each node in $u \in S$, and if u has a negative test report, we remove u from S.
- We find node 3 and 6 have negative test reports, and we update $S^+ = \{5, 33\}$.
- Next, we add this S^+ in I_{T_j}. We have updated $I_{T_j} = \{4, 5, 13, 25, 31, 33\}$.
- We recompute the infection parameter for each node in G. We get $\mathcal{P} = \{1, 1.05, 1.05, 0, 1, 1, 0, 0.75, 1.05, 0.57, 1, 0.75, 0.75, 1, 0.48, 0.48, 0.57, 0.75, 0.48, 1.05, 0.48, 0.75, 0.48, 0.78, 0.78, 1, 0.48, 0.66, 0.87, 0.57, 0.57, 1, 0.87, 1\}$.
- We again compute the final paths P:

$P_{0,31} : \{0, 2, 8, 33, 31\}$ $\qquad$ $P_{10,31} : \{10, 0, 19, 33, 31\}$
$P_{0,13} : \{0, 19, 1, 2, 13\}$ $\qquad$ $P_{10,13} : \{10, 0, 19, 1, 13\}$
$P_{0,4} : \{0, 10, 5, 6, 4\}$ $\qquad$ $P_{10,4} : \{10, 0, 5, 6, 4\}$
$P_{0,25} : \{0, 19, 33, 31, 25\}$ $\qquad$ $P_{10,25} : \{10, 0, 31, 24, 25\}$
$P_{0,33} : \{0, 19, 33\}$ $\qquad$ $P_{10,33} : \{10, 0, 2, 8, 33\}$
$P_{0,5} : \{0, 10, 4, 6, 5\}$ $\qquad$ $P_{10,5} : \{10, 0, 4, 6, 5\}$

- We get the suspected node list $S' = \{1, 2, 8, 19, 24\}$.
- Next, we test each node in $u \in S'$ and find node 8 has a negative test report. Hence, we remove 8 from S'. The updated $S^{+'}$ is $\{1, 2, 19, 24\}$.

- Finally, we find the carrier nodes $C = S^+ \cup S^{+'} = \{1, 2, 5, 19, 24, 33\}$, as shown in Fig. 1(d). The nodes having negative test reports are shown by green color in Fig. 1(d).

4   Complexity Analysis

In this section, we analyze the complexity of Procedure 1. There are three main parts of the algorithm for which we estimate the running time separately. We have I_{T_i} and I_{T_j} nodes as inputs. First, we determine the infection parameter for a node. If we consider the neighbors up to h hop, then in the worst case, we need to find all the neighbors of a node at hop distance h. A node can have at most Δ neighbors. Thus, the total number of neighbors up to h is Δ^h. We repeat this process for all infected nodes in the graph and thus gain the complexity of $O((|I_{T_i}| + |I_{T_j}|)\Delta^h)$. Second, we compute all simple paths between two nodes that are part of the input. The paths are computed using iterative deepening Depth First Search up to a cutoff Φ. Here, we compute all paths smaller or equal to length Φ for a pair of nodes u and v, where $u \in I_{T_i}$ and $v \in I_{T_j}$. There can be at most Δ^Φ nodes at a distance Φ from a node. Thus we can find all paths with an iterative deepening DFS with time complexity $O(\Delta^\Phi)$ for a node $u \in I_{T_i}$. Iterating through all the paths, we can determine the paths that end at $v \in I_{T_j}$, and compute the corresponding infection parameter of the path. Hence, we arrive at a time complexity of $O((|I_{T_i}| + |I_{T_j}|)\Delta^h + \Delta^\Phi |I_{T_i}|)$ time.

5   Performance Evaluation

Extensive simulation studies have been done to evaluate the performance of the proposed algorithm. In our simulation study, we use small real-world benchmark datasets as the contact graphs like, Zachary karate club, Dolphin, Football and Facebook ego networks having 34, 62, 115, 4039 nodes and 78, 159, 613, 88234 edges, respectively. The algorithm is implemented using python3. Initially, for each of the datasets, we generate a random tree treated as the actual infection transmission tree to show how the infection spreads over the network.

Infection Transmission Tree Generation. We consider the persons as a node in the graph. We first randomly select a root node for the infection transmission tree. We assume that there is a single source of infection for the virus in a community. A node can spread the virus to its neighbors with a certain probability. We choose random neighbors of an infected node to select the next neighbor that is infected with a probability of 30%. We continue to grow the infection transmission tree subsequently. As an example, Fig. 1(b) shows the infection transmission tree of the Zachary Karate club network.

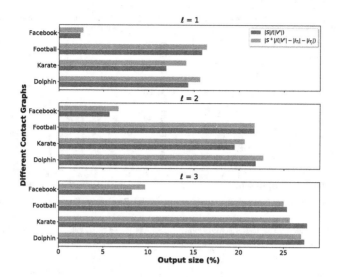

Fig. 2. Size of suspected nodes ($|S|$) and nodes tested positive among the suspected ($|S^+|$) with respect to number of total infected nodes ($|V'|$) and the remaining positive nodes ($|V'| - |I_{T_i}| - |I_{T_j}|$) for different contact graphs based on Zachary karate club, Dolphin, Football and Facebook ego networks.

Input Data Generation. We take T_i and T_j as the two time instances. The infection transmission tree contains all the nodes that are infected. Now we choose the subset of nodes from the tree which are tested positive. We choose a subset of the nodes that are infected before T_i with higher probability (80% for simulation), which becomes the set I_{T_i}, since it is highly likely for nodes infected earlier to show symptoms and get tested. Next, we similarly choose nodes for I_{T_j} with moderate to low probability (30% for simulation), because the onset of the symptoms takes time as well as in most cases, the symptoms are very mild.

Suspected Node Identification. Procedure 1 takes the two sets of nodes (I_{T_i} and I_{T_j}) as input and returns a set of nodes (S) suspected of having been infected. We choose the first ℓ paths with highest infection parameter based on the computed infection parameter of a path with maximum length $\Phi = 4$ between a node from I_{T_i} and a node from I_{T_j}.

We show in Fig. 2 the ratio of the size of suspected nodes to the size of the infected nodes, i.e., $|S|/(|V'|)$. We also show the ratio of the size of positive suspected nodes to the size of remaining positive undetected nodes, i.e., $|S^+|/(|V'| - |I_{T_i}| - |I_{T_j}|)$. We run our algorithm 100 times for different I_{T_i} and I_{T_j} for the same infection transmission tree and take the average. We plot it against the value of ℓ chosen from $\{1, 2, 3\}$. Observe that we can safely choose a higher value of ℓ to get more suspected nodes and correspondingly also get more positive nodes.

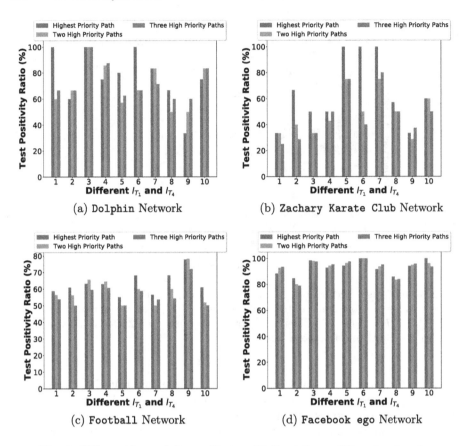

Fig. 3. Different I_{T_1} and I_{T_4} vs. Test positivity ratio on different networks.

We show the comparison between the *test positivity ratio* for the highest priority path, two high priority paths, and three high priority paths in Dolphin, Zachary karate club, Football, Facebook ego networks, as shown in Fig. 3(a–d). We define test positivity ratio as the ratio of the number of nodes that is tested positive to the number of suspected nodes, i.e., $|S^+|/|S|$.

We observe that our proposed method results in a better positivity ratio for the highest priority path. In contrast, if we consider two or three high priority paths for finding the suspected nodes, then the positivity ratio decreases a little. For example, in the Dolphin networks, considering the highest priority path, we get on an average 77% positivity ratio. When we consider the two and three high priority paths, we get the positivity ratio 70% and 72%.

In the real world, as of 17 August 2020, we have around 3,09,41,264 samples tested in India as per the data from the Indian Council of Medical Research website [8] with 27,01,604 people tested positive [9,10]. It is interesting to observe that our proposed method results in a significant positivity ratio as compared to

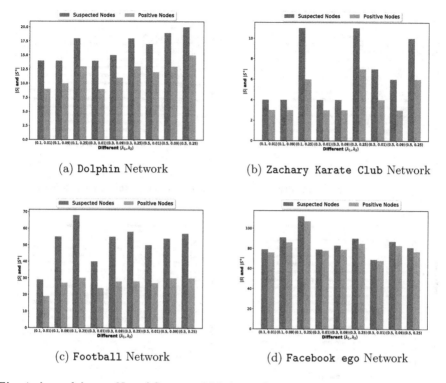

(a) **Dolphin** Network

(b) **Zachary Karate Club** Network

(c) **Football** Network

(d) **Facebook ego** Network

Fig. 4. λ_1 and λ_2 vs. No. of Suspected Nodes and No. of Positive Nodes out of the suspected nodes between time interval T_1 and T_4 on different networks.

the real-world test positivity ratio, which is around 10% in India [10], whereas it was as low as 1% in some states at the initial stages of the pandemic.

Variation of Infection Multiplier λ. We compute the infection parameter of a node by Eq. 1(a–d). For simulation, we have considered infection parameters up to two hops. Specifically, we vary the value of λ_1 and λ_2 for the same infection transmission tree, and input node set I_{T_i} and I_{T_j}. We present the results of the variation in Fig. 4. Here, our target is to find suitable values for λ_1 and λ_2. We find that for the different values of (λ_1, λ_2) such as $(0.1, 0.01)$, $(0.1, 0.09)$, $(0.1, 0.25)$, $(0.3, 0.01)$, $(0.3, 0.09)$, $(0.3, 0.25)$, $(0.5, 0.01)$, $(0.5, 0.09)$, $(0.5, 0.25)$, the variation between the number of identified positive nodes and the total number of the suspected nodes is minimal. We choose $(0.3, 0.09)$ as the default values of λ_1, λ_2 for other simulations presented in this paper.

Algorithmic Feedback. We can run our algorithm repeatedly with added input to arrive at more and more suspected nodes. If we get entirely correct feedback, i.e., all test results of suspected nodes are accurate (be it positive or negative), we can run it again to get more suspected nodes. As of now, some of the test kits used for detection of the virus is not very accurate. So, in the feedback

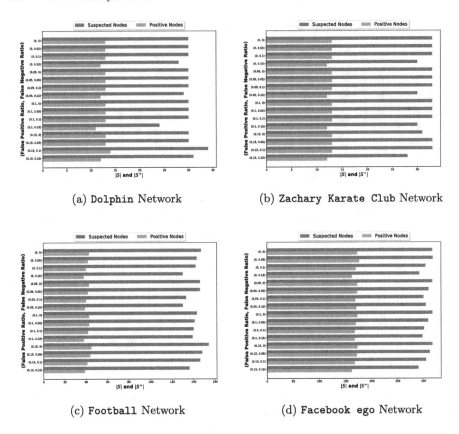

(a) **Dolphin** Network

(b) **Zachary Karate Club** Network

(c) **Football** Network

(d) **Facebook ego** Network

Fig. 5. (False Positive Ratio, False Negative Ratio) vs. No. of Suspected Nodes/No. of Positive Nodes out of the suspected between time interval T_1 and T_4 on different networks.

input, we vary the false positive and false negative percentages for the values $\{5\%, 10\%, 15\%\}$. We plot the suspected node list and the corresponding positive node list in Fig. 5(a–d).

In this study, Fig. 5 show how the number of suspected nodes varies with the False Positive Ratio, False Negative Ratio. We see that size of the suspected nodes increases as we increase the false positive ratio and the actual positive nodes decrease as we increase the false negative ratio. Notice that, even with high false positive and false negative ratios, our algorithm performs well, and the test positivity ratio remains high.

Assuming that the test results are entirely correct, we determine the total number of runs of Algorithm 1 required before all the positive nodes are detected. We execute the algorithm 100 times with different tree sizes and different input data to show the number of runs Algorithm 1 requires before it stops in Fig. 6(a). We observe from the simulation that the algorithm may not find all the positive nodes. We stop the algorithm when Procedure 1 returns an empty set.

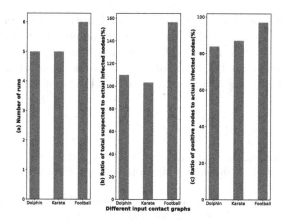

Fig. 6. (a) The number of runs of the algorithm, (b) total suspected, and (c) total positive nodes detected with respect to total infected nodes for different contact graphs based on Dolphin, Zachary karate club and Football networks

In Fig. 6(b), we plot the ratio of total suspected nodes that have been generated from the algorithm and the total infected nodes in the infection transmission tree. In Fig. 6(c), we plot the ratio of total positive nodes that have been found by testing the suspected nodes and the total infected nodes. Observe that, for the contact graph based on Dolphin network, we need on an average of 5 rounds to determine 83.84% of the infected nodes on an average, whereas the total suspected nodes generated by the algorithm is 109.88% of the total infected nodes on an average. Similarly for Zachary Karate Club and Football networks.

6   Conclusion

In this paper, we identify suspected persons infected with the virus so that they can be tested or quarantined to prevent the spreading of the virus. Our proposed approach works by determining a path connecting one infected person to another in the underlying contact graph. We simulate our proposed method on some benchmark datasets considered as the contact graph, such as Dolphin, Zachary karate club, Football, and Facebook ego.

We show that our proposed method of finding suspected nodes results in a significantly higher test positivity ratio (around 70%) than the real world (around 10%). Our assumptions rely on the availability of location data as well as testing data of previous days. The real world test positivity ratio is small due to various factors, including the testing criteria and tracing mechanism. Depending on the availability of the test kits, we can run our algorithm multiple times to get more suspected nodes. Since the suspected node size is directly correlated with the input size, we get more suspected nodes as output as we include the test results of the previously suspected nodes. We show the robustness of our algorithm with different infection multiplier (λ). Even when false positive and false negative test results are included, our algorithm maintains a high test positivity ratio. Finally, we also determine the number of runs our algorithm needs to terminate, which is very small. We show that our algorithm, when run to completion, finds more than 80% of the positive nodes on an average. This is also helpful in identifying asymptomatic carriers that may be infectious.

References

1. Cooper, I., Mondal, A., Antonopoulos, C.G.: A SIR model assumption for the spread of COVID-19 in different communities. Chaos, Solitons Fractals **139**, 110057 (2020)
2. Ye, F., et al.: Delivery of infection from asymptomatic carriers of COVID-19 in a familial cluster. Int. J. Infect. Dis. **94**, 133–138 (2020)
3. Bai, Y., et al.: Presumed asymptomatic carrier transmission of COVID-19. JAMA **323**, 1406–1407 (2020)
4. Lauer, S.A., et al.: The incubation period of coronavirus disease 2019 (COVID-19) from publicly reported confirmed cases: estimation and application. Ann. Internal Med. **172**(2020), 577–582 (2019)
5. He, X., et al.: Author correction: temporal dynamics in viral shedding and transmissibility of COVID-19. Nat. Med. **26**, 1491–1493 (2020)
6. He, X., et al.: Temporal dynamics in viral shedding and transmissibility of COVID-19. Nat. Med. **26**, 672–675 (2020)
7. Widders, A., Broom, A., Broom, J.: SARS-CoV-2: the viral shedding vs infectivity dilemma. Infect. Dis. Health **25**, 210–215 (2020)
8. Indian Council of Medical Research: Samples tested in India (2020). https://www.icmr.gov.in/. Accessed 17 Aug 2020
9. Ministry of Health and Family Welfare: COVID-19 Status in India (2020). https://www.mohfw.gov.in/. Accessed 17 Aug 2020
10. covid19india.org: Coronavirus Outbreak in India (2020). https://www.covid19india.org/. Accessed 17 Aug 2020

Cost Effective Method for Ransomware Detection: An Ensemble Approach

Parthajit Borah[1]([✉]), Dhruba K. Bhattacharyya[1], and J. K. Kalita[2]

[1] Department of Computer Science, Tezpur University, Tezpur, Assam, India
parthajit@tezu.ernet.in
[2] Department of Computer Science, University of Colorado,
Colorado Springs, CO 80918, USA

Abstract. In recent years, ransomware has emerged as a new malware epidemic that creates havoc on the Internet. It infiltrates a victim system or network and encrypts all personal files or the whole system using a variety of encryption techniques. Such techniques prevent users from accessing files or the system until the required amount of ransom is paid. In this paper, we introduce an optimal, yet effective classification scheme, called ERAND (Ensemble RANsomware Defense), to defend against ransomware. ERAND operates on an optimal feature space to yield the best possible accuracy for the ransomware class as a whole as well as for each variant of the family.

Keywords: Malware · Feature · Optimal · Classification · Static · Dynamic · Analysis

1 Introduction

With rapid advances in technology, more than one third of the world's population has now entered the digital world. The Internet provides the backbone to the digital world where people constantly make use of beneficial services and applications available on the Internet. The Internet is used for basic communication purposes as well as for numerous online transactions. The services available on the Internet can be exploited by people with destructive intentions. Malicious software or Malware is used to further increase the harmful intentions of such people. There are various types of malware available in the wild and each of them has been designed for specific purpose. Ransomware is a type of malware which has been emerged as one of the most sophisticated malware in the recent past.

Locker and *Crypto* are primarily the two categories of ransomware. Both kinds of ransomware utilize the same infection vectors like drive by download, social engineering, phishing, spam emails, or removable media to get into the information devices and systems, including mobile and Internet of Things devices. However, the way of compromising the victim's system is different for both types of ransomware. The *locker* ransomware is designed to lock the target

© Springer Nature Switzerland AG 2021
D. Goswami and T. A. Hoang (Eds.): ICDCIT 2021, LNCS 12582, pp. 203–219, 2021.
https://doi.org/10.1007/978-3-030-65621-8_13

system and denies user access to the system without making any modification to the file system and then a certain amount of ransom is demanded from the victim. On the other hand, *crypto* ransomware, after getting into the victim's system, encrypts all or selected files in the system using various encryption techniques like AES or RSA [1]. After encryption, a message with all the payment instructions is displayed to the users. To gain access to the system, a required ransom need to be paid to the attackers and in return a decryption key is obtained. The cyber-attacks carried out by ransomware is growing and becoming more sophisticated to defend against.

This paper presents a fast, yet reliable ransomware defense solution, referred to as ERAND, powered by an optimal feature selection method to discriminate the ransomware class as a whole, as well as the eleven variants of the ransomware family from the goodware instances.

The proposed solution is significant, considering the following clauses.

1. It is able to identify an optimal subset of Indicator of Compromises (IoCs) for the ransomware as a family as well as its individual variants to ensure better accuracy.
2. It is able to classify or discriminate instances of ransomware class (as a whole) from non ransomware as well as instances corresponding to individual variants from one another with high accuracy.

The rest of the paper is organised as follows. Section 2 discusses background and related work. In Sect. 3, we present our defense solution, ERAND. Section 4 discusses about performance comparison of ERAND with other recent approaches. Section 5 contains implementation and discusses the results. Finally, in Sect. 6, we give the concluding remarks.

2   Background and Related Work

Cyber threats involving ransomware or ransom malware are growing at an exponential rate to extort money from individual users or organizations. In the recent past, several defense solutions have been proposed to combat ransomware. To combat malware, it is necessary to analyze the malware binaries properly to extract the IoCs to distinguish malware from goodware. As shown in Fig. 1, malware files are fed as input to the host machine of the analysis framework, which executes the binaries in an emulated environment and records their static and dynamic characteristics, and provides an output report to the user. These reports are finally used to extract the IoCs.

Gazet et al. [14] made first attempt at analysing ransomware families. The authors carried out a technical review on quality of ransomware codes and its functionality. The authors concluded that the ransomware under analysis were designed for mass propagation but not for mass extortion.

Scaife et al. [18] propose a ransomware detection system called *Cryptodrop* which promises to give early warnings in case of breach. It also combines three IoCs related to ransomware for rapid detection of ransomware.

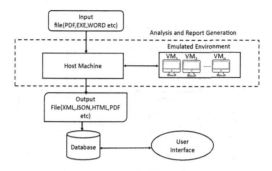

Fig. 1. A generic architecture of malware analysis framework

Homayoun et al. [16] propose a sequential pattern mining approach for combating ransomware. The approach helps to identify best features for classification of ransomware applications from benign apps as well as identifying a ransomware sample family.

2.1 Discussion

We observe the following, based on the conducted review.

- Both supervised and semi-supervised learning approaches have been used for detection of known and unknown malware.
- Among supervised approaches, there is scope for further enhancement of detection performance in terms of classification accuracy. Recently, several faster and effective classifiers as well as ensemble approaches have been proposed to address the issue.
- Identification of an appropriate and optimal subset of IoCs can improve the performance of the detection method in terms of both accuracy and cost effectiveness.
- Most learning approaches fail to perform well for all kinds of malware due to non-availability of adequate training instances. Active learning approaches could be a better alternative for detection of both known as well as unknown malware with a low rate of false alarms.

3 Proposed Framework

This section presents the proposed detection framework, referred to as ERAND, and discusses its components. Figure 2 illustrates the architecture of the proposed framework and its components.

3.1 Data Collection

We evaluate our method using two datasets. For the first, we collect 2288 ransomware samples from [7]. In addition to that, we also collect 933 goodware

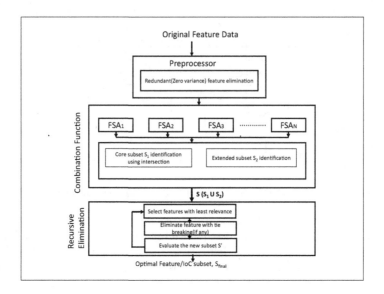

Fig. 2. ERAND Detection framework for Ransomware and its variants

samples from Google Play Store[1]. After this, we analyse the collected samples for feature extraction. We extract two categories of features: a) Permission and b) API. A total of 241 features are extracted out of which 214 features belong to permission based and the remaining 27 belong to API category. The whole process of feature dataset generation is represented in Fig. 3. The final description of the dataset is given in Table 1.

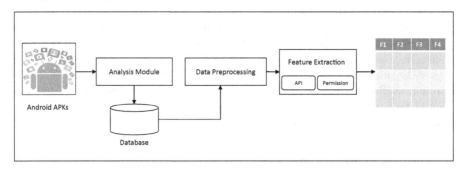

Fig. 3. The ransomware feature dataset generation framework

For our experiment, we use another feature dataset from Sgandurra et al. [19]. The dataset contains 582 samples of ransomware with 11 variants and 942 samples of benign programs. The dataset has 30,962 attributes which represent all instances both goodware and ransomware present in the dataset. A detailed description of the dataset is given in the Table 2.

---

[1] https://play.google.com/.

Table 1. Ransomware dataset with two classes

No. of instances		No. of classes	No. of features	
Ransomware	2288	2	Permission-based	214
Goodware	933		API-based	27
Total instances:	3221		Total features:	241

Table 2. Ransomware dataset with Normal and 11 ransomware subclasses

Sl no.	Class	No. of samples
1	Goodware	942
2	Critroni	50
3	CryptLocker	107
4	CryptoWall	46
5	KOLLAH	25
6	Kovter	64
7	Locker	97
8	MATSNU	59
9	PGPCODER	4
10	Reveton	90
11	TeslaCrypt	6
12	Trojan-Ransom	34
		Total samples: 1524
		Total features: 30962

3.2 Data Preprocessing

Data preprocessing helps convert the input data into an appropriate format to make it suitable for further analysis. In our work, we preprocessed our original dataset before performing subsequent analysis. In the preprocessing phase, we removed all those attributes whose variance is zero. In addition to that, we have discarded all those malware binaries that are failed to execute during analysis phase.

3.3 Ensemble Feature Selection

Data mining or machine learning algorithms may face the curse of dimensionality issues while dealing with high dimensional data. Additionally, the learning models may overfit in the presence of a large number of features which may lead to performance degradation, in addition to increased memory requirements and computational cost. Therefore, it is necessary to remove irrelevant features. Since both the datasets have large number of features (241 for dataset 1 and 30,962 for dataset 2), we perform feature selection to find an optimal subset of features.

Each variant of ransomware exhibits different characteristics and as such feature selection techniques are used for each of them present in our dataset. More specifically, we use an ensemble feature selection approach, where the results of the base feature selection algorithms are combined with a consensus to generate an optimal subset of features.

Selection of the Base Feature Selection Algorithms. Ensemble feature selection eliminates the biases of individual participating feature selection methods to yield the best possible output using an appropriate consensus function. Similar to other ensemble approaches, there are two steps in ensemble feature selection. First, we need a set of well-performing feature selectors, each of which provides a subset of features found relevant. Second, based on the output received from each ranker or feature selection algorithm, we apply an appropriate consensus function to yield the best possible subset of relevant features. Guided by our experimental results, we use the following three feature selectors, namely, CMIM [12], MIFS [3], and ReliefF [17].

(a) **Conditional Mutual Information Maximization (CMIM)** [12]: For a given set of selected features, CMIM feature selector functions in an iterative manner by selecting features with maximum mutual information with the class labels. In other words, CMIM discards those features which are similar to the previously selected features even though its predictive power is strong concerning the class labels. For each unselected feature X_i, the feature score is calculated using Eq. 1.

$$J_{CMIM}(X_i) = min_{X_j \epsilon S}[I(X_i; Y|X_j)] \qquad (1)$$

(b) **Mutual Information Feature Selection (MIFS)** [3]: A good feature should be highly correlated with the class label, but it should not have high correlation with other features. Both feature relevance and feature redundancy are taken into consideration by MIFS during feature selection phase. The feature score is calculated for each unselected feature X_k using Eq. 2.

$$J_{MIFS}(X_K) = I(X_k; Y) - \beta \sum_{X_j \epsilon S} I(X_j; X_k) \qquad (2)$$

(c) **ReliefF** [17]: ReliefF selects features to efficiently separate instances from different classes. Assume that l data instances are randomly selected among all n instances, then the feature score of any feature f_i in ReliefF is estimated using Eq. 3.

$$ReliefFscore(f_i) = 1/c \sum_{j=1}^{l} (-1/m_j) \sum_{x_r \epsilon NH(j)} d(X(j,i) - X(r,i))$$

$$+ \sum_{y \neq y-j} 1/h_{jy} p(y)/(1 - p(y)) \sum_{x_r \epsilon NM(jy)} d(X(j,i)X(r,i)) \qquad (3)$$

where $NH(j)$ and $NM(j,y)$ are the nearest instances of x_j in the same class and in class y, respectively. Their sizes are m_j and h_{jy}, respectively. $p(y)$ is the ratio of instances with class label y.

Combination Function to Generate Initial Feature Subset. In this work, we introduce a 3-step consensus building process to identify an initial optimal subset of features for the subsequent recursive optimality test.

C1 Consider the intersection of selected feature subsets given by each base feature selection algorithm to obtain a core subset of features, which we denote as S_1.

C2 Consider the scores of all features given by all individual algorithms and select those features (other than those included in S_1) for each algorithm with scores higher than a user defined threshold (say, α). We consider all those features whose score value is greater than 0. Finally, this step outputs a feature set S_2 based on contributions from all the feature selection algorithms.

C3 Obtain the initial optimal feature subset S by taking union of S_1 and S_2 for consideration of the recursive optimality test, described next, towards generation of the final optimal feature subset, i.e., S_{final}.

Generation of Final Optimal Feature Subset Using Recursive Optimality Test. In this section, a recursive elimination method is applied to get the final optimal feature subset S_{final} based on S. There are three steps in this process, which are stated below.

O1 Consider the feature subset, i.e., S as input and identifies one or more features with least relevance score.

O2 Eliminate the feature(s) to obtain a new subset, S'. In case of tie, based on relevance score estimated for an identified pair of candidate features, we choose feature for elimination given by an inconsistent performing ranker algorithm.

O3 Evaluate S' in terms of classification accuracy. It terminates the elimination process if and only if a significant performance degradation is observed in terms of accuracy due to the elimination of a feature, and considers the recent S_i as S_{final}.

Optimal Feature Subset for Each Class and for the Whole Family. Initially, the three feature selection algorithms namely: CMIM, MIFS and ReliefF generate 3 feature subsets for each variant of ransomware. The naming convention for each subset is Ran_sub_{ij}, where i goes from 1 to n and j goes from 1 to 3. Next, we apply a consensus function (described in Sect. 3.3) on these subset of features to generate a common subset for each class of ransomware. This generates n feature subsets for each variant of ransomware present in the dataset. Now, for each of the n feature subsets, an optimal feature subset is

Table 3. Number of optimal features for each ransomware dataset

Dataset	No. of optimal features
Dataset 1	15
Dataset 2 (class 1)	23
Dataset 2 (class 2)	36
Dataset 2 (class 3)	19
Dataset 2 (class 4)	42
Dataset 2 (class 5)	20
Dataset 2 (class 6)	36
Dataset 2 (class 7)	31
Dataset 2 (class 8)	4
Dataset 2 (class 9)	32
Dataset 2 (class 10)	8
Dataset 2 (class 11)	25

Table 4. List of selected features for dataset 1

Feature rank	Feature name
1	$SEND\_SMS$
2	$RECEIVE\_BOOT\_COMPLETED$
3	GET_TASKS
4	$Ljava/net/URL; -> openConnection$
5	$VIBRATE$
6	$WAKE\_LOCK$
7	$KILL\_BACKGROUND\_PROCESSES$
8	$SYSTEM\_ALERT\_WINDOW$
9	$ACCESS\_WIFI\_STATE$
10	$DISABLE\_KEYGUARD$
11	$Landroid/location/LocationManager; -> getLastKnownLocation$
12	$READ\_PHONE\_STATE$
13	$RECEIVE\_SMS$
14	$CHANGE\_WIFI\_STATE$
15	$WRITE\_EXTERNAL\_STORAGE$

Table 5. List of top ranked feature categories for dataset 2

Feature rank	Feature category
1	$RegistryKeysOperations$
2	$APICalls$
3	$Strings$
4	$Filesoperations$
5	$Fileextensions$
6	$Directoryoperations$
7	$Droppedfiles$

identified using the process described in the Sect. 3.3. The number of optimal features identified for each dataset with each variant of ransomware is given in the Table 3. Table 4 lists all the optimal features for ransomware dataset 1 and Table 5 lists top ranked feature categories for dataset 2.

Correctness of Feature Selection Results. To establish the correctness of our feature selection results, we propose the following two lemmas.

Lemma 1. *For discrimination of each ransomware variant, i.e., R_i from benign instances, selected feature subset, i.e. Ran_sub_i is optimal.*

Proof: Suppose for the sake of contradiction, we assume that for a ransomware variant R_i, Ran_sub_i is non optimal and $|Ran\_sub_i| = k$. Also, assume that $|Ran\_sub_i| + 1$ gives us the best possible accuracy. However, as shown in Table 12 and also stated in Sect. 3.3, the highest possible accuracy to discriminate R_i from normal or goodware after recursive elimination is for the subset of features Ran_sub_i. Any addition or deletion of features from Ran_sub_i does not improve accuracy. Hence, the assumption is false and it contradicts the non-optimality assumption. Hence, Ran_sub_i is optimal.

Lemma 2. *The accuracy given by Ran_sub_{all} cannot be greater than the overall highest accuracy given by the individual optimal subset of features i.e., Ran_sub_i.*

Proof: A feature subset Ran_sub_i for each ransomware variant R_i is identified and its optimality as stated in the Lemma 1 is established. Ran_sub_{all} includes Ran_sub_i and some additional features. In other words, for discrimination of R_i, Ran_sub_{all} includes some additional redundant features with reference to Ran_sub_i. Such additional features cannot improve classifier performance for R_i (as substantiated by Lemma 1). Hence, the accuracy given by $Ran\_sub_{all} \not> Ran\_sub_i$ (where i varies from 1 to 11).

3.4 Classification of Ransomware Family and Its Variants

After obtaining the dataset using an optimal feature subset, it is necessary to establish the performance of the features to distinguish the ransomware from the goodware and supervised approach can be used to achieve the same. To avoid biases of classifiers, we consider an ensemble approach for unbiased evaluation of the optimality of the subset of IoCs given by the previous step. However, ensemble methods are also not totally free from drawbacks due to the limitations of the inherent combination/consensus function used. Therefore, in our study, we consider a number of consistent performing ensemble classifiers for optimal classification. The five ensemble classifiers used in our work are Random forest [5], Extra Tree [15], Adaboost [13], Gradient boosting [4], and XGBoost [8].

To avoid individual biases of these ensemble methods, we combine their outputs to yield best possible classification performance by minimizing false alarms.

Balancing of Classes. Data balancing is a technique to make an approximately balanced number of instances in each class. An imbalanced data distribution may lead to unusual model performance. Our dataset is highly imbalanced as shown in Table 2 of class distribution and hence, it needs to be balanced. For data balancing, we need additional class specific instances which are difficult to collect because ransomware data are not readily available due to various other reasons in addition to security reasons. Therefore, we use a sampling technique to handle the class imbalance problem. In general, there are three sampling techniques: undersampling, oversampling, and hybrid sampling. In our case, we use an oversampling technique called SMOTE [6], where the minority class is oversampled by creating "synthetic" examples rather than by over-sampling with replacement. Finally, in the dataset all the class instance distributions become 50:50. In addition to that, we also validate our method's performance in other data distributions also like 60:40, 70:30 and 80:20.

Classification of Ransomware Variants. The above mentioned classifiers, i.e., Random forest, Extra tree, Adaboost, Gradient boosting, and XGboost are used to build a predictive model for each Ran_sub_i dataset, where i goes from 1 to 11 and each dataset includes the instances of goodware and ransomware variants.

Classification of Ransomware Family. The classifier models are also built using the Ran_sub_{all} dataset, where all the instances of ransomware variants are included as a single ransomware class along with the goodware instances.

4   Comparison with Existing Methods

In this section, we compare our method with some of the existing ransomware detection methods. The similarity and dissimilarity of our method with the existing methods can be described in the following ways. Table 6 presents comparative study of the proposed method with some of the existing methods.

– Like [2,21,22], our method also employ the various supervised approaches for classification of ransomware instances into their respective families.
– Like [2,21,22], our work is also based on multi-class classification ransomware instances. But in [2,21,22], the proposed method is experimented against 8, 9, and 7 families of ransomware whereas our method uses 11 families of ransomware for validation.
– Like [22], our dataset is also not balanced in terms of goodware and ransomware samples. But unlike [22], we apply data balancing technique to validate our method with different class distributions.
– Unlike [2,22], our method uses the different platform specific ransomware for which both dynamic and static behaviors of ransomware are extracted as features to discriminate ransomware from goodware.
– In [21], the stable performance is obtained for 131 features which is too high in comparisons to ours. The maximum feature dimension used by our method is 45 and minimum feature dimension is 4 for which we get the stable performance among the ransomware families.
– In [22], the stable performance is obtained for 123 features which is too high in comparisons to ours. The maximum feature dimension used by our method is 45 and minimum feature dimension is 4 for which we get the stable performance among the ransomware families.
– In [2], the highest accuracy is obtained with 8 features which 97.10 but our method achieves highest accuracy of 98.7 with only 4 features for Dataset 2 (class 8).

– Unlike [2,22], our method achieves better accuracy in terms of classification. The best possible accuracy obtained by the method [22] is 91.43% while our method obtained 98.7%.

5 Results

The experimental analysis is performed in a Python environment. The experiments are carried out on a workstation with 64 GB main memory, 2.26 Intel(R) Xeon processor and Ubuntu operating system.

To build consensus based on decisions given by the individual classifiers, we use a weighted majority approach. The approach uses individual weights of the classifiers given by a multiobjective optimization technique for unbiased combinations of the individual decisions to achieve best possible accuracy.

5.1 Computation of Weights for Classifiers Using NSGA-II

We use multiobjective evolutionary method to compute best possible set of weighting factors for the participating classifiers based on their classification performances on each of the 11 variants of ransomware. Since none of the classifiers has been found to give winning performance consistently for all the variants of ransomware, we decided to exploit weighted majority based combination function to achieve best possible classification accuracy. A good number of multiobjective evolutionary algorithms are available in the literature and some of their comparisons are available at [9,23]. NSGA-II has already been established as a promising optimization method to handle multiobjective problem due to its elitist approach. An arithmetic crossover and Gaussian mutation operators generates offspring population from parent population. Offspring populations are then added to the current population. The NSGA-II algorithm uses (i) non-dominated sorting method for ranking individuals into different non-domination levels and (ii) crowding distance method to sort individuals within the same level. An individual dominates another individual if it is strictly better in at least one objective and no worse in all the other objectives.

In this work, we exploit the NSGA-II to compute an optimal set of weighting factor for the five classifiers (c_1 to c_5) based on their individual performances for 11 variants. We use their $5 \times 11 = 55$ performance values as input to the NSGA-II for computation of the optimal set of weights. The optimal weights obtained are given in Table 7.

Table 6. Comparison of the proposed method with existing methods

Methods	Ransomware samples	Total class	Features (S/D)	Total features	Accuracy (%)
[22]	1787	10	S	123	91.43
[2]	210	10	D	8	97.1
[10]	500	6	D	23	97.03
[11]	256	2	D	8	87
[21]	755	8	D	131	98
[20]	574	12	S/D		98.25
Proposed	2288 (Dataset 1)	2	S	15	98.2
	582 (Dataset 2)	12	D	Min:4 Max:42	98.8

Table 7. Weightage of the classifiers given by NSGA-II

Classifier, c_i	Weightage
ExtraTree (c_1)	0.35
Gradient Boosting (c_2)	0.28
AdaBoost (c_3)	0.15
XGBoost (c_4)	0.12
Random Forest (c_5)	0.10

5.2 Weighted Majority Based Combination Function

To generate an unbiased classification output, ERAND uses 'weighted majority voting' to build consensus among the outputs given by the individual classifiers. We initially carry out an exhaustive experimentation with these classifiers using the datasets described in Sect. 3.1 and consider their performance as the basis for subsequent processing to decide their weights while building the consensus. Our experimental study based on weighted majority voting uses Eq. 4 to decide the class label of a test instance. It computes anomaly score, S_i for each test instance given by Eq. 4 to recognise either as 'goodware' or 'malware' with respect to a user defined threshold, β.

$$S_i = w_1c_1 + w_2c_2 + w_3c_3 + w_4c_4 + w_5c_5 \tag{4}$$

If the value of $S_i \geq \beta$ (a user-defined threshold), the instance is considered anomalous or belonging to a malware class. In our experimentation, we consider $\beta = 0.63$. Because if any two best performers (like (c_1,c_2) or (c_1,c_3) agree, then their total weights are used as threshold. The value of c_i for a given class can be either 1 (if belongs to the class) or 0 (if not). In case of tie, we give priority to the decision of the best performers. For example, if c_1 and c_4 are on one side and c_2, c_3 and c_5 are on the other side, we prefer the decision of (c_1, c_4).

5.3 Classification of Ransomware Variants

We evaluate the performance of the selected subset of features to distinguish the instances of the ransomware family from the goodware, using five classifiers individually. The classification results of dataset 1 and dataset 2 are given in Tables 8 and 9. It can be observed from Tables 8 and 9 that ERAND consistently performs well like ExtraTree and Gradient Boosting in classifying each variant of the ransomware malware.

Table 8. Classification accuracies of dataset 1

Classifiers	Accuracy
Gradient Boosting	97.5
Adaboost	96.47
Random Forest	98
Extra Tree	98.27
XGBoost	97.2
ERAND	98.2

Table 9. Classification accuracies of dataset 2 for each variant

Ransomware family Classifiers	Gradient Boosting	Adaboost	Random Forest	Extra Tree	XGBoost	ERAND
Critroni	98.7	98.7	98	98.1	98.7	98.8
CryptLocker	96.8	96.8	96.7	96.8	96.7	96.8
CryptoWall	96.3	96.17	96.23	96.44	96.33	96.42
KOHLER	98.6	98.56	98.61	98.8	98.7	98.83
Kovter	98.76	97.88	97.8	98.1	98.23	98.78
Locker	96.39	96.34	96.50	96.92	96.39	96.55
MATSNU	97.61	97.70	97.77	97.70	97.88	97.88
PGPCODER	98.12	98.12	98.43	98.7	98.43	98.7
Reveton	98.40	98.72	98.84	97.7	98.72	98.79
TeslaCrypt	98.87	98.62	98.77	98.6	97.88	98.86
Trojan-Ransom	98.43	97.78	98.32	98.61	97.86	98.67

5.4 Classification of Ransomware Family

To calculate the performance of the selected features to distinguish whole ransomware family from the goodware, we used five classifiers namely, Random forest, Gradient boosting, Adaboost, Extratree and XGboost. The classification results of whole ransomware family with respect to goodware are enlisted in Table 10.

5.5 Metrics and Cross Validation

For effective evaluation of our method, four machine learning performance metrics are used namely: Accuracy, Recall, Precision and F-Measure. The precision, recall and F1 Score values of each classifier are reported in Table 11. On the other hand, the classification accuracies of each classifier are reported in Table 9 for 50:50 class distribution.

– *Accuracy*: The no of instances correctly detected by a classifier divided by the total of goodware and ransomware instances gives the accuracy.

$$Accuracy = \frac{TP + TN}{TP + TN + FP + FN}$$

– *Precision*: It defines what proportion of predicted ransomware are actually correct. Thus, Precision of a model is calculated as follows:

$$Precision = \frac{TP}{TP + FP}$$

Table 10. Classification accuracies of whole ransomware family

Goodware	Ransomware	Classifiers					ERAND
		Random Forest	Extra Tree	AdaBoost	XGBoost	Gradient Boosting	
942	618	97.8	98.7	97.9	98.1	98.6	98.6

Table 11. Precision, Recall, and F1 score of all the classifiers

Datasets	Precision					Recall					F1-Score				
	Gradient Boosting	Adaboost	Random Forest	Extra Tree	XGBoost	Gradient Boosting	Adaboost	Random Forest	Extra Tree	XGBoost	Gradient Boosting	Adaboost	Random Forest	Extra Tree	XGBoost
Dataset 1	98.1	97	98.9	98.7	98.4	97.9	97.5	98.1	98	97.6	98	97.22	98.5	98.6	97.8
Dataset 2 (Class 1)	98.9	98.89	98.89	98.88	98.89	98	98.3	98.3	98	98.4	98	98.1	97.9	98.7	98.4
Dataset 2 (Class 2)	95.7	95.9	96.8	96.2	95.8	98.8	98.8	97.5	98.7	98.3	97.2	97.4	96.7	97.2	97.1
Dataset 2 (Class 3)	94.3	93.2	93.4	93.3	93.1	98.7	98.6	98.5	98.8	98.7	96.5	96.2	96.4	96.5	96.3
Dataset 2 (Class 4)	98.7	98.7	98.7	98.8	98.8	98.6	98.6	98.6	98.6	98.7	98.7	98.7	98.7	98.7	98.7
Dataset 2 (Class 5)	98.5	98.7	98.2	98.6	98.6	98.3	98.6	98	98.5	98	98.9	98.6	98.7	98	98.8
Dataset 2 (Class 6)	95.4	94.5	94.7	94.6	94.3	98.1	98.3	98.6	98.2	98.7	96.7	96.5	96.6	96.8	96.4
Dataset 2 (Class 7)	98.6	98.4	98.7	98.5	98.6	98	98.8	98.2	98.7	98.9	98.3	98.1	98.2	98.1	98.3
Dataset 2 (Class 8)	97.7	98.8	98.76	98.8	98.88	97.8	97.8	97.7	98.8	97.8	97.8	97.9	97.8	98.7	97.9
Dataset 2 (Class 9)	98.1	98.6	98.3	98.4	98.2	98.2	98.5	98.6	98.7	98.2	98.6	98	98.89	98.89	98.7
Dataset 2 (Class 10)	98.4	98.7	98.8	98.8	97.3	98.7	98.6	98.5	98.88	97.5	98.6	98.7	98.8	97.8	98.4
Dataset 2 (Class 11)	98.5	98.4	98.8	98.6	98.4	98.4	98.3	98.3	98.5	98.6	98.5	98.4	98.5	98.6	98.5

– *Recall*: It defines what proportion of all ransomware samples are correctly predicted. The recall of a model is calculated as follows:

$$Recall = \frac{TP}{TP + FN}$$

– *F1-score* is calculated by taking the weighted average of precision and recall. F1-score is defined as follows:

$$F1\ Score = \frac{2 * (Recall * Precision)}{(Recall + Precision)}$$

Where TP: True Positive, TN: True Negative, 1.65 cm FP: False Positive, FN: False Negative. In order to evaluate the performance of the proposed method, we used the K-Fold cross validation where we set the value of K = 10. Table 11 presents the Precision, Recall, and F1 score of all the classifiers.

6 Conclusion

In order to counter the ransomware, a cost effective method is proposed based on the dynamic features of ransomware. For identification of most discriminative features of ransomware families, an ensemble approach is introduced. Finally, a weighted majority based combination function is proposed to get highest possible classification accuracy in ransomware detection. ERAND performs consistently well on all the malware datasets. As a future work, we are developing an unsupervised approach to counter zero-day ransomware.

Table 12. Result of Recursive Optimality test for ransomware variant 1

No. of features	Classification accuracy	No. of features	Classification accuracy	No. of features	Classification accuracy	No. of features	Classification accuracy
1	0.883264278	10	0.954893617	19	0.977217245	28	0.982049272
2	0.892821948	11	0.954893617	20	0.977743561	29	0.982575588
3	0.911394177	12	0.954893617	21	0.978269877	30	0.982575588
4	0.907183651	13	0.954893617	22	0.978226204	31	0.982575588
5	0.926254199	14	0.954893617	23	0.982049272	32	0.982575588
6	0.935828667	15	0.954893617	24	0.982575588	33	0.982049272
7	0.953309071	16	0.954893617	25	0.982575588	34	0.982575588
8	0.953309071	17	0.954893617	26	0.982575588	35	0.982049272
9	0.954367301	18	0.96393617	27	0.982575588		

References

1. The Evolution of Ransomware (2008). https://www.symantec.com/content/en/us/. Accessed 14 Feb 2019
2. Alhawi, O.M.K., Baldwin, J., Dehghantanha, A.: Leveraging machine learning techniques for windows ransomware network traffic detection. In: Dehghantanha, A., Conti, M., Dargahi, T. (eds.) Cyber Threat Intelligence. AIS, vol. 70, pp. 93–106. Springer, Cham (2018). https://doi.org/10.1007/978-3-319-73951-9_5
3. Battiti, R.: Using mutual information for selecting features in supervised neural net learning. IEEE Trans. Neural Netw. **5**(4), 537–550 (1994)
4. Breiman, L.: Arcing the edge. Technical report (1997)
5. Breiman, L.: Random forests. Mach. Learn. **45**(1), 5–32 (2001)
6. Chawla, N.V., Bowyer, K.W., Hall, L.O., Kegelmeyer, W.P.: Smote: synthetic minority over-sampling technique. J. Artif. Intell. Res. **16**, 321–357 (2002)
7. Chen, J., Wang, C., Zhao, Z., Chen, K., Du, R., Ahn, G.: Uncovering the face of android ransomware: characterization and real-time detection. IEEE Trans. Inf. Forensics Secur. **13**(5), 1286–1300 (2018). https://doi.org/10.1109/TIFS.2017.2787905
8. Chen, T., Guestrin, C.: XGBoost: a scalable tree boosting system. In: Proceedings of the 22nd ACM SIGKDD International Conference on Knowledge Discovery and Data Mining, KDD 2016, pp. 785–794. ACM, New York (2016). https://doi.org/10.1145/2939672.2939785, http://doi.acm.org/10.1145/2939672.2939785
9. Coello, C.A.: An updated survey of GA-based multiobjective optimization techniques. ACM Comput. Surv. **32**(2), 109–143 (2000). https://doi.org/10.1145/358923.358929
10. Cohen, A., Nissim, N.: Trusted detection of ransomware in a private cloud using machine learning methods leveraging meta-features from volatile memory. Exp. Syst. Appl. **102**, 158–178 (2018). https://doi.org/10.1016/j.eswa.2018.02.039. http://www.sciencedirect.com/science/article/pii/S0957417418301283
11. Cusack, G., Michel, O., Keller, E.: Machine learning-based detection of ransomware using SDN. In: Proceedings of the 2018 ACM International Workshop on Security in Software Defined Networks & Network Function Virtualization, pp. 1–6. ACM (2018)
12. Fleuret, F.: Fast binary feature selection with conditional mutual information. J. Mach. Learn. Res. **5**, 1531–1555 (2004)
13. Friedman, J., Hastie, T., Tibshirani, R., et al.: Additive logistic regression: a statistical view of boosting (with discussion and a rejoinder by the authors). Ann. Stat. **28**(2), 337–407 (2000)
14. Gazet, A.: Comparative analysis of various ransomware virii. J. Comput. Virol. **6**(1), 77–90 (2010). https://doi.org/10.1007/s11416-008-0092-2
15. Geurts, P., Ernst, D., Wehenkel, L.: Extremely randomized trees. Mach. Learn. **63**(1), 3–42 (2006)
16. Homayoun, S., Dehghantanha, A., Ahmadzadeh, M., Hashemi, S., Khayami, R.: Know abnormal, find evil: frequent pattern mining for ransomware threat hunting and intelligence. IEEE Trans. Emerg. Top. Comput. **8**, 341–351 (2017)
17. Robnik-Šikonja, M., Kononenko, I.: Theoretical and empirical analysis of relieff and rrelieff. Mach. Learn. **53**(1–2), 23–69 (2003)
18. Scaife, N., Carter, H., Traynor, P., Butler, K.R.: Cryptolock (and drop it): stopping ransomware attacks on user data. In: 2016 IEEE 36th International Conference on Distributed Computing Systems (ICDCS), pp. 303–312. IEEE (2016)

19. Sgandurra, D., Muñoz-González, L., Mohsen, R., Lupu, E.C.: Automated dynamic analysis of ransomware: benefits, limitations and use for detection. CoRR abs/1609.03020 (2016). http://arxiv.org/abs/1609.03020
20. Shaukat, S.K., Ribeiro, V.J.: Ransomwall: a layered defense system against cryptographic ransomware attacks using machine learning. In: 2018 10th International Conference on Communication Systems Networks (COMSNETS), pp. 356–363 (January 2018). https://doi.org/10.1109/COMSNETS.2018.8328219
21. Vinayakumar, R., Soman, K., Velan, K.S., Ganorkar, S.: Evaluating shallow and deep networks for ransomware detection and classification. In: 2017 International Conference on Advances in Computing, Communications and Informatics (ICACCI), pp. 259–265. IEEE (2017)
22. Zhang, H., Xiao, X., Mercaldo, F., Ni, S., Martinelli, F., Sangaiah, A.K.: Classification of ransomware families with machine learning based on N-gram of opcodes. Future Gener. Comput. Syst. **90**, 211–221 (2019). https://doi.org/10.1016/j.future.2018.07.052. http://www.sciencedirect.com/science/article/pii/S0167739X18307325
23. Zitzler, E., Deb, K., Thiele, L.: Comparison of multiobjective evolutionary algorithms: empirical results. Evol. Comput. **8**(2), 173–195 (2000)

Social Networks and Machine Learning

Exploring Alzheimer's Disease Network Using Social Network Analysis

Swati Katiyar⬤, T. Sobha Rani$^{(\boxtimes)}$, and S. Durga Bhavani$^{(\boxtimes)}$⬤

School of Computer and Information Sciences,
University of Hyderabad, Hyderabad, India
swatikatiyarcs0107@gmail.com, {sobharani,sdbcs}@uohyd.ac.in

Abstract. Alzheimer's is a degenerative disease with changes occurring in different regions of the brain at different rates resulting in progressive deterioration. A lot of functional brain connectivity is altered, the process itself is insufficiently understood. In this work, an attempt is made to understand the progressive deterioration of the brain by locating the regions that show significant changes in the connectivity in the five lobes of the brain at different stages of the disease. Methods available in social network analysis like community and maximal clique analysis along with degree distributions, and centrality measures have been used to observe the network evolution of these regions at different stages. Networks of four diagnostic stages i.e., Normal, Early MCI (eMCI), Late MCI (lMCI), and Alzheimer's Disease (AD), taken from ADNI (Alzheimer's Disease Neuroimaging Initiative) database, are used for this study. Nine Regions of Interest (ROIs) from the five lobes are identified and a higher degree of change is observed in the connections of regions from the temporal and frontal lobes. There is a splurge of new connections in the eMCI stage for all regions except for those from the frontal lobe. We also observed more rearrangement among the left hemisphere nodes as compared to the right hemisphere nodes. There is an overall loss of edges between the normal and AD stages. This confirms that the study is able to identify the regions that are affected by the progression of the disease.

Keywords: Disease progression · Differential degree · Community discovery · Regions of the brain

1 Introduction

Alzheimer's is a degenerative disease that destroys memory and other important mental functions. It is an irreversible process, which may ultimately lead to the inability to perform even simple tasks [12]. Main focus of this work is on understanding these functional changes caused by the Alzheimer's Disease. An attempt to gain insights into the effects of this disease on the brain including the changing connectivity patterns as the disease progresses from one stage to the next is being attempted here. The concept of Network biology [3] is used for the purpose of visualising the brain as a network where the regions of interest

© Springer Nature Switzerland AG 2021
D. Goswami and T. A. Hoang (Eds.): ICDCIT 2021, LNCS 12582, pp. 223–237, 2021.
https://doi.org/10.1007/978-3-030-65621-8_14

(ROI) of the brain become nodes wherein two nodes are connected if there is a pathway between these regions.

1.1 Motivation

More than 4 million people are estimated to be suffering from Alzheimer's in India (the third highest caseload in the world). In most cases the patients' lives are characterised by a total loss of independence in the last years [1,11]. Through this work we aim to identify changes which could be indicative of early signs of the disease onset in the brain network.

1.2 Objectives

The goal as mentioned earlier, is to understand the changes in the brain network as the Alzheimer's disease progresses. For this purpose we have used methods available in social network analysis literature: community analysis, maximal clique, degree distributions and centrality measures. We also locate specific regions from the five lobes of the brain that show significant changes and visualise their connections through the stages.

2   Related Literature

Barabasi and their group of co-authors have pioneered the work on network biology [3]. A biological network is built using concerned entities as nodes and interactions between the respective molecular components as edges. Many a time, if the strength of the interaction can be captured then these are weighted networks. Network medicine is a branch of network biology that studies and analyzes human diseases using a network based approach. This enables a possibility of personalised therapies and treatment [2].

Disease modelling refers to the quantification of the features of any disease along with an understanding of the underlying patterns of the disease growth. The network analysis of cancer disease has been carried out in [7,13,15].

In [16], the authors model diseases and symptoms which are the phenotype manifestations of a disease in a network. They construct a symptom-based network of human diseases (HSDN) in which two diseases are linked if they exhibit similar symptoms. The authors study the complex network obtained by integrating HSDN with disease—gene interactions along with the corresponding protein-protein interaction (PPI) data to obtain interesting results of shared genes among diseases and disease clusters.

In an interesting work [6], using network analysis, a disease is linked to a well-defined local neighbourhood of the human interactome, known as the disease module. It is shown that the modules extracted are distinct for each disease.

There is less work regarding Alzheimer's disease with network analysis. Our work considers the data set extracted by [14] in which the authors construct the disease networks for Alzheimer's disease in various stages. They apply the important problem of link prediction from social network analysis in order to discern the patterns of links lost and gained in various stages of the disease using measures like Adamic Adar, Preferential attachment etc.

In a study to understand the changes in brain laterization in patients with MCI and Alzheimer's disease conducted by Liu and Zhang [8] they have used the intrinsic laterality index approach to compute the functional laterality of the brain hemispheres.

It is important to mention the key work of [5] who crafted Desikan-Killiany atlas. In an effort to aid clinical investigation, an automated labeling system was developed. This was used for the subdivision of the cerebral cortex into various gyri. 35 ROIs were manually identified in each hemisphere on a data set of 40 MRI scans. This was encoded as an atlas which could be used to label the cortical regions automatically. A comparison between the automated and the manual labelling of ROIs was done using both ICC (intra-class correlation coefficients) and mean distance measures to guage the percentage of mismatch between them. It turned out that the automated labelling was extremely accurate, with an average ICC of 0.835 and a mean distance error of less than 1 mm [5]. These metric values suggest that the system developed was both valid and reliable. Figures 1 shows the identified ROIs using the Desikan-Killiany atlas.

ROI	Node pair	ROI	Node pair
Banks of Superior Temporal Sulcus	(0, 35)	Caudal Anterior Cingulate Cortex	(1, 36)
Caudal Middle Frontal Gyrus	(2, 37)	Corpus Callosum	(3, 38)
Cuneus Cortex	(4, 39)	Entorhinal Cortex	(5, 40)
Fusiform Gyrus	(6, 41)	Inferior Parietal Cortex	(7, 42)
Inferior Temporal Gyrus	(8, 43)	Isthmus Cingulate Cortex	(9, 44)
Lateral Occipital Cortex	(10, 45)	Lateral Orbital Frontal Gyrus	(11, 46)
Lingual Gyrus	(12, 47)	Medial Orbital Frontal Gryrus	(13, 48)
Middle Temporal Gyrus	(14, 49)	Parahippocampal Gyrus	(15, 50)
Paracentral Lobule	(16, 51)	Pars Opercularis	(17, 52)
Pars Orbitalis	(18, 53)	Pars Triangularis	(19, 54)
Pericalcarine Cortex	(20, 55)	Postcentral Gyrus	(21, 56)
Posterior Cingulate Cortex	(22, 57)	Precentral Gyrus	(23, 58)
Precuneus Cortex	(24, 59)	Rostral Anterior Cingulate Cortex	(25, 60)
Rostral Middle Frontal Gyrus	(26, 61)	Superior Frontal Gyrus	(27, 62)
Superior Parietal Cortex	(28, 63)	Superior Temporal Gyrus	(29, 64)
Supramarginal Gyrus	(30, 65)	Frontal Pole	(31, 66)
Temporal Pole	(32, 67)	Transverse Temporal Cortex	(33, 68)
Insular Cortex	(34, 69)		

Fig. 1. Cortical Representations of the ROIs in one Hemisphere (L) and their Index (R) [5,9].

3   Data Set

3.1   Initial Data Set

Data used in this work is taken from ADNI (Alzheimer's Disease Neuroimaging Initiative) database [14]. The main goal of ADNI has been to assess the progression of early Alzheimer's and MCI (Mild Cognitive Impairment) from PET (Positron Emission Tomography), MRI (Magnetic Resonance Imaging), and other biological markers. DWIs (diffusion-weighted images) of 202 participants are scanned for this purpose. Table 1 shows the demographic information for the 202 participants [14]. Here, N is the number of participants in each category, age is the age of the participants, MMSE (Mini Mental State Exam) scores.

Table 1. Demographic information.

	Normal	eMCI	lMCI	AD	Total
N	50	72	38	42	202
Age (mean $\pm$ SD in years)	72.6 $\pm$ 6.1	72.4 $\pm$ 7.9	72.6 $\pm$ 5.6	75.5 $\pm$ 8.9	73.1 $\pm$ 7.4
MMSE (mean $\pm$ SD)	28.9 $\pm$ 1.4	28.1 $\pm$ 1.5	26.9 $\pm$ 2.1	23.3 $\pm$ 1.9	27.1 $\pm$ 2.7
Sex	22M/28F	45M/27F	25M/13F	28M/14F	120M/82F

3.2   Final Data Set

Applying whole-brain tractography using the Hough transform on every scan recovered 10000 fibers for each participant. 35 regions of interest(ROI) are extracted from each hemisphere from MRI scans using the Desikan-Killiany atlas. A connectivity matrix of size 70 × 70 (35 from each hemisphere) was obtained for each one of the 202 participants. Mean of matrices from each diagnostic group is obtained and are converted into boolean values. Four matrices of size 70 × 70, one for each diagnostic group: Normal, eMCI, lMCI, and AD are obtained. The corpus callosum region is eliminated by replacing rows 3 and 38 by 0s which represents the region in left and right hemispheres respectively.

3.3   Network Construction

Here, a method is described to convert the given data-set into a form useful for our experimentation. Also the nodes of our networks are mapped to the regions of interest of the brain.

Four binary matrices of dimensions 70 × 70 are obtained, where every row and column index corresponds to a ROI of the brain, deduced from the Desikan-Killiany atlas, and each matrix corresponds to a stage of the Alzheimer's disease i.e., normal, eMCI, lMCI and AD.

These four matrices are taken and visualised as graphs containing 70 nodes, connected to each other by non-weighted edges. These were our four networks of the brain corresponding to the different stages of the Alzheimer's disease. All experiments and observations are a result of analysis done on these four networks.

4 Experiments and Results

Our analysis focuses on three broad categories: Network Analysis, Node-wise analysis, Edge-wise analysis.

Network Analysis. Number of Edges, Average Path Length, Average Clustering Coefficient

Node-Wise Analysis. Degree Distribution, Eigenvector Centrality, Maximal Clique Analysis, Community Analysis - Girvan Newman (GN) algorithm and Louvain methods, Degree Differential Analysis

Edge Distribution. Visualisation of connections for chosen ROIs from the five lobes based on the above analysis.

4.1 Global Network Analysis

These are dense networks with high clustering coefficients and small path lengths therefore satisfying the small-world property. This goes with our previous knowledge of brain networks being small-world networks. Table 2 shows the values obtained for each stage.

Table 2. Observations of Global Network Properties.

Stage	Normal	eMCI	lMCI	AD
No. of edges	1490	1510	1380	1364
Avg. path length	1.346	1.337	1.397	1.402
Avg. clustering coefficient	0.753	0.751	0.738	0.736

4.2 Degree Distribution

Figure 2 shows degree distribution for the 4 stages. It is surprising to observe a *Normal* distribution instead of *power law* distribution which is observed in many biological networks. There is a possible loss of the *Normal* behaviour as the disease progresses. A number of edges are lost in the later stages.

4.3 Eigenvector Centrality

Figure 3 shows the plots for degree vs. eigen vector centrality. Wider range of values are observed for degree as compared to eigenvector centrality. High degree

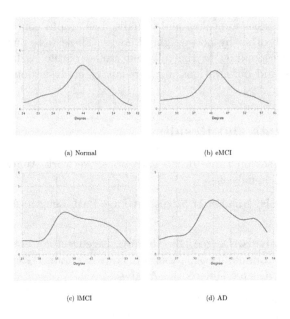

(a) Normal   (b) eMCI

(c) lMCI   (d) AD

Fig. 2. Degree Distribution Plots for various stages.

nodes are connected to the other high degree nodes signifying the assortativity property. An observable drop in the highest degree can be noticed from normal to AD stages. eMCI and AD have more nodes with 0.08 eigenvector centrality. Entorhinal Cortex and Frontal Pole belong to this case. Eigenvector centrality for the Temporal Pole is 0.08 in normal which decreases to 0.06 in AD. Posterior Cingulate Cortex has eigenvector centrality 0.17 in normal which drops to 0.15 in AD. Eigenvector centrality is not varying much. Hence, it can be concluded that the shortest paths are not disturbed if a rewiring happens in normal to AD stages, still it is maintaining the connections in such a way to retain the shortest paths.

4.4   Maximal Clique Analysis

Maximal cliques are those cliques which cannot be extended any further by including another adjacent vertex. Then it becomes a maximal clique, meaning it is not a subset of a larger clique. Again a sizable loss of connections can signify the loss of functionality as the disease progresses. Total number of maximal cliques observed in each stage are:

- Normal - 414
- eMCI - 611
- lMCI - 424
- AD - 333

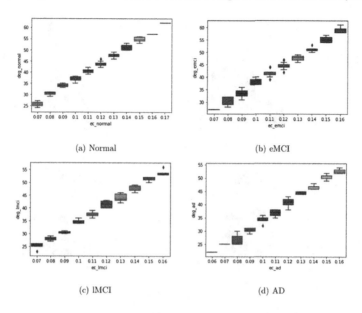

(a) Normal

(b) eMCI

(c) lMCI

(d) AD

Fig. 3. Degree vs Eigenvector centrality of nodes.

Figure 4 shows the number of cliques and the size of the clique. Two size 1 cliques are nodes 3 and 38 (Corpus Callosum). The frequency of maximal cliques is higher for bigger sizes in normal and eMCI. In stages lMCI and AD more number of maximal cliques appear for comparatively smaller size values.

4.5 Community Analysis

The **GN algorithm** [10] is run until the highest modularity value was found. This resulted in the formation of two major communities i.e., the left and right hemispheres along with a few isolated node communities. On applying the **Louvain method** [4], the entire network was divided into left and right hemispheres as communities with higher modularity values. Table 3 shows the modularity values using GN and Louvain community discovery algorithms. Communities that are obtained when the modularity is highest are chosen as the best communities.

Table 3. Modularity values for communities.

Community discovery method	Normal	eMCI	lMCI	AD
Girvan Newman	0.169	0.176	0.214	0.225
Louvain	0.207	0.198	0.232	0.242

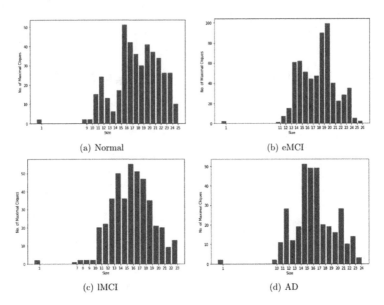

Fig. 4. Count vs. Size of Maximal Cliques.

4.6   Degree Differential Analysis

Degree differential analysis is taken up between each of the stages for all the 70 nodes. From the Fig. 5, it is evident that eMCI to lMCI and Normal to AD has similar structure where there is loss of edges almost for all nodes. Loss of connections between the nodes may signify the loss of functionality that is experienced in the progression of the disease.

5   List of Selected ROIs

In order to carry out a deeper analysis, nine ROIs (at least one ROI from each of the five lobes of the brain) are chosen based on the eigen vector centrality and degree differential analysis explained earlier. These are chosen on the basis of the change in their network properties and their functionalities. Each ROI is represented by a node pair (x, y) where $x \in [0, 34]$ and $y \in [35, 69]$. They are listed in Fig. 6 which provides the change of connections for each node pair in all the 4 stages. That is, the node pair (22,57) has 64 and 59 connections in Normal stage, 63 and 60 in eMCI, 58 and 55 in lMCI, 53 and 52 in AD stages respectively.

On visualising their connections we observed a significant amount of rearrangement between the normal state and the disease stages. We describe this rearrangement for three selected ROIs in the following sections. There is a certain degree of randomness in the way connections are changing in the disease stages.

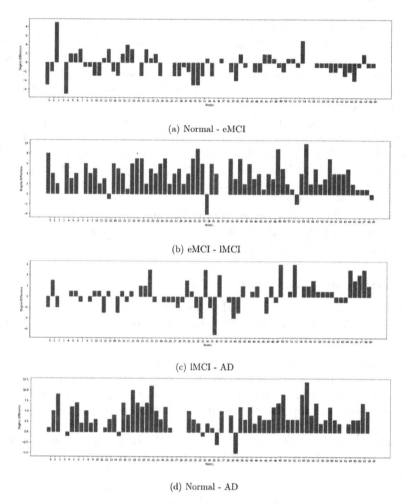

(a) Normal - eMCI

(b) eMCI - lMCI

(c) lMCI - AD

(d) Normal - AD

Fig. 5. Degree difference plots.

5.1   Posterior Cingulate Cortex (22, 57)

The Posterior Cingulate Cortex participates in diverse functions and communicates with various regions in the brain. It was identified as one of the significant regions from Eigenvector centrality analysis. Refer Fig. 7.

- 22 and 57 are connected to each other in Normal stage. 57 is connected to the entire map of the region's connections in all the stages.
- It is also connected to all the regions in the parietal lobe through all the four stages.
- In AD, 22 lost its connection with the cuneus cortex which is responsible for *visual processing*.

- 22 lost many connections after the eMCI stage with the temporal lobe. Only connects to parahippocampal gyrus responsible for*memory encoding and retrieval,* fusiform gyrus responsible for *object recognition* and banks of superior temporal sulcus which plays a role in (*social perception* remained in lMCI. It still connects to middle temporal gyrus and transverse temporal cortex, *involved in processing of tone* in AD.
- This region has links to every region of the frontal lobe except for the left hemispheres of lateral orbital frontal gyrus, frontal pole and pars orbitalis in normal and eMCI. Links are lost with pars opercularis and pars triangularis, both having functions in *language formation and semantic processing*, in lMCI and to pars orbitalis *language processing* and rostral middle frontal gyrus *attention switch* in AD.
- It is connected to all the regions within the cingulate cortex in the first three stages, lost it's link to left hemisphere node of insular cortex in AD. Insular cortex is *involved in consciousness.*

5.2 Parahippocampal Gyrus (15, 50)

This surrounds the hippocampus and contains the entorhinal cortex hence plays an important role in the memory function. This region is selected because of the role it plays in memory related tasks. Refer Fig. 8.

- 15 and 50 are connected to each other in all the four stages.
- A lot of rearrangement occurred in the connections with Occipital lobe. In the eMCI stage, both 15 and 50 got linked to all its regions. They got divided by hemispheres again in lMCI except for lingual gyrus *vision and dreaming; visual processing of the written word.*
- Connections with every region in the parietal lobe are maintained until AD stage. 15 got linked to the right hemisphere node of inferior parietal cortex (*perception of facial stimuli*) and 50 gained connections to the left hemispheres of supramarginal gyrus and superior parietal cortex (*involved in spatial orientation*) in eMCI which are lost again in lMCI.
- It's connection to the caudal anterior cingulate cortex is lost in lMCI stage. It gains a connection to the left hemisphere of rostral anterior cingulate cortex in AD.
- With the frontal lobe, 50 lost its connections to the left hemisphere nodes of caudal middle frontal gyrus (*reorients attention*) and pars opercularis (*language production*) in eMCI. 15 lost its connections with the left hemispheres of frontal pole and rostral middle frontal gyrus whereas 50 gained a link to the right hemisphere of the frontal pole in lMCI. Frontal pole *controls the ability to communicate.*
- Within the temporal lobe it was connected to every other region in the normal and lMCI states, divided by hemispheres. eMCI showed formation of links from 15 to right hemispheres of fusiform gyrus (*facial recognition*), middle temporal gyrus (*semantic memory processing*) and inferior temporal gyrus (*Sensory integration*). In AD, 15 gets linked to the right hemisphere of entorhinal cortex.

5.3 Caudal Middle Frontal Gyrus (2, 37)

This region from the frontal lobe is chosen since it displayed a high degree difference in the differential analysis of nodes. It acts as a circuit breaker and diverts attention towards external stimuli. Refer Fig. 9.

- 2 and 37 are linked to each other till the last stage.
- In eMCI, 37 lost its link to the right hemisphere of the precuneus cortex *memory recollection* but regained it in lMCI. 2 lost all its connections to the parietal lobe in lMCI.
- In the occipital lobe it had connections to every region except for the cuneus cortex, divided by hemispheres, in the normal stage. 2 lost all it's connections in eMCI and 37 gained a link to the right hemisphere of the cuneus cortex in AD.
- Both 2 and 37 are completely connected to the cingulate cortex in the Normal stage. 2 lost it's links to the right hemispheres of the insular cortex and isthmus cingulate cortex in eMCI. Both 2 and 37 lost their connections to the left hemispheres of insular cortex and isthmus cingulate cortex in lMCI. Insular cortex has many functions in *self-awareness, empathy, cognition, etc.*

Regions of Interest (Node Pair)	Normal	eMCI	lMCI	AD	Functions
Occipital Lobe					A visual processing center.
Cuneus Cortex (4, 39)	(37, 41)	(44, 43)	(38, 36)	(38,37)	Site for visual processing.
Parietal Lobe					- Integrates sensory inputs with visual cortex. - Damage to RH can cause visuo-spatial loss.
Supramarginal Gyrus (30, 65)	(46, 47)	(48, 51)	(44, 49)	(41, 44)	Language and mathematical computations.
Cingulate Cortex					Integral part of the limbic system.
Rostral Anterior Cingulate Cortex (25, 60)	(49, 45)	(49, 47)	(42, 40)	(43, 39)	Emotion formation; Automatic motor responses
Posterior Cingulate Cortex (22, 57)	(64, 59)	(63, 60)	(58, 55)	(53, 52)	Intense activity during access of autobiographical memory.
Temporal Lobe					Processing of sensory inputs into meanings.
Entorhinal Cortex (5, 40)	(33, 26)	(31, 30)	(28, 27)	(27, 31)	Hub of the memory network.
Parahippocampal Gyrus (15, 50)	(41, 42)	(44, 44)	(39, 39)	(42, 33)	- Surrounds the hippocampus. - Memory encoding and retrieval.
Temporal Pole (32, 67)	(29, 31)	(34, 29)	(25, 28)	(24, 24)	- Site for primary auditory perception. - LH: semantic memory; RH: personal memory
Frontal Lobe					- Memory functions, motor function, judgement, language, problem solving, social behavior, and impulse control. - Damage can cause an inability to regulate behavior.
Caudal Middle Frontal Gyrus (2, 37)	(52, 49)	(43, 48)	(41, 48)	(43, 44)	Reorients attention to external stimuli.
Pars Triangularis (19, 54)	(43, 46)	(43, 41)	(36, 37)	(36, 37)	- Language semantic processing.

Fig. 6. List of selected ROIs.

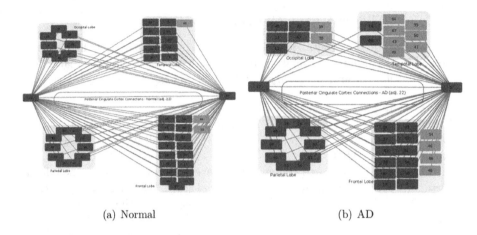

(a) Normal   (b) AD

Fig. 7. Connections of Posterior Cingulate Cortex to other lobes.

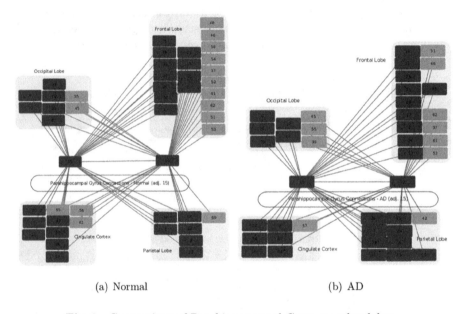

(a) Normal   (b) AD

Fig. 8. Connections of Parahippocampal Gyrus to other lobes.

- In the temporal lobe it is connected to all regions except the temporal pole.
  2 lost all its connections in the eMCI stage. Temporal Pole is the *site for
  auditory perception and also has functions in semantic and personal memory.*
- Within the frontal lobe they kept their connections to every other region but
  the number of common nodes kept decreasing with every stage. 37 lost its
  connections with the left hemispheres of pars opercularis, pars orbitalis, pars
  triangularis *the language processing regions* and frontal pole. 2 lost its link to
  the right hemisphere of the paracentral lobule which has *motor functions.*

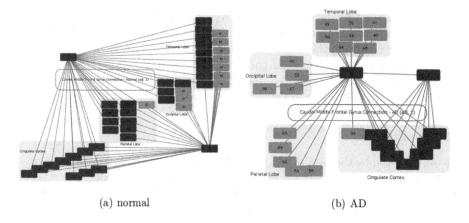

(a) normal   (b) AD

Fig. 9. Connections of Caudal Middle Frontal Gyrus to other lobes.

6   Conclusion

6.1   Conclusions from the Node Wise Analysis and Network Analysis Experiments

A significant loss of edges can be observed from Normal to AD stage. Loss of Normal distribution through the disease stages can be observed from global network properties and degree distribution. High degree of rearrangement can be seen from maximal clique analysis. It is highly plausible that the rearrangement in the network occurs in a way that it gives the brain a false impression of working properly but in hindsight, some secondary or tertiary connections could be missing which causes some malfunction.

6.2   Conclusions from Edge Distribution and Visualisation

Rostral anterior cingulate cortex lost connections with regions responsible for motor functions. Entorhinal cortex and parahippocampal gyrus lost connections with major regions of the cingulate cortex and regions responsible for communication (among others) in the frontal lobe. Temporal lobe is a region of auditory perception which loses its links with the language processing unit. Pars triangularis loses links with the memory hub and other regions of the language processing unit.

Regions from the temporal lobe and the frontal lobe had connections divided by hemispheres which are disturbed in the disease stages. The connections of a region with the right hemisphere nodes in Normal are replicated in lMCI. This is most prominent in the parietal lobe. An explosion of new connections happened in the eMCI stage for all regions except for those from the frontal lobe. High loss of edges in lMCI and AD stages can be seen in every lobe. Higher degree of rearrangement and loss of connections happens among the left hemisphere nodes as compared to the right hemisphere. In another work by Liu and Zhang [8], they found an abnormal rightward dominance in the patients with MCI and AD. According to them this could be indicative of such patients using additional brain resources to compensate for the loss of cognitive function. Disappearance of the leftward laterality was also observed in the patients with AD. This was associated with the damage in the left hemisphere.

6.3 Limitations

We were limited by the data set we used which only gave us binary information in the form matrices averaged over N subjects. For a work as this one it is possible to get better results if data is made available per subject hence, all of the results we produce are obtained from a generalised perspective.

References

1. Alzheimer's Association: 10 early signs and symptoms of alzheimer's (2020). https://www.alz.org/alzheimers-dementia/10_signs. Accessed 26 Jun 2020
2. Barabási, A.L., Gulbahce, N., Loscalzo, J.: Network medicine: a network-based approach to human disease. Nat. Rev. Genet. **12**(1), 56–68 (2011). https://doi.org/10.1038/nrg2918
3. Barabási, A.L., Oltvai, Z.N.: Network biology: understanding the cell's functional organization. Nat. Rev. Genet. **5**(2), 101–113 (2004). https://doi.org/10.1038/nrg1272
4. Blondel, V.D., Guillaume, J.L., Lambiotte, R., Lefebvre, E.: Community structure in social and biological networks. J. Stat. Mech. Theor. Exp. (2008). https://doi.org/10.1088/1742-5468/2008/10/P10008
5. Desikan, R.S., et al.: An automated labeling system for subdividing the human cerebral cortex on MRI scans into gyral based regions of interest. NeuroImage **31**(3), 968–980 (2006). https://doi.org/10.1016/j.neuroimage.2006.01.021
6. Ghiassian, S.D., Menche, J., Barabási, A.L.: A disease module detection (DIAMOnD) algorithm derived from a systematic analysis of connectivity patterns of disease proteins in the human interactome. PLOS Comput. Biol. **11**(4), e1004120 (2015)
7. Hanahan, D., Weinberg, R.A.: The hallmarks of cancer. Cell **100**(1), 57–70 (2000)
8. Hao, L., et al.: Changes in brain lateralization in patients with mild cognitive impairment and Alzheimer's disease: a resting-state functional magnetic resonance study from Alzheimer's disease neuroimaging initiative. Front. Neurol. **9**, 3 (2018). https://doi.org/10.3389/fneur.2018.00003
9. Lisowska, A., Rekik, I.: Joint pairing and structured mapping of convolutional brain morphological multiplexes for early dementia diagnosis. Brain Connect. **9**(1), 22–36 (2019). https://doi.org/10.1089/brain.2018.0578
10. Girvan, M., Newman, M.E.J.: Community structure in social and biological networks. Proc. Natl. Acad. Sci. **99**, 7821–7826 (2002)
11. NIA: Alzheimer's disease fact sheet (2020). https://www.nia.nih.gov/health/alzheimers-disease-fact-sheet. Accessed 26 Jun 2020
12. NIA: What is Alzheimer's disease? (2020). https://www.nia.nih.gov/health/what-alzheimers-disease. Accessed 26 Jun 2020

13. Sahoo, R., Rani, T., Bhavani, S.: Differentiating cancer from normal protein-protein interactions through network analysis, Chap. 17. In: Arabnia, H., Tran, Q.N. (eds.) Emerging Trends in Applications and Infrastructures for Computational Biology, Bioinformatics, and Systems Biology (2017)
14. Sulaimany, S., Khansari, M., Zarrineh, P., Daianu, M., Thompson, N.J.P.M., Masoudi-Nejad, A.: Predicting brain network changes in Alzheimer's disease with link prediction algorithms. Mol. BioSyst. **13**(4), 725–735 (2017). https://doi.org/10.1039/c6mb00815a
15. Wu, G., Feng, X., Stein, L.: A human functional protein interaction network and its application to cancer data analysis. Genome Biol. **11**, 1 (2010)
16. Zhou, X., Menche, J., Barabási, A.L., Sharma, A.: Human symptoms-disease network. Nat. Commun. **5**, 4212 (2014)

Stroke Prediction Using Machine Learning in a Distributed Environment

Maihul Rajora[1], Mansi Rathod[1(✉)], and Nenavath Srinivas Naik[2]

[1] Department of Electronics and Communication Engineering, IIIT Naya Raipur,
Naya Raipur, India
{maihul17101,mansi17101}@iiitnr.edu.in
[2] Department of Computer Science and Engineering, IIIT Naya Raipur,
Naya Raipur, India
srinu@iiitnr.edu.in

Abstract. As with our changing lifestyles, certain biological dimensions of human lives are changing, making people more vulnerable towards stroke problem. Stroke is a medical condition in which parts of the brain do not get blood supply and a person attains stroke condition which can be fatal at times. As these stroke cases are increasing at an alarming rate, there is a need to analyze about factors affecting the growth rate of these cases. There is a need to design an approach to predict whether a person will be affected by stroke or not. This paper analyse different machine learning algorithms for better prediction of stroke problem. The algorithms used for analysis include Naive Bayes, Logistic Regression, Decision Tree, Random Forest and Gradient Boosting. We use dataset, which consists of 11 features such as age, gender, BMI (body mass index), etc. The analysis of these features is done using univariate and multivariate plots to observe the correlation between these different features. The analysis also shows how some features such as age, gender, smoking status are important factors and some feature like residence are of less importance. The proposed work is implemented using Apache Spark, which is a distributed general-purpose cluster-computing framework. The Receiver Operating Curve (ROC) of each algorithm is compared and it shows that the Gradient Boosting algorithm gives the best results with the ROC area score of 0.90. After fine-tuning, certain parameters in Gradient Boosting algorithm like optimization of the learning rate, depth of the tree, the number of trees and minimum sample split. The obtained ROC area score is 0.94. Other performance parameters such as Accuracy, Precision, Recall and F1 score values before fine-tuning are 0.867, 0.8673, 0.866 and 0.8659 respectively and after fine-tuning the values are 0.9449, 0.9453, 0.9449 and 0.9448 respectively.

Keywords: Stroke · Distributed environment · Apache spark · Machine learning

© Springer Nature Switzerland AG 2021
D. Goswami and T. A. Hoang (Eds.): ICDCIT 2021, LNCS 12582, pp. 238–252, 2021.
https://doi.org/10.1007/978-3-030-65621-8_15

1 Introduction

A stroke is a cerebrovascular disease in which arteries carrying oxygen and nutrients to the brain gets ruptured and there is no blood supply to the parts of the brain. This result in complete damage of blood cells in the brain [6]. A Fairly large number of people are losing life, especially in developing countries [5]. According to the reports of the American Heart Association [10], the mortality rate for 2017 was 37.6 in every 100,000 stroke cases. According to the World Health Organization [12], stroke has been classified under non-communicable disease. The reports of 2012 say that Stroke was the main cause of death due to non-communicable disease, causing 17.5 million deaths.

Stroke is also the fourth major cause of death in India [16]. It is also the fifth major cause of death in the United States. Nearly 800,000 people have a stroke per year which equates to one person every 40 s. As this issue is increasing at an alarming rate, there is an emergent need to examine the health data and develop a system which could predict whether a person is likely to suffer a stroke or not. As with the advancement in maintaining medical data [4], it is easier to maintain Electronic Health records. As with growth in data, the importance of big data analytic [1] comes into play. The data used to make decisions in this system consists of various attributes like age, gender, BMI, smoking status, glucose level etc. The objective of the paper is to maximize the stroke detection rate of the patient i.e. correctly categorize the patients who are at risk of stroke and reduce the false alarms rate which will reduce the number of patients visiting hospitals if not necessary. The parameter SaveLife is the number of people who were saved due to correct prediction made by the system. MissLife is the number of people who had chances of stroke but were predicted of not having the stroke. FalseAlarm is the number of people who didn't have the chances of stroke but were predicted as having the stroke. Hence, the two terms i.e detection rate and false alarm rate can be described as

$$DetectionRate = \frac{Savelife}{saveLife + MissLife}$$

$$FalseAlarmRate = \frac{FalseAlarm}{SaveLife + FalseAlarm}$$

To develop a robust system, stroke detection rate should maximize and false alarm rate should minimize. Hence this trade-off is shown in Fig. 1. As the data is growing at an alarming rate, the importance of big data is comprehended. With this, the need for frameworks to process this enormous data is rapidly increasing, especially in the healthcare field. Apache Hadoop [2,17] is the emerging big data technology framework for distributed data storage and parallel processing. Apache Spark [9,15] is one of the framework which is designed for fast processing using in-memory computation.

In this paper, we use Apache spark as a data processing framework. Spark provides abstraction known as Resilient distributed dataset [18]. Spark executes operation 10 times faster on disk and 100 times faster in-memory than Hadoop.

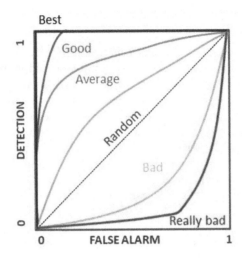

Fig. 1. Trade-off between stroke detection and false alarm rate

The Spark stack currently consists of Spark core engine along with libraries i.e MLlib for executing machine learning task in spark, Cluster Management to acquire cluster resource for performing jobs and Spark SQL which combines relational processing with Spark functional API.

The rest of the paper is organized as follows. In Sect. 2, the related work is described by comparing it with the proposed system performance. In Sect. 3, an elaborate description of the proposed solution is presented. It contains details about the data used and explanation of the system model. Section 4 contains the experimental analysis and results and also performance analysis of different models and Sect. 5 concludes the paper.

2   Related Work

In [13], an artificial neural network was used to predict the thrombo-embolic stroke disease. The dataset consisted of eight important features to be considered for prediction. Simple ANN model was built which evaluated the accuracy score of 0.89. It uses a relatively smaller dataset as it should use when working with deep learning models.

In [14], Support vector machine algorithm with all its four kernels i.e linear, quadratic, polynomial and RBF were used. The dataset consisted of features like - age, sex, atrial fibrillation, walking symptoms, face deficit, arm deficit, Leg deficit, dyphasia, visuospatial disorder, hemianopia, infarct visible on CT and cerebellar signs. They worked with 300 training samples and 50 testing samples. Accuracy score of the four kernels are as follows: linear was 91%, quadratic was 81%, RBF was 59% and polynomial was 87.9%.

In [8], authors used the dataset which consisted the attributes like Sex, Age, Province, Marital status, Education and occupation. They used three machine learning algorithms i.e. naive bayes, decision tree and neural network with six input layer, one hidden layer and two output layer to predict the stroke. The accuracy score obtained from decision tree was 75%, by naive bayes was 72% and by neural network it was 74%.

In [11], the data set consisted of 29074 records, of which 30% was used for testing and 70% training. The algorithm used was decision tree, random forest and neural network. The accuracy presented by decision tree was 74.31%, by random forest was 74.53% and 75.02% by neural network.

The limitation of the paper [8] and [11] is their accuracy score. The result depicts the predictions on which person's life depends and risking accuracy in medical domain costs high.

Among the related works, the accuracy predicted by our model has better results. We compared six models to choose the best performing model and then tuned the parameter to reach the state of art. The main contribution of our work is implanting Gradient Boosting algorithm and then tuning various parameters to reach an accuracy of 0.9449.

3   Proposed Solution

The objective of the paper is to build the robust system which can accurately detect whether a person will suffer from stroke or not. For this purpose, machine learning classification algorithms are applied on processed data in Apache spark framework. The proposed model works in a pseudo distributed environment. A Detailed description is given in following sub-sections.

3.1   Data Description

The dataset consists of 43400 entries of patients and 12 attributes as shown in Table 1. These attributes can be majorly divided into three parts i.e lifestyles factors, medical risk factors and non-controllable factors. Lifestyle factors constitutes the habit and indulgence of a person in a certain activity due to his own will. They consist of smoking, drinking habits, eating habits and physical activities. Medical risk factors are those factors for which chances of stroke can be controlled like high blood pressure, atrial fibrillation, high cholesterol, diabetes and circulation problems. Non-controllable factors include age, gender and ethnicity.

The data set contains various attributes like: gender, age, hypertension, heart disease, marital status, kind of occupation, residence area (rural or urban), average glucose level, Body Mass Index (BMI), smoking status and the stroke status.

3.2   System Architecture

The System architecture explains elaborately about each step as shown in Fig. 2. It is carried out from importing libraries to predicting whether patients will suffer from stroke or not. It explains the step by step process of the implementation

Table 1. Data set description

Attributes	Description
ID	Patients ID to avoid duplicity
Gender	Gender of patient
Age	Age of patient
Hypertension	No hypertension-0 Suffering hypertension-1
Heart disease	No heart disease-0 Suffering heartdisease-1
Marital status	Married or not
Work-type	Kind of Occupation person is involved
Residence area	Lives in urban or rural area
Avg-Glucose	Average glucose level of patient measured after meal
BMI	Body Mass Index of patient
Smoking-status	Patient smoking status
Stroke status	No Stroke-0 Stroke suffered-1

of stroke prediction system architecture. The very first step includes importing certain spark libraries. As we work with columnar data, we import Spark SQL libraries. The first point to use spark SQL is an object called Spark Session. It initializes the spark application and sets up the session where we can process data. After the session is created we load our data into the session. As the data is loaded into the session, we perform exploratory data analysis.

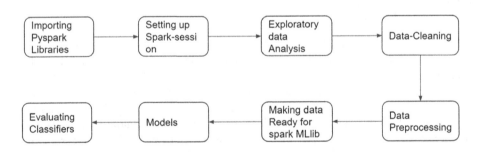

Fig. 2. System architecture

Exploratory Data Analysis. We analyse the uni-variate plots for six features such as Age, Avg-Glucose, BMI, heart disease, hypertension and stroke. From Fig. 3, we can observe that heart disease and hypertension happens to show correlation with each other. The plot of average glucose is slightly bi-modal in nature and not normal distribution as it seems to be. The standard deviation of average glucose is 43 with an average value of 140. The BMI plot is slightly skewed to the right and age is not uniform distribution but comes out that stroke is common around the age of 42 and a spike for old age and infants.

Next, we check the influence of Gender, BMI and Age on predicting the stroke percentage. It comes out that age is an important factor to be considered while evaluating the probability of stroke. In Fig. 4, it shows there is an abrupt increase in the stroke rate above the age of 40 years and diminishing rate below 20 years. The plots also help us to conclude that BMI is a relevant feature as it has less number of outliers and also high BMI value contributes to the greater probability of stroke than people with lower BMI values. Gender is also another factor, as per the data of 43400 people, 25665 are females and 17724 are males with females having 2.89% and males having 3.49% chances of getting a stroke.

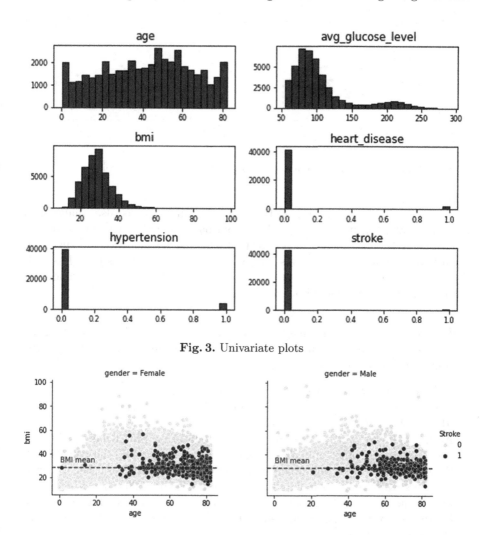

Fig. 3. Univariate plots

Fig. 4. Influence of age, gender and BMI on stroke

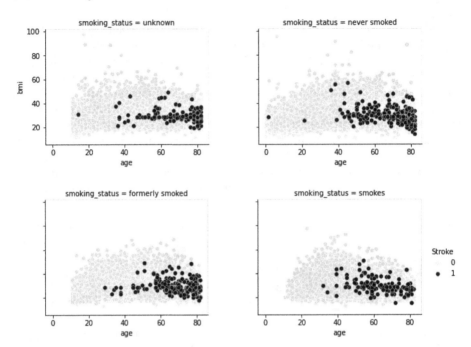

Fig. 5. Influence of age, smoking status and BMI on stroke

The effect of Smoking status, BMI and age on stroke is also analysed in Fig. 5. The smoking status is divided into four parts i.e. unknown, never smoked, formally smoked and smokes. It reveals that smoking is a factor to be considered when looked upon smokers versus non-smokers. Present smokers have less BMI than people who never smoked or older in age. The risk of stroke is highest for former smokers having age above 40.

Data Cleaning. After the analysis of data in the above section, there is a need to remove the outliers, duplicate values and also fill the missing values. In the dataset, it is observed that

- Age values range from negatives to values above 100.
- Patients-Ids which are duplicated, need to be resolved. Here we have 43400 Ids out of which 38713 unique Ids.
- Also, we ponder over the missing data and found that 1461 fields of BMI feature are missing. Since only 3% of BMI data is missing, we fill these fields with the mean value. This marginally reduces the correlation with other features.
- The missing data for a smoking status attribute is about 30% hence we fill the missing fields with new category which is unknown except with the intuitive knowledge we put "never smoked" for children of age below 10. Hence data cleaning is required.

Table 2. Statistical description of data.

	Id	Age	Hypertension	Heart-disease	Avg-glucose-level	BMI	Stroke
Count	43400.00	43400.00	43400.00	43400.00	43400.00	41938.00	43400.00
Mean	36326.14	42.22	0.09	0.05	104.48	28.61	0.02
Std	21072.13	22.52	0.29	0.21	43.11	7.77	0.13
Min	1.00	0.08	0.00	0.00	55.00	10.10	0.00
25%	18038.50	24.00	0.00	0.00	77.54	23.20	0.00
50%	36351.50	44.00	0.00	0.00	91.58	27.70	0.00
75%	54514.25	60.00	0.00	0.00	112.07	32.90	0.00
Max	72943.00	82.00	1.00	1.00	291.05	97.60	1.00

Table 2 gives the statistical description of the dataset. It shows total count, mean, standard deviation, minimum value, maximum value and quartile division. These quartile are made on the values of features present in the dataset.

Data Preprocessing. As we have cleaned the data, with no outliers and missing values, now we proceed to eradicate the issue of imbalance. If a class is imbalanced then the predicted output will always be biased. To address the issue, SMOTE technique has been used. Instead of directly oversampling the minority class, it first randomly selects a point from minority class and find the nearest neighbour. Now, among the neighbours, a point is chosen and a synthetic instance is created between these two. In this way, enumerable synthetic points can be generated [3] and the class imbalance can be re-balanced. This is shown in Figs. 6 and 7.

Preparing Data for PySpark to Process. After the data is processed, PySpark does not process the data in this form for implementation of machine learning algorithms. Machine learning algorithms cannot work solely with categorical data, it has further requirements which are fulfilled through String Indexer, One-hot encoder and Vector assembler. These are the steps for machine learning pipeline [7] as shown in Fig. 8.

Machine Learning Models. For this stroke Prediction Model, we used five ML models such as Naive Bayes, Logistic Regression, Decision Tree, Random Forest, Gradient Boosting algorithms.

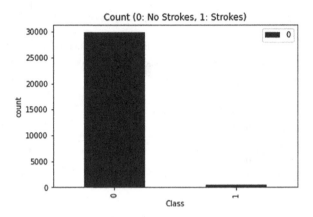

Fig. 6. Before class rebalancing

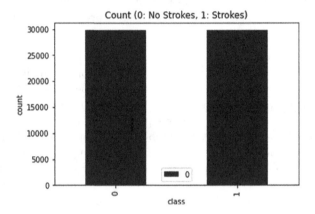

Fig. 7. After class re-balancing using SMOTE

Evaluating Classifiers. To evaluate the classifiers, we use the concept of confusion matrix. We define its four terms as below

TP (True Positive): Stroke is predicted, the person actually suffers from a stroke. We call it "Save Life".

TN (True Negative): No stroke is predicted, there is actually no stroke. We call it "Save Time".

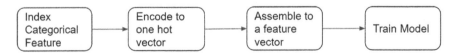

Fig. 8. Machine learning pipeline

FP (False Positive): Stroke is predicted but actually there is no Stroke. We call it "False Alarm".

FN (False Negative): No stroke is predicted but there is actually a stroke. We call it "Missed Life".

In order to evaluate the classifier and find out the most robust and efficient of all, we aim to maximize the Detection rate as

$$DetectionRate(Recall) = \frac{TP}{TP + FN}$$

To maximize Detection Rate term, we need to minimize FN i.e missed life. Also, we aim to reduce the False alarm rate such as

$$FalseAlarmRate = \frac{FP}{TN + FP}$$

To view the results, we use Receiver Operating Characteristic curve (ROC). Few parameters for performance criteria are defined as below

$$Accuracy = \frac{TP + TN}{TP + FP + FN + TN}$$

$$Precision = \frac{TP}{FP + TP}$$

$$Recall = \frac{TP}{TP + FN}$$

$$F1Measure = \frac{2 \times Recall \times Precision}{Recall + Precision}$$

Optimization of Algorithm. After evaluating various classifiers, an algorithm with the best result is chosen for further optimization. The ROC score of different machine learning algorithms is 0.66 for Naive Bayes, 0.83 for Decision Tree, 0.82 for Random Forest, 0.78 for Logistic Regression and 0.90 for gradient boosting as described in Fig. 13. The results show that the gradient boosting algorithm has the best ROC score of 0.90 and hence it is further optimized. The parameter optimized for gradient boosting algorithm are learning rate, tree depth, number of trees and minimum sample leaf. The optimal value for these parameters is chosen such that overfitting and underfitting are avoided. Figure 9 shows the performance of the model with varying learning rates. The value of the learning rate is varied from 0.0 to 1.6. The optimal value chosen is 0.9, for which model produces the best results.

Figure 10 shows the performance of the model with a varying number of trees. Increasing the number of trees results in more learning. This increases the training time, hence an optimal value is chosen. The number of trees is varied from 1 to 900. 600 is chosen for which model produces the best results.

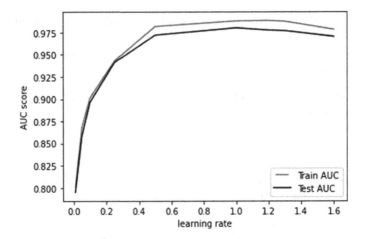

Fig. 9. Optimizing learning rate.

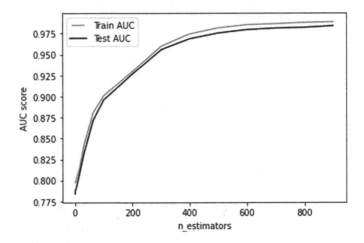

Fig. 10. Optimizing number of trees.

Figure 11 shows the performance of the model with varying the depth of the tree. Deeper the tree, better it learns. But increasing too much depth increases the overfitting. Hence the optimal value is 8 for this case. Figure 12 shows the performance of the model with varying the number of samples required to split an internal node. The value is varied from 1% to 30% and it is observed the increasing the value results in underfitting of data. Hence, the optimal value chosen is 0.04.

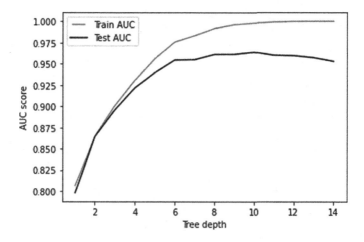

Fig. 11. Optimizing depth of the tree.

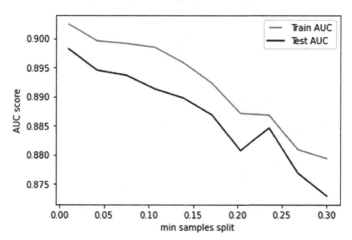

Fig. 12. Optimizing number of sample at node split.

4   Results and Analysis

In this section, we evaluate the ROC curve for each of the machine learning algorithms as shown in Fig. 13. We observe that Gradient Boosting algorithm has the highest accuracy of the value of 0.867. The ROC score obtained is 0.90. The precision, recall and F1 score are 0.8673, 0.866 and 0.8659 respectively. In order to predict more precisely, we tune the parameters of gradient boosting algorithm by optimizing the learning rate, tree depth, minimum number of samples required at the node split and the number of trees. After these tuning, the accuracy is 0.9449. The ROC score obtained is 0.94. The precision, recall and F1 scores are 0.9453, 0.9449, 0.9448. The ROC curve before and after fine tuning is as shown in Fig. 14.

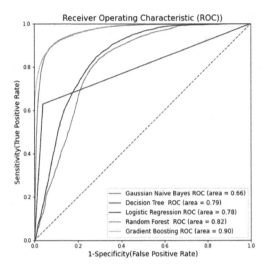

Fig. 13. Receiver operating curve

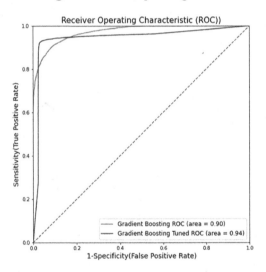

Fig. 14. Receiver pperating curve before and after tuning

Table 3 describes the classification report of Gradient boosting algorithm before tuning and Table 4 describes the classification report after tuning. The class 0 and class 1 represents No stroke and Stroke respectively. Figure 14 gives the insight about ROC value of each algorithm with gradient boosting performing the best and naive-bayes performing the least as it is a simple classification technique and requires data with no least correlating feature. The ROC score of different machine learning algorithm is 0.66 for Naive Bayes, 0.83 for Decision Tree, 0.82 for Random Forest, 0.78 for Logistic Regression and 0.90

Table 3. Classification report before tuning

	Precision	Recall	F1
Class 0	0.89	0.83	0.86
Class 1	0.84	0.90	0.87
Avg/Total	0.87	0.87	0.87

Table 4. Classification report after tuning

	Precision	Recall	F1
Class 0	0.93	0.96	0.95
Class 1	0.96	0.93	0.94
Avg/Total	0.95	0.95	0.94

for gradient boosting as described in Fig. 14. Figure 14 gives the insight about the comparative performance before and after tuning parameters in gradient boosting algorithm.

5   Conclusion

As the stroke disease is ranked fourth major cause of death in the category of non-communicable diseases, it is the need of the hour to bring this stroke prediction system which can predict the chances of whether the person can suffer from a stroke or not. Based on the results and extensive analysis of the data, preventive measures can be advised to patients to avoid the chances of suffering from a stroke. The system is built in a distributed machine learning environment using the Apache Spark framework. Among various classifiers, the gradient boosting algorithm performed the best with ROC of 0.88 score before tuning and 0.9449 score after tuning. The novel work contributed is training gradient boosting algorithm and improvising the accuracy from 0.867 to 0.9449 and ROC score from 0.90 to 0.95 by optimizing various parameters of gradient boosting algorithms. The future work will be to attain the state of art results by training deep learning models for a larger dataset.

References

1. Bates, D.W., Saria, S., Ohno-Machado, L., Shah, A., Escobar, G.: Big data in health care: using analytics to identify and manage high-risk and high-cost patients. Health Aff. **33**(7), 1123–1131 (2014)
2. Borthakur, D.: The Hadoop distributed file system: architecture and design. Hadoop Proj. Website **11**(2007), 21 (2007)
3. Chawla, N.V., Bowyer, K.W., Hall, L.O., Kegelmeyer, W.P.: SMOTE: synthetic minority over-sampling technique. J. Artif. Intell. Res. **16**, 321–357 (2002)

4. Chen, M., Hao, Y., Hwang, K., Wang, L., Wang, L.: Disease prediction by machine learning over big data from healthcare communities. IEEE Access **5**, 8869–8879 (2017)
5. Donaldson, M.S., Corrigan, J.M., Kohn, L.T., et al.: To Err is Human: Building a Safer Health System, vol. 6. National Academies Press, Washington, D.C. (2000)
6. Hafermehl, K.T.: High spatial resolution diffusion-weighted imaging (DWI) of ischemic stroke and transient ischemic attack (TIA) (2016)
7. Haihong, E., Zhou, K., Song, M.: Spark-based machine learning pipeline construction method. In: 2019 International Conference on Machine Learning and Data Engineering (iCMLDE), pp. 1–6. IEEE (2019)
8. Kansadub, T., Thammaboosadee, S., Kiattisin, S., Jalayondeja, C.: Stroke risk prediction model based on demographic data. In: 2015 8th Biomedical Engineering International Conference (BMEiCON), pp. 1–3. IEEE (2015)
9. Karau, H., Konwinski, A., Wendell, P., Zaharia, M.: Learning Spark: Lightning-Fast Big Data Analysis. O'Reilly Media, Inc., Sebastopol (2015)
10. Roger, V.L., et al.: Heart disease and stroke statistics—2012 update: a report from the American heart association. Circulation **125**(1), e2 (2012). Writing Group Members
11. Nwosu, C.S., Dev, S., Bhardwaj, P., Veeravalli, B., John, D.: Predicting stroke from electronic health records. In: 2019 41st Annual International Conference of the IEEE Engineering in Medicine and Biology Society (EMBC), pp. 5704–5707. IEEE (2019)
12. World Health Organization, et al.: Global status report on noncommunicable diseases 2014. No. WHO/NMH/NVI/15.1. World Health Organization (2014)
13. Shanthi, D., Sahoo, G., Saravanan, N.: Designing an artificial neural network model for the prediction of thrombo-embolic stroke. Int. J. Biometric Bioinform. (IJBB) **3**(1), 10–18 (2009)
14. Singh, M.S., Choudhary, P., Thongam, K.: A comparative analysis for various stroke prediction techniques. In: Nain, N., Vipparthi, S.K., Raman, B. (eds.) CVIP 2019. CCIS, vol. 1148, pp. 98–106. Springer, Singapore (2020). https://doi.org/10.1007/978-981-15-4018-9_9
15. Apache Spark: Apache spark: lightning-fast cluster computing, pp. 2168–7161 (2016). http://spark.apache.org
16. Subha, P.P., Geethakumari, S.M.P., Athira, M., Nujum, Z.T.: Pattern and risk factors of stroke in the young among stroke patients admitted in medical college hospital, Thiruvananthapuram. Ann. Indian Acad. Neurol. **18**(1), 20 (2015)
17. White, T.: Hadoop: The Definitive Guide. O'Reilly Media, Inc., Sebastopol (2012)
18. Zaharia, M., et al.: Resilient distributed datasets: a fault-tolerant abstraction for in-memory cluster computing. In: Presented as Part of the 9th {USENIX} Symposium on Networked Systems Design and Implementation ({NSDI} 2012), pp. 15–28 (2012)

Automated Diagnosis of Breast Cancer with RoI Detection Using YOLO and Heuristics

Ananya Bal[1], Meenakshi Das[2], Shashank Mouli Satapathy[1(✉)]🆔,
Madhusmita Jena[3], and Subha Kanta Das[4]

[1] School of Computer Science and Engineering, Vellore Institute of Technology,
Vellore, Tamil Nadu 632014, India
shashankamouli@gmail.com
[2] Department of Computer Science and Engineering, Indraprastha Institute of
Information Technology Delhi, New Delhi 110020, India
[3] Department of Pathology, East Point College of Medical Sciences and Research
Centre, Bengaluru, Karnataka 560049, India
[4] Department of Pathology, MKCG Medical College,
Brahmapur, Odisha 760004, India

Abstract. Breast Cancer (specifically Ductal Carcinoma) is widely diagnosed by Fine Needle Aspiration Cytology (FNAC). Deep Learning techniques like Convolutional Neural Networks (CNNs) can automatically diagnose this condition by processing images captured from FNAC. However, CNNs are trained on manually sampled RoI (Region of Interest) patches or hand-crafted features. Using a Region Proposal Network (RPN) can automate RoI detection and save time and effort. In this study, we have proposed the use of the YOLOv3 network as an RPN and supplemented it with image-based heuristics for RoI patch detection and extraction from cytology images. The extracted patches were used to train 3 CNNs - VGG16, ResNet-50 and Inception-v3 for classification. YOLOv3 identified 164 RoIs in 26 out of 27 images and we achieved 96.6%, 98.8% and 98.9% classification accuracies with VGG16, ResNet-50 and Inception-v3 respectively.

Keywords: Breast cancer · Computer aided diagnosis · Deep learning · RoI extraction and classification · YOLO

1 Introduction

The most common cancer among Indian women is breast cancer. In 2018, more than 1,60,000 new incidences of breast cancer were reported in India [5]. Ductal carcinoma is a cancer originating from the cells that line the milk ducts in breasts. More than 80% of all breast cancer cases are Ductal Carcinomas [4]. The National Cancer Registry Programme by the Indian Council of Medical Research estimates the rate of growth per decade of breast cancer in India lies within 15% and 20% [14]. Additionally, breast cancer prognosis in India is far worse than

© Springer Nature Switzerland AG 2021
D. Goswami and T. A. Hoang (Eds.): ICDCIT 2021, LNCS 12582, pp. 253–267, 2021.
https://doi.org/10.1007/978-3-030-65621-8_16

the prognosis in developed countries with merely 50% women surviving [13]. The lack of awareness and screening are two major causes for this dismal statistic. India also has very burdened diagnostic systems. Therefore, creating intelligent CAD (Computer-Automated Diagnosis) systems is necessary to improve breast cancer diagnosis and treatment.

Fine Needle Aspiration Cytology (FNAC) is the industry standard to diagnose breast cancer (Ductal Carcinoma). Pathologists use a narrow-gauge needle to collect a tissue sample from the breast for microscopic examination. The aspirated sample is fixed onto a slide and stained (common stains are Haematoxylin and Eosin (H&E), Pap, and Giemsa). A cytopathologist views stained slides under a microscope and makes a diagnosis. FNAC is preferred as it is minimally invasive and quick. While the process of FNAC remains manual, diagnosis from the microscopic images can be automated with the help of Computer Vision techniques.

Deep Learning can be used to extract features for visual context and classify cytology images from FNAC lesions. Convolutional Neural Networks (CNN), a class of deep learning models, yield state-of-the-art results for image classification problems. They are increasingly being adopted for digital diagnosis. While CNNs can tackle medical image classification, they require a lot of data preparation and manually extracted RoIs which contain the objects that need to be classified. Most medical and cellular images have a lot of irrelevant data. Thus, extracting RoIs from these images is time-consuming and is mostly done manually. A Region Proposal Network (RPN) can automatically detect RoIs which can then be classified by CNNs. We aimed to build a pipeline that could automatically detect RoIs, extract them and classify them. We have achieved this by using YOLOv3, heuristics and CNNs.

We present related literature in Sect. 2 and then outline our framework in detail in Sect. 3. This is followed by results and discussion in Sect. 4 and 5.

2   Prior Work

Given that mammograms usually have a single mass to be detected, YOLO has performed well in tumour detection in mammograms. Al-masni et al. [3] trained a YOLO-based CAD model that detected masses in mammograms and classified them as benign or malignant. The proposed system detected mass locations with 96.33% accuracy and distinguished between benign and malignant lesions with an accuracy of 85.52%. Mugahed A. et al. [2] proposed an integrated CAD system for lesion detection and classification from entire mammograms. A deep learning YOLO detector was used and evaluated for breast lesion detection. Then, three deep learning classifiers, a regular feedforward CNN, ResNet-50, and InceptionResNet-V2, were used for classification. Mugahed A. et al. [1] have utilized YOLO, a full-resolution convolutional network (FrCN) and Alexnet for RoI detection, segmentation and classification respectively. They achieved 98.96% mass detection accuracy, 92.97% segmentation accuracy and 95.64% classification accuracy.

YOLO is especially effective in identifying RoIs in video frames. Gao et al. [7] proposed an approach to detect Squamous Cell Carcinomas from Oesophageal Endoscopic Videos using mask-RCNN and YOLOv3. They have used a Non-Maxima Technique to ensure the detection of a single bounding box. The bounding box region is classified into three classes. YOLOv3 gave a detection accuracy of 85% and a classification accuracy of 74%. Ding et al. [6] proposed a novel approach for lesion localization in gastroscopic videos with a cloud-edge collaborative framework. They have detected upper gastrointestinal disease with a Tinier-YOLO algorithm and have improved the model performance by integrating lesion RoI segmentation into the YOLOv3 algorithm. Their results exhibit superior performance in mean Average Precision (mAP) and Intersection over Union (IOU) of lesion detection.

Spanhol et al. [19] used deep learning on histopathological images from BreakHis public dataset. They concluded that CNN performed better than other machine learning models. They also tested the combination of different CNNs using simple fusion rules, obtaining some improvement in performance. Saikia et al. [17] used CNNs for the diagnosis of cell samples from FNAC images and tested VGG16 and other network architectures for a comparative study. The results showed that GoogLeNet-V3 achieved 96.25% accuracy. Vesal et al. [22] fine-tuned the Inception-v3 and ResNet-50 networks and used transfer learning with weights from the ImageNet competition to classify the BACH 2018 challenge data. They achieved 97.08% classification accuracy for Inception-v3 and 96.66% classification accuracy for ResNet-50.

3 Proposed Framework

The workflow of our proposed framework can be seen in Fig. 1. The framework can be divided into six modules which are as follows:

3.1 Data Collection

Pathologists view slides with stained tissue from FNAC under microscopes for diagnosis. The microscopic lesions, as viewed under the microscope, can be captured by a camera to produce digital images. For this study, FNAC images of breast lesions with Giemsa stain were captured in the pathology labs at East Point College of Medical Sciences and Research Centre, Bangalore, India and Maharaja Krushna Chandra Gajapati Medical College, Brahmapur, Odisha, India following all ethical protocols.

Benign FNAC samples collected from 40 patients and malignant FNAC samples (Ductal Carcinoma NOS) collected from 30 patients were used. These samples were observed at 400x magnification by certified cytopathologists using a CH-20i Olympus Binocular Microscope and an LM-52–6000 Lawrence and Mayo Multi viewing Microscope. The diagnosis for each sample has been confirmed by histopathology. Image collection methods were consistent.

On an average, 1 to 2 images were taken per patient's sample. This produced 79 images of benign lesions and 56 images of malignant lesions. Roughly 80% of these images were used for training (64 benign images and 44 malignant images) the YOLOv3 network after annotation. The remaining images were used for testing (15 benign images and 12 malignant images). All test images belonged to different patients. For training the CNN, 4 to 8 RoI patches of size 256 × 256 pts were extracted from each image in the training set depending on the cellular content. This resulted in 389 benign patches and 300 malignant patches as presented in Table 1.

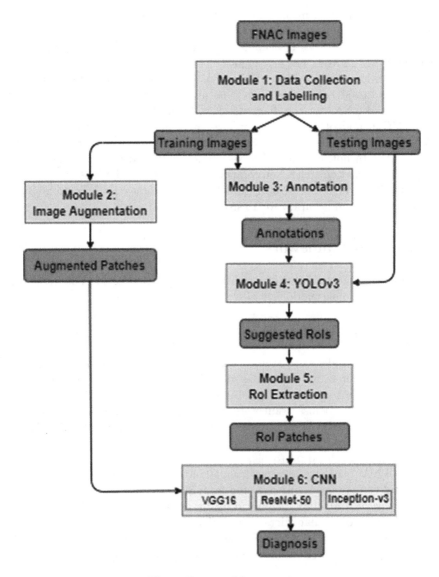

Fig. 1. Proposed framework

Table 1. Data distribution

Category	Benign	Malignant
Slide Images	79	56
Images for training YOLO	64	44
Images for testing YOLO	15	12
RoI patches for training CNN	389	300
Augmented patches for training CNN	2334	1800

3.2 Image Augmentation for CNNs

Neural networks can overfit on small datasets, rendering them unable generalize to larger unseen test data. To avoid this and to obtain good classification accuracy, we have increased the cardinality of our training data for the CNN classifiers through data augmentation. We applied geometric transformations, i.e., flipping, mirroring and rotation. Microscopic cellular images are rotationally invariant i.e., a pathologist will be able to make a diagnosis irrespective of the angle of rotation of the image. Therefore, our image patches were rotated by 90° three times, resulting in 4 images. Similarly, flipped or mirrored images of cells can still be diagnosed by a pathologist. As a result of the augmentation, the cardinality of our training data grew by a factor of 6, resulting in 2334 benign training patches and 1800 malignant training patches. Nearly 75% of these RoI patches were placed under the training set and the remaining were placed under the validation set as provided in Table 1.

3.3 Annotation for YOLOv3

The training images need to be annotated to define ground truth for the RoI detection model. Annotation is the process of identifying an object in an image with a box and tagging the object with a label. This was done with the help of the Microsoft Visual Object Tagging Tool (VoTT) software. This process saves the x and y coordinates of the boxes we draw to enclose the RoIs. The process is seen in Fig. 2.

Object annotation is largely subjective. There is no set method for annotating irregularly-shaped cell clusters. Many cell clusters are big and occupy a large part of the image. These clusters were not annotated with single large boxes as this would pick up more background information than is desirable. Instead, as seen in Fig. 2, multiple smaller and tight-fitting boxes were used to cover the entire cell cluster. This resulted in higher object to background ratio.

3.4 RoI Detection with YOLO

YOLO (You Only Look Once) is a unified CNN-based architecture that can identify and classify objects [15]. It is faster than other networks used for object

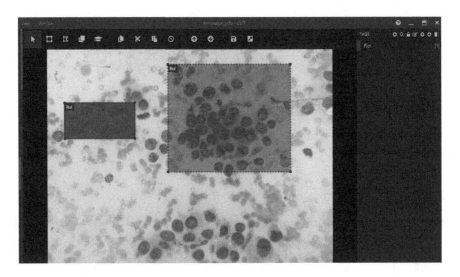

Fig. 2. Image annotation with Micrsoft VoTT

detection and is therefore uniquely suited to object detection in video frames. As the name suggests, YOLO looks at the entire image to learns context instead of looking at smaller parts of the image. Object detection is formulated as a regression problem in the YOLO architecture.

An image is divided into a grid and each grid cell detects bounding boxes for objects whose centres lie within the cell. The grid cells predict bounding boxes for objects by resizing a fixed number of boxes of different aspect ratios called anchors. After this, confidence values for the boxes are calculated (Eqs. 1 and 2). They indicate the model's confidence in the accuracy of the box's fit to an object.

Duplicate boxes or boxes having a high degree of overlap with other boxes are discarded by Non-maximal Suppression (NMS) which looks at the Intersection Over Union (IOU) between proposed bounding boxes. In NMS, the proposed bounding box with the highest confidence is added to a list and other proposed bounding boxes which have a high IOU with the boxes already in the list are discarded on the grounds of duplicity. This process is done iteratively and an IOU threshold is set for the same.

$$IOU = \frac{Area\ in\ intersection}{Area\ in\ union} \tag{1}$$

$$ConfidenceValue\ (cv)\ =\ P(RoI) \times IOU \tag{2}$$

where,

$P(RoI)$ is the probability of the object being in the bounding box.

A CNN is used to learn the parameters of bounding boxes - the coordinates of the centre of the box relative to the grid cell, height, width and the confidence value (x, y, h, w, cv). The class of the object can also be learned by the CNN. But in our framework, taking inspiration from studies [1,2], we test YOLO as a region proposal network only. Hence, we have used it for RoI detection solely and not to classify the suggested RoIs. Features are extracted in the first few layers while the fully-connected layers at the end predict bounding box coordinates as well as class probabilities, if classification is also to be done. The loss function of the CNN is a modified sum squared error function. This is similar to the squared error losses (Root Mean Squared error and Mean Squared Error) in regression.

Since FNAC is the conclusive diagnostic test for breast cancer, testing the efficiency of YOLO as an RPN on cytology images is crucial. We have not found literature which has attempted this. There are certain challenges associated with cytological images because they contain cell clusters that do not have clearly demarcated boundaries. They vary a lot in size and shape. But the biggest challenge with these images is the presence of multiple RoIs in close proximity, unlike in the case of most radiological images, where there is only one RoI. Hence, multiple bounding-boxes are required to cover all and many of these overlap. To conclude, identifying RoIs in these images is a complex problem and required modifications in the YOLO network.

YOLOv3 Network

The YOLOv3 network is an improved version of YOLO. It has two parts - a Feature Extractor and a Detector. The architecture can be seen in Fig. 3.

DarkNet53 is the feature extractor [16] and has 53 layers - 52 convolution layers and one fully-connected layer. There are 23 residual blocks which contain residual layers. Residual blocks use skip connections [8]. The convolution layers use the Leaky ReLU activation function (Eq. 3) [12] to avoid dying neurons which occur with the ReLU (Eq. 4) function when the input is lower than 0.

The detector module has 53 layers consisting of 1×1 and 3×3 convolution layers and two upsampling layers. The feature extractor downsizes the input and the detector module applies 1×1 detection kernels on feature maps from the last layers of the last three residual blocks. The detection occurs at three different scales. The feature map from the first scale is upsampled (enlarged) by a factor of 2 for the second scale and the feature map from the second scale is upsampled by a factor of 2 for the third scale. Each grid cell predicts three bounding boxes using three anchors at each scale, making the total number of anchors used 9. The different scales help the network detect objects of all sizes, especially small ones.

The confidence values are calculated for all detected boxes and the best fitting box is retained by NMS. The final output is a list of detected bounding boxes which enclose RoIs. We used transfer learning by leveraging the pre-trained DarkNet53 weights on ImageNet data. The training continued for 50 epochs with an initial learning rate of 0.0001 which was gradually reduced. We implemented the network with Keras and Tensorflow in Python.

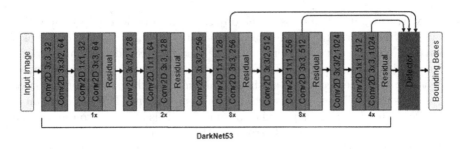

Fig. 3. YOLOv3 architecture

Leaky ReLU activation function :

$$f(x) = \begin{cases} x & if \ x > 0; \\ 0.1x & otherwise \end{cases} \tag{3}$$

After fine-tuning hyperparameters, we established a batch size of 12 for the network and used the RMSprop optimizer [9] instead of Adam [11] which is the default optimizer in DarkNet53. 15% of the training data was used for validation. The key change in our implementation was the choice of the confidence value threshold. Traditionally, a value (0.5-0.95) is used to retain the best-fitting bounding boxes that have confidence scores above the threshold. However, given the complex nature of our images and RoIs, the threshold was lowered to 0.1 to retain a few poorly fit bounding boxes. This ensures that bounding boxes are retained for most RoIs and a sufficient number of RoIs are detected for diagnosis by classification.

3.5 Heuristic RoI Patch Extraction

The YOLOv3 network performed reasonably well in detecting RoIs in the test images. To use CNNs for classification, all RoI patches need to be of a uniform size. However, the bounding boxes and their respective RoIs, vary in size and shape. One solution to overcome this hurdle is to resize all RoIs to a single dimension. However, resizing alters the shape of cells especially if the aspect ratio of the RoI is not maintained. The RoIs vary in shape and so resizing them all to a single fixed size (256 × 256 in our case) would stretch the cells in the patches. Since the distinction in shape between benign and malignant cells is important in interpreting features for a diagnosis, it is not wise to resize the RoIs. The other solution is to take a smaller, fixed-size patch from each RoI. But this approach leads to loss of data. The cells which are in the RoI but not in the patch may be essential features. Therefore, our objective was to extract a minimum number of patches from any suggested RoI such that we maximized the features covered, while having minimum overlap among patches. We tackled this with heuristics.

Upon examination of the dimensions of all bounding boxes, we identified 10 categories of RoIs based on variations in width (x) and height (y). The number of 256×256 patches that could be extracted from an RoI depended on the category into which the RoI fell. The categories are:

- *Category 1 ($x < 256$ and $y < 256$): RoIs* in this category had x and y values which were nearly equal and only slightly less than 256 pts. Thus, they could be enlarged to 256×256 pts without significant changes to their aspect ratios. The enlarged RoI was taken as a single 256×256 patch.
- *Category 2 ($256 \leq x \leq 350$ and $256 \leq y \leq 350$):* Due to the square-like shape and smaller size, a single patch was taken from the centre of RoIs in this category.
- *Category 3 ($256 \leq x < 350$ and $350 \leq y < 500$):* RoIs in this category were rectangles since their heights are larger than their widths. For these RoIs, two patches were taken vertically along the midpoint of the width.
- *Category 4 ($350 \leq x < 500$ and $256 \leq y < 350$):* RoIs in this category were also rectangles since their widths are larger than their heights. For these RoIs, two patches were taken horizontally along the midpoint of the height.
- *Category 5 ($350 \leq x < 500$ and $350 \leq y < 500$):* RoIs in this category were square-like in shape. Four patches were taken from the corners for these RoIs.
- *Category 6 ($300 \leq x < 500$ and $500 \leq y$):* RoIs in this category were rectangles. For these RoIs, four patches were taken from the corners and two patches were taken horizontally along the midpoint of the height.
- *Category 7 ($500 \leq x$ and $300 \leq y < 500$):* RoIs in this category were also rectangles. For these RoIs, four patches were taken from the corners and two patches were taken vertically along the midpoint of the width.
- *Category 8 ($500 \leq x$ and $500 \leq y$):* These RoIs could be square or rectangles but since we know that most of the cells lie in the centre of the RoI, we take one patch from the centre and four other patches along the sides of the central patch.
- *Category 9 ($256 \leq x < 300$ and $500 \leq y$):* Three patches are taken vertically for these RoIs along the midpoint of the width.
- *Category 10 ($500 \leq x$ and $256 \leq y < 300$):* Three patches are taken horizontally for these RoIs along the midpoint of the height.

The visual representation of heuristic categories is presented in Fig. 4.

3.6 Classification with CNNs

We have tested three different CNNs on the extracted RoI patches. The networks use the 256×256 patches taken from the training images and predicts class labels (benign and malignant) for all the RoI patches from the previous module.

VGG16: VGG stands for Visual Geometry Group, the team that submitted the network for the ILSVRC-2014 [18]. VGG16 comprises of 16 layers - 13 convolution layers and three fully-connected layers. All layers, except the last, use the ReLU (Eq. 4) activation function. The layers can be segregated into blocks where the first two blocks have two layers each, and the next three blocks have

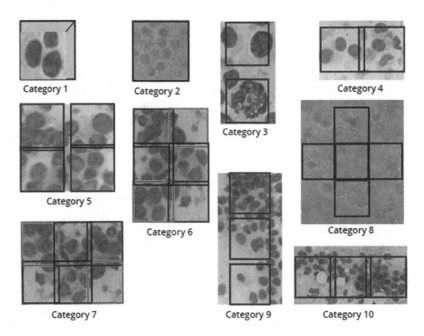

Fig. 4. Suggested RoIs and their Heuristic categories

three layers each. The number of filters in the convolution layers block-wise is 64, 128, 256, 512, and 512. There are five max-pooling layers, one at the end of each block. The network uses 3 × 3 sized filters and 2 × 2 max pooling. The first two fully-connected layers have 4096 nodes each. The last fully-connected layer has a single node and uses the Sigmoid activation function. The VGG16 architecture is presented in Fig. 5.

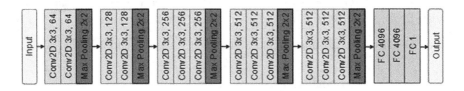

Fig. 5. VGG16 architecture

ResNet-50: ResNet-50 is a deep CNN which employs residual learning via skip connections. This helps solve the vanishing gradient problem [8]. The network architecture has two types of blocks - convolution blocks and identity blocks. The convolution block has four convolution layers. Three are positioned back to back and the fourth convolution layer is along the skip connection. The identity block has three convolution layers back to back and a skip connection to bypass these layers. The network starts with a 7 × 7 convolution layer which is followed by 4 residual blocks and 12 identity blocks where multiple identity blocks follow one residual block. This is followed by a global average-pooling layer and a fully-connected layer with a single node. The activation function is ReLU. The last layer uses Sigmoid function. The architecture is seen in Fig. 6.

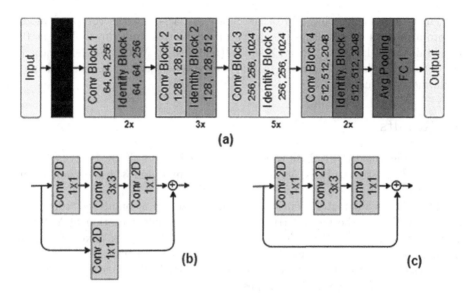

Fig. 6. (a) ResNet-50 network (b) Convolution block (c) Identity block

Inception-V3: This network was first introduced during the ImageNet Recognition challenge. It stacks inception modules [20], where each module consists of convolutional layers with ReLU activation function and pooling layers in parallel. Inception modules are used in CNNs for efficient computation through dimensionality reduction. They have sparsely connected with 1 × 1, 1 × 3, 3 × 1, 3 × 3, 1 × 7, and 7 × 1 sized convolution layers whose outputs are concatenated into a single vector and used as the input for the next layer [21]. The network is faster to train than previous Inception networks due to the addition of Batch Normalization [10]. The architecture of inception modules and the network can be seen in [20]. Before the last fully-connected layer, we have added an average pooling layer followed by batch normalization and dropout of 0.5, respectively.

All the three networks have a single node in the last fully-connected layer and use the sigmoid activation function (Eq. 5) here because ours is a binary classification problem. All networks were implemented with Keras and Tensorflow in Python. They were trained for 50 epochs using NVIDIA Tesla P100 GPU support from Kaggle. We used the RMSprop optimizer and a learning rate of 0.0001

ReLU (Rectified Linear Unit) activation function :

$$f(x) = \begin{cases} 0 \; if \; x < 0 \\ x \; if \; x \geq 0 \end{cases} \tag{4}$$

Sigmoid Activation function $f(x) = \dfrac{1}{1 + e^{-x}}$ (5)

The test set consisting of RoI patches was passed to the compiled model to produce class probabilities (0–1). The probabilities were thresholded at 0.5 to obtain class labels 0 (benign) and 1 (malignant). With another vector of the actual class labels, confusion matrices were generated and used to calculate evaluation parameters.

4   Results

YOLOv3 identified 164 RoIs in 26 images. It failed to identify RoIs in one image. Applying heuristics to RoIs, 584 patches (240 benign and 344 malignant) were extracted.

The YOLOv3 detector identified 164 RoIs that had a confidence score > 0.1 and an IOU with the ground truth >= 0.5. Our implementation of YOLOv3 generated an Average Precision of 29.3% with 560 bounding boxes, failing to predict any RoI with confidence score > 0.1 for one image in 27 images. This indicates the complexity of cytology images and that YOLOv3 was 96% effective in detecting RoIs in cytological images.

Table 2. Results

Metric	Formula	VGG16	ResNet-50	Inception-v3
Accuracy	$\frac{(TP + TN)}{Total\ Cases}$	0.966	0.988	0.989
Precision	$\frac{TP}{(TP + FP)}$	0.996	0.985	1
Recall (or Sensitivity)	$\frac{TP}{(TP + FN)}$	0.944	0.994	0.982
Specificity	$\frac{TN}{(FP + TN)}$	0.996	0.979	1
False Positive Rate	$\frac{FP}{(FP + TN)}$	0.004	0.021	0
False Negative Rate	$\frac{FN}{(FN + TP)}$	0.055	0.005	0.017

The final diagnosis was the majority class from the predicted labels for all RoIs in images from a patient's sample. We tested the system for accuracy in diagnosing a patient's sample. The framework gave the correct diagnosis for all but one patient's test image, failing only when the YOLO detector could not find any RoIs.

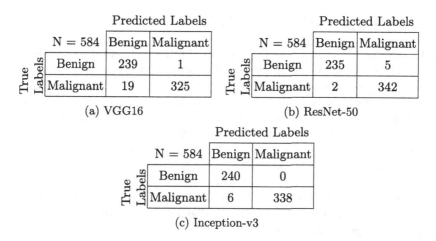

(a) VGG16   (b) ResNet-50

(c) Inception-v3

Fig. 7. Confusion matrices for VGG16, ResNet-50 and Inception-v3

Among the CNN classifiers, Inception-v3 performed the best for our data shown in Table 2. Sensitivity and specificity are especially important for assessing the performance of medical tests and while all three networks give above-satisfactory values, Inception-v3 and ResNet-50 are the obvious choices, because their sensitivity and specificity values are both high. Inception-v3 has a slight edge over Resnet-50 as it does not falsely classify any benign patches as malignant (False positive rate is 0). While VGG16 has a high specificity value, its sensitivity value is low. This combined with its lower accuracy value makes VGG16 an inferior model. Refer Table 2. All metrics provided in Table 2 are calculated from the confusion matrices shown in Fig. 7.

5 Conclusion

Our implementation of YOLOv3 is 96% effective in suggesting RoIs. It fails for one image only but since the diagnosis is dependent on RoIs, having zero RoIs from an image will result in no diagnosis. This needs to be overcome with further improvements to the YOLOv3 detector network. The addition of more data to the pipeline will also certainly improve the bounding box detection.

Overall, our framework performed very well in detecting and classifying RoIs in cytology images from breast FNAC lesions. The diagnostic accuracy of our framework lies between 96.6% and 98.9% depending on the choice of classifier network. High precision, sensitivity and specificity values make the framework suitable for industry applications. We conclude that the YOLOv3 network is an effective Region Proposal Network for cytological images. The combination of YOLOv3, heuristics and CNNs fully automates the diagnosis of Ductal Carcinoma with good classification accuracy and with further improvement, can be used in medical laboratories.

6   Discussion and Future Work

While lowering the confidence threshold in YOLO can retain more bounding boxes, unless the RPN is improved in terms of training and/or architecture, there can be cases where no RoIs are detected and a diagnosis is not possible. The RPN can either be trained on datasets which are similar to ours or be trained on more data. Also, other RPN architectures such as SSD (Single Shot Detector) and Faster RCNN can be tested in the pipeline. In the future, we will work on integrating detection and classification into a single network.

YOLOv3 detects more bounding boxes for the malignant test images even though they are lesser in number than the benign test images. Therefore, the number of malignant patches is also higher. This shows that the learning is skewed and that the network identifies malignant cells better than it identifies benign cells. Again, the addition of more data is expected to resolve this issue.

Acknowledgment. We acknowledge the help and support of lab technicians and pathologists at East Point College of Medical Sciences and Research Centre and Hospital, Bengaluru, India, and Maharaja Krushna Chandra Gajapati Medical College, Brahmapur, Odisha, India. Their diligent efforts and coordination have made this study possible.

This research did not receive any specific grant from funding agencies in the public, commercial, or not-for-profit sectors.

References

1. Al-Antari, M.A., Al-Masni, M.A., Choi, M.T., Han, S.M., Kim, T.S.: A fully integrated computer-aided diagnosis system for digital x-ray mammograms via deep learning detection, segmentation, and classification. Int. J. Med. Inf. **117**, 44–54 (2018)
2. Al-antari, M.A., Kim, T.S.: Evaluation of deep learning detection and classification towards computer-aided diagnosis of breast lesions in digital x-ray mammograms. Computer Methods and Programs in Biomedicine p. 105584 (2020)
3. Al-masni, M.A., et al.: Detection and classification of the breast abnormalities in digital mammograms via regional convolutional neural network. In: 2017 39th Annual International Conference of the IEEE Engineering in Medicine and Biology Society (EMBC). pp. 1230–1233. IEEE (2017)
4. Breastcancer.org: Invasive ductal carcinoma: Diagnosis, treatment, and more. https://www.breastcancer.org/symptoms/types/idc (2019)
5. Cancer Today: International Agency for research on Cancer: Iarc world cancer report 2020. https://www.iccp-portal.org/sites/default/files/resources/IARC-World-Cancer-Report-2020.pdf (2018). Accessed: 20 Feb 2020
6. Ding, S., Li, L., Li, Z., Wang, H., Zhang, Y.: Smart electronic gastroscope system using a cloud-edge collaborative framework. Future Generation Comput. Syst. **100**, 395–407 (2019)
7. Gao, X., Braden, B., Taylor, S., Pang, W.: Towards real-time detection of squamous pre-cancers from oesophageal endoscopic videos. In: 2019 18th IEEE International Conference on Machine Learning and Applications (ICMLA). pp. 1606–1612. IEEE (2019)

8. He, K., Zhang, X., Ren, S., Sun, J.: Deep residual learning for image recognition. In: Proceedings of the IEEE Conference on Computer Vision and Pattern Recognition. pp. 770–778 (2016)
9. Hinton, G., Srivastava, N., Swersky, K.: Coursera: Neural networks for machine learning: Lecture 6(a)–overview of mini-batch gradient descent. https://www.cs.toronto.edu/~tijmen/csc321/slides/lecture_slides_lec6.pdf (2014)
10. Ioffe, S., Szegedy, C.: Batch normalization: Accelerating deep network training by reducing internal covariate shift. arXiv preprint arXiv:1502.03167 (2015)
11. Kingma, D.P., Ba, J.: Adam: A method for stochastic optimization. arXiv preprint arXiv:1412.6980 (2014)
12. Maas, A.L., Hannun, A.Y., Ng, A.Y.: Rectifier nonlinearities improve neural network acoustic models. In: Proceedings of ICML. vol. 30, p. 3 (2013)
13. National Cancer Institute (NCI-AIIMS: Cancer statistics — drupal. http://nciindia.aiims.edu/en/cancer-statistics (2020)
14. National Centre for Disease Informatics and Research: NCPR three-year report of population based cancer registries 2012–2014. https://ncdirindia.org/NCRP/ALL_NCRP_REPORTS/PBCR_REPORT_2012_2014/ALL_CONTENT/PDF_Printed_Version/Chapter10_Printed.pdf (2020)
15. Redmon, J., Divvala, S., Girshick, R., Farhadi, A.: You only look once: Unified, real-time object detection. In: Proceedings of the IEEE Conference on Computer Vision and Pattern Recognition. pp. 779–788 (2016)
16. Redmon, J., Farhadi, A.: Yolov3: An incremental improvement. arXiv preprint arXiv:1804.02767 (2018)
17. Saikia, A.R., Bora, K., Mahanta, L.B., Das, A.K.: Comparative assessment of cnn architectures for classification of breast fnac images. Tissue Cell **57**, 8–14 (2019)
18. Simonyan, K., Zisserman, A.: Very deep convolutional networks for large-scale image recognition. arXiv preprint arXiv:1409.1556 (2014)
19. Spanhol, F.A., Oliveira, L.S., Petitjean, C., Heutte, L.: Breast cancer histopathological image classification using convolutional neural networks. In: 2016 International Joint Conference on Neural Networks (IJCNN), pp. 2560–2567. IEEE (2016)
20. Szegedy, C., et al.: Going deeper with convolutions. In: Proceedings of the IEEE Conference On Computer Vision And Pattern Recognition. pp. 1–9 (2015)
21. Szegedy, C., Vanhoucke, V., Ioffe, S., Shlens, J., Wojna, Z.: Rethinking the inception architecture for computer vision. In: Proceedings of the IEEE Conference On Computer Vision And Pattern Recognition, pp. 2818–2826 (2016)
22. Vesal, S., Ravikumar, N., Davari, A.A., Ellmann, S., Maier, A.: Classification of breast cancer histology images using transfer learning. In: Campilho, A., Karray, F., ter Haar Romeny, B. (eds.) ICIAR 2018. LNCS, vol. 10882, pp. 812–819. Springer, Cham (2018). https://doi.org/10.1007/978-3-319-93000-8_92

Short Papers

An Efficient Approach for Event Prediction Using Collaborative Distance Score of Communities

B. S. A. S. Rajita$^{(\boxtimes)}$ ⓘ, Bipin Sai Narwa, and Subhrakanta Panda ⓘ

CSIS, BITS-Pilani, Hyderabad Campus, Pilani, India
{p20150409,f20170030,spanda}@hyderabad.bits-pilani.ac.in

Abstract. An effective technique for prediction of events can capture the evolution of communities and help understand the collaborative trends in massive dataset applications. One major challenge is to find the derived features that can improve the accuracy of ML models in efficient prediction of events in such evolutionary patterns.

It is often observed that a group of researchers associate with another set of researchers having similar interests to pursue some common research goals. A study of such associations forms an essential basis to assess collaboration trends and to predict evolving topics of research. A hallmarked co-authorship dataset such as DBLP plays a vital role in identifying collaborative relationships among the researchers based on their academic interests.

The association between researchers can be calculated by computing their collaborative distance. Refined Classical Collaborative Distance (RCCD) proposed in this paper is an extension of existing Classical Collaborative distance (CCD).

This computed RCCD score is then considered as a derived feature along with other community features for effective prediction of events in DBLP dataset.

The experimental results show that the existing CCD method predicts events with an accuracy of 81.47%, whereas the accuracy of our proposed RCCD method improved to 84.27%. Thus, RCCD has been instrumental in enhancing the accuracy of ML models in the effective prediction of events such as trending research topics.

Keywords: Social networks · Community mining · Event prediction · Collaboration distance · Machine learning

1 Introduction

A massive data set is a collection of voluminous data that can be represented in the form of a *social network (SN)* to understand relations among the data such as associations, behavior, interactions, and collaborative trends etc. A SN is a graphical representation of the dataset consisting of nodes interconnected

© Springer Nature Switzerland AG 2021
D. Goswami and T. A. Hoang (Eds.): ICDCIT 2021, LNCS 12582, pp. 271–279, 2021.
https://doi.org/10.1007/978-3-030-65621-8_17

through edges. Such graphical representation of these SNs consists of nodes that correspond to individual entities, and edges correspond to the relationship between the nodes (entities) [8].

A community is defined to be a subset (subgraph) of the graphical representation of a social network. A community represents dense intra-connection among its nodes and sparse inter-connection with the nodes that are outside the community. The structure of these communities change according to the occurrence of different events, such as *Form*, *Dissolve*, *Same*, *Split*, and *Merge* [2].

Researchers often form different collaborations in order to discover new knowledge, improve individual skills or specialization, and also for pursuing inter-disciplinary research goals. Such association is an essential basis to assess collaborative trends and to identify trending (evolving) topics of research. Supposing a researcher X switches to another research domain (community) then it will certainly impact the structure of both parent and host communities. Such structural changes (transitions) also reflect a collaborative change that attributes to SN evolution [4,9]. Therefore, prediction of events is essential in many areas of SN applications related to mining the underlying structure and detection of the network's structural properties. Thus prediction of the future state of the communities have recently drawn significant attention of the researchers [11].

This paper aims to improve the accuracy in the prediction of events that are likely to occur within the communities. But, one of the major challenges in such evolutionary patterns, in a massive dataset, is finding the derived features of communities that improve the accuracy of ML models for efficient prediction events [6]. This paper envisages to calculate the collaborative change by calculating the distance between community of researchers (Authors of research articles), who change their publishing pattern (area of interest). Thereby influences a collaborative change in the communities (occurrence of an event) of a co-authorship dataset. For this purpose, collaborative distance is proposed as an additional feature along with other community features to train the machine learning models for better accuracy in prediction.

The organization of the rest of the paper is as follows: Sect. 2 gives the details of the background and the proposed methodology. The performance and comparative analysis of the experimental results of our proposed approach are available in Sect. 3. Section 4 concludes the work with some insights into our future work.

2 Background and Proposed Methodology

In this section, we give a basic understanding of the SNs and our methodology. A SN can be represented as a set of graphs over a set of timestamps, {1,2, ..., T}. Thus, a SN can be represented in the form of $\{G^t\}_{t=1}^T$, where each $G^t = (V^t, E^t)$ represents the entire snapshot (graphical representation) at timestamp t, $V^t = \{v_1, v_2, v_3, ...v_m\}$ is the set of m vertices and $E^t = \{e_1, e_2, e_3, ...e_n\}$ is the set of n edges. The timestamp considered in this paper to construct the graphs is one year.

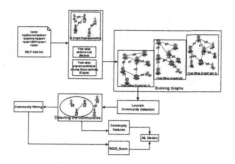

Fig. 1. A proposed framework for event prediction in a social network.

Table 1. Comparative analysis of nine community detection algorithms

Community Algorithm	CC	M	Time(sec)
Louvain	**0.83**	**0.96**	**20**
Multilevel	0.73	0.96	40
Fastgreedy	0.73	0.95	756
Label propagation	0.88	0.88	831
Infomap	0.67	0.87	3433
Walktrap	0.65	0.84	5996
Eigenvector	0.61	0.77	533
Spinglass	0.55	0.78	42083
Edgebetweeness	0.45	0.36	44592

A community, C_G, where $C_G \subseteq G$, is a sub-graph having densely connected internal nodes and these nodes have a sparse connection with other $G - C_G$ nodes. The density is computed as the average degree of vertices in C_G, given as $D_{C_G} = \frac{\sum_{i=1}^{N}(d_{C_G}^{+}(V_i)+d_{C_G}^{-}(V_i))}{N}$, to find the communities of G. So, a set of i communities of Graph G for year t is represented as $C_{Gt} = \{C_{1t}, C_{2t}, C_{3t}, ...C_{it}\}$.

Community mining refers to the detection of structural changes in a sequence of communities over a period of time [5,13]. Supposing C_{G1} to C_{Gt} are sequence of communities over the years, y_1 to y_t, $1 \leq t \leq T$. Next we need a technique to identify the dependence of changes in these communities on the behavior of the nodes in the community [1,10]. This can be depicted by finding *direct features (Community features)* and *Derived features*.

The proposed framework (shown in Fig. 1) is to detect the communities, extract features from the communities, compute RCCD values, and predict events using ML (Machine Learning) models. The first step in Fig. 1 is to convert XML format of DBLP data into a vector format. The second step is to graphically represent the temporal data of each year. In the third step, we detect the communities for each year of data using the Louvain approach. The results proves that Louvain detects communities in less *Time* with high *Clustering Co-efficient(CC)* and *Modularity(M)* as compared to the other eight methods (refer Table 1). In the fourth step, we applied the algorithm in [2] to mine (identify the events) detected communities in previous step. These identified events are labeled with their communities using LDA approach [7]. In the fifth step, we compute the community features (Sect. 2.1) and the RCCD score (Sect. 2.2) of the communities. These scores are then used as feature of the ML model for the prediction of events.

2.1   Community Features

The extraction of community features is significant in identifying the evolutionary patterns of the communities. In this work, we identified 13 categorical community features [12] for better internal connectivity. The identified community features are *Year, Node Degree, Edge Degree, Number of Inter edges, Number of Inter edges, Degree, Conductance, Density, Connected components, Clustering Co-efficient, Activeness, Aging,* and *Events*. Experiments were carried out to justify the relevance of these 13 community features using the *Pearson correlation heatmap* [12]. The plot of the *Pearson correlation heatmap* in Fig. 2(a) shows the correlation of the community features (independent variables) with the Events (output variable). Generally, the correlation coefficient ranges between -1 to 1, but Fig. 2(a) shows that the correlation coefficient values of community features range between -0.8 to 0.8. Therefore, it is inferred from the experimental results in Fig. 2(a) that our identified community features are beneficial for predicting events of the communities.

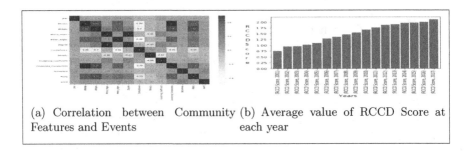

(a) Correlation between Community   (b) Average value of RCCD Score at
Features and Events   each year

Fig. 2. Scores

This work focuses on calculating the relationships among authors (nodes) involved in the change of interactions and derive properties to predict the events of communities. The association between authors can be calculated by computing their collaborative distance. The proposed Refined Classical Collaborative Distance (RCCD) is an extension of existing Classical Collaborative distance. Collaborative distance between two nodes is the shortest edge length between them in a given community. It signifies how similar nodes influence a community to change its structure (number of edges necessary to reach a node from another node). Existing approaches are based on similarity measure within the community only.

Refined Classical Collaboration Distance of a node (author) is calculated by using intersection between two authors based on paper publication on same topic in a given graph. $RCCD = \sum_{i=0}^{n} \dfrac{1}{|p(a_i) \cap p(a_{(i+1)})|}$. Where $p(a_i)$ is the set of papers of author a_i and $|\cdot|$ is the cardinality operator. RCCD score of the community is calculated by considering the centrality of the community : $\sigma^2 = \dfrac{\sum_{i=1}^{n}(RCCD_i - \mu)^2}{n}$.

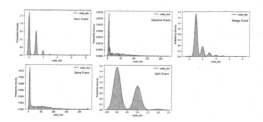

Fig. 3. Probability distribution function between RCCD and events

2.2   RCCD Score

Observation. How to know the RCCD Score could be a good measure for detecting event changes? The above question is answered by the usage of two strategies called PDF and Poisson distribution.

First Strategy: We added a new feature called RCCD to improve the accuracy of the ML model. Before that we needed to check whether the newly derived feature affects the target variable (Events). This effect can be identified by identifying relation between newly derived feature and the target variable. Relation can be identified by using two steps [3]. Step one calculates the average value of new feature at each time-interval. Figure 2(b) shows the outcome of the first step. The inference from Fig. 2(b) is that the average value of RCCD increased every year (this justifies the first step). In second step we identified impact of RCCD on each Event by calculating *probability density function (PDF)*. The outcome of this step is represented in Fig. 3 and shows the PDF values of *Merge* (which is 1.6), *Split* (which is 1.6), *Form* (which is 2.5), *Same* (which is 0.012), and *Dissolve* (which is 0.0035) events. The average values of RCCD (from Fig. 2(b)) are matching with these PDF values. It is expected as RCCD score signifies the

Table 2. Poisson multiple regression results

Parameters	Beta value	Std. err
RCCD score	0.0289	0.008
Conductance	0.4086	0.173
Connected components	0.0016	0.000
Degree	0.0155	0.002
Density	0.0138	0.004
Aging	0.2086	0.113

tendency of nodes to link with other nodes that have a similar degree distribution (authors tend to collaborate with other authors having similar paper publications). The inference from Fig. 3 is that RCCD score is considerably impacting *Merge, Split* and *Form* events and has less impact on *Same* and *Dissolve* events.

Second Strategy: In this strategy, we observed the effect of independent variables on dependent variables by using *Poisson regression* model [5]. We start by assigning weights to the event changes. The higher weight associated with RCCD Score (0.0289) in Table 2 proves that it indeed is a good measure for detecting event changes. So, based on above justifications, we included RCCD Score as an additional feature along with community features. The pseudo-code of our proposed algorithm to compute the RCCD score of all the communities is given in Algorithm 1.

Algorithm 1: RCCD Algorithm

   Input   : Features_Data frame=df{}
   Output: RCCD Score
1   n = 0
2   auth_ano = []
3   list_ind = int(df[year][index])-2001
4 **for** auth in df[names][index]

$$RCCD = \sum_{i=0}^{n} \frac{1}{p(a_i) \cap p(a_{(i+1)})}$$

$$RCCD\ Score = \frac{\sum_{i=1}^{n} (RCCD_i - \mu)^2}{n}$$

7 **end for**
8 **return** RCCD Score

---

3 Performance and Comparative Analysis of Results

We conducted experiments on several ML multi-classification algorithms to find the best accuracy model for predicting the events of the communities. We used *Decision Tree, Naive Bayes, Neural Networks, SVM*, and *Logistic Regression* ML models for our experimentation. For all the ML models, all the classifiers are evaluated by 10-fold cross-validation approach.

3.1   Performance Analysis

We included all sets of community and derived features in our experimentation. We compared the results obtained by considering only the community features (shown in Table 3) with the results obtained by considering RCCD scores as an additional feature along with community features. Accuracy gives the measure of the correctness of predicted events based on the training events. As can be inferred from Table 3, the addition of the RCCD score as a feature improved the performance of the Logistic Regression model from 81.47% to 84.27% (aprox. 3.43% improvement). Precision gives the measure of the positivity of the correctly predicted events based on the training events. Our results in Table 3 show that the precision of the Logistic Regression model improved from 79.68% to 83.62% (aprox. 4.94% improvement). The recall is the ratio of correctly predicted positive events to all the predicted events. It measures the completeness (how relevant the results are) of the ML models. Recall value of the Logistic Regression model improved from 76.37% to 83.53% (aprox. 9.37% improvement). F-measure or F1 score is the weighted average of Precision and Recall. Our results in Table 3 show that the F-score of the Logistic Regression model improved from 76.83% to 83.57% (aprox. 11.67% improvement).

Table 3. Experimental comparison of ML models.

Classifiers	Accuracy		Precision		Recall		F-measure	
Approach	CF	RCCD	CF	RCCD	CF	RCCD	CF	RCCD
Decision Tree	52.92	77.82	51.98	70.48	50.98	73.41	51.24	71.79
Naive Bayes	73.92	79.91	72.61	72.31	71.72	73.71	72.16	72.89
NN	81.84	79.34	72.14	78.63	75.53	77.24	74.25	77.94
SVM	81.17	82.17	79.92	81.57	71.82	81.59	70.85	81.58
LR	81.47	84.27	79.68	83.62	76.37	83.53	76.83	83.57

3.2   Comparative Analysis with Existing Work

Classical Collaborative Distance (CCD) method [8] finds common neighbors.

And verified a correlation between the number of common neighbors of v_i and v_j at the time t, and the probability that they will collaborate in the future. So, it identified collaboration of only two nodes in the future.

Table 4. Performance analysis of RCCD and CCD on Logistic Regression Model.

Metrics	Accuracy		Precision		Recall		F-measure	
Approach	CCD	RCCD	CCD	RCCD	CCD	RCCD	CCD	RCCD
LR	82.54	**84.27**	81.12	**83.62**	82.67	**83.53**	81.45	**83.57**

Whereas, the novelty in our proposed RCCD approach is that it considers the similarity measure of both intra- and inter- communities and is Table 3 infers that the logistic regression (LR) model predicted events more accurately compared to the remaining four ML models. In Table 4, we compared logistic regression model with the performance of our proposed model. Our model predicts events approximately with 2.09% more accuracy than CCD approach. The precision of our prediction is approximately 3.08 % more compared to CCD approach. Our proposed method predicts events with **83.53%** recall, which is approximately 1.04% improvement over CCD approach. Similarly, the F-measure for our model is **83.57%**, which is approximately 2.60% better than CCD approach.

4   Conclusion and Future Work

This paper presented a **scalable and parallel** framework for modeling a co-authorship SN and demonstrated how the proposed new feature, called RCCD score, improved the performance of the ML models for the prediction of the events in social network communities. The performance and effectiveness of the proposed framework show that the addition of the RCCD score as a feature improved the accuracy of the ML model. Thus, the accuracy of the proposed approach in prediction of the events improved from 81.47% to 84.27%.

In the future, we plan to design a strategy to measure similarity using GAN and stochastic gradient methods for further improvement in accuracy.

References

1. Alamuri, M., Surampudi, B.R., Negi, A.: A survey of distance/similarity measures for categorical data. In: 2014 IJCNN, pp. 1907–1914. IEEE (2014)
2. Bommakanti, S.R., Panda, S.: Events detection in temporally evolving social networks. In: 2018 ICBK, pp. 235–242. IEEE (2018)
3. Chakraborty, T., Srinivasan, S., Ganguly, N., Mukherjee, A., Bhowmick, S.: On the permanence of vertices in network communities. In: Proceedings of the 20th ACM SIGKDD, pp. 1396–1405. ACM (2014)
4. Kong, X., Shi, Y., Yu, S., Liu, J., Xia, F.: Academic social networks: modeling, analysis, mining and applications. J. Network Comput. Appl. **132**(3), 86–103 (2019)
5. Leskovec, J., Lang, K.J., Dasgupta, A., Mahoney, M.W.: Statistical properties of community structure in large social and information networks. In: Proceedings of the 17th ICWWW, pp. 695–704. ACM (2008)
6. Newman, M.E.: Co-authorship networks and patterns of scientific collaboration. In: Proceedings of the National Academy of Sciences 101(1), pp. 5200–5205. National Acad Sciences (2004)
7. Papanikolaou, Y., Foulds, J.R., Rubin, T.N., Tsoumakas, G.: Dense distributions from sparse samples: improved gibbs sampling parameter estimators for LDA. J. Mach. Learn Res. **18**(1), 2058–2115 (2017)
8. Pereira, F.S., de Amo, S., Gama, J.: Detecting events in evolving social networks through node centrality analysis. In: ECML, pp. 47–60 (2016)

9. Pradhan, A.K., Mohanty, H., Lal, R.P.: Event detection and aspects in twitter: a bow approach. In: Fahrnberger, G., Gopinathan, S., Parida, L. (eds.) ICDCIT 2019. LNCS, vol. 11319, pp. 194–211. Springer, Cham (2019). https://doi.org/10.1007/978-3-030-05366-6_16

10. Rajita, B.S.A.S., Kumari, D., Panda, S.: A comparative analysis of community detection methods in massive datasets. In: Goel, N., Hasan, S., Kalaichelvi, V. (eds.) MoSICom 2020. LNEE, vol. 659, pp. 174–183. Springer, Singapore (2020). https://doi.org/10.1007/978-981-15-4775-1_19

11. Rajita, B.S.A.S., Ranjan, Y., Umesh, C.T., Panda, S.: Spark-based parallel method for prediction of events. Arabian J. Sci. Eng. **45**(4), 3437–3453 (2020). https://doi.org/10.1007/s13369-020-04437-2

12. Saganowski, S., Bródka, P., Koziarski, M., Kazienko, P.: Analysis of group evolution prediction in complex networks. PLoS ONE **14**(10), e0224194 (2019)

13. Sharma, A., Bhavani, S.D.: A network formation model for collaboration networks. In: Fahrnberger, G., Gopinathan, S., Parida, L. (eds.) ICDCIT 2019. LNCS, vol. 11319, pp. 279–294. Springer, Cham (2019). https://doi.org/10.1007/978-3-030-05366-6_24

A Distributed System for Optimal Scale Feature Extraction and Semantic Classification of Large-Scale Airborne LiDAR Point Clouds

Satendra Singh and Jaya Sreevalsan-Nair$^{(\boxtimes)}$ (iD)

Graphics-Visualization-Computing Lab, International Institute of Information Technology, 26/C, Electronics City, Bangalore 560100, Karnataka, India
jnair@iiitb.ac.in
http://www.iiitb.ac.in/gvcl

Abstract. Airborne LiDAR (Light Detection and Ranging) or aerial laser scanning (ALS) technology can capture large-scale point cloud data, which represents the topography of large regions. The raw point clouds need to be managed and processed at scale for exploration and contextual understanding of the topographical data. One of the key processing steps is feature extraction from pointwise local geometric descriptors for object-based classification. The state of the art involves finding an optimal scale for computing the descriptors, determined using descriptors across multiple scales, which becomes computationally intensive in the case of big data. Hence, we propose the use of a widely used big data analytics framework integration of Apache Spark and Cassandra, for extracting features at optimal scale, semantic classification using a random forest classifier, and interactive visualization. The visualization involves real-time updates to the selection of regions of interest, and display of feature vectors upon a change in the computation of descriptors. We show the efficacy of our proposed application through our results in the DALES aerial LiDAR point cloud.

Keywords: Big data framework · Apache Spark · Cassandra · LiDAR point cloud · Multiscale feature extraction · Semantic classification

1 Introduction

Three-dimensional (3D) topographical data for large expanses of region is captured effectively using airborne Light Detection and Ranging (LiDAR) technology. The data is procured in the format of point clouds, which are unstructured. Contextual understanding of such data is necessary to make sense of the environment and its constituents. Hence, semantic classification is a key processing

Supported by Early Career Research Award, Science and Engineering Research Board, Government of India.

D. Goswami and T. A. Hoang (Eds.): ICDCIT 2021, LNCS 12582, pp. 280–288, 2021.
https://doi.org/10.1007/978-3-030-65621-8_18

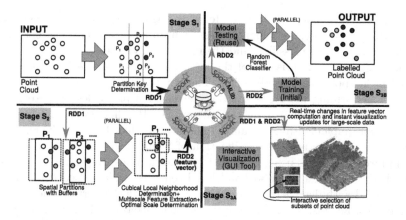

Fig. 1. Our proposed 3-stage workflow for data management, optimal scale feature extraction, and visual analytics involving interactive visual exploration and semantic classification of large-scale airborne LiDAR point clouds using Apache Spark-Cassandra integrated framework, with Datastax Spark-Cassandra Connector. The processed data is managed using resilient distributed datasets (RDDs).

method applied on the point clouds. The state of the art in semantic classification of LiDAR point clouds is mostly supervised learning including ensemble learning techniques, such as random forest classifiers [12], and deep learning techniques [11]. The feature vector for the learning task is obtained using local geometric descriptors computed using local neighborhood, which is determined at multiple scales [1,12]. The combination of feature extraction at optimal scale of local neighborhood and a random forest classifier has been recommended as an appropriate framework for semantic classification in terms of both accuracy and computational efficiency [12]. Upon evaluating multiple scales, the optimal scale is determined at the *argmin* of Shannon entropy computed from eigenvalues of the covariance matrix representing the local neighborhood at the scale.

However, the existing solutions for this compute-intensive combination do not directly scale for large-scale point clouds in data analytic applications, such as, interactive feature visualization and semantic classification. As an example, DALES (Dayton Annotated LiDAR Earth Scan) [11] is one of the largest publicly available annotated point cloud dataset acquired using aerial laser scanning, with ~0.5 billion 3D points at considerably high point resolution of 50 ppm (points per meter). The dataset spans a region of 10 km² in the city of Surrey in British Columbia, stored in 40 tiles, with each tile containing 12 million points. That said, existing big data tools and frameworks can be tapped into and re-purposed for addressing this gap. In our previous work, we have proposed an integrated framework of Apache Spark and Cassandra to perform semantic classification using feature extraction from local geometric descriptors using multiscale aggregation of saliency map [10]. Here, we extend the framework for optimal scale feature extraction, and interactive visualization (Fig. 1). Our main contributions are in extending framework for: (a) feature extraction from large-scale point clouds at optimal scale, for semantic classification using conventional classifiers, such as random forest classifier; and (b) interactive visualization.

Local neighbor search is one of the most compute-intensive steps in feature extraction for point cloud processing. The computational requirements multiply when performing feature extraction across multiple scales by determining an optimal scale based on Shannon entropy [1]. Parallel processing has been exploited for implementing semantic classification has been implemented on large-scale point clouds. The classification of Semantic3D has been done using random forest classifiers using OpenMP [3], and deep learning frameworks, such as Torch [2]. k-nearest neighborhood has been used widely used type of local neighborhood with deep learning methods to optimize the performance of these architectures. For instance, Adam optimizer has been used in RandLA-Net [5], which also performs down-sampling of the point cloud on the GPU. While parallelized and optimized machine learning frameworks can improve computational efficiency, the big data frameworks have been largely used for both dataset management and processing. Apache Spark has been used for extraction of tree crowns from LiDAR point cloud, using spherical neighborhood [7].

Background: Apache Spark is a unified data analytics engine for large-scale data using in-memory processing [13]. Integration of Spark with storage systems, such as key-value stores, e.g., Cassandra [6], provides persistent storage. Both Spark and Cassandra are horizontally scalable, as more distributed systems, or *nodes*, can be added to the cluster. Spark uses Resilient Distributed Data (RDD) distributed across multiple cluster nodes for loading data in logical partitions across many servers for parallel processing on the cluster nodes. Apache Spark-Cassandra Connector from Datastax[1] is used to query Cassandra tables from RDDs, after which the query results are stored in Cassandra. The connector leverages data locality to mitigate the network latency. Apache Spark also integrates complex tools such as MLlib, for machine learning.

2   Methodology

We use an integrated Apache Spark-Cassandra framework for semantic classification of large-scale airborne LiDAR point clouds using optimal scale feature extraction, and interactive visualization. We design an appropriate 3-stage workflow for utilizing this framework effectively. Here, the choice of Apache Spark with Cassandra has been made for: (a) parallelizing and scaling with data as well as nodes, and (b) optimized performance in semantic classification using tools like Spark ML, and interactive visualization. The persistent storage using Cassandra serves two purposes in our case: (a) storage of processed data in compute-intensive interactive applications, e.g., visualization, (b) distributed data management, as, in a multi-partitioned node, only a single partition can be in-memory in Spark at any given time. A partition key is needed for partitioning

---

[1] https://github.com/datastax/spark-cassandra-connector.

data across nodes, and is computed based on the user-defined strategy on Spark. A hash value of the partition key is needed for inserting and retrieving data and it is computed using a function Partitioner in Apache Spark during the read-write operations on the cluster. We exploit the feature in Cassandra to store the data in distributed nodes based on the partition key and optimize the search using *clustering columns*. In our work, we partition 3D data in the x-y plane, assign the partitions a region-ID, use the region-ID as the partition key, and assign the x, y, z variables as the clustering columns. When the Spark executor and Cassandra nodes are deployed on the same machine, the integrated framework processes the region data without incurring any network traffic, owing to the use of Spark-Cassandra Connector.

2.1 Our Proposed Workflow

Our workflow implemented on the integrated framework comprises of the following three stages (Fig. 1): the partition assignment of large-scale point cloud on the framework [$\mathbf{S_1}$], spatial partitioning and feature extraction [$\mathbf{S_2}$], and visual analytics [$\mathbf{S_3}$]. Within $\mathbf{S_3}$, the framework performs interactive visualization of features in the point cloud, $\mathbf{S_{3A}}$, and semantic classification, $\mathbf{S_{3B}}$. Compared to our previous work [10], here, we compute more features, modify $\mathbf{S_2}$ to determine the optimal scale, and include $\mathbf{S_{3A}}$.

Stage $\mathbf{S_1}$: For initializing the framework, we load the 3D point cloud $\mathcal{P}$ into the Apache Spark as an RDD. We normalize all points in $\mathcal{P}$ to be contained inside a cube of size 2 units centered at $(0,0,0)$, without altering its aspect ratio. We then partition only along one axis, referred to as the *principal axis*, to strategize the partition layout with fewer partition boundaries. The partition boundaries pose an overhead of inter-node communication, as, for the points close to the boundaries, their local neighborhoods are split across different partitions, and hence, across different nodes. Thus, fewer partition boundaries are used to reduce the inter-node communication for collating neighborhood information. We select the axis with maximum range as principal axis p, either x or y axes, here. Spatial partitions of $\mathcal{P}$ into N contiguous regions along the p axis, have partition boundaries at p_i, for $i = 0, 1, 2, \ldots, N$, where N is determined using the maximum scale value, l_{max}, range of data along p-axis in $\mathcal{P}$ ($\Delta p = p_{max} - p_{min}$), and the number of available cluster nodes n. Thus, $N = \frac{\Delta p}{l_{max} \cdot n}$, and the ith partition boundary $p_i = p_{min} + i * n * l_{max}$. A region-ID assigned to each point x in $\mathcal{P}$, serves as the partition key in Spark, K, where the p-coordinate of the point satisfies the boundary condition, $p_{(K-1)} \leq x_p < p_{(K)}$ for $K = 1, 2, \ldots, N$. For each partition, a buffer region is introduced by extending the right and left boundaries to $p_i \pm l_{max}$, respectively. Buffer regions provide *complete* local neighborhood information for boundary points, and features are extracted for all points except those in buffer regions. We store the resultant RDD in the Cassandra cluster using partition key, K.

Stage $\mathbf{S_2}$: We create partitions with the assigned K in $\mathbf{S_1}$ using our custom partitioner in the RDD. The custom partitioner enforces our computed partitioning, thus, overriding the default random one on Spark. The partition key is crucial for the spatial contiguity in $\mathcal{P}$ as it ensures that a partition is contained in a single node without being split across nodes. A single node can still load multiple partitions, and process them in parallel. The feature extraction algorithm consists of four sequential processes implemented for each point, namely, local neighborhood determination, descriptor computation, its eigenvalue decomposition, and feature vector computation. Point-wise processing makes the algorithm embarrassingly data-parallel. Here, we use the cubical neighborhood [8] over the conventional spherical or k-nearest, to reduce computations. Cubical neighborhood uses Chebyshev distance (infinity (L_∞) or maximum norm) for neighbor-search, instead of Euclidean distance (L_2 norm). A spherical neighborhood of radius r is approximated by the cubical neighborhood of $l = 2r$.

Definition 1. *l-cubical neighborhood N_l of a point x in $\mathcal{P}$, such that $\mathcal{P} = \{p \in \mathbb{R}^d\}$, is a set of points which satisfy the criterion based on Chebyshev distance,*

$$N_l(x) = \{y \in \mathcal{P} \mid \max_{\{0 \leq i < d\}} (|x_i - y_i|)\}.$$

The local geometric descriptor provides the shape of the local neighborhood, e.g. the covariance tensor T_{3DCM} [10], and its size is the *scale*. The eigenvalue decomposition of the descriptor gives the likelihood of the corresponding point being on a surface, line, or junction (point) type feature [10], given by the saliency map $[C_l, C_s, C_p]$. For eigen values of the descriptor, such that, $\lambda_1 \geq \lambda_2 \geq \lambda_3$:

$$C_l = (\lambda_1 - \lambda_2)/\sum\lambda, C_s = 2(\lambda_2 - \lambda_3)/\sum_\lambda, C_p = 3(\lambda_3)/\sum_\lambda; \text{for} \sum_\lambda = (\lambda_1 + \lambda_2 + \lambda_3).$$

There are different 3D features computed using geometric and the shape properties [12]. The eight different local 3D shape features using eigenvalues of the descriptors are: omnivariance O_λ, eigen-sum $\sum_\lambda$, eigen-entropy E_λ, change of curvature C_λ, linearity L_λ, planarity P_λ, scattering S_λ, and anisotropy A_λ. O_λ and $\sum_\lambda$ are tensor invariants of second-order tensor, namely, determinant and trace; with $O_\lambda = \sqrt[3]{\lambda_1\lambda_2\lambda_3}$. Eigen-entropy gives the Shannon entropy in descriptor shape, given by $E_\lambda = -\sum_{i=1}^{3} \lambda_i \ln(\lambda_i)$. Other measures are: $C_\lambda = \lambda_3/\sum_\lambda$, $L_\lambda = (\lambda_1 - \lambda_2)/\lambda_1$, $P_\lambda = (\lambda_2 - \lambda_3)/\lambda_1$, $S_\lambda = \lambda_3/\lambda_1$, $A_\lambda = (\lambda_1 - \lambda_3)/\lambda_1$. Since C_p and C_λ are equivalent, we ignore C_λ. The semantics of the saliency map $[C_l, C_s, C_p]$ and the descriptor shape $[L_\lambda, P_\lambda, S_\lambda]$ are the same; thus, we keep $[C_l, C_s, C_p]$. Of four geometric features we use, three are height-based, namely, the absolute height z of each point, and the range z_Δ and standard deviation z_σ of the height distribution in the local neighborhood of the point. The fourth feature is local point density D [12], given by $D = (n_p + 1)/(\frac{4}{3}\pi r^3)$, where n_p is the number of points in the l-cubical neighborhood, and $r = 0.5l$. Thus, we get a 11-feature vector at each point in $\mathcal{P}$ as:

$$\mathbf{v}_f = [z, z_\Delta, z_\sigma, D, C_l, C_s, C_p, O_\lambda, \sum\lambda, E_\lambda, A_\lambda].$$

In the case of annotated data, the class label for each point is stored along with $\mathbf{v}_f$ in an RDD in Spark and the Cassandra cluster, using K. The class label is used for training data for the classifier, and validation.

Optimal Scale Determination: We compute the feature vector at different scales, i.e., size of the cubical neighborhood, l, such that $l_{min} \leq l \leq l_{max}$, using n_s uniform scales. Thus, scale step-size is $\Delta l = \frac{(l_{max} - l_{min})}{(n_s - 1)}$. The optimal scale is the *argmin* of E_λ. We then use the feature vector $\mathbf{v}_f^{(i)}$ at the optimal scale at each point as the feature vector for the concerned point in the classification stage (**S3B**). These point-wise feature vectors at different scales are stored in the same RDD to determine the global minimum of E_λ [1], and thus, the optimal scale.

Stage S3A: Our visualization tool is inspired by Potree [9], a browser-based visualization tool for large-scale point clouds using WebGL. It loads the data from file, organizes data in the octree data structure, and stores on the local disk on the web server. Potree provides interactive visualization of the point clouds loaded from file, using Poisson disk sampling. Potree, however, does not perform real-time analytics. To facilitate real-time analytics and visualization, we load the Cassandra-resident data on the local disk as required, and render the point clouds using OpenGL on a desktop application. We propose the system architecture to perform not just interactive visualization but also perform selective analytics on the fly using Apache Spark. The real-time performance is facilitated by Cassandra storage, and the Spark-Cassandra Connector. As an example usage of our visualization tool, we change scale on the fly and visualize the features computed for the scale, using parallel processing.

Stage S3B: For training, the feature RDD of the training data is loaded into Apache Spark ML. Then, any classifier on Spark ML, e.g. random forest classifier (RFC) or gradient boost tree classifier (GBT), is initiated, and stored as a classifier model in file. For testing the model, the feature RDD of the testing data is loaded, and the classifier is run on $\mathbf{v}_f$ to determine point-wise class labels. The resultant RDD with the $\mathbf{v}_f$ and the class label is stored in the local Cassandra node, and efficiently retrieved using the Connector. We perform training/testing using 80/20 split, and for labelled data, we validate the model seamlessly.

3 Experiments and Results

We have used Apache Spark 2.4 integrated with Cassandra 3.0., with three executor nodes on Apache Spark, of which one executor node runs on master node. All the four nodes use Intel i7 processor @2.80 GHz, 4 cores, 8 logical processors, and 8 GB RAM. For our experiment, we have used the DALES dataset [11], with 0.5 billion points across 8 semantic classes, stored in 40 tiles. In our distributed system, there are five spatially contiguous partitions (Fig. 2), of which one partition is loaded on the executor running on master node, and two each in the other executor nodes. We have used feature vectors computed at optimal scale determined cubical neighborhood sizes l = 1m, 2m, 3m, 4m, 5m, 6m, 7m, 8m, 9m, 10m in metric space. We have trained the RFC on Spark ML using ~34 million points in tiles 5110_54460, 5110_54475, and 5110_54495 of DALES (Fig. 2), and tested on ~11 million points in 5080_54470.

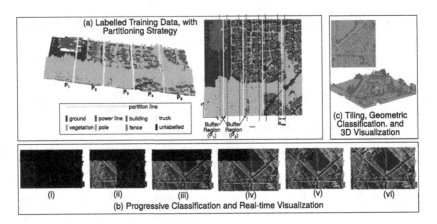

Fig. 2. Visualization of a region 5110_54495 of DALES dataset (~12 million points) – (a) Labeled data for training, and our customized partitioning strategy; (b) real-time updates of semantic classification in our visualization system, (i)–(vi), from unlabeled points (black) to class labels; (c) tiling of the point cloud, computation of saliency map on the fly, and point rendering with color (RGB) corresponding to the saliency map (C_l, C_s, C_p), with its interactive rotation using our visualization system.

In our case study, we observe that the buffer regions add data for 10 m, on either side of each partition. This implies each partition has up to $8K$ points (~1.3 MB) overhead, with 50 ppm. This becomes a significant overhead when we consider massive point cloud datasets, as the buffer region grow proportional to the point cloud size. However, we observe that the local descriptor used for generating a predominant part of the vector is an additive tensor. Hence, when the local neighborhood is truncated for the boundary points in a partition, the local descriptor is a coarser approximation. The overall accuracy (OA) of semantic classification is not expected to be affected drastically owing to the low percentage of boundary points. As an experiment, we estimate the trade-off. We have determined the Intersection Over Union (IoU) values for mean, overall accuracy (OA), and per class (Table 1). RFC gives an OA of 81.7%, with 78.1% for ground class. We observe that the absence of buffer region gives us an OA of 79.8% with 76% for ground class. For each square tile of 0.5 km, the total buffer region with 5 partitions is 0.1 km. Thus, we observe that we can have a trade-off of 16% of additional storage by 2% reduction in overall accuracy in semantic classification. RFC and GBT classifier perform comparably. We demonstrate the use of our visualization system in progressive rendering of the progression in semantic classification as the results get updated; and the visualization of saliency map in the point cloud, on the fly after sectioning (Fig. 2).

Overall, we have explored the use of an integrated Apache Spark-Cassandra framework as a distributed system for optimal scale feature extraction from a point cloud and its semantic classification, using customized region-based spatial partitioning. Our proposed 3-stage workflow for interactive visualization and

Table 1. Semantic classification result for our case study of DALES point cloud, using 33,825,345 training points, using different classifiers in a distributed system

Buffer Region (# test points)	OA	Mean	Ground	Vegetation	Cars	Trucks	Power line	Fence	Pole	Building
Random Forest Classifier (RFC)/Gradient Boost Tree Classifier										
With	0.817	0.357	0.781	0.739	0.154	0.199	0.238	0.159	0.190	0.395
(10,773,000)	0.792	0.351	0.746	0.626	0.030	0.110	0.447	0.177	0.206	0.464
Without	0.798	0.327	0.760	0.703	0.155	0.186	0.153	0.134	0.182	0.346
(12,654,558)	0.773	0.341	0.719	0.657	0.041	0.133	0.487	0.217	0.149	0.321

semantic classification has been effectively implemented on the integrated framework using our design choices. We found that not using buffer region saves the additional 16% of storage needed, with only 2% reduction in overall accuracy.

References

1. Demantké, J., Mallet, C., David, N., Vallet, B.: Dimensionality based scale selection in 3D LiDAR point clouds. In: The International Archives of the Photogrammetry, Remote Sensing and Spatial Information Sciences, vol. 38(Part 5), W12 (2011)
2. Hackel, T., Wegner, J.D., Savinov, N., Ladicky, L., Schindler, K., Pollefeys, M.: Large-scale supervised learning for 3D point cloud labeling: semantic3D. Net. Photogram. Eng. Remote Sens. **84**(5), 297–308 (2018)
3. Hackel, T., Wegner, J.D., Schindler, K.: Joint classification and contour extraction of large 3D point clouds. ISPRS J. Photogram. Remote Sens. **130**, 231–245 (2017)
4. Hoppe, H., DeRose, T., Duchamp, T., McDonald, J., Stuetzle, W.: Surface reconstruction from unorganized points. Siggraph Comp. Graph. **26**(2), 71–78 (1992)
5. Hu, Q., et al.: RandLA-Net: efficient semantic segmentation of large-scale point clouds. In: Proceedings of the IEEE/CVF Conference on Computer Vision and Pattern Recognition, pp. 11108–11117 (2020)
6. Lakshman, A., Malik, P.: Cassandra: a decentralized structured storage system. ACM SIGOPS Operating Syst. Rev. **44**(2), 35–40 (2010)
7. Liu, K., Boehm, J.: Classification of big point cloud data using cloud computing. ISPRS-Int. Arch. Photogram. Remote Sens. Spat. Inf. Sci. **40**, 553–557 (2015)
8. Olofsson, K., Holmgren, J.: Single tree stem profile detection using terrestrial laser scanner data, flatness saliency features and curvature properties. Forests **7**(9), 207 (2016)
9. Schütz, M.: Potree: Rendering Large Point Clouds in Web Browsers. Technische Universität Wien, Wiedeń (2016)
10. Singh, S., Sreevalsan-Nair, J.: A distributed system for multiscale feature extraction and semantic classification of large-scale LiDAR point clouds. In: Proceedings of the IEEE India Geoscience and Remote Sensing Symposium (INGARSS) (to appear) (2020)
11. Varney, N., Asari, V.K., Graehling, Q.: DALES: a large-scale aerial LiDAR data set for semantic segmentation. In: Proceedings of the IEEE/CVF Conference on Computer Vision and Pattern Recognition Workshops, pp. 186–187 (2020)

12. Weinmann, M., Jutzi, B., Hinz, S., Mallet, C.: Semantic point cloud interpretation based on optimal neighborhoods, relevant features and efficient classifiers. ISPRS J. Photogram. Remote Sens. **105**, 286–304 (2015)
13. Zaharia, M., et al.: Apache spark: a unified engine for big data processing. Commun. ACM **59**(11), 56–65 (2016)

Load Balancing Approach
for a MapReduce Job Running
on a Heterogeneous Hadoop Cluster

Kamalakant Laxman Bawankule$^{(\boxtimes)}$, Rupesh Kumar Dewang$^{(\boxtimes)}$,
and Anil Kumar Singh$^{(\boxtimes)}$

Department of Computer Science and Engineering, Motilal Nehru National Institute
of Technology Allahabad, Prayagraj, India
{kamalakant,rupeshdewang,ak}@mnnit.ac.in
http://www.mnnit.ac.in/

Abstract. Hadoop MapReduce has become the de-facto standard
in today's Big data world to process the more prominent data sets on
a distributed cluster of commodity hardware. Today computing nodes
in a commodity cluster do not have the same hardware configuration,
which leads to heterogeneity. Heterogeneity has become common in the
industry, research institutes, and academics. Our study shows that the
current rules for calculating the required number of Reduce tasks (Reducers) for a MapReduce job are fallacious, leading to significant computing
resources' overutilization. It also degrades MapReduce job performance
running on a heterogeneous Hadoop cluster. However, there is no definite answer to the question: What is the optimal number of Reduce tasks
required for a MapReduce job to get Hadoop's most accomplished performance in a heterogeneous cluster? We have proposed a new rule that
decides the required number of reduce tasks for a MapReduce job running on a heterogeneous Hadoop cluster accurately. The proposed rule
balances the load among the heterogeneous nodes in the Reduce phase of
MapReduce. It also minimizes computing resources' overutilization and
improves the MapReduce job execution time by an average of 18% and
28% for TeraSort and PageRank applications running on a heterogeneous
Hadoop cluster.

Keywords: Heterogeneous cluster · Hadoop · Load balancing ·
MapReduce · Reduce tasks

1 Introduction

An enormous amount of data is generated every day through various platforms
such as the world wide web, social media, news channels, and research institutes.
The traditional databases and computational models cannot store and compute
this vast amount of data [3]. Distributed storage and parallel processing is an
intelligent way to store and process Big data [15]. Google proposed the most
popular and significant computational model, MapReduce, capable of handling

© Springer Nature Switzerland AG 2021
D. Goswami and T. A. Hoang (Eds.): ICDCIT 2021, LNCS 12582, pp. 289–298, 2021.
https://doi.org/10.1007/978-3-030-65621-8_19

massive data [5]. It processes large scale data in a parallel fashion on the cluster of commodity machines.

Hadoop is the most popular open-source framework developed by Yahoo [16]. It is used for the implementation of Google's MapReduce. Facebook, Amazon, Yahoo, and many other industry giants use it to store and process the data in terabytes. MapReduce is a simple model that a programmer can use without any prior knowledge of distributed and parallel data processing. The model is very efficient that can handle the failures automatically.

We have observed that the model's performance degrades in a heterogeneous Hadoop cluster where nodes are of different computing capabilities. The existing rule to calculate the Reduce tasks (Reducers) is not efficient in calculating the exact number of required Reducers for a MapReduce job running on a heterogeneous Hadoop cluster [13]. The model creates the load imbalance in the Reduce phase of a MapReduce by either generating more Reducers or fewer Reducers for a job running on a heterogeneous Hadoop cluster [14]. The existing rule either use 0.95 or 1.75 multiplication factor to calculate the required number of Reducers for a MapReduce job running on a heterogeneous Hadoop cluster.

We have proposed a new rule for calculating the required number of Reducers for a MapReduce job by combining the existing rules. The proposed rule generates an accurate number of required Reducers for a MapReduce job running on a heterogeneous Hadoop cluster. It balances the load among the slower and faster nodes to complete the job execution simultaneously. In the experiment, we have compared the proposed rule with the default Hadoop's rule. We have used HiBench benchmark suite [7] workloads such as a Micro benchmark TeraSort workload and a Websearch benchmark PageRank workload to test the proposed rule's performance in a heterogeneous Hadoop cluster [7].

The remaining paper is organized as Sect. 2 presents the related work. Section 3 presents a brief overview of background and motivation. Section 4 presents a detailed study of the proposed rule. Section 5 presents the performance evaluation with little information on experimental results and graphs. Section 6 concludes the paper with some future work.

2   Related Work

MapReduce model is capable of large scale data processing on the cluster of commodity hardware. The commodity hardware used to create a cluster can be of the same or different hardware configuration [18]. A MapReduce job running on a heterogeneous Hadoop cluster creates a load imbalance in the Reduce phase of MapReduce [14]. Several efforts have been made to improve the performance of a MapReduce in the Reduce phase. Wei Yan et al. [17] proposed a dynamic load balancing algorithm for the heterogeneous Hadoop clusters that allocates the data based on the nodes' computation power. However, the authors do not balance a MapReduce program, but it balances the complete heterogeneous Hadoop cluster.

Wei Lu et al. [11] designed a new partitioner for YARN to balance the load between the Reducers in a heterogeneous Hadoop cluster. The proposed partitioner balances the workload among the Reducers efficiently and improves the performance of MapReduce in a heterogeneous Hadoop cluster. Xiaofei Hou et al. [6] finds the workload imbalance for a MapReduce application and proposed the algorithm for balancing the workload among different racks on a Hadoop cluster based on information gathered by investigating the log files of Hadoop. However, the proposed method balances the workload of the Hadoop job. Rohan Gandhi et al. [4] investigated the MapReduce program's key design issues running on a heterogeneous Hadoop cluster and proposed an algorithm to articulate the load adjustment tradeoff between the estimation accuracy versus wasted work to rebalance the load. Zhihong Liu et al. [10] reports the Hadoop schedulers load imbalance issue in the Reduce phase. However, the proposed approach predicts the workload of each Reducer at run time for the assignment of the Reduce tasks on the particular machine. Still, it fails to balance the load of a heterogeneous Hadoop cluster.

Rohit Paravastu et al. [14] proposed Flubber the new rule for deciding the number of reducers before running the job on a homogenous Hadoop cluster. However, authors have calculated the required reducers on a homogeneous Hadoop cluster. Peter P et al. [13] proposed an algorithm that finds the optimal number of task resources for any workload running on Hadoop MapReduce. It also verifies that current thumb rules for calculating the required number of reduce tasks. It finds the current rule is inaccurate and could significantly waste energy and computing resources. However, the authors proposed the work for a MapReduce program running on a homogeneous Hadoop cluster. We have found that limited works have been proposed to estimate the required number of Reducers for a MapReduce job running on a heterogeneous Hadoop cluster.

3   Background and Motivation

The section provides a background study related to the MapReduce computation model and also presents the motivation behind the work.

3.1   MapReduce

In 2008, Google proposed MapReduce for data-intensive computation [3]. MapReduce data computation is divided into two phases Map and Reduce, as shown in Fig. 1. The client submits the MapReduce job to the JobTracker, and then it divides the job into multiple Map and Reduce tasks [2]. Finally, Job-Tracker assigns these tasks to TaskTraker based on the available slots to complete their execution. In the Map task, the Mapper function is applied to the input data to generate a list of key-value pairs [1]. The Reduce task calls the Reducer function to copy the intermediate data to the Reducer node that acts as input to the reducer function [3]. It applies the Reducer function to the key-value pairs having the same key [5]. Reducer function generates the final output as a key-value pair by performing sort, shuffle, and reduce operation [3].

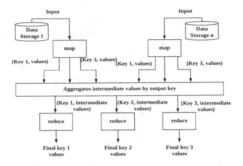

Fig. 1. MapReduce computation model

A MapReduce program has only 1 Reducer by default. But by using Job.setNumReduceTasks(int) function, the user can set the number of Reducers for a MapReduce program. When the number of Reducers is more, it reduces the cluster overhead and improves load balancing by lessening the cost of failures [12]. A MapReduce job needs to set the number of Reducers correctly. If Reducers are not set correctly, it may lead to load imbalance and increase the job execution time [6].

3.2 Motivation

The user sets the required number of reducers for the job using a function Job.setNumReduceTasks(int) [13]. It uses JobConf for the Reducer implementations via the JobConfigurable.configure(JobConf) method. Each Reducer in MapReduce has three phases: shuffle, sort, and reduce [14].

The existing thumb rule uses Eqs. 1 or 2 to decide the number of Reducers for each MapReduce job. When the multiplication factor is 0.95, all the reduces can launch immediately and start transferring the map outputs as the maps finish its execution [14]. When the multiplication factor is 1.75, the faster nodes end their first-round and begin a second wave of reduces to perform a better load balancing job [13]. The rule works and balances the load perfectly in a homogeneous cluster where compute nodes in the cluster are of the same capabilities [9]. When we increase the number of reducers, the framework reduces the overhead and enhances load balancing by lowering the cost of failures. The user sets mappers and Reducers values before MapReduce job execution.

Example: job.setNumReduceTasks(2); // 2 reducers
Example: Suppose a heterogeneous cluster consists of 12 nodes, and each node has a maximum of 2 containers. Then using the thumb rule required number of Reducers for a MapReduce job will be:

$$= 0.95 * (< no.of nodes > * < no.of the maximum container per node >) \quad (1)$$

$=0.95 * (12 * 2) = 22.8$

$$= 1.75 * (< no.ofnodes > * < no.ofthemaximumcontainerpernode >) \quad (2)$$

$=1.75 * (12 * 2) = 42$

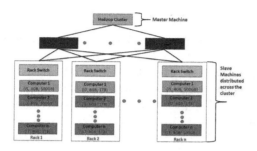

Fig. 2. Heterogeneous Hadoop cluster

In the heterogeneous cluster, the thumb rule creates fewer required Reducers when multiplied by the factor 0.95, and creates more required Reducers when multiplied by factor 1.75 [17]. Nodes with higher computing capabilities complete their first round of reduces and launch a second stream of reduces. In contrast, nodes with lower computing capabilities will near-complete their first round of reduces and start a second stream of reduces when the first-round gets complete [8]. This uneven estimation of Reducers for a MapReduce job running on a heterogeneous Hadoop cluster motivates us to correctly estimate the specified number of Reducers for a MapReduce job in a heterogeneous Hadoop cluster [10].

4 Proposed Approach to Estimate Required Number of Reducers for a MapReduce Job Running on a Heterogeneous Hadoop Cluster

The existing rule does not estimate the correct number of required Reducers for a MapReduce job running on a heterogeneous Hadoop cluster. It creates the load imbalance by wasting the computing resources. To improve a MapReduce job's performance in a heterogeneous Hadoop cluster, we have modified the existing rule to calculate the required number of Reducers. The existing rule uses either 0.95 or 1.75 multiplication factors to estimate the required number of Reducers. The rule either overload the cluster or underutilizes the cluster resources, leading to load imbalance in a heterogeneous Hadoop cluster.

We have proposed a new rule by modifying and combining the existing rules. While changing the rule for a heterogeneous cluster, we have assumed that some nodes are faster, and other nodes are slower. The proposed rule uses both Eqs. 3

and 4 with the above assumption to modify the existing rule for calculating the required number of Reducers. Finally, the values obtained from Eqs. 3 and 4 are added to estimate the required number of Reducers for a MapReduce job running on a heterogeneous Hadoop cluster.

$$= 0.95 * (< no.of fasternodes > * < no.of the maximum container per node >) \tag{3}$$

$$= 1.75 * (< no.of slowernodes > * < no.of the maximum container per node >) \tag{4}$$

We will take the same above examples to understand the proposed rule. Suppose a heterogeneous cluster consists of 12 nodes, and each node has a maximum of 2 containers. Using the proposed rule, we assumed some nodes as faster and other nodes as slower.

Example 1: We assume that out of 12 nodes, 4 nodes as faster nodes and 8 nodes as slower nodes. So the required number of Reducers for a MapReduce job will be:
=0.95 * (4 * 2) = 7.6
=1.75 * (8 * 2) = 28
Number of required Reducers = 7.6 + 28 = 35.6

Example 2: We assume that out of 12 nodes, 6 nodes as faster nodes and 6 nodes as slower nodes. So the required number of Reducers for a MapReduce job will be:
=0.95 * (6 * 2) = 11.472
=1.75 * (6 * 2) = 21
Number of required Reducers = 11.472 + 21 = 32.472

For a heterogeneous cluster, the proposed rule estimates an exact number of required Reducers when multiplied by both the factor 0.95 and 1.75. The proposed rule distribute more Reducers to the faster nodes and less number of Reducers to slower nodes. The above Example 1 creates a total of 36 Reducers in a heterogeneous cluster, out of which it will assign 28 Reducers to the faster nodes and 8 Reducers to slower nodes. The above Example 2 creates 32 Reducers in a heterogeneous cluster, out of which it will assign 21 Reducers to the faster nodes and 11 Reducers to slower nodes.

Faster nodes complete their first round of reduces and launch a second wave of reduces, whereas all the Reducers scheduled on slower nodes start simultaneously. The new rule helps to complete the execution of all the Reducers at the same time. The proposed rule works well for a MapReduce job running on a heterogeneous Hadoop cluster and balances the MapReduce's job load in the Reduce phase of MapReduce.

5 Performance Evaluation

The section presents the information regarding the experimental environment, the benchmark programs, and the experimental results.

5.1 Experimental Environment

In our experiment, we have tested the performance of the proposed rules by simulating a heterogeneous environment. To simulate the heterogeneous environment, we have used four physical machines. Each physical device has 20 GB of memory, 4 CPUs, and 500 GB of disk. Table 1 provides the detailed specification of all the seven VMs (virtual machines) used to simulate a heterogeneous environment. Except for one physical node where the Master node is running, other physical nodes run two slave nodes. For varying each node's computing capabilities, we used the Oracle VM VirtualBox 5.2 platform for simulation of a heterogeneous environment. We have used Ubuntu 16.04 LTS operating system VMs and installed a stable version of Hadoop-2.7.2.

Table 1. Virtual machines specification

SrNo	Node	CPU	Memory	Disk
1	Master	6	10 GB	40 GB
2	Slave1	2	6 GB	30 GB
3	Slave2	4	8 GB	40 GB
4	Slave3	3	4 GB	30 GB
5	Slave4	6	8 GB	40 GB
6	Slave5	3	3 GB	30 GB
7	Slave6	5	10 GB	20 GB

We have evaluated the proposed rule's performance on a micro benchmark workload and a websearch benchmark such as TeraSort and PageRank of HiBench benchmark suite [7]. These benchmark programs are realistic and widely used to test the performance of Hadoop. We have tested the proposed rule's performance on data sizes 5 GB, 10 GB, and 20 GB. We have varied data sizes to analyze the proposed rule's performance in the Reduce phase of MapReduce.

In this section, the proposed rule's performance is measured on the MapReduce jobs running on a heterogeneous Hadoop cluster by performing a series of experiments. For each set of tests, the Reduce tasks execution time is recorded by varying the data sizes. We evaluate the performance of the proposed rule by using the execution time metric:

Execution Time: Total time required from submission of Reduce task until the end of its execution. It can be formalized as follows:

$$ExecutionTime(ret) = EndTimeofReducetask(ert) - StartTimeofReducetask(srt) \tag{5}$$

To calculate the total time required to execute all the Reduce tasks, we have added the execution time of each Reduce task completed on heterogeneous Hadoop cluster.

Total Execution Time: Sum of total turnaround time required to execute all the Reduce tasks of a MapReduce job in a heterogeneous cluster.

$$TotalExecutionTime(tet) = ret(rt1) + ret(rt2) + ... + ret(rtn) \tag{6}$$

5.2   Results

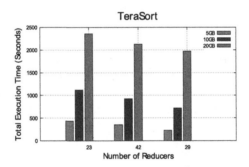

Fig. 3. Total execution time of a TeraSort application

We have performed a series of experiments by varying the number of Reducers and data sizes to measure the total execution time required to execute all the Reduce tasks. In the first iteration, the total execution time of TeraSort and PageRank is recorded for different data sizes. Figure 3 and 4 shows the total execution time required to execute all the Reduce tasks for TeraSort and PageRank application on 5 GB, 10 GB, and 20 GB data.

In Fig. 3 and 4, we have compared the results of the existing rule with the proposed rule using total execution time. For the current rule of 0.95, it creates 23 Reducers, while using the 1.75 factor, it creates 42 Reducers. Subsequently, by using the proposed rule, it creates 29 Reducers. For the TeraSort application, we improved the execution time by nearly 18%, and for the PageRank application, we improved the execution time by nearly 28%. Based on the test results, regardless of the data sizes, the proposed rule generates the exact number of Reducers. It balances the heterogeneous Hadoop cluster's workload and improves the MapReduce Reduce phase's total execution time.

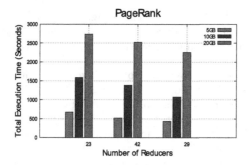

Fig. 4. Total execution time of a PageRank application

6 Conclusion and Future Work

In a heterogeneous Hadoop cluster, load imbalance in the Reduce phase of MapReduce delays the job execution. The current rule is not proficient in calculating the required number of Reducers for a heterogeneous Hadoop cluster. We have proposed a new rule by modifying the existing rule to balance a load of a MapReduce program in a heterogeneous cluster. It calculates the exact number of required Reducers for a MapReduce program running on a heterogeneous Hadoop cluster. Experimental results prove that the proposed rule balances the load and improves the execution time of all the Reducers of a MapReduce job running on a heterogeneous Hadoop cluster compared to the existing rule on all data sizes and minimizes computing resources' overutilization. Our future research will focus on scheduling more Reduce tasks on faster processing nodes and fewer Reduce tasks on the slower processing nodes in a heterogeneous cluster.

References

1. Ahmad, F., Chakradhar, S.T., Raghunathan, A., Vijaykumar, T.: Tarazu: optimizing mapreduce on heterogeneous clusters. In: ACM SIGARCH Computer Architecture News, vol. 40, pp. 61–74. ACM (2012)
2. Anjos, J.C., Carrera, I., Kolberg, W., Tibola, A.L., Arantes, L.B., Geyer, C.R.: Mra++: scheduling and data placement on mapreduce for heterogeneous environments. Future Gen. Comput. Syst. **42**, 22–35 (2015)
3. Dean, J., Ghemawat, S.: Mapreduce: simplified data processing on large clusters. Commun. ACM **51**(1), 107–113 (2008)
4. Gandhi, R., Xie, D., Hu, Y.C.: {PIKACHU}: how to rebalance load in optimizing mapreduce on heterogeneous clusters. In: 2013 {USENIX} Annual Technical Conference ({USENIX}{ATC} 13), pp. 61–66 (2013)
5. Ghemawat, S., Gobioff, H., Leung, S.T.: The google file system. In: Proceedings of the Nineteenth ACM Symposium on Operating Systems Principles, pp. 29–43 (2003)
6. Hou, X., Thomas, J.P., Varadharajan, V.: Dynamic workload balancing for Hadoop mapreduce. In: Proceedings of the 2014 IEEE Fourth International Conference on Big Data and Cloud Computing, pp. 56–62 (2014)

7. Huang, S., Huang, J., Dai, J., Xie, T., Huang, B.: The hibench benchmark suite: characterization of the mapreduce-based data analysis. In: 2010 IEEE 26th International Conference on Data Engineering Workshops (ICDEW 2010), pp. 41–51. IEEE (2010)

8. Kwon, Y., Balazinska, M., Howe, B., Rolia, J.: Skewtune: mitigating skew in mapreduce applications. In: Proceedings of the 2012 ACM SIGMOD International Conference on Management of Data, pp. 25–36. ACM (2012)

9. Lee, C.W., Hsieh, K.Y., Hsieh, S.Y., Hsiao, H.C.: A dynamic data placement strategy for Hadoop in heterogeneous environments. Big Data Res. 1, 14–22 (2014)

10. Liu, Z., Liu, Y., Wang, B., Gong, Z.: A novel run-time load balancing method for mapreduce. In: 2015 4th International Conference on Computer Science and Network Technology (ICCSNT), vol. 1, pp. 150–154. IEEE (2015)

11. Lu, W., Chen, L., Yuan, H., Wang, L., Xing, W., Yang, Y.: Improving mapreduce performance by using a new partitioner in yarn. In: The 23rd International Conference on Distributed Multimedia Systems, Visual Languages and Sentient Systems, pp. 24–33 (2017)

12. Naik, N.S., Negi, A., BR, T.B., Anitha, R.: A data locality based scheduler to enhance mapreduce performance in heterogeneous environments. Future Gen. Comput. Syst. 90, 423–434 (2019)

13. Nghiem, P.P., Figueira, S.M.: Towards efficient resource provisioning in mapreduce. J. Parallel Distrib. Comput. 95, 29–41 (2016)

14. Paravastu, R., Scarlat, R., Chandrasekaran, B.: Adaptive load balancing in mapreduce using flubber. Duke University Project Report (2012)

15. Shvachko, K., Kuang, H., Radia, S., Chansler, R., et al.: The Hadoop distributed file system. MSST. 10, 1–10 (2010)

16. White, T.: Hadoop: The Definitive Guide. O'Reilly Media, Inc., Massachusetts (2012)

17. Yan, W., Li, C., Du, S., Mao, X.: An optimization algorithm for heterogeneous Hadoop clusters based on dynamic load balancing. In: 2016 17th International Conference on Parallel and Distributed Computing, Applications and Technologies (PDCAT), pp. 250–255. IEEE (2016)

18. Zaharia, M., Konwinski, A., Joseph, A.D., Katz, R.H., Stoica, I.: Improving mapreduce performance in heterogeneous environments. In: Osdi, vol. 8, p. 7 (2008)

Study the Significance of ML-ELM Using Combined PageRank and Content-Based Feature Selection

Rajendra Kumar Roul[1(✉)] and Jajati Keshari Sahoo[2]

[1] Department of Computer Science and Engineering,
Thapar Institute of Engineering and Technology, Patiala 147004, Punjab, India
raj.roul@thapar.edu
[2] Department of Mathematics,
BITS-Pilani, K.K.Birla Goa Campus, Zuarinagar 403726, Goa, India
jksahoo@goa.bits-pilani.ac.in

Abstract. Scalable big data analysis frameworks are of paramount importance in the modern web society, which is characterized by a huge number of resources, including electronic text documents. Hence, choosing an adequate subset of features that provide a complete representation of the document while discarding the irrelevant one is of utmost importance. Aiming in this direction, this paper studies the suitability and importance of a deep learning classifier called Multilayer ELM (ML-ELM) by proposing a combined PageRank and content-based feature selection (*CPRCFS*) technique on all the terms present in a given corpus. Top $k\%$ terms are selected to generate a reduced feature vector which is then used to train different classifiers including ML-ELM. Experimental results show that the proposed feature selection technique is better or comparable with the baseline techniques and the performance of Multilayer ELM can outperform state-of-the-arts machine and deep learning classifiers.

Keywords: Classification · Deep learning · Feature selection · Machine learning · Multilayer ELM · PageRank

1 Introduction

Modern web society is characterized by a huge number of resources, including electronic text documents, and a large number of end users as active participants. In order to personalize vast amounts of information to the needs of each individual user, systematic ways to organize data and retrieve useful information in real time are necessary. Document classification is a machine learning technique which can handle a huge volume of data very efficiently by categorizing the unseen test data into their respective groups. Different research on classification methods can be found in [1–4]. The problem with classification technique is that visualizing the data becomes more difficult when the dataset size increases, and it needs a large storage size. In order to handle such problem, *feature selection* technique is essential which selects the important features from a large corpus and removes the unnecessary features during the model construction [5–7]. A good feature selection technique is not enough to make the classification process faster. Along with the feature selection technique, choice of a good classifier also affects the

© Springer Nature Switzerland AG 2021
D. Goswami and T. A. Hoang (Eds.): ICDCIT 2021, LNCS 12582, pp. 299–307, 2021.
https://doi.org/10.1007/978-3-030-65621-8_20

entire classification process. There are many traditional machine and deep learning classifiers exist, but they face many limitations such as need a high amount of training time, require more parameters, unable to manage a huge volume of data etc. Multilayer ELM [8], a deep learning network architecture is one of the most popular classifiers among them because of its good characteristics such as being able to manage a huge volume of data, no backpropagation, faster learning speed, maximum level of data abstraction etc. Keeping all these things in mind, a novel feature selection technique named as *CPRCFS* along with the Multilayer ELM classifier is introduced for text classification, which is the main motivation of this paper. The novelty of this feature selection technique is that it is very simple to understand, easy to implement, and comparable to the conventional feature selection technique. Although much work has been done in text classification, the realm of Multilayer ELM provides a relatively unexplored pool of opportunities. The major contributions of the proposed approach are as follows:

  i. A novel feature selection technique (*CPRCFS*) is introduced by combining the PageRank mechanism with the content-based similarity measures to select the important features from the corpus which improves the performance of the classification technique.
 ii. The proposed *CPRCFS* technique is compared with the conventional feature selection technique to measure its efficacy.
iii. The performance of Multilayer ELM using the proposed *CPRCFS* technique is compared with state-of-the-arts machine and deep learning classifiers to justify its competency and effectiveness.

Rest of the paper is as follows: Sect. 2 highlights the methods and materials used for the proposed approach. The methodology of the proposed work is discussed in Sect. 3. Section 4 discusses the experimental work and finally, Sect. 5 concludes the work with some future enhancements.

2   Materials Used

2.1   Multilayer ELM

Multilayer ELM (ML-ELM) is an artificial neural network having multiple hidden layers [8] and it is shown in Fig. 1. Equations 1, 2 and 3 are used for computing β (output weight vector) in ELM Autoencoder where H represents the hidden layer, X is the input layer, n and L are number of nodes in the input and hidden layer respectively.

  i. $n = L$

$$\beta = H^{-1}X \tag{1}$$

 ii. $n < L$

$$\beta = H^T(\frac{I}{C} + HH^T)^{-1}X \tag{2}$$

iii. $n > L$

$$\beta = \left(\frac{I}{C} + H^T H\right)^{-1} H^T X \tag{3}$$

Here, $\frac{I}{C}$ generalize the performance of ELM [9] and is known as regularization parameter.

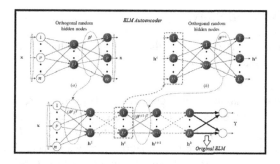

Fig. 1. Architecture of Multilayer ELM

Multilayer ELM uses Eq. 4 to map the features to higher dimensional space and thereby makes them linearly separable [9].

$$
h(\mathbf{x}) =
\begin{bmatrix} h_1(\mathbf{x}) \\ h_2(\mathbf{x}) \\ \cdot \\ \cdot \\ \cdot \\ h_L(\mathbf{x}) \end{bmatrix}^T
=
\begin{bmatrix} g(w_1, b_1, \mathbf{x}) \\ g(w_2, b_2, \mathbf{x}) \\ \cdot \\ \cdot \\ \cdot \\ g(w_L, b_L, \mathbf{x}) \end{bmatrix}^T.
\tag{4}
$$

where, $h_i(\mathbf{x}) = g(w_i.\mathbf{x} + b_i)$. $h(\mathbf{x}) = [h_1(\mathbf{x})...h_i(\mathbf{x})...h_L(\mathbf{x})]^T$ can directly use for feature mapping [10, 11]. w_i is the weight vector between the input nodes and the hidden nodes and b_i is the bias of the ith hidden node, and $\mathbf{x}$ is the input feature vector with g as the activation function. ML-ELM takes the benefit of the ELM feature mapping [9] extensively as shown in Eq. 5.

$$
\lim_{L \to +\infty} ||y(\mathbf{x}) - y_L(\mathbf{x})|| = \lim_{L \to +\infty} ||y(\mathbf{x}) - \sum_{i=1}^{L} \beta_i h_i(\mathbf{x})|| = 0
\tag{5}
$$

Using Eq. 6, Multilayer ELM transfers the data between the hidden layers.

$$
H_i = g((\beta_i)^T H_{i-1})
\tag{6}
$$

3 Proposed Methodology

The following steps are used to select the important features from a given corpus to generate the training feature vector.

1. *Document Pre-processing*:
   Consider a corpus P having a set of classes $C = \{c_1, c_2, \cdots, c_n\}$. At the beginning, the documents of all the classes of P are merged into a large document set called $D_{large} = \{d_1, d_2, \cdots, d_b\}$. Then all documents of D_{large} of P are pre-processed using lexical-analysis, stop-word elimination, removal of HTML tags, stemming[1], and then index terms are extracted using Natural Language Toolkit[2].

2. *Calculation of content-based similarities:*
   The content-based similarities between every pair of terms (t_p and t_q) of the corpus P are calculated using the following four conventional techniques.

   i. *Dice Coefficient* is calculated as follows:
   $$dice(t_p, t_q) = \frac{2(t_p.t_q)}{||t_p||^2 + ||t_q||^2}$$

   ii. *Extended Jaccard Coefficient* is computed as follows:
   $$e\text{-}jac(t_p, t_q) = \frac{t_p.t_q}{||t_p||^2 + ||t_q||^2 - (t_p.t_q)}$$

   iii. *Cosine Similarity* is a similarity measure and computed as follows:
   $$cosine(t_p, t_q) = \frac{t_p.t_q}{||t_p|| * ||t_q||}$$

   iv. *Euclidean Distance* is computed as follows:
   $$eucl(t_p, t_q) = \sqrt{\sum_{p=q=1}^{n} (a_p - b_q)^2}$$

   where $t_p = \{a_1, a_2, \cdots, a_n\}$ and $t_q = \{b_1, b_2, \cdots, b_n\}$ are the co-ordinates of t_p and t_q respectively. The average similarity between every pair of terms t_p and t_q of P are calculated using the Eq. 7.
   $$Avg_{sim}(t_p, t_q) = \frac{dice(t_p, t_q) + e\text{-}jac(t_p, t_q) + cosine(t_p, t_q) + eucl(t_p, t_q)}{4}$$
   $$(7)$$

3. Graph Creation:
   An undirected graph is created where each term represents a node and the average similarity value ($Avg_{sim}(t_p, t_q)$) is the edge between two terms t_p and t_q of the corpus P. Now all the term-pairs (i.e., edges) are arranged in the descending order of their average similarity values. Of this, the top $n\%$ similarity values are selected. If a term-pair (both inclusive) is not present in the top $n\%$ similarity values then there will be no edge between that term-pair.

---

[1] https://pythonprogramming.net/lemmatizing-nltk-tutorial/.
[2] https://www.nltk.org/.

4. PageRank calculation:
PageRank [12] is an algorithm used to determine the relevance or importance of a web page and rank it in the search results. The rank value indicates the importance of a particular page. We have modified the existing PageRank algorithm so that it can be used on terms where each term is assumed to be a web page in the real PageRank algorithm. Assume that term T has incoming edges from terms $T_1, T_2, T_3, \cdots, T_n$. The PageRank of a term T is given by Eq. 8 where 'd' represents the damping factor and its value lies between 0 and 1 and $C(T)$ represents the number of edges that leaving out from the term T. The PageRanks form a probability distribution over the terms, hence the sum of the PageRank of all the terms $PR(T)$ will be one.

$$PR(T) = (1 - d) + d\Big(\frac{PR(T_1)}{C(T_1)} + \cdots + \frac{PR(T_n)}{C(T_n)}\Big) \qquad (8)$$

If there are a lot of terms that link to the term T then there is a common belief that the term T is an important term. The importance of the terms linking to T is also taken into account, and using PageRank terminology, it can be said that terms $T_1, T_2, T_3, \cdots, T_n$ transfer their importance to T, albeit in a weighted manner. Thus, it is possible to iteratively assign a rank to each term, based on the ranks of the terms that point to it. In the proposed approach, the PageRank algorithm is run on the graph created in the previous step, with damping factor $d = 0.5$.

5. *Generating the training feature vector:*
All the terms of the corpus P are sorted in descending order based on their PageRank score and out of these, top $k\%$ terms are selected. The *TF-IDF* values of these terms will act as the values of the features for the documents. Finally, all these top $k\%$ terms are merged into a new list L_{new}, which constitute the training feature vector for the classifiers.

6. *Performance evaluation*
With the known class labels, the unknown documents are tested against each classifier to predict their performances.

4 Experimental Framework

4.1 Dataset Used

To conduct the experiment, two benchmark datasets (20-Newsgroups[3] and Classic4[4]) are used. The details about these two datasets are shown in the Table 1.

4.2 Experimental Setup Details

Parameter settings of different deep learning classifiers are depicted in the Table 2. Approximate sizes of feature vectors used for ELM and Multilayer ELM is shown in the Table 3, where 'ILN' represents input layer nodes and 'HLN' indicates hidden layer nodes. The values of the parameters for these classifiers are decided based on the best results that are obtained by experiment.

---

[3] http://qwone.com/~jason/20Newsgroups/.
[4] http://www.dataminingresearch.com/index.php/2010/09/classic3-classic4-datasets/.

Table 1. Details of the datasets

Dataset	No. of training docs	No. of testing docs	No. of terms used for training
20-NG	11293	7528	32270
Classic4	4257	2838	15971

Table 2. Parameters used for deep learning classifiers

Classifiers	No. of hidden layers	Activation function	Dropout	Optimizers	Epochs
ANN	3	Sigmoid	0.1	SGD	500
CNN	3	Relu	0.2	SGD	500
RNN	3	Tanh	0.2	SGD	400
ML-ELM	20-NG = 4, Classic4 = 3	Sigmoid	0.1	SGD	450

Table 3. Approximate size of the feature vectors of ELM and ML-ELM

Dataset	Terms used for training	ILN (Top 1%)	HLN (Top 1%)	ILN (Top 5%)	HLN (Top 5%)	ILN (Top 10%)	HLN (Top 10%)
20-NG	32270	320	350	1610	1630	3230	3250
Classic4	15971	160	195	800	870	1600	1650

Table 4. Top 1% (20-NG)

ML Classifier	MI	IG	Chi-square	BNS	CPRCFS
SVC (linear)	0.89122	0.87161	0.87362	0.88947	0.87515
SVM (linear)	0.89234	0.88967	0.89151	0.89444	0.89428
Gradient Boosting	0.85583	0.83784	0.84084	0.86063	0.85224
Decision Trees	0.88227	0.86307	0.86992	0.87514	0.87782
NB(Multinomial)	0.86303	0.83860	0.83796	0.85794	**0.88662**
Adaboost	0.87322	0.88314	0.88381	0.88472	0.87335
Random Forest	0.85993	0.85847	0.85902	0.84243	0.85584
Extra Trees	0.89672	0.87606	0.88643	0.88235	0.88762
ELM	0.89242	0.87041	0.87542	0.89575	0.88420
MLELM	0.91703	0.91237	0.90511	0.91668	**0.93802**

Table 5. Top 5% (20-NG)

MI	IG	Chi-square	BNS	CPRCFS
0.93460	0.92817	0.92815	0.93015	0.93454
0.94377	0.93461	0.93729	0.93375	**0.95509**
0.89954	0.88561	0.89489	0.89591	0.87908
0.93516	0.88816	0.90252	0.92878	0.93314
0.93122	0.90103	0.91607	0.92511	0.92191
0.89075	0.88366	0.86261	0.87112	0.87184
0.85997	0.86254	0.85813	0.85763	0.85618
0.90426	0.88001	0.90223	0.89423	0.89717
0.93551	0.92673	0.93012	0.93682	0.92331
0.93873	0.94882	0.94664	0.95584	**0.96746**

Table 6. Top 10% (20-NG)

ML Classifier	MI	IG	Chi-square	BNS	CPRCFS
SVC (linear)	0.94742	0.93732	0.93648	0.94377	**0.94921**
SVM (linear)	0.94286	0.94559	0.93647	0.94654	0.94536
Gradient boosting	0.90147	0.89582	0.89861	0.90510	0.89582
Decision trees	0.93996	0.91012	0.93353	0.93992	0.91133
NB (Multinomial)	0.93822	0.92344	0.93272	0.93732	0.91937
Adaboost	0.88266	0.86261	0.86341	0.87253	0.87686
Random Forest	0.86372	0.84923	0.86605	0.85911	0.85641
Extra Forest	0.89293	0.89242	0.89472	0.89273	**0.90572**
ELM	0.93228	0.94051	0.93443	0.94672	0.92886
MLELM	0.95636	0.96882	0.95567	0.95814	**0.96928**

Table 7. Top 1% (Classic4)

MI	IG	Chi-square	BNS	CPRCFS
0.91491	0.88286	0.89942	0.91784	0.90147
0.92632	0.90663	0.92185	0.92799	0.91670
0.90966	0.83336	0.88875	0.88188	0.88345
0.83281	0.79881	0.87911	0.86601	0.83021
0.84197	0.76852	0.80705	0.85317	**0.88163**
0.89162	0.88094	0.88437	0.88986	0.88393
0.86046	0.84001	0.85312	0.86365	0.85874
0.91773	0.89212	0.91534	0.91801	0.88714
0.90286	0.88143	0.89944	0.92382	0.90182
0.94651	0.92222	0.91885	0.94563	**0.95707**

4.3 Comparison of the Performance ML-ELM Using *CPRCFS* with other machine learning classifiers

The proposed *CPRCFS* is compared with the traditional feature selection techniques such as mutual information (MI), Information Gain (IG), Chi-square, and Bi-normal separation (BNS) (shown in Tables 4, 5, 6, 7, 8, 9) where a bold result indicates the maximum F-measure achieved by a feature selection technique. From the results, it can be concluded that Multilayer ELM can outperform the conventional machine learning classifiers.

Table 8. Top 5% (Classic4)

ML Classifier	MI	IG	Chi-square	BNS	CPRCFS
SVC (linear)	0.94596	0.92333	0.94105	0.94302	**0.95655**
SVM (linear)	0.96511	0.93916	0.94052	0.94794	0.96021
Gradient boosting	0.93412	0.92598	0.92952	0.93951	0.93278
Decision trees	0.92632	0.90763	0.91492	0.90218	0.90987
NB (Multinomial)	0.93814	0.92327	0.93095	0.94525	**0.94667**
Adaboost	0.87345	0.88184	0.84973	0.85482	0.84585
Random Forest	0.84925	0.84846	0.84887	0.85559	0.84849
Extra Trees	0.91893	0.91891	0.91656	0.91921	0.89554
ELM	0.94532	0.92522	0.94676	0.94172	0.94578
MLELM	0.96668	0.94888	0.96253	0.96548	0.96541

Table 9. Top 10% (Classic4)

MI	IG	Chi-square	BNS	CPRCFS
0.94547	0.92125	0.92338	0.96869	0.96551
0.94542	0.92652	0.92758	0.97287	0.96768
0.94021	0.93594	0.93951	0.94238	0.93991
0.92031	0.90688	0.91548	0.91054	0.89722
0.95097	0.94561	0.94778	0.95352	**0.96918**
0.85482	0.85482	0.85482	0.84587	0.84587
0.85072	0.84735	0.85205	0.84573	0.85087
0.91525	0.92688	0.91851	0.91436	0.91675
0.92333	0.94672	0.95634	0.96948	0.95633
0.97106	0.95877	0.96886	0.97944	**0.98077**

4.4 Comparison of the Performance ML-ELM Using *CPRCFS* with other deep learning classifiers

The existing deep learning techniques have high computational cost, require massive training data and training time. The F-measure and accuracy comparisons of Multilayer ELM along with other deep learning classifiers such as Recurrent Neural Network

(RNN), Convolution Neural Network (CNN), and Artificial Neural Network (ANN) using *CPRCFS* technique on top 10% features are depicted in Figs. 2 and 3 respectively. Results show that the performance of Multi-layer ELM outperforms existing deep learning classifiers. Reason behind the good performance of ML-ELM is that, using the universal approximation [13] and classification capabilities [14] of ELM, it can able to map a huge volume of features from a low to high dimensional feature space and can separate those features linearly in higher dimensional space with less cost.

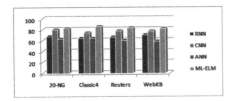 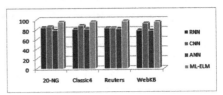

Fig. 2. Deep learning (F-measure)   **Fig. 3.** Deep learning (Accuracy)

5 Conclusion

A novel feature selection technique named as *CPRCFS* is introduced in this paper which combined the ranking ability of PageRank with four similarity measures to select the relevant features from a corpus of documents. By using the similarity measures, top $n\%$ of term-pairs are selected. A graph is created based on this selected term-pair set, and the PageRank algorithm is run on it which gives the most relevant features. Performance of different machine and deep learning classifiers using this relevant features are measured. Empirical results indicate that the proposed *CPRCFS* is comparable with the conventional techniques and the performance of Multilayer ELM outperformed the state-of-the-arts machine and deep learning classifiers. This work can be extended by running the machine learning classifiers on the feature space of Multilayer ELM which can further enhance the classification results.

References

1. Du, J., Vong, C.-M., Chen, C. P.: Novel efficient RNN and LSTM-like architectures: Recurrent and gated broad learning systems and their applications for text classification. IEEE Trans. Cybern. (2020)
2. Sambasivan, R., Das, S.: Classification and regression using augmented trees. Int. J. Data Sci. Anal. 7(4), 259–276 (2019)
3. Joseph, S.I.T., Sasikala, J., Juliet, D.S.: A novel vessel detection and classification algorithm using a deep learning neural network model with morphological processing (m-dlnn). Soft Comput. 23(8), 2693–2700 (2019)
4. Roul, R.K., Asthana, S.R., Kumar, G.: Study on suitability and importance of multilayer extreme learning machine for classification of text data. Soft Comput. 21(15), 4239–4256 (2017)

5. Sayed, G.I., Hassanien, A.E., Azar, A.T.: Feature selection via a novel chaotic crow search algorithm. Neural Comput. Appl. **31**(1), 171–188 (2019)
6. Tsai, C.-J.: New feature selection and voting scheme to improve classification accuracy. Soft Comput. **23**(15), 1–14 (2019)
7. Roul, R.K., Rai, P.: A new feature selection technique combined with elm feature space for text classification. In: Proceedings of the 13th International Conference on Natural Language Processing, pp. 285–292 (2016)
8. Kasun, L.L.C., Zhou, H., Huang, G.-B., Vong, C.M.: Representational learning with extreme learning machine for big data. IEEE Intell. Syst. **28**(6), 31–34 (2013)
9. Huang, G.-B., Zhou, H., Ding, X., Zhang, R.: Extreme learning machine for regression and multiclass classification. IEEE Trans. Syst. Man Cybern. Part B (Cybern.) **42**(2), 513–529 (2012)
10. Huang, G.-B., Chen, L., Siew, C.K., et al.: Universal approximation using incremental constructive feedforward networks with random hidden nodes. IEEE Trans. Neural Netw. **17**(4), 879–892 (2006)
11. Roul, R.K.: Suitability and importance of deep learning feature space in the domain of text categorisation. Int. J. Comput. Intell. Stud. **8**(1–2), 73–102 (2019)
12. Page, L., Brin, S., Motwani, R., Winograd, T.: The pagerank citation ranking: Bringing order to the web. Tech. Rep, Stanford InfoLab (1999)
13. Huang, G.-B., Zhou, H., Ding, X., Zhang, R.: "Extreme learning machine for regression and multiclass classification. IEEE Trans. Syst. Man Part B Cybern.(Cybern.) **42**(2), 513–529 (2011)
14. Huang, G.-B., Chen, Y.-Q., Babri, H.A.: Classification ability of single hidden layer feedforward neural networks. IEEE Trans. Neural Netw. **11**(3), 799–801 (2000)

Author Index

Bal, Ananya 253
Basappa, Manjanna 114
Bawankule, Kamalakant Laxman 289
Bhattacharyya, Dhruba K. 203
Bhavani, S. Durga 223
Biswas, Girish 160
Borah, Parthajit 203

Das, Meenakshi 253
Das, Rajib K. 65
Das, Satyabrata 81, 98
Das, Subha Kanta 253
Dewang, Rupesh Kumar 289
Dinesha, K. V. 129

Gaikwad, Ajinkya 175
Gogolla, Martin 24

Jena, Madhusmita 253

Kalita, J. K. 203
Karmakar, Kamalesh 65
Kasyap, Harsh 145
Katiyar, Swati 223
Khatua, Sunirmal 65
Kshemkalyani, Ajay D. 3
Kulkarni, Parth Parag 145

Maity, Soumen 175
Mandal, Partha Sarathi 188
Mishra, Sudeepta 114
Misra, Anshuman 3

Mitra, Debarati 188
Mukherjee, Nandini 160

Naik, Nenavath Srinivas 238
Narwa, Bipin Sai 271
Nayak, Sanjib Kumar 81
Nguyen, Le-Minh 44

Panda, Sanjaya Kumar 81, 98
Panda, Subhrakanta 271
Pande, Sohan Kumar 81, 98
Pattanayak, Debasish 188

Rajesh Kumar, R. 129
Rajita, B. S. A. S. 271
Rajora, Maihul 238
Rani, T. Sobha 223
Rathod, Mansi 238
Roul, Rajendra Kumar 299

Saha, Dibakar 188
Sahoo, Jajati Keshari 299
Satapathy, Shashank Mouli 253
Shanbhag, Vivek 129
Singh, Anil Kumar 289
Singh, Satendra 280
Sreevalsan-Nair, Jaya 280

Tarafdar, Anurina 65
Tran, Xuan-Chien 44
Tripathi, Shuvam Kant 175
Tripathy, Somanath 145

ted in the United States
ɔkmasters